CULTURES OF PSYCHIATRY AND
MENTAL HEALTH CARE
IN POSTWAR BRITAIN
AND THE NETHERLANDS

THE WELLCOME INSTITUTE SERIES IN THE HISTORY OF MEDICINE

Forthcoming Titles

Constructing Paris Medicine
edited by Caroline Hannaway and Ann La Berge

The Beast in the Mosquito:
the Correspondence of
Ronald Ross and Patrick Manson
edited by W. F. Bynum and Caroline Overy

Drugs On Trial:
Experimental Pharmacology and Therapeutic Innovation
in the Eighteenth Century
Holger Maehle

Academic enquiries regarding the series should be addressed
to the editors W. F. Bynum, V. Nutton and Roy Porter at
the Wellcome Institute for the History of Medicine,
183 Euston Road, London NW1 2BE, UK

I ... is largely ignored.

much of the analyses in this group of articles is invalidated if one includes a the existence of religious anti psychiatry

CULTURES OF PSYCHIATRY AND
MENTAL HEALTH CARE
IN POSTWAR BRITAIN
AND THE NETHERLANDS

new age is ... entirely, one brief noncommittal reference p. 31.

Edited by
Marijke Gijswijt-Hofstra and Roy Porter

II There is also a disturbing lack of willingness to face the above issue; to evaluate critically, by many authors, fundamentalism, anti-science, etc. Some ... critici, RD Laing for his egoism and abandonment of ... in favor of a commitment to the counter culture movement world reform etc or Foudraine's abandonment of the struggle. Psychoanalyses, & psychotherapies are ... discussed as but not evaluated — nor is chemotherapy ...

Rodopi

Amsterdam – Atlanta, GA 1998

what of opposition of Courts & Jurists to psychiatry re medical jurisprudence .... M'Naghten rule. its concept of moral treatment

First published in 1998
by Editions Rodopi B. V., Amsterdam – Atlanta, GA 1998.

© 1998 Marijke Gijswijt-Hofstra and Roy Porter

Design and Typesetting by Alex Mayor, the Wellcome Trust.
Printed and bound in The Netherlands by Editions Rodopi B. V.,
Amsterdam – Atlanta, GA 1998.

British Library Cataloguing in Publication Data
A catalogue record for this book is available from the British Library
ISBN 90-420-0652-8 (Paper)
ISBN 90-420-0662-5 (Bound)

Gijswijt-Hofstra, Marijke and Porter, Roy
Cultures of Psychiatry and Mental Health Care
in Postwar Britain and the Netherlands –
Amsterdam – Atlanta, GA:
Rodopi. – ill.
(Clio Medica 49 / ISSN 0045-7183;
The Wellcome Institute Series in the History of Medicine)

Front cover:
Design by A. Mayor: 'Family Group' by Henry Moore, adapted
from a print used on the cover of 'The Politics of the Family'
by R. D. Laing, Pelican, 1976.

© Editions Rodopi B. V. Amsterdam – Atlanta, GA 1998

Printed in The Netherlands

Contents

Notes on Contributors

Jonathan Andrews is a Wellcome University Award Holder and Senior Lecturer in the History of Medicine at Oxford Brookes University. His main research interests are in the history of psychiatry in Britain from the 17th to the early 18th centuries. His publications include *The History of Bethlem* (jointly authored: 1997) and *Let There Be Light Again. A History of Gartnavel Royal Hospital* (jointly edited: 1993). He is currently working on a Wellcome funded research project on the history of criminal insanity and forensic psychiatry in Britain *c.* 1863–1913.

Peter Barham's books include *Schizophrenia and Human Value* (Blackwell, 1984; second edition, Free Association Books, 1993); with Robert Hayward, *Relocating Madness: From the Mental Patient to the Person* (Routledge, 1991; second edition, Free Association Books, 1995); and *Closing the Asylum: The Mental Patient in Modern Society* (second edition, Penguin Books, 1997). Currently he is working on a social history of the insane servicemen of the First World War. He is a Research Associate, Wellcome Institute for the History of Medicine, and Hon. Research Fellow in the History of Medicine, University College London.

Hans Binneveld is Professor of History at Erasmus University, Rotterdam. He has published books and articles on the history of psychiatry and on military affairs.

Gemma Blok studied history at the University of Amsterdam. Her final thesis on general paralysis of the insane won her the Frederik van Eeden Prize. Since 1995 she has been working at the Trimbos

Instituut, the Netherlands Institute of Mental Health and Addiction in Utrecht where she is currently writing on the history of Dutch mental hospitals.

Joan Busfield is a Professor in the Department of Sociology at the University of Essex. She trained initially as a clinical psychologist at the Tavistock Clinic and then moved into sociology. Her book *Managing Madness: Changing Ideas and Practice* (Hutchinson, 1986), offered an historical and sociological account of the development of psychiatry. More recently she has focused on issues relating to gender illness and psychiatry, resulting in her book, *Men, Women and Madness: Understanding Gender and Mental Disorder* (Macmillan, 1996). She is currently completing *Health and Health Care Policy in Britain* (OUP, 1999). She has been a non-executive Director of the North East Essex Mental Health NHS Trust since 1992.

Leonie de Goei, historian, is Senior Associate at the Trimbos Instituut, Netherlands Institute of Mental Health and Addiction in Utrecht. Her main fields of interest are the history of Dutch mental health care, the mental hygiene movement and child psychiatry in the twentieth century.

Marijke Gijswijt-Hofstra is Professor of Social and Cultural History at the University of Amsterdam. She has published on the granting of asylum in the Dutch Republic, deviance and tolerance (16–20th centuries), witchcraft and cultures of misfortune (16–20th centuries), the reception of homœopathy in the Netherlands (19–20th centuries), and on women and alternative health care in the Netherlands (20th century). She has recently edited in English, with Hilary Marland and Hans de Waardt, *Illness and Healing Alternatives in Western Europe* (London: Routledge, 1997).

David Ingleby began his career working as a research psychologist for the Medical Research Council and subsequently taught in Social and Political Sciences at Cambridge University. In 1982 he moved to Holland to take up a chair in Developmental Psychology at Utrecht University. His publications include 'Critical Psychology: The Politics of Mental Health' and numerous articles on psychology and its interface with other disciplines.

Colin Jones is Professor of History at Warwick University, and specializes in French history, especially from the seventeenth to the nineteenth century. His books include *Charity and Bienfaisance: the Treatment of the Poor in the Montpelier Region, 1740-1815* (1982), *The Charitable Imperative* (1989), *The Longman Companion to the French Revolution* (1989), *Medicine and Charity before the Welfare State* (edited with Jonathan Barry, 1991), *The Cambridge Illustrated History of France* (1993), *Reassessing Foucault: Power, Medicine and the Body* (edited with Roy Porter), and (with Laurence Brockliss), *The Medical World of Early Modern France*.

Harry Oosterhuis is Assistant Professor of History at the University of Maastricht. He has published books on the history of Catholicism and homosexuality in the Netherlands and on the early homosexual movement and male bonding in pre-Nazi Germany. He is currently researching the work of the German-Austrian psychiatrist Richard von Krafft-Ebing (1840-1902).

Paul Schnabel is Professor of Mental Health and Public Health at the Faculty of Social Sciences, Utrecht University. From 1977 to 1991 he was Director of Research at the Netherlands Institute of Mental Health (now Trimbos Institute) and from 1992 to 1996 Dean of the Netherlands School of Public Health. He is Editor-in-chief of the *Maandblad Geestelijke volksgezondheid* (Mental Health Monthly) and columnist for the *NRC-Handelsblad*, a leading Dutch newspaper. He is a member of the Health Council of the Netherlands, the State Council for Social Development (RMO) and the National Committee for People with Chronic Diseases (NCCZ). His latest book is *De weerbastige geestesziekte. Naar een nieuwe sociologie van de geestelijke gezondheidszorg* (Nijmegen: SUN, 1995).

Roy Porter is Professor in the Social History of Medicine at the Wellcome Institute for the History of Medicine. Recent books include *Doctor of Society: Thomas Beddoes and the Sick Trade in Late Enlightenment England* (London: Routledge, 1991), *London: A Social History* (Hamish Hamilton, 1994), and the *'Greatest Benefit to Mankind': A Medical History of Humanity* (London: HarperCollins, 1997). He is currently working on a general history of the Enlightenment in Britain. He is interested in eighteenth century medicine, the history of psychiatry and the history of quackery.

Stephen Snelders studied history at the University of Utrecht. He is currently working on his PhD thesis on 'LSD and psychiatry in the

Netherlands' at the Vrije Universiteit, Amsterdam. He has written articles on the history of the use of hallucinogenic drugs.

Tilli Tansey studied Octopus brain chemistry for her PhD and spent many years working in neuroscience laboratories in Plymouth, Naples, Edinburgh, and St Thomas' Hospital, London. In 1986 she spent a period of sabbatical leave at the Wellcome Institute for the History of Medicine in London, and decided to refocus her career, completing a PhD on the scientific career of Sir Henry Dale FRS (1875-1968) in 1990. She is currently Historian of Modern Medical Science at the Wellcome Institute, where her research is principally in modern physiology and pharmacology; an Honorary Senior Lecturer in the Department of Anatomy, University College London; and the Convenor of the Wellcome Trust's History of Twentieth Century Medicine Group.

Mathew Thomson is a Lecturer in the History Department at Sheffield University. Since 1993 he has held a Wellcome Award in the History of Medicine. He has published articles on the history of mental deficiency and mental health care in Britain during the first half of the twentieth century. His *The Problem of Mental Deficiency: Eugenics, Democracy and Social Policy in Britain, 1870-1959* was published by Oxford University Press. He is currently preparing a book on the impact of psychological ideas in Britain between 1900 and 1950.

Keir Waddington completed his PhD on nineteenth-century metropolitan hospitals and then worked at the Wellcome Institute for the History of Medicine on the *History of Bethlem* with Roy Porter, Jonathan Andrews, Penny Tucker, and Asa Briggs. He is currently a Research Fellow at Queen Mary and Westfield College, working on the history of St Bartholomew's Medical School and medical education in London.

Ido Weijers wrote his dissertation, *Terug naar het behouden huis. Romanschrijvers en wetenschappers in de jaren vijftig* (Back to the Safe House. Novelists and Scientists in the Fifties). Since 1996 he has been teaching history of education in the Department of Education, University of Utrecht. He has written extensively on the history of mental retardation. His current research interest is in the history and theory of juvenile justice.

Saskia Wolters studied Cultural Studies at the University of Maastricht which she completed in 1997 with a thesis on 'The Changing Professional Identity of the Dutch Psychiatrist, 1960-1997'. This has furnished the material for her contribution together with Harry Oosterhuis to this book.

* There is a considerable literature on post WWI psychiatry and mental health care; at least in the USA & France

Introduction:
Cultures of Psychiatry and Mental Health Care
in Postwar Britain and the Netherlands

Marijke Gijswijt-Hofstra

Psychiatry and mental health care have their histories. Ideas about what constitutes the normal and the abnormal, or the sane and the insane, have changed over time. This also goes for the diagnoses, labels, interpretations and explanations of mental problems, and, not surprisingly, for the ways in which these problems have been treated and countered by the various parties concerned. Histories of psychiatry and mental health care, moreover, form part of and therefore also reflect cultural histories in the broadest sense of the word.

However, historical research into the development of psychiatry and mental health care in the twentieth century is fairly scarce.[1] Most research has been concentrated on the nineteenth century. This implies that important developments such as the introduction of psychopharmaceuticals, the changing cultural and psychiatrical climate during the 1960s and 1970s, 'anti-psychiatry', the experience of de-institutionalization, but also the recent change towards a more biological, natural science orientated psychiatry have not until now been illuminated. This has changed only recently. This collection of essays, and the preceding workshop (see below), fits in with this development.

This book offers many examples of what it implies to say that psychiatry and mental health care have their histories, and are embedded in broader cultural histories. It will be shown that postwar British and Dutch conceptions and measures in the field of psychiatry and mental health care were (and still are) closely interwoven with, or were, in other words, a function of, British or Dutch culture at large. The different war experiences, the different social and religious make-up, the different political cultures in both countries have all had an impact on the shaping of distinct British

1

and Dutch cultures of psychiatry and mental health care.

This being said, there is no denying that these cultures also have much in common. Not least this is the case because there has been a more or less institutionalized scientific exchange in the field of psychiatry since the second quarter of the nineteenth century (first travelling, then psychiatric journals, and still later conferences). From the beginning, countries such as France and England have served as points of orientation for reforms in psychiatric care. Notwithstanding the many national differences, a West-European psychiatric 'culture' came into being from a fairly early stage onwards. Moreover, all these countries have sooner or later shared in similar economic and social developments, which to a certain extent furthered similarity with respect to psychiatry and mental health care. Western culture has increasingly become an international business. Entertainment, information, youth- and counter-cultures, to mention but a few examples, have all become exported and spread over the whole Western world, if not globally. And yet we are confronted with partly different modes of reception and appropriation, modes which may indeed vary per nation, but also within and across nations, for instance according to generation, socio-economic status, or religious affiliation.

It hardly needs saying that the past histories of psychiatry and mental health care form no exception in this respect. Indeed, internal cultural differences and ensuing attempts to secure a following for one's own convictions and to refute or ridicule the ideas of the other party, have been part and parcel of these histories, the British and the Dutch not excluded.

One of the postwar issues which has particularly stirred the world of psychiatry and mental health care, and to some extent society at large as well, was 'anti-psychiatry'. Coined as a concept by the British psychiatrist David Cooper in 1967, Britain's most influential advocate of psychiatric reforms at that time undoubtedly was Ronald D. Laing. His fame, moreover, far outreached Britain. The Dutch also had their own idol of 'anti-psychiatry', the psychiatrist Jan Foudraine. They, and others with them, fiercely criticized current psychiatric ideas and practice, and propagated as well as applied their own, radically different conceptions.

However, 'anti-psychiatry' was not directed at the aboliton of psychiatry as such. 'Anti-psychiatry' was a kaleidoscopic movement which aimed to bring about fundamental changes, if not a psychiatric revolution. For some this meant a thoroughly different view of what constituted the normal. It was not the mental patient

2

who should be considered as abnormal, but society at large. It was society and the family, not biological deficiencies of the sufferer, that were the cause of mental problems. This implied that a radical change of society was required. For others 'anti-psychiatry' primarily meant a fundamental critique of the traditional psychiatric hospital, a call for de-hospitalization, and the abolishment of 'inhuman' methods of treatment, like ECTs and the administering of psychopharmaceuticals. Instead of being isolated and subjected to an objectionable medical regime, 'patients' should be allowed more individual freedom, brought back into society, and treated humanely, without being stigmatized. Indeed, patients were expected and stimulated to stand up for their own rights and organize themselves. *what of Laing's view that psychotics in some cases were or could become sane*

Although 'anti-psychiatry' was presented as a clean break with the then current psychiatry, most of the propagated ideas and practices were not as new as it may have seemed at the time. What was new was indeed, the response these ideas had outside the professional circle, in society at large, as they were mediated by the press. Especially the counter-cultural circles of the sixties offered a fertile soil and stimulants for psychiatric reform and revolt, for their aim was a more humane, democratic and tolerant world. *what of religious anti psy etc.*

Centred around this colourful episode of 'anti-psychiatry' in the sixties and seventies a workshop was held in June 1997 in Amsterdam (once the European capital of hippie culture), organized by the Dutch Huizinga Institute for Cultural History and the Wellcome Institute for the History of Medicine (London).[2] British and Dutch historians and social scientists presented all in all fourteen papers, most of them matched in Anglo-Dutch pairs on a particular aspect of the respective postwar histories of psychiatry and mental health care, while all of them were discussed during the workshop from a comparative point of view. This volume presents the results, including conclusions by Colin Jones and David Ingleby who attended the workshop as commentators and accepted the challenge of gathering up the threads. *origin of this book: not a party not conference*

The comparative, cross-national approach has proved to be both rewarding and difficult, for complicated reasons. It was rewarding not in the least place because comparison provides an extra dimension to otherwise simple, possibly too matter-of-course thought of national histories. In other words, comparison offers an antidote for the one-sided 'solipsism' of a purely national view. Thus it appeared that anti-psychiatry's impact may well have been stronger in the Netherlands than in Britain. Although the extent to

3

which this was the case remains to be settled, the intriguing question as to why such differences occurred began already to be tackled during the workshop. Preceding developments in the field of mental hygiene, mental health, and psychiatry proved to be enlightening, developments which partly ran parallel in both countries, partly diverging. It was suggested that the different impact of World War II (German occupation or not) may well have contributed to different accents in mental health care, just as the different political, social, and religious make-up of both countries may have done.

On the other hand, it became clear that both Britain and the Netherlands also experienced similar changes in mental health concepts and policy which paved the way for an 'anti-psychiatry' that after all was not as new or revolutionary as has been thought. The concept of the therapeutic community and the sociogenetic perspective, which both gained importance after World War II, and the sociological analyses of the psychiatric hospital around 1960, were all of them developments which, as it were, anticipated anti-psychiatry. Instead of a break or rupture in the history of psychiatry and mental health care, the episode of 'anti-psychiatry' should therefore rather be seen in terms of continuity, be it a continuity including undeniable changes, as will be shown in this volume.

Joan Busfield (University of Essex) and Paul Schnabel (University of Utrecht) open this book with contributions on the main lines of the provision, organization, and financing of mental health care in Britain (from the late nineteenth century onwards) and the Netherlands (after 1945). Mathew Thomson (University of Sheffield) and Leonie de Goei (Trimbos Institute, Utrecht) follow with contributions on respectively the idea of mental health as it was developed in wartime Britain, and the Dutch mental hygiene movement between 1924 and 1960. While in Britain most attention seems to have been paid to the causes of the war and the crucial importance of mental health, both as a product of and a basis for a democratic society, was stressed, the Dutch were primarily occupied with the consequences of the war and with individual mental disorders. These first four chapters provide the setting for what follows.

This begins with two contributions on psychopharmaceuticals. Tilli Tansey (Wellcome Institute, London) tackles the problem of what the introduction of psychopharmaceuticals has meant for psychiatric practice and science, and to what extent this introduction was a function of industrial interests. Stephen Snelders (Free University, Amsterdam) concentrates on the role that a particular drug, LSD, has played in the development of two different concepts of the origin and nature of mental illness in the 1970s, namely the so-called biomedical and the social theories of mental illness. In this context anti-psychiatry's hero R.D. Laing as well as a number of Dutch psychiatrists are introduced.

The acquaintance with Laing is continued in the contribution by Jonathan Andrews (Brookes University, Oxford). Attention is focused on Laing's early career in the Glasgow Gartnavel Hospital and his therapeutical experiments with chronically schizophrenic patients in 1953-55. Gemma Blok (Trimbos Institute, Utrecht) discusses Jan Foudraine's anti-psychiatric Dutch best-seller, *Wie is van hout* (1971). Both Andrews and Blok do a good job of debunking Laing's and Foudraine's self-representations.

From anti-psychiatric idols it is but a small step to psychiatric hospitals, especially in the case of the Dutch contribution on the Dennendal affair in 1971-74. Ido Weijers (University of Utrecht) reports on how Carel Muller, the young, alternative, long-haired and occasional joint-smoking psychological director of this institution for the mentally handicapped, attempted, with part of his staff, to do away with the medical regime, an attempt which was eventually aborted after the right-wing press had succeeded in alarming the political scene at the Hague. Interestingly, nothing of the sort occured at the Joint Hospital, the postwar merger of the Bethlem and the Maudsley Hospital, described by Keir Waddington (St Barts Medical School). It is as though this merger and the defence of each party's material interests absorbed most attention.

Internal strife within the psychiatric profession, this time within the Dutch profession as a whole, is also discussed by Harry Oosterhuis (University of Maastricht) and his former student Saskia Wolters. In 1974 it all culminated in a split between the two sections of the Dutch Association for Psychiatry and Neurology. It appears that at least part of the Dutch psychiatrists favoured a multidisciplinary and multicausal approach in psychiatry, whereas other psychiatrists preferred to adhere to the medical approach as promoted by their neurological colleagues. Anti-psychiatrical ideas obviously had their appeal for a number of Dutch psychiatrists.

Instead of focussing on the psychiatric profession, Peter Barham (Wellcome Institute, London) is the only one who has given a voice to psychiatric patients. He interviewed young schizophrenic 'clients' in Northern England after deinstitutionalization had been effected. Although no longer locked up in an asylum, their problems with joining in with the community should not be underestimated.

The next two contributions have much less in common, although each one in its own way attempts to provide a more encompassing view which proves to be very helpful in understanding postwar psychiatry and mental health care. Hans Binneveld (Erasmus University Rotterdam) shows how military psychiatry has developed from World War I onwards. The parallels between military psychiatric insights and practice and anti-psychiatrical criticism of, for instance, hospitalization are remarkable. Roy Porter (Wellcome Institute) closes with a thought-provoking essay on madness, the family and anti-psychiatry in a long-term perspective.

Finally, Colin Jones (University of Warwick) and David Ingleby (University of Utrecht) demonstrate what they consider to be the distinctive features of the British and Dutch postwar cultures of psychiatry and mental health care. And what they do with Colin Jones's humorous attempt at characterizing anti-psychiatry, offered towards the end of the workshop: anti-psychiatry as 'the carnavalesque celebration of the symbolic inversion of medical authority and legitimacy'! The last words have not been spoken on these intriguing issues, but at least the opening statements have been made. Hopefully they will serve as an inspiration and stimulus for future comparative research.

Acknowledgement

With many thanks to Joost Vijselaar for his useful comments.

Notes

1. A small selection of recent literature on, or including, the twentieth century:
   Leonie de Goei & Joost Vijselaar (eds), *Proceedings 1st European Congress on the History of Psychiatry and Mental Health Care* (Rotterdam: Erasmus Publishing, 1993).
   Gerald N. Grob, *The Mad among Us. A History of the Care of America's Mentally Ill* (New York etc.: The Free Press, 1994).
   Mark S. Micale, *Approaching Hysteria. Disease and Its Interpretations* (Princeton, New Jersey: Princeton University Press, 1995).
   Mark S. Micale & Roy Porter (eds), *Discovering the History of Psychiatry* (New York & Oxford: Oxford University Press, 1994).
   Edward Shorter, *A History of Psychiatry. From the Era of the Asylum to the Age of Prozac* (New York etc.: John Wiley & Sons, Inc., 1997).
   Joost Vijselaar (ed.), *Gesticht in de duinen. De geschiedenis van de provinciale psychiatrische ziekenhuizen van Noord-Holland van 1849*

tot 1994 (Hilversum: Verloren, 1997).

Hanneke Westhoff, *Geestelijke bevrijders. Nederlandse katholieken en hun beweging voor geestelijke volksgezondheid in de twintigste eeuw* (Nijmegen: Valkhof Pers, 1996).

2. Anglo-Dutch Workshop on Postwar Psychiatry and Anti-Psychiatry from a Social-Cultural Perspective, Amsterdam 13-14 June 1997. The organizers of this workshop were Marijke Gijswijt-Hofstra (Huizinga Institute, Amsterdam), Joost Vijselaar (Trimbos Institute, Utrecht), and Roy Porter (Wellcome Institute, London). This workshop was the first of a series of Anglo-Dutch workshops on 'The Diversity of Medicine in England and the Netherlands in the Twentieth Century'. The University of Warwick will also take an active part in the organization.

1

Restructuring Mental Health Services in Twentieth Century Britain

Joan Busfield

This paper offers an overview of twentieth century developments in mental health services in Britain. It is intended to provide a context for the more specific papers on Britain which are included in this volume. I have chosen to look at mental health services in general, not just psychiatry, since the place of psychiatry itself has changed throughout the century and this becomes more visible if psychiatry is located within the context of mental health services as a whole. My basic disciplinary approach is that of a sociologist who believes that we need to look at history if we are to understand the ideas, practices and institutions of present-day society.

In examining twentieth century developments in the mental health services in Britain, I want to begin by setting out the key assumptions that underpin my analysis. There are four. First, my starting point for thinking about developments in mental health services in Britain this century, or indeed any other time or place, is to see them as institutions in the broadest sense of the term that are intended to deal with, and try to solve, the problem of what we now call mental illness, but in the past has been called, mental disease, madness, lunacy or insanity, though these concepts are not of course exactly equivalent. In that respect there are parallels with society's attempts to deal with social problems such as poverty, crime or ill-health more generally, all problems that pose in different ways some threat to the social order. In the case of the mental disorder this threat includes the risk of dangerous behaviour from some who are severely disturbed.

Second, and following on from this, I also take it as axiomatic that mental health services are partly shaped by the welfare system, broadly defined, of a society – that is, if we are to understand the

9

character of mental health services in a particular society at a particular point in time, we need to locate these services within the institutional arrangements, and the ideas underpinning them, for dealing with the welfare of its members. This is a point demonstrated very effectively in this volume by Paul Schnabel in his discussion of developments in psychiatry in the Netherlands.

Third, in thinking about mental illness or, to use a somewhat more neutral term, mental disorder, and the related mental health services, including the legal and administrative arrangements which give them shape, I find Foucault's conceptualisation, which links madness with irrationality and unreason, the most helpful, though I disagree with many of his other ideas.[1] In my view the concept of mental illness is applied to what is regarded within a society as some form of 'unreason' – a formulation that defines mental disorder firmly in terms of mind and mental processes rather than of body or behaviour, so allowing differentiation between physical disease, mental disorder and deviance.[2] What is clear, however, is that the boundaries of madness and mental illness are not set with any great precision, change over time, and are highly contested.

Fourth and finally, I assume that notions such as Charles Rosenberg's 'framing of disease', or the standard sociological notion of 'social construction', are crucial to any understanding of changes and developments in mental health services.[3] The ways in which a society, or groups within a society, think about mental disorder helps to structure and shape the responses that are made to it as well as the ways psychological difficulties are expressed within a given population. Changing conceptualisations of mental disorder and the emergence of new categories influence the ways services are structured and the treatments that are offered. Equally service arrangements themselves contribute to the way in which mental disorder is framed.

Having set out these four assumptions I want now to consider the major developments in mental health services in Britain this century. In examining this history I think it is helpful to highlight three ongoing struggles that pervade twentieth century ideas and services. The first is that between physical, psychological and social explanations and treatments of mental disorder. This is, of course, first and foremost a competition at the level of ideas, but it also needs to be seen as a competition between professional groups, such as psychiatrists, psychologists, psychotherapists and social workers in which the standard techniques of professional closure and exclusion are deployed to try and enhance power and status.[4] Second, and

10

[left margin handwritten notes:] No! what of Moral Insanity. Then behavior itself may define mental disorder even when irrationality itself is not evident! Then mental disorder or insanity could & was seen as a physical disorder. even by m.I. advocates in mid 19 Sth cent USA

[right margin handwritten notes:] No! thy inability to make these distinct. or separate plagued the Courts & led to innumerable disputes

related to this, there has been a battle over the extent to which mental health services should be integrated with other health services. And third, there has been an ongoing struggle between care and control. It is fashionable in the post-Foucauldian era to see power and control as all pervasive. In my view, whilst we need to reject Whiggish histories of psychiatry that present a somewhat simple trajectory of scientific progress, there is no need to abandon the values and standards which allow us to make judgements between more supportive, caring environments and more coercive, repressive ones.

How have these struggles played themselves out in twentieth-century Britain? For convenience I have divided the century into four periods treating it, contra Hobsbawm, as the long twentieth century.[5] The four periods with their respective labels are: 'Custodialism under Attack, 1890-1929'; 'Integration and Medical Innovation, 1930-1953'; 'Community Care in the Public Sector, 1954-1978' ; and 'Privatisation and Competition, 1979-1997'. As will be apparent, I use a range of criteria for distinguishing the four periods and do not see any one dimension as determinate – legal, cultural, political or therapeutic.

Custodialism under Attack, 1890–1929

This first period I have identified begins with the 1890 Lunacy Act – an act which is usually seen as symbolising the highpoint of a legalistic, custodial approach to madness which extended across Europe in this period.[6] The Act, designed to protect the liberty of the citizen and not the rights of the lunatic, codified the various procedures and arrangements for the certification of any lunatic admitted to an asylum, whether public or private.[7]

In 1890, as during the previous half century and the early decades of the twentieth century, the public asylum, developed within the framework of the Poor Law was undoubtedly the centre point of the mental health services in Britain as it was in other parts of Europe. Little formal care was available for those with psychiatric problems outside it, other than through private physicians, some of whom specialised in the care and treatment of mental disorder. By the final decade of the nineteenth century the number of patients confined in public asylums was already large. In England and Wales in 1900, when the population was around 32 million, some 107 thousand people were officially identified as insane, over 69 per cent of whom were in public asylums (around 11 per cent were in workhouses and others were to be found in charitable asylums or private madhouses, or were registered as in private care).[8] Fifty-four per cent were women, a difference that resulted largely from women's lower mortality in comparison with men and their greater economic dependence which meant that they were more likely to end up in Poor Law institutions.[9] The custodial nature of the public asylums was reflected in their scale (with by then over 800 inmates on average), the legal powers of detention, the lengthy stays of many of the residents (though a significant proportion were discharged quite quickly), the fact that most people were admitted only when their problems were long standing (because of the need for clear evidence of disturbance to satisfy certification criteria and the reluctance of the Poor Law authorities to provide help except as a last resort), as well as the lack of much in the way of active therapeutic intervention.

Amongst psychiatrists, usually resident doctors whose numbers were limited and whose activities largely focussed on legal and administrative requirements, hereditarian ideas predominated and little was expected in the way of cure.[10] Whilst public asylums had been founded on reformist, therapeutic principles and it was widely assumed by their advocates that inmates could be cured, by the end of the century custodialism and bureaucratic management of the insane were pervasive. Though medical powers over patients were very extensive, it was the Poor Law authorities, with their overriding concern to keep a firm hand on budgets, who ultimately reigned supreme.

Yet in this first period there were signs of challenge to the old orthodoxy. First and very importantly, the principles on which state welfare was grounded began to shift, evidenced most clearly by the reforms initiated by the Liberal Governments of 1906-1914.[11] Public asylums were rooted in the ninteenth century Poor Law system and its principles (especially from 1834 onwards) of last resort. The Liberal reforms introduced into public welfare arrangements the principles of insurance already established in the private sector where voluntary and commercial insurance were quite common. These reforms helped to undermine, although they did not destroy, the last resort principles of the Poor Law system which was formally abolished only in 1929. But the Liberal reforms meant that the possibility of additional welfare provision outside the framework of the Poor Law system was increasingly accepted – a development that facilitated a shift away from custodial models of mental health care. One example was the decision by the London County Council, using funds that Henry Maudsley had made available, to establish the Maudsley Hospital for the early treatment of mental disorder on an in- and out-patient basis without certification (special legislative provision was secured in 1915, the year the hospital opened). The advent of the First World War meant that the hospital was initially used for military purposes, but after the war it reverted to the original intention of serving as a hospital for the early treatment of mental disorder.

Another challenge came from major shifts in the framing of mental disorder. Central here was the introduction of the concept of shell-shock in the First World War. The effects of shell-shock reverberated across psychiatry, just as C.S. Myers, who first identified the condition in 1915, believed the physical impact of the shells reverberated through the afflicted soldiers. In the first place, shell-shock challenged assumptions of inherited weakness and degeneration as the key to mental disorder and the belief that those who became disturbed necessarily had 'tainted family histories'.[12] This was not least because officers, though fewer in number than lower ranks in absolute terms, actually manifested higher rates of disorder than non-commissioned officers.[13] Moreover the numbers involved overall (at least 80,000 during the war if not more) made assumptions of tainted stock seem less and less plausible.[14]

In a similar vein shell-shock challenged legal and institutional assumptions about the appropriateness of compulsory detention and the necessity for treatment in a public asylum, with its requirement that if care were to be provided free the individual would have to be deemed a pauper. Even soldiers suffering from shell-shock, who were open to charges of either cowardice or malingering from those who doubted whether they were genuinely ill, nonetheless belonged to a group who collectively, if not always individually, were considered the heroes of war and whose sacrifices, frequently in the form of their lives, were well-known. The dual stigma of certification and pauperisation did not seem, in the minds of many, an apt reward for facing up to the dangers of war. And again they seemed peculiarly ill-fitting for officers and gentlemen. Instead most soldiers suffering from shell-shock were sent to military hospitals, including a few specifically focusing on the treatment of shell-shock, such as Craiglockhart in Scotland and the new Maudsley Hospital in London. As a result both during and after the war a number of attempts were made to pass bills permitting voluntary admission nationally, but none was successful before 1930.[15]

Shell-shock also provided an opportunity for the application of psychodynamic ideas about the causes and treatment of mental disorder in Britain. In the first decade of the century, Freud's books and papers began to be translated into English and began to gain currency amongst intellectual and educational elites, but psychoanalysis as a form of treatment was confined to a few specialist physicians.[16] With the advent of shell-shock, sympathetic doctors found an occasion to apply psychoanalytic ideas and treatments in an institutional setting. In Britain the work of W.H. Rivers, who first worked as an anthropologist, is one such example. Rivers and his colleagues argued that shell-shock was a flight into illness occasioned by the conflict between fear and duty and contended that 'sexual factors take a comparatively small place in the production of war neuroses'.[17]

During the 1920s some of these ideas were taken up in the private and voluntary sectors by psychoanalysts (most of whom were medically qualified). The Tavistock Clinic was established in London in 1920 and opened a Children's Department in 1926. This provided the model for a number of child guidance clinics which were set up in the late 1920s.[18] These new clinics employed psychologists and social workers as well as psychotherapists, and operated with ideas about the causation and treatment of mental disorder which moved away from the emphasis on physical causes and treatment and instead focused on the importance of psychological and social processes, developing a set of ideas about prevention often referred to as mental hygiene. These new psychological and social models of illness influenced a number of psychiatrists.[19] In Britain, the influential work of the US psychiatrist Adolf Meyer was taken up by Henderson and Gillespie whose *Textbook of Psychiatry*, first published in 1927, introduced British psychiatry to notions such as reaction type as a way of framing mental disorder.[20] They viewed mental disorder as the reaction of the individual mind to its environment, emphasising bio-psychological processes and the importance of looking at the individual case and the setting in which symptoms occur. A good case history which included psychological and social information became all important.

These challenges did not, however, lead to immediate, radical changes in public sector mental health services. The difficulty, of course, was that the introduction of voluntary admission, the development of new types of services that did not involve pauperisation, and the psychodynamic and social models of mental disorder, largely conflicted with the ideas and practices that underpinned public sector provision centred on the custodial asylums. There was scope for experimentation in the private and voluntary sector where funds were available, but little in the public sector, as long as the poor law retained its stranglehold. During the 1920s the struggles for reform continued, but the legal and administrative changes were limited until the end of the decade.

Integration and Medical Innovation, 1930–1954

The nineteenth century asylum was legally, administratively and institutionally separate from the rest of medicine and, as we have seen, though doctors were employed, their powers, except over patients, were tightly curtailed and they had little time for, or indeed belief in, the value of therapeutic interventions. The period 1930-54 was marked by two major changes from the old pattern. On the one hand, there were the first signs of a restructuring of mental health services and their integration into the rest of medicine; on the other hand, there was a burgeoning of medical treatments for the mentally ill. Both helped significantly to increase the power and influence of the medical profession.

The 1929 Local Government Act which formally abandoned the language, if not all the practices and procedures, of the Poor Law heralded the beginning of this second period. The 1930 Mental Treatment Act which followed has been seen by many as the start of a new, more distinctively medical era for the mental health services.[21] The Act was grounded in the ideas and recommendations of the 1924-6 Royal Commission on Lunacy and Mental Disorder. Taking the view 'that there is no clear line of demarcation between mental illness and physical illness', the 1926 Report emphasised the need to treat mental illness and physical illness in a similar fashion, which the authors believed inevitably meant a greater role for the medical profession.[22]

The 1930 Mental Treatment Act not only incorporated the new language of 'rate-aided persons' instead of paupers, it also symbolically relabelled asylums mental hospitals. In addition, it introduced two other important changes. First, it introduced a new category of voluntary treatment for those who were willing and able to indicate that they would agree to enter a mental hospital on a voluntary basis, as well as the possibility of temporary certification for no more than six months. Significantly this change, which was designed to facilitate early treatment, was specifically modelled on practices in medicine where the objective was to get the patient into hospital as quickly as possible without any cumbersome process of certification. Second, the Act also gave local authorities powers to set up out-patient clinics. A number of out-patient clinics for the treatment of mental disorder had already been established in the voluntary hospitals – at this stage the main hospital in most localities. Once public funds could be used for psychiatric out-patient clinics, the same model was usually adopted, thereby linking mental health services more closely to other health services (the clinics were often staffed by doctors who worked at the local public asylum). As a result the asylum was no longer the exclusive location for the treatment of mental illness within the public sector. The development of publicly funded out-patient clinics represents therefore an important step towards the integration of the mental health services into the medical mainstream. Yet there was no sign during the 1930s of any decline in the numbers confined in the mental hospitals. Rather the overall numbers of resident patients continued a steady increase as did in particular the percentage of the elderly.

The decision to incorporate the mental health services into the National Health Service when it was enacted in 1946 was a further and even more significant step towards integration and expansion. The inclusion of mental health services into the NHS was by no means a foregone conclusion. Mental health services were not included in early plans for the NHS, first featuring in the 1944 Plan. Aneurin Bevan, the Minister of Health in the new Labour Government, supported their inclusion, echoing the 1926 Royal Commission Report in his statement that 'The separation of mental from physical treatment is a survival from primitive conceptions and is a source of endless cruelty and neglect'.[23] Ironically, although this was the most visible and most significant step towards the integration of the mental health services into the rest of medicine, and initially increased psychiatrists' power, it also put them in direct competition with other hospitals for funds and for managerial power and potentially contributed to a diminution of their power. Significantly for patients it opened up access to medical services, especially in relation to less severe disorders such as the neuroses, which were often dealt with by general practitioners and where women were usually over-represented.

The innovations in physical treatments for mental disorder that characterised the 1930s constitute the second major feature of this period; they also brought psychiatry closer to other areas of medicine and helped to increase its legitimacy as a field of medical practice. Medical innovations in treatment for mental hospital patients were extensive. Whereas throughout the second half of the nineteenth century and the first three decades of the twentieth century, the use of physical treatments had been limited and medical innovations rare (the significant exception was work on the treatment of general paresis of the insane (GPI) which resulted from syphilitic infection spreading to the brain), in the 1930s new physical treatments proliferated, many of them highly controversial. These included the use of insulin-induced comas in Britain from 1933 onwards, and then Metrazol-induced convulsions from 1937. The use of convulsive therapies was based on the belief, which proved to be mistaken, that there was an antagonism between epilepsy and schizophrenia.. The use of electricity to induce convulsions by applying electrodes to the brain was first tried out by Cerletti and Bini in Italy in 1938 and was first used in Britain the following year. It was regarded as a more satisfactory method of producing the necessary convulsions than Metrazol since its use required little training and experience, though at this stage rather little in the way of anaesthetics and muscle relaxants were used and fractures and physical injuries were not uncommon . It was initially considered of value in the treatment of a range of psychiatric conditions including schizophrenia, but later was largely used in the treatment of so-called endogenous (psychotic) depression.

Even more controversial than ECT were the forms of psychosurgery involving severing of the frontal lobes developed by the Portuguese neurologist, Moniz, in 1936 and first used in Britain in 1941.[24] However, the Second World War delayed the widespread use of both ECT and psychosurgery in Britain and it was not until the end of the 1940s and early 1950s that their use became common. ECT was an attractive treatment in state-funded mental hospitals not least because it was cheap and relatively easy to administer. In that respect it had a major advantage over psychotherapy which, though quite popular, in part because it allowed patients to talk about their experiences, was largely confined to the private sector. Psychosurgery unlike ECT required an experienced neurologist and mental hospitals could often employ one only on a sessional basis.[25] The numbers of operations carried out increased in the 1950s but it was generally a treatment of last resort. One important consequence of these new physical treatments was that they helped to undermine any remaining belief, which had been so important to the initial establishment of the asylums, that a stay in the insitution had therapeutic value in itself.

Community Care in the Public Sector, 1954–1979

I have chosen to treat 1954 as the beginning of the third period in the twentieth century restructuring of the mental health services in

Britain for three reasons. First, it is the year when the resident mental hospital population was at its peak. From then on resident numbers started to decline. Second, it was the year when the second Royal Commission on mental disorder of the century began its work: the Royal Commission on the Law relating to Mental Illness and Mental Deficiency. And third, it was the year when the use of chlorpromazine under its trade name Largactil, the first chemically-synthesised, anti-psychotic drug began to be used quite widely in Britain.

The three events, which together make 1954 a turning point in the history of mental health services in Britain, are all intimately related to the development of community care. The decline in the resident population of mental hospitals has been treated by Andrew Scull as the marker of decarceration and the move into the community.[26] The Royal Commission transformed various local initiatives that had been taken to provide alternative services outside the mental hospital into a national policy. And drugs such as Largactil made the possibility of care beyond the walls of the mental hospital seem more and more possible.

Community care is, of course, an elusive concept whose meaning changes over time. It is most simply defined as the policy of treating mental disorder outside the mental hospital, and in the 1950s in Britain, when it was adopted as national policy, this was its dominant, overriding meaning. There was no very explicit or distinctive model of community care in operation. The implicit model derived from other health services with their distinction between three stages of care and three types of service: first, general practice (the key element of what we would now call primary care) for those with less serious problems and the identification of those needing specialist care; second, hospital or secondary care which was the province of the medical specialists and those in the acute stages of illness; and third, after-care for those who needed some form of rehabilitation or long-term care. Community care in its early formulations was frequently about the third stage of care: after care. Consequently it was typically envisaged as services for those who had already had a stay in a mental hospital, although reference was also made in the literature to those who might have mental illness requiring longer term support but not need in-patient treatment. Community care was, however, primarily about services for people who could be discharged from the mental hospital and about expanding these services so that more people, especially those with chronic problems, could be discharged and could be discharged at an earlier stage. It was also in Britain primarily a model of public sector provision, particularly services provided by local authorities such as social services and housing and therefore required cooperation between local and health authorities.

The contemporary interpretation of the term community care in this period had therefore three facets: it meant services *outside* the mental hospital, it particularly meant *after-care* services for those with long-standing problems, and it meant services provided in the *public sector*. We can see these features in the 1957 Report of the Royal Commission on Mental Illness and Deficiency.[27]

However, a further adaptation of this model of mental health care came with the argument, first put forward as clear policy by the Minister of Health in 1961, and repeated in the 1962 Hospital Plan, that there should be acute psychiatric units for the treatment of the mentally ill in general hospitals – a policy no doubt facilitated by the incorporation of mental health services into the NHS.[28] The implication of this was that psychiatrists would work alongside their medical colleagues in the same hospitals. The development of such units represented in fact only a modification of a long-standing belief in the need for special units to concentrate on the early treatment of acute cases, but these units had been attached to mental hospitals. To have them outside the mental hospital as units within a general hospital was a very significant modification: symbolically and practically it meant the mental hospital was no longer to be the centre of service provision. Mental hospitals would still deal with chronic cases; the new units those in the acute stages of illness. As a result the acute general hospital unit was to replace the mental hospital as the appropriate location for the second stage of care.

The policy shift away from the old mental hospital was further reinforced by the advent of anti-psychotic drugs in the 1950s. The new drugs reawakened assumptions about the curability of mental disorder and led to (over)optimistic talk about the eradication of the old long-stay patients. Whilst existing patients with chronic disorders would disappear only with time as they died, many claimed that there would be no new generations of long-stay patients. Consequently the old Victorian mental hospitals would no longer be needed and could gradually be closed. This was the vision put forward by Enoch Powell as Minister of Health in the Conservative Government in 1960 when he predicted the closing down of the old mental hospitals 'isolated, majestic, imperious, brooded over by the gigantic watertower and chimney combined, rising unmistakable and daunting out of the countryside'.[29]

In the event the movement towards community care in this period was halting and many psychiatrists sought to reform rather than to close down the old mental hospitals.[30] The slow progress in the introduction of community care in this period was primarily due to the fact that community care as it was then interpreted meant the addition of new services requiring capital investment – psychiatric units in general hospitals and the development of more after care services in the form of half-way houses, residential homes and so forth.[31] The financial constraints faced by the NHS since its inception ensured a slow pace of change in the provision of new services, given the public sector assumptions underpinning community care. Significantly, too, in Britain there was no real attempt in the 1960s to develop a distinctive model of community care centred on the Community Mental Health Centre as there was in the United States – the model that was adopted in the Netherlands in the 1970s.

The slow pace of change in terms of establishing new services did not preclude other important changes in the mental health services in this period. Most obviously the numbers actually resident in the mental hospitals began to decline, although no mental hospitals actually closed. Instead the number of discharges increased significantly, partly facilitated by the 1959 Mental Health Act which replaced voluntary admission with informal admission, shifting the onus from establishing a willingness to enter voluntarily to presuming a willingness unless there was evidence to the contrary.[32] But admissions also increased and there were signs of the emergence of a 'revolving door' with patients being discharged and then readmitted only to be discharged once more after a period in hospital.

Of equal importance were the changes in the balance of power between professional groups in this period. The 1959 Act has been seen by many as the high point of medical power, and certainly as regards compulsory detention and treatment medical powers were largely unchecked. Moreover the introduction of the expanding gamut of psychotropic medications gave a new rationale for, and legitimacy to, psychiatric intervention. Nonetheless the post-war developments posed an enormous threat to psychiatry. On the one hand, within the mental hospitals themselves the overriding power of the medical superintendent was diminished and the post began to be phased out in the 1960s. Moreover integration with other parts of medicine often led to a loss of power to other health bodies. On the other hand, the development of community mental health services arguably led to a diffusion and gradual diminution of psychiatric power as other mental health facilities became more widespread, facilities in which psychiatrists were often in more direct competition with other mental health professionals, such as psychologists, social workers and the emerging group of community psychiatric nurses.[33] In addition, the direct criticisms of psychiatry also became vocal. Whilst the new drugs seemed to offer a weapon that strengthened psychiatrists' power, critics of a physically-oriented psychiatry were very strong, including voices from within the profession. In Britain, R. D. Laing and David Cooper's conceptualisations of mental disorder focused on the experiences of those deemed disordered and questioned bio-medical models of mental sickness.[34] Such ideas helped to sustain and reinforce, though they did not initiate, the policy of community care since they called into question the value of medical treatment in mental hospitals.

Privatisation and Competition, 1979–1997

The final period in the history of twentieth century psychiatry in Britain is defined in terms of the emergence of the new Conservative Government in 1979 and the rapid development of the ideology of the New Right which explicitly encouraged both privatisation and competition. Of course there was no sudden break in 1979. In particular we can trace many of the efforts to reduce public expenditure that characterise the Thatcherite era to the early years of the decade and to the oil crises and the fiscal crises they generated. What is distinctive however from 1979 onwards is the ideological commitment to cutting back public sector provision and the welfare state and to encouraging the private sector and competition. Private provision and a competitive market were seen as necessarily superior and preferable to public sector provision.

This ideological shift had a very significant impact on the policy of community care which had by then been in existence for over twenty years. Most importantly of all it undermined the taken for granted assumption that community care services would as far as possible be publicly provided services. Instead the private sector was to be crucial – a private sector that was itself defined negatively as simply 'not the public sector'. In practice this meant three very different forms of provision all to be encompassed within the new meaning of community care: services provided on a commercial basis, such as commercially-run psychiatric hospitals, boarding houses and nursing homes; voluntary sector services, which already played a role in community provision; and informal care provided by family and friends. This shift in meaning is clear from a range of policy documents of the period which begin to refer to the importance of family and friends and voluntary services and concentrate far less on formal care. It is also reflected in a new policy language where terms such as client or even customer replace that of patient.

Ironically this new reliance on the private sector accelerated the move towards community care since it meant that more people could be discharged from mental hospitals without the need to provide publicly-funded alternatives. Consequently the cost of providing new publicly-funded alternatives to mental hospital care became less and less of a deterrent to early discharge. Indeed pressure to reduce public expenditure encouraged the run down of psychiatric hospitals whose unit costs (costs per capita) increased as the numbers of patients declined since there were fixed costs in maintaining buildings and so forth. Patients could be discharged almost anywhere and this would still count as community care. Increasingly those discharged from mental hospitals were to be found in other institutions: private boarding houses, nursing homes and homes for the elderly, or sometimes with their families, or living rough in large cities without work or homes. Sometimes the new location was of a high standard and appropriate; often it was not. And with more patients being discharged including, very importantly, those whose problems were long-standing, for the first time mental hospitals could actually be closed down. Over the last two decades many have been shut: in 1960 there were 130 mental hospitals in England; by 1993, 89 had closed leaving only 41 open.[35] In their place there has been a growth in private provision as well as an increasing dependence on informal care.

Increased competition, so central to New Right ideology, has been encouraged within the mental health field in three main ways. First, through the increase in private sector provision as a result of direct support by government to the private sector.[36] Significantly this has not been by any means been free and open competition, since requirements have been introduced or targets set for the level of private provision so that the public sector has not always been able to compete against private companies. Second, there have been attempts to introduce competition within the public sector itself by the establishment of the so-called internal market within the National Health Service – attempts which the change of government in 1997 look set to curtail. And third, there have been explicit attempts to reduce the power of professionals and to limit and reduce their 'restrictive practices'. Here the power of the medical profession has been a major focus of attack across the health services, with new management structures put in place designed to limit the power of the profession.

It is not entirely clear however whether psychiatrists' power has been diminished over the last two decades, notwithstanding the Conservative Governments' explicit endeavours. Certainly psychiatrists, like other medical specialists, have been subject to greater non-medical, managerial control and this reduction in managerial power has coincided with the very significant loss of their specific empire – the mental hospital. Mental hospitals not only provided the location in which psychiatry emerged as a distinctive discipline of medicine, they also provided a demarcated domain over which psychiatrists could reign, albeit within the constraints set by funding bodies. The movement away from mental hospitals represented therefore a potential loss of empire for psychiatrists. Furthermore, as I noted in the previous section, with the move to community care psychiatrists have increasingly to compete with a range of other mental health professionals. And, like other medical specialists involved in secondary care, psychiatrists are facing the redirection of power towards a primary care-led health service that has been part of explicit government policy over the last decade and is likely to continue with the new administration. In the case of mental health, one consequence has been the employment of counsellors within primary care, though GPs, like psychiatrists retain their bias towards psychotropic medication as the standard treatment for mental disorder. This shift of emphasis towards primary care, which is partly motivated by a concern for cost-effectiveness, is not likely to disappear with any movement from general practice fundholding to local commissioning that may follow from the recent change of government in Britain.

Against these changes, all of which have the potential to reduce psychiatrists' power, should be set two counter-tendencies. First, whilst the old empire of the mental hospital has been disappearing it is being replaced by new empires – a range of smaller but more numerous satellite states. Consequently psychiatrists can now, with the move to community care, potentially spread their tentacles more widely across a wide range of services for a far greater range of patients, and in so doing they can formulate and disseminate new ideas about mental disorder and new treatments. This is part of the process that has been described as the psychiatrisation of society.[37] Second, developments in genetics, in the neurosciences and in the biochemistry of mental disorder have strengthened the hand of psychiatrists in their competition with other professionals; they have given a new legitimacy to bio-medical models of mental disorder and led to new drug treatments.[38] Certainly there is no doubt that within psychiatry biological ideas are very much in the ascendancy and physical forms of treatment which are under medical control are now very widely used in the treatment of all types of mental disorder and are expanding the boundaries of mental disorder.[39] But it needs to be noted that the new scientific developments may lead to a loss of some psychiatric territory to neurology and that the biological reductionism on which much biological psychiatry is founded is likely in the longer term to prove inadequate.

Privatisation and market competition have not eradicated all public sector mental health services in Britain. Significant transformations are, however, occurring in these services. I want to mention three. The first is that publicly-funded specialist mental health services are now highly selective: they are targeted (or rationed) on those whose problems are most severe, and in particular those who are considered most dangerous or, to use the newer language, most at risk of harming either themselves or others.[40] One consequence of this is that the numbers of those admitted on a compulsory basis has now increased after the very low level of the 1970s.[41] In addition new procedures in the form of supervisory orders have been introduced to regulate the freedoms of those discharged into the community who are considered difficult and potentially dangerous.

The second change is that during the second half of the 1970s and the 1980s the United States model of the community mental health centres has been introduced in a modified form, as it has elsewhere in Europe, as one model of community care. In the US the model of mental health services developed in the 1970s placed the Community Mental Health Centre not the mental hospital as the centre point of the new health services – a CMHC which provided a diverse range of services including acute beds, emergency and drop-in services, out-patient clinics and was staffed by a diverse range of professionals. However, when CMHCs were introduced in the UK they did not have any beds, so excluding the second stage of health care and those with the most severe problems. This ensured that they could not be the centre of service provision but developed alongside other types of service. Indeed, instead of being set up as a distinctive type of facility they were often developed simply as groupings of mental health professionals who worked together – as

24

community mental health teams (not centres) delivering services across a range of different locations.

The third important development in public sector provision in Britain in this period is that, in an effort to co-ordinate care for the individual across a range of services, we have seen the development of the so-called 'care programme approach', the CPA. Care programmes or plans of care are supposed to be devised for every individual client specifying the appropriate plan of action for them across a range of services. This individualisation of the programme of care fits with the individualistic ideology that underpins the commitment to the free market and with post-Fordist models of customised production.[42] Yet it is not clear how far how developments like this, or those such as the allocation of 'key workers', actually improve the quality of care that is provided or make it more responsive to individual needs.

Conclusion

Comparison with other European countries and the United States shows important similarities in the trajectories of twentieth century psychiatry. Most notable has been the movement from custodial care centred on the asylum catering for those deemed to be lunatics, primarily amongst the poor and marginal in society, to a more therapeutically-oriented psychiatry delivered to a far wider group of the population across a wider range of services in which psychiatrists are but one group amongst a number of mental health professionals. Nonetheless, despite the significant correspondences in the trajectories across different countries, the character of services do differ as does the precise timing of key changes. In particular the precise balance between physical, psychological and social approaches varies at a particular period of time as do the degree of integration of psychiatry and mental health services with other health services, and the balance between custody and repression versus care and treatment. These balances are the result of ongoing struggles and reflect the influence of a range of changing political, economic, social and cultural forces which affect the shape of welfare provision, including mental health services. There can be little doubt that these same struggles over competing explanations and treatments of disorder, over the degree of integration there should be with other medical services, and between care and control will continue over the next century.

25

Notes

1. Michel Foucault, *Madness and Civilization* (London: Tavistock, 1967).
2. See Joan Busfield, *Men, Women and Madness: Understanding Gender and Mental Disorder* (London: Macmillan, 1996), Chapter 3.
3. Charles E. Rosenberg and Janet Golden (eds), *Framing Disease: Studies in Cultural History* (New Brunswick: Rutgers University Press, 1992); see also Erving Goffman, *Frames of Mind* (New York: Harper & Row, 1974).
4. See, for instance, Frank Parkin, *Marxism and Class Theory* (London: Tavistock, 1979); Anne Witz, *Professions and Patriarchy* (London: Routledge, 1992).
5. Eric Hobsbawm, *The Age of Extremes: The Short Twentieth Century* (London: Michael Joseph, 1994). Hobsbawm's century began in 1914.
6. Kathleen Jones, *A History of the Mental Health Services* (London: Routledge, 1972).
7. See Clive Unsworth, *The Politics of Mental Health Legislation* (Oxford: Clarendon Press, 1987).
8. Commissioners in Lunacy, *Fifty-Fourth Report* (London: HMSO, 1900); Peter R. Cox, *Demography*, Fourth Edition (London: Cambridge University Press, 1970), p. 322.
9. Joan Busfield, 'Is Mental Illness a Female Malady? Men, Women and Madness in Nineteenth Century England', *Sociology*, 29:259-77.
10. Andrew Scull, *The Most Solitary of Afflictions: Madness and Society in Britain, 1700-1900* (New York: Yale University Press, 1993).
11. See, for instance, Pat Thane, *The Foundations of the Welfare State*, Second Edition (London: Longman, 1982).
12. G. Elliot Smith and T .H. Pear, *Shell-Shock and Its Lessons* (Manchester: The University Press, 1917).
13. J. T. MacCurdy, *War Neuroses* (Cambridge: Cambridge University Press, 1918), p.9.
14. Martin Stone, 'Shellshock and the Psychologists', in W.F. Bynum, R. Porter and M. Shepherd (eds), *The Anatomy of Madness, II: Institutions and Society* (London: Tavistock, 1985), 249.
15. Philip Bean, *Compulsory Admissions to Mental Hosptials* (New York: Wiley, 1980).
16. Henri F. Ellenberger, *The Discovery of the Unconscious: The History and Evolution of Dynamic Psychiatry* (New York: Basic Books, 1970).
17. W. H. Rivers, 'Preface'. G. Elliot Smith and T. H. Pear, *op.cit.*
18. Nikolas Rose, *Psychology, Politics and Society in England, 1869-1939* (London: Routledge and Kegan Paul, 1985), Chapter 8.
19. Kelly Loughlin, *Gender and Schizophrenia in British Psychological*

Medicine, 1880-1930 (University of Essex, Ph.D. 1996).

20. D. K Henderson and R. D. Gillespie, *Textbook of Psychiatry* (Oxford: Oxford University Press, 1927).

21. P. Bean, *op. cit.*

22. *Royal Commission on Lunacy and Mental Disorder* (London HMSO, 1926), p. 20.

23. Quoted in Michael Foot, *Aneurin Bevan, 1945-1960* (St. Albans: Paladin, 1975), p.137.

24. Elliot S. Valenstein, *Great and Desperate Cures: The Rise and Decline of Psychosurgery and Other Radical Treatments* (New York: Basic Books, 1986).

25. Diana Gittins outlines both the growth of ECT and the use of lobotomies in a provincial mental hospital, Severalls Colchester, in *Madness in its Place* (London: Routledge, 1998), Chapter 7.

26. Andrew Scull, *Decarceration: Community Treatment, A Radical View*, Second Edition (Cambridge: Polity Press, 1984).

27. *Royal Commission on the Law Relating to Mental Illness and Mental Deficiency, 1954-1957, Report* (London: HMSO, 1957), p. 208.

28. Geoff Baruch and Andrew Treacher, *Psychiatry Observed* (London: Routledge & Kegan Paul, 1978), Chapters 4 and 5.

29. Quoted in MIND *Co-ordination or Chaos? The Run-down of Psychiatric Hospitals* (London: MIND, 1974), p.1.

30. See, for instance, Russell Barton, *Institutional Neurosis* (Bristol: John Wright, 1959).

31. The 1959 Mental Health Act did not make their provision mandatory.

32. In this the 1959 Act followed the recommendation of the Report of the Royal Commission.

33. Colin Samson, 'The Fracturing of Medical Dominance in British Psychiatry?', *Sociology of Health and Illness*, 17 (1995), 245-68; Peter Nolan, *A History of Mental Health Nursing* (London: Chapman and Hall, 1993).

34. R. D. Laing, *The Bird of Paradise and the Politics of Experience* (Harmondsworth: Penguin, 1967); David Cooper, *Psychiatry and Anti-psychiatry* (London: Paladin, 1970).

35. Department of Health, *Annual Report of the Health Service in England, 1994-5* (London: HMSO,1995).

36. This support included tax concessions to those over 65 who paid for private health insurance, as well as requiring some services to be put out to tender.

37. Peter Miller and Nikolas Rose (eds), *The Power of Psychiatry* (Cambridge: Polity Press, 1986), p.15.

38. Philip Bean and Patricia Mounser, *Discharged from Mental Hospitals* (London: Macmillan, 1993).

39. On the last point see, Peter D. Kramer, *Listening to Prozac* (London: Fourth Estate, 1994).

40. See Audit Commission, *Finding A Place* (London: HMSO, 1994), p. 5.

41. Department of Health *Statistical Bulletin*, 10 (1996).

42. Sylvia Walby and June Greenwell, *Medicine and Nursing: Professions in a Changing Health Service* (London: Sage, 1994), Chapter 6.

2

Dutch Psychiatry after World War II:
An Overview

Paul Schnabel

Life as Usual

As in many other areas of social and political life in the Netherlands, Dutch psychiatry resumed its pace after World War II as if nothing had happened in those five dreadful years. Of what really *had* happened, there was nothing left to see: the deportation of patients and staff of the 'Apeldoornsche Bosch', the psychiatric hospital of the Jewish community in the Netherlands, to Auschwitz in 1943. On arrival, most of them were immediately killed. On the site of the Apeldoornsche Bosch there is now an institution for the mentally handicapped. The name has been changed and the rather austere buildings of the old hospital have all been replaced by friendly low-rise buildings and family-home type dwellings.

For most of the other Dutch psychiatric hospitals – still called 'gestichten' at the time, a word that in Dutch social life exactly conveys the meaning Erving Goffman tried to encompass in his concept of the 'total institution' – the war had simply meant hardship and sometimes evacuation to another mental hospital in a safer area. After the war, many buildings were in bad shape and most wards were overcrowded. Generally, there was a severe shortage of staff – doctors and nurses – and a persistent lack of money. But in practice this was the case throughout the health care system, and psychiatry was understandably not a priority in the first years after the war (the same low priority can be witnessed now in the countries of Eastern Europe). It took more than 20 years before building work could start on the first new mental hospital. Its buildings still bear the modernist touch of the sixties, but the whole concept of the institution, its remote location and its rather traditional layout, is considered now to be completely obsolete. This last 'old' psychiatric hospital (St. Franciscushof, Raalte) is now, together with the first 'new' hospital of the nineteenth century (Santpoort, near Haarlem, founded in 1849), one of the first to close its doors for good.

Major Developments in the Provision of Mental Health Care since 1945

Of course, as elsewhere in the fifties, Dutch psychiatry eagerly took up the new treatment possibilities offered by the first psychotropic agents: antipsychotic drugs like Largactil, followed later by the first antidepressants, anxiolytica, sedatives and antimanic agents (lithium carbonate). The so-called somatic therapies, desperate attempts in the pre-war years to disguise the psychiatrist in the surgeon's gown and mask, were soon forgotten. Only ECT (electro-convulsive therapy) survived to become the target of anti-psychiatric attention in the seventies. Now ECT is accepted again as a treatment of last resort in severe depression, administered to a few hundred patients each year under strict conditions.

Between 1953 and 1963, medical (i.e. pharmacological) interventions for a broad spectrum of mental disorders became generally available, and on this solid base all kinds of new social and psychological therapies could flourish. For many patients, even those with the most severe mental illnesses, life outside the institutions became a real option. However, more than a decade would pass before this option became a real alternative to hospitalization for a growing number of patients.

Psychotherapy was introduced in the Netherlands before the turn of the century, at about the same time as the first chair in psychiatry was established at Utrecht University (1890) and the first psychiatrists took up private practice. Of course, since there were no possibilities as yet for reimbursing health care costs, access to this type of care was strictly reserved for the more affluent layers of society. Psychotherapy turned into psychoanalysis and it would take another fifty years before behavioral therapy or Carl Rogers' ideas put an end to this monopoly. At present more than 2,200 licensed psychotherapists (mainly psychologists) and about 1,700 psychiatrists provide mental health care. Most of them are employed by the regular mental health institutions, but a growing number are (full-time or part-time) in private practice. Although traditional psychoanalysis has become rare as a treatment modality (between 50 and 100 new patients each year), the psychodynamic approach still dominates the field, followed by the behavioral and cognitive

30

therapies, the Rogerian approach and systems theory. The existential therapies are quite popular, but not acknowledged by the professional bodies and not eligible for third party payment.

Social psychiatric and psychosocial services (providing care for children, alcohol abusers, the demented elderly, people with disrupted marriages etc.) began offering outpatient care in the years before the Second World War. Many of them were part of the 'pillarization' system so typical for the structure of Dutch society up to 1975. So the same types of social psychiatric services were offered through separate institutions to Roman Catholic, Protestant or 'non-confessional' clients and patients. In 1982 all ties with the religious denominations were severed: outpatient services for social psychiatry, psychosocial counselling and psychotherapy were integrated in the new RIAGG ('Regional Institute of Ambulatory Mental Health Care'), the Dutch equivalent of the American Community Mental Health Centers. Each RIAGG was responsible for mental health care delivery in a designated catchment area and financed by an annual budget based on the number of inhabitants (about 40 guilders – then equivalent to 10 pounds or so – per person per year). Services providing for alcohol- and drug-addicts were organised separately.

Within a few years, the almost 60 RIAGGs developed into the main providers of outpatient mental health care in the country. They now deal with about 500,000 patients each year. As the waiting lists for the RIAGGs have come to be long, a growing number of people prefer to look for therapy in the private sector, in many cases at their own expense. There are indications that the so-called 'alternative therapists' – many of them of a distinct 'New Age' orientation – enjoy a fast-growing clientèle. Of course, the differentiation in healing practices between problems of the mind and problems of the body is here less relevant.

Facts and Figures

At first, the only external indication that the situation inside the hospitals was changing was the diminishing growth in the number of 'real' hospital beds. Admittedly, the actual number of beds in use for the care of psychiatric patients rose in the fifties and sixties, as ever more mentally handicapped patients could be transferred to their 'own' institutions. Between 1970 and the present the number of places increased threefold and now stands at 43,000. In the seventies the newly-built nursing homes for the demented elderly also took over part of the function of the traditional psychiatric hospitals: today, these comprise more than 31,000 beds.

The general psychiatric hospitals (current bed capacity about 23,000) gradually came to focus on the care of psychiatric patients alone, and at the same time a process of internal differentiation led to the development of new therapeutic régimes for specific subgroups of patients. Beginning in the sixties, most psychiatric hospitals witnessed an astounding proliferation of all kinds of therapeutic communities, rehabilitation units, short and long term treatment programs, substance abuse clinics and services for people with behavioral problems and personality disorders. Hardly any of these new developments brought relief to the group of the chronically mentally ill. Approximately half of the total number of hospital beds was (and still is) taken up by the more than 10,000 chronic patients already hospitalized for at least two consecutive years. Even today the psychiatric hospitals provide accommodation for more than 5,000 patients staying there for at least 10 and up to more than 65 years, i.e. their whole life as an adult.

Most of the long-stay patients are now people who have grown old in the hospital. For those who still remain there, the chances of successful reintegration in society are virtually non-existent. Their living conditions in hospital, however, are now generally more in line with the standard considered acceptable in the wider society. Many of them have their own room in one of the sheltered housing projects developed by the psychiatric hospitals as part of a nationwide scheme for the renovation of old psychiatric institutions. In 1978 less than 8,000 of the psychiatric beds were rated as 'good' and 9,000 as 'bad', in terms of quality of the buildings they were located in. In 1991 the number of beds rated 'good' had been doubled and less than 2,000 beds earned the label 'bad'.

The majority of people in psychiatric care remain outside the psychiatric hospitals. Most new chronic patients are only intermittently hospitalized, if at all. Even in situations where it is quite clear that they have great difficulty managing their own life, most of them prefer to stay outside hospital. The RIAGGs, outpatient clinics of psychiatric and general hospitals, psychiatrists or psychologists in private practice and general practitioners, provide 'extramural' (outpatient, ambulatory) care for their problems. Short-term hospitalization is possible in the PAAZ, the psychiatric department of the general hospital, and partial hospitalization programs ('semimural care') are available in many places. The whole gamut of psychiatric, psychotherapeutic and psychosocial services is provided for by the present mental health system. In 1996 the intramural services in mental health accounted for 140,000 patient episodes, the semimural services for 50,000 episodes and the extramural services – the general practitioner and social worker not included – for more than 750,000 patient episodes. As many patients make use of the services of more than one institution every year, with a population of 15.5 million inhabitants these nearly 950,000 patient episodes relate to about 4% of the population.

Only recently, a national survey made it clear that in the adult population the 12-month prevalence of all mental disorders is about 23.5%; the prevalence 'ever' is 41.2%. Thus, the majority of people with mental disorders are not referred to specialized mental health care institutions. Many of them (especially in cases of depression or anxiety) are seen by general practitioners, but epidemiological studies have revealed that in many cases – alcohol abuse and dependence is an obvious example – neither the services of the general practitioner, nor those of the mental health system are sought. Sometimes patients, like their doctors, fail to recognize their somatic symptoms as indicators of an underlying mental disorder.

Mental Health Care as Part of Welfare Policy

The present level of service provision and the meticulously planned distribution of services by way of regional mental health networks is the outcome of a specific welfare policy on the national level. This could be implemented only through the allocation of a comparatively generous budget specifically for mental health. Traditionally, care for the mentally ill was subsumed under a city council's obligation to take care of the needs of its own poor. In that respect, a mental hospital was not so much a medical institution as an asylum for the poor with a mental illness, a mental handicap, a dementia or a substance disorder. It was only in the fifties that the last battle was resolved between psychiatrists and hospital managements – many still run by religious orders – as to who was primarily responsible for the patients. The doctors won, and with them a medical model that would soon be contested by the proponents of a more socially-oriented model and by the first patient advocates. Nobody, however, contested the by then practically complete coverage of a stay in a psychiatric hospital by the Sickness Fund, the national health insurance scheme.

Attempts in the twenties and the thirties to introduce a national system of compulsory insurance for health care costs always failed. The Germans introduced their own system during the war in an attempt to gain the support of the working population, and at the same time to prevent Dutch industries from working at a lower level of labour cost than their German counterparts. Essentially the same system was continued after the war. In the early fifties, short-term psychiatric hospitalization was made eligible for coverage by the Sickness Fund Act (ZFW). Gradually, the number of days reimbursed was increased. From 1968 onward, through the new Exceptional Medical Expenses Act (AWBZ) – an additional compulsory health insurance system for the population as a whole – much more money became available for the care of the chronically mentally ill than could ever have been provided by the city councils. The first year of stay in a mental hospital was covered by the ZFW; thereafter, the AWBZ took over.

The extramural or ambulatory services, many of them founded back in the thirties, always had difficulty making ends meet. Their budget was meagre and very insecure, highly dependent from year to year on fluctuating state subsidies, additional grants from private foundations and the scant fees they could impose on (some of) their patients. To stimulate the development of the RIAGGs the government decided in 1982 to allocate additional AWBZ funds for the new ambulatory services. An initially generous budget system (based on capitation) fuelled the development of over 60 RIAGGs all over the country and provided the basis for sustainable growth of the ambulatory services over a number of years.

In 1989 all services provided by mental hospitals, ambulatory services and private practitioners became eligible for reimbursing from AWBZ funds. Thereby the mental health sector as a whole could benefit from the same advantages as the institutions for the mentally handicapped and the nursing homes for the demented elderly had enjoyed since the inception of the AWBZ in 1968. In 1996 the total cost for the mentally handicapped amounted to six billion guilders, for the services for the demented elderly about three billion guilders had to be spent, while five billion guilders was needed for mental health care (about 8% of the total health care bill and 0.8% of the national income).

Money – or to be more precise, the funds allocated for psychiatry by the AWBZ – is the fertilizer of the soil on which Dutch psychiatry blooms. As the AWBZ was introduced long after the Sickness Funds were established, the moment of take-off for the development of psychiatry and mental health care in the modern sense of the word came rather late: at the end of the sixties for the psychiatric hospitals, at the end of the seventies for the predecessors of the RIAGGs. Many developments in care provision were in themselves not that new: what was new was above all the availability of the means to *implement* new ideas – or, for that matter, old ones – on a relatively grand scale.

Public Funds, Private Providers

Interestingly enough, successive increases in the funding of the mental health services (in 1950, 1986 and 1989) were not the consequence of a major political change in the public-private mix of funding. Admittedly, the contribution of private out-of-pocket payments to the budget of mental health institutions has become less and less significant, to the point where it is today marginal; yet the main locus of change is to be found in the mode of public funding. Poor relief, paid for by local authorities out of their own budgets, made way for a national health insurance system entitling every citizen to access to services of good quality and guaranteeing budgetary continuity for the service providers. Health insurance money cannot be used for other purposes than the provision of health care and this provision is only possible if its delivery can be guaranteed over time. The insurance system makes health care relatively immune to the vicissitudes of rapidly changing political priorities: the entitlements of patients can only be restricted by law, and it is not easy to find a political majority willing to do that.

The acceptance of mental health care as an integral part of the health care system, as a medical enterprise, typically meant a rise in status and budget to a middle-class level. Compared to the social sector, salaries in the medical sector are higher, the buildings better in style and decoration, the level of care more professional and there is more differentiation in the services offered. In psychiatry just as in the medical sector as a whole, there is – certainly at the hospital level – no demand for an extended private service system. As the majority of the Dutch population considers itself to be 'middle class', the level, style and layout of the medical sector is completely in accordance with their expectations. It not only reflects middle-class values; it *is* middle-class. The main reason why quite a few people prefer to go to a private practitioner, and are even willing to pay for his or her services out of their own pocket, is that in this way they can avoid the waiting lists for psychotherapy and counselling which confront them at many RIAGGs. Due to the emphasis now placed on public mental health and social psychiatric services for chronic patients, the centers can no longer sustain their original balance between psychosocial and social psychiatric services, at least not without a substantial rise in their yearly budget. At present, this budget is only allowed to grow by a very limited amount each year.

Mental health care institutions – be they hospitals, RIAGGs, or sheltered housing projects – are typically private not-for-profit organisations. The few state institutions in this sector have now all been privatized. However, the autonomy of these institutions is not unrestricted. The Ministry of Health issues quite detailed guidelines and the Sickness Fund Council – responsible for the execution of the provisions of the AWBZ Act – is a formidable controller of the money spent. The regional sickness funds are responsible for contracting the services to be provided to the population and they also have influence, albeit limited, on the budgets of the different institutions. The planning of services (new sites, number of beds and places) is a major responsibility of the government. All in all, the growing diversity of checks and balances, the mix of autonomy and dependence, the interface between private and public, have made the (mental) health care system extremely complex. As with many Dutch welfare state arrangements one might say that it functions relatively well and works rather smoothly, but even the single most important agent, the Ministry of Health, would not be able to say precisely by what rules and in what way.

Mental Health as Public Health.

More than in other areas of health care the Ministry of Health is directly involved in mental health. Inevitably, mental health contains a strong element of public health: involuntary admission to mental hospital (certification) is a judicial and not a medical decision; the care for the homeless with a mental illness is a responsibility of local government; the civil rights of psychiatric patients have to be safeguarded; mental health prevention is dependent on government subsidies; and so on. In the days when mental health care was paid for out of the social services budgets of the city councils, one might say that nearly all psychiatry belonged to the area of public health. Now this area is confined to the responsibility for the safeness and well-being of the community, the collection of epidemiological data and the development of community-oriented prevention programmes for mental health.

Public mental health has long been neglected, but as it became more and more clear that mental health care is more than just providing cure and care, there arose a new interest in the custodial and preventive functions of mental health care. The Ministry of Health is now developing new policies to stimulate city councils to

become more active in these areas. Proposals are even in preparation
to change the new law on involuntary admission (BOPZ). The
present 'lunacy act' is just three years old and is the unhappy
outcome of a parliamentary debate that took more than 20 years. At
present, the only criterion for involuntary admission is imminent
danger to others or the patient, occasioned by the patient as a direct
consequence of his or her mental illness. Even then, it has to be
made plausible that only placing the patient in a mental institution
will remove the danger. To make matters even more complicated,
involuntary admission does not entitle the psychiatrist to use force
in treatment: patients may refuse drugs or any other kind of
treatment. About 15% of all admissions in psychiatric hospitals take
place under the BOPZ Act.

However, most patients in need of treatment but refusing it are
not at all dangerous and there is now a strong lobby in favour of
reinstating the old 'for your own good' clause in the new law. In
modern psychiatric institutions, strongly treatment-oriented as they
are, the right to refuse treatment is experienced as a real dilemma in
cases of involuntary commitment, especially when the patient is
psychotic and violent at the same time. In most of these cases there
is hardly any doubt that it is possible to relieve the patient of his or
her symptoms. It is not at all easy to get around the strict
stipulations of the law, for in every hospital the patients'
'ombudsman' (an independent patient advocate working in the
hospital, but employed by a national authority) closely watches over
the rights of patients. By law, medical treatment is (with very few
exceptions) only possible by informed consent of the patient; the use
of force and isolation cells, or any curtailment of a patient's civil
rights, is kept under strict surveillance.

At the other end of the public mental health spectrum, we find
the preventive programmes in mental health, sometimes organized
by the municipal health authority (GG&GD), but in most cases by
the (private) RIAGGs. Typical areas of prevention and mental
health education are support for people taking care of a demented
parent, psycho-education for families with a schizophrenic son or
daughter, community work with depressed patients, or prevention
of bullying in schools. Characteristic of mental health prevention is
a strong orientation to people at risk and secondary prevention.
The ideas of the mental health movement of the fifties and sixties
(primary prevention, even societal change) have lost their appeal
due to lack of empirical data and an appropriate technology to back
up the lofty humanistic ideals. As a sector within the health care

system, mental health chose for a future of professionalization (especially in the area of psychotherapy) and medicalization. Very soon after its introduction in 1980 the new DSM system of classification became generally accepted, and in the present decade we witness the emergence of an 'evidence-based medicine' movement with a plethora of protocols, standards and consensus statements.

The Welfare State: Idea and Ideal

The Dutch welfare state was modelled after the English example, but retained some of the traditional Bismarckian traits that prevailed in most West European countries. The economic growth and the discovery of huge natural gas reserves in the early sixties provided the funds necessary for the creation of a welfare state of hitherto unforeseen dimensions. In fact, the development of a fully-fledged welfare state became for the first time a political goal in itself. Political parties were looking for gaps to be filled and the idea of the perfection of society by way of a skilful combination of political will, unlimited means and professional knowledge gained a remarkable popularity. The major political parties all more or less endorsed this idea in the years between 1965 and 1975.

In this attempt to end history by establishing a complete and all-encompassing welfare state, it was unavoidable that politicians, journalists and activists would at some point stumble on the mental hospitals and their population. It was a shock to the public eye to find them in such a poor state. Mental health was quickly discovered as a domain too long forgotten. At the same time that the government tried to gain control over the skyrocketing costs of the health care system in general, it decided to invest in mental health care. Building schemes for the renewal of psychiatric hospitals were developed and psychotherapy became the object of great expectations.

In 1974 the State Secretary of Health, J.H. Hendriks, presented his "Structuurnota Gezondheidszorg" (Plan for a new structure in the health care system), the first policy document ever on the organisation of the health care system. In this White Paper he endorsed, among many other changes, a mental health care system that would provide all citizens with high quality mental health care in their own community and on all necessary levels: outpatient, part-time, inpatient. What he envisaged was a system of regionalized mental health care with the general practitioner as a gatekeeper, the

RIAGG as community mental health center for outpatient care, the psychiatric hospital as a major treatment facility and the psychogeriatric nursing home as a facility for the care of the demented elderly.

More than twenty years later we can say that a major part of his plan has become reality. In a country with a multiparty system (about 12 parties!) and a notoriously difficult coalition system that allows a government to survive only as long as it is prepared to look for compromise, this is rather astonishing. In fact, outside the field of mental health practically none of Hendriks' great plans to restructure the health care system have been realised. The same fate was suffered by most of the grand designs of his successors, Veder-Smit, Gardeniers-Berendsen, Van der Reijden, Dees, and Simons. Perhaps one has to include in this list Borst-Eilers, the present Minister of Health and the first to deny any penchant for thinking in grand designs ('Dutch health care is nearly perfect', she likes to say while trying to push a major change through parliament in the guise of a minor adjustment!)

The welfare state ideology is not only interesting in relation to its effects on the place allotted to mental health services, but also in its influence on the definition of mental health. The psychiatric hospital had always been considered to be a marginal place for marginal people. The rise of ambulatory services outside the hospital and without direct connections to the hospital was a first step towards a more socially integrated position for mental health. It has something to offer to people who were obviously not 'mad', but suffered nonetheless as victims of enduring and painful problems in living. Previously, neurotic, disturbed or unhappy people with sufficient financial means could rely on a highly individualized 'talking cure', i.e. psychotherapy (until 1960 mainly psychoanalysis), but for the majority of the population psychotherapy or even psychosocial counselling was hardly available and certainly not something they could pay for themselves.

The welfare state combined these different types of services under the heading 'mental health' and declared this area of care to be guided by the same principles as health care in general: available, accessible and acceptable to every citizen who might benefit from the services. A national insurance scheme would secure a safe financial basis for the care providers, independent of the income of the individual clients. Under these circumstances, psychiatry was quite willing to join forces with other professions under the aegis of mental health.

By way of spoiling this rosy picture I would like to add the hypothesis that in psychiatry, as in society in general, the sudden positive acceptance of mental illness and psychological problems was greatly enhanced by the growing tendency in the sixties to deny the harsh reality of mental illness, in particular its stubborn resistance to easy cures and good intentions. The rising popularity of psychotherapy and all kinds of experiential therapies was an important second factor. Looking back, it is difficult to grasp now the exceptionally high status awarded in those days to psychotherapists. Without any empirical evidence, their work was considered to be highly effective, even in the most difficult cases. A third factor that gave the new mental health its sudden upswing was the growing popularity of the labelling theory of mental illness and the romantic fervour of the antipsychiatric movement. Together they provided the ideological underpinning.

Psychiatry Then and Now

In 1974, Dutch mental health care was a fragmented system, consisting of about 40 mental hospitals (400 – 1200 beds), several hundred mainly small and autonomous ambulatory services, and a limited number of psychiatrists in private practice, some of them heading the psychiatric department (PAAZ) of a general hospital. In some places there were facilities for sheltered living and part-time treatment and there was an exciting proliferation noticeable in the area of psychotherapy, especially in the big cities and the university towns. Psychiatry was certainly not a popular choice for medical doctors wishing to become a medical specialist; the resulting shortage of psychiatrists opened the door to clinical psychologists and non-medical psychotherapists. The whole idea of a catchment area or of regionalization of care was unheard of. Cities like Amsterdam and Utrecht were very well equipped with all kind of services and practitioners, in Rotterdam there was next to nothing and in many areas of the country it would have been very difficult to find a psychotherapist or psychiatrist at all. Psychiatric hospitals were very unevenly distributed over the country and mainly situated in wooded areas far from the big cities. Many of them still cherished their confessional identity, but all of them arbitrarily accepted (and refused) patients of any denomination from every corner of the country. The divide between inpatient and outpatient services was practically unsurmountable.

The picture today is quite different. In this chapter I have set

40

out the changes which have been brought about, but it may still be useful to ask again what made these changes possible. The answer is quite simple: money. The mental health sector was impoverished and the Ministry of Health offered the possibility of renewing long derelict buildings, attracting more and better staff, getting more permanent funding, differentiating between patient categories, and specializing within the array of services provided. The bottom line, sometimes very implicit, was always the same: adherence to the new principles of the organization of mental health care as *an integrated system providing comprehensive care to a community in a circumscribed area.*

Even today, with the regionalization of services entering a new phase (one regional provider instead of a number of autonomous organizations in the different echelons), money is again the catalyst of the new developments. Several years ago, a small part of the budget of the psychiatric hospitals was placed in the 'Zorgvernieuwingsfonds' (a regional budget for the renewal of mental health care). To get hold of this money again, the different mental health care providers in a region had to devise new projects, in collaboration with each other and with a strong component of de-institutionalisation. Literally hundreds of these projects landed on the doormat at the offices of the regional Sickness Funds. In many regions this was the final impetus needed to bring the partners together in a new comprehensive organisation for mental health care.

Today, the danger of regional monopolies of care would seem to be imminent. Superficially, it may even seem that at the end of the century just as at its beginning, psychiatry will be the domain of some 40 large institutions; and in the eyes of some critics, the word institution is synonymous with 'psychiatric hospital'. However, even if one labels the institutions in this way, in reality they bear no resemblance to the old psychiatric hospital. They are 'virtual' organizations, coordinating structures governing a loose network of small, highly differentiated and socially integrated centres of care. Most patients will live in society permanently, making use of the services they need to continue doing just that.

Notes

There is a rich and extensive literature in Dutch on mental health and mental health care in this country and although Dutch researchers regularly publish in international journals, they hardly ever do so on specifically 'Dutch' topics such as the organisation of mental health care. Readers who would like to have access to the references in Dutch relating to this article can contact the author for a bibliography. English readers are advised to consult the following books:

1. A.J.P. Schrijvers (ed.), *Health and Health Care in the Netherlands. A Critical Self-Assessment by Dutch Experts in the Medical and Health Sciences* (Utrecht: De Tijdstroom, 1997). This book provides the most up-to-date overview of developments in all areas of health and health care.
2. G.H. Okma, *Studies on Dutch Health Politics, Policies and Laws* (Utrecht University: Ph.D. thesis, 1997).
3. A. de Swaan, *In Care of the State. Health Care, Education and Welfare in Europe and the USA in the Modern Era* (Cambridge: Polity Press, 1988).
4. J. Goudsblom, *Dutch Society* (New York: Random House, 1967).

The Dutch Ministry of Health, Welfare and Sport regularly publishes in English informative brochures and fact sheets on Dutch health (care) issues (P.O. Box 5406, NL 2280 HK Rijswijk). The national library on mental health is at the Trimbos Instituut, the Netherlands Institute of Mental Health and Addiction, P.O. Box 725, NL 3500 AS Utrecht).

42

3

Before Anti-Psychiatry:
'Mental Health' in Wartime Britain

Mathew Thomson

British anti-psychiatry was very much a child of its own age: shaped by, and a shaper of, the era of the 'counter-culture'. As such, it is perhaps unsurprising that a search for roots earlier in the century at first bears meagre results. There was, for instance, no Clifford Beers-style lay critique of psychiatry in the interwar British mental hygiene movement,[1] and though there was a continuing suspicion of psychiatry as a threat to individual liberties, this was a well-established tradition, stronger fifty years earlier, and to an extent notable for its relative weakness in interwar Britain as more and more control was quite eagerly passed to the increasingly respected psychiatric profession. A substantial critique emerged only in the 1950s with the campaign for legislative reform which led to the 1959 Mental Health Act; significantly, however, this Act placed more, rather than less, power in the hands of the psychiatric profession – hardly an 'anti-psychiatric' development.[2] However, the intellectual basis for anti-psychiatry did not emerge out of thin air; and even those ideas and political positions which were novel, can only properly be understood if we know what they were reacting against. This essay suggests that the mid-century crisis which centred on the Second World War reorientated the psychological sciences and their position within society, and that this was important in setting the stage for the later emergence of anti-psychiatry.

The War provided an environment for problematising the normal in a new way.[3] Interwar mental hygiene had established the notion of a continuous spectrum of mental abilities, and had thus blurred the division between normality and abnormality, health and illness, but as a spectrum it still set mental fitness and unfitness at opposite poles. The War encouraged a shift towards problematising normality at every point on this spectrum. Key in this transition was the challenge of explaining the disintegration of interwar Europe into nationalism, fascism, and ultimately World War. Psychoanalytic modes of thought, well established already during the interwar period, now came to the fore to explain this disintegration. The instinctive or unconscious drive of aggression, evident in the mass psychology of fascism, anti-semitism, and warfare, and the innate need for identity beyond the self – evident in the mass appeal of dictators such as Hitler, in the appeal of ideology, and the power of nationalism and racism – were recognised as a very part of what had been seen as 'normality'. Those drawn towards antisemitism, nationalism, Fascism and war could not simply be dismissed as suffering from some kind of mental illness, nevertheless the unconscious psychological root of their behaviour was clearly a vital problem for mental hygienists; in fact, far more so than that of the mentally ill, since the whole future of society rested on it.[4] In fact, all 'human science' disciplines – psychology, politics, economics, sociology – had to reorientate themselves to acknowledge the power of unconscious drives. The sense of revelation is captured in Labour intellectual, Evan Durbin's, 1940 text *The Politics of Democratic Socialism*:

> Nothing is quite the same again. Those who come to see themselves, their friends, and the societies in which they live, through the categories of modern psychology experience the same kind of shock as those who look for the first time at some common object through a microscope, or at the moon through a telescope.[5]

The fact that the first hundred pages of Durbin's influential account was dominated by psychological ideas indicates how important this influence had become.[6]

A second impact of the war was that it focused attention on the relationship between culture and mental health, and on that between the health of society and the individual. There was a great desire to explain the apparent differences as well as similarities between nations. Compared to studies in the era of the First World War, there was far less emphasis on biological difference; instead it was the shaping role of culture which was emphasised, with the concept of 'national character' therefore attracting much interest.[7] As psychiatrist, William Brown, put it:

> the cumulative effect of history within the nation, the interaction of philosophical, political and economic conceptions built up by the

thinkers of the nation, and the interplay of psychological forces at any given time produce a "psychological field of force" within which the individual becomes orientated and conditioned in very definite ways. This is the real psychological problem of the German nation.'[8]

Not only were culture, traditions, and history depicted as shaping forces behind national character, but it was recognised that these forces became even more powerful as 'propagandist' techniques emerged to manipulate the masses. In such circumstances, it was no longer possible or desirable to confine the scope of the psychological sciences to the individual: the individual and his psychology was indivisible from that of the group.[9]

One possible implication of viewing individual psychology as a product of culture was a relativism about mental health: mental health simply becoming equivalent to a functional fit between culture and the individual, and as such specific rather than general. Such reasoning would have led to the conclusion that Nazis were actually well-adjusted, mentally healthy people within the context of their own cultural situation: that no society was more mentally healthy than any other. Because of the almost universal consensus that Nazism was morally despicable, such a relativism was resisted in Britain. Instead, mental health was conceptualised as both the product of and the foundation stone for a democratic (and often also a socialist or at least 'planned') society. Rather than accepting a relativist position, the science of mind appeared to offer the possibility of defending mental health as having an absolute and provable value. The society which fostered mental health could therefore be regarded as ethically superior to that which did not, with the search for an idealised mental health providing the basis for a humanist ideology which could be defended as ethically superior to the political ideologies of the era. 'Mental health' thus provided an apparently value neutral way to evaluate the good life and the good society: an answer to the 'crisis of valuation' which faced those disillusioned with political ideology and religion yet still searching for values to tackle what was perceived as a long-term politico-moral crisis, beginning with the First World War, leading to totalitarianism and the Second World War, and in Britain's case continuing with the prospect of a rapid decline in Imperial power. This sense of crisis is clear in the post-war British psychological literature: the defeat of Germany provided no neat resolution as one might have expected. Psychologists recognised that they had a key role to play in ensuring that an understanding of human nature became a core feature of the politics and international relations of the future, but they also recognised that the problems and therefore the answers must be ethical as well as psychological. The great hope was that an ethical value system could be found in the science of psychology; that psychology could reveal the values which humans carried, psycho-biologically, within themselves from the earliest age, and that society would be organised to encourage the healthy development of these natural values.[10]

Having accepted that culture and society were key forces in shaping the individual mind, yet also having accepted that an understanding of mental health could provide ethical answers to broader social issues, British mental hygienists recognised that it was their own responsibility to promote a culture and society which would foster mental health. This had implications on both the national and international stages. During the war such thinking informed the work of psychologists in the provision of propaganda. A 'British way' in propaganda emerged, in which propaganda was conceptualised as promoting mental health, and contrasted to the repressive, dictatorial style of Goebbels and the Nazis.[11] British propaganda was to defeat 'the Hitlerism within'. It was to be educational, placing the individual in an assertive position where mental breakdown and poor morale could be resisted.[12] Psychoanalyst Edward Glover was called on for advice on the Ministry of Information's 'Social Survey'. Undertaken on a daily basis, this record of popular opinion on attitudes to the war and on virtually every aspect of daily life was regarded by Glover as a path to a more democratic form of government which could truly respond to the people and thereby lead to a psychotherapeutic form of government – an era of 'social psychiatry'.[13] Another key field of application for the new ideas was in the management of the armed forces, which acted as a testing ground for the importation of techniques into the domestic arena. J.R. Rees, Consulting Psychiatrist to the British Army, felt that the war had placed psychiatry at the very centre of a new discipline of social medicine.[14]

More generally, the new ideas about mental health influenced wartime and postwar reconstruction.[15] The argument that man had innately destructive drives which had to be controlled and directed constructively rather than destructively was an influential factor in the acceptance of a planned society, and one which seems to have been ignored in existing studies of the intellectual roots of the welfare state.[16] The influence can be clearly traced in the work of Evan Durbin. In a rebuff to Marxists within the Labour movement, he used psychology to argue for a human and ethical dimension to socialism. His account demonstrated that education had to have a central role in the construction of citizens who could build a democratic socialism, with channels for free play and release of aggressive tendencies vital to avoid repression and the storage of mental problems into adult life. Following his friend psychologist John Bowlby, he asserted the importance of maintaining a close bond between mother and child if the latter was to develop into a healthy citizen.[17] As such, psychology contributed to the promotion of a maternalist style of 'family values' at the heart of the welfare state.[18] Durbin recognised the potential value of psychoanalysis as a tool of mass education and therapy, but he also realised that the expense of such a policy made it completely unfeasible. Instead, preventive techniques were needed. Education provided one of these, and the whole political process provided another. As such, psychology and the search for mental health influenced Durbin's whole vision of a democratic socialism. For instance, it suggested that the security of private property had to be at the heart of the British vision of socialism. With the prospect of a Labour government in 1945, Durbin turned his thoughts towards the psychology of leadership, contributing to a weekend conference on 'the Psychological and Sociological Problems of Modern Socialism' with an impressive list of invited participants, including Karl Mannheim, T. H. Marshall, G.D.H. Cole and Margaret Cole, John Ryle, Leonard Woolf, Michael Young, John Bowlby, and a young Harold Wilson. Hitlerism had demonstrated the continuing appeal of a strong leader to an educated population, and psychology suggested that the explanation could be found in an unconscious search for a father figure. If democracy was to succeed, then a substitute which served the same sort of purpose had to found. Ideally, libidinisation in the dictator would be replaced by libidinisation in the group. The latter was always going to be harder, and therefore the group needed to be clearly in the interests of all (for that reason he regarded the Tory philosophy of supremacy of private interests as inadequate). Democracy was a key, as it provided the mechanism for libidinisation in the political process; so too was the idea of a common plan.[19]

A further example of the influence of psychology in the post-war reconstruction is provided by the highly influential Karl Mannheim, Professor of Sociology at the LSE, editor of the postwar Sociology and Social Reconstruction series, author of *Diagnosis of Our Time*, and a leading actor in cross-party discussion about welfare reform.[20]

Mannheim placed the idea of an innately destructive dimension to human nature at the heart of his case for accepting planning. This was important for it provided a route for conservatives to accept the post-war settlement. The war had been immensely destructive to the social fabric, leaving a desperate need for psychological integration. Education, planning, even ideology, could all play a psychotherapeutic role: he urged a new age of 'socio-analysis' to replace the psycho-analysis of the age of individualism. The Nazis had demonstrated the immense power of such techniques, but they had abused them, using the state's power to repress individual drives; the new 'democratic personalism' would be based on an advance in self understanding. Planning would provide the essential environment for this new regime (the healthy development of youths was a priority – he recognised the extremist movements of the interwar period as in part youth movements, and he saw the gang age as a threat to western society). A degree of planned social control was therefore essential for a healthy society. However, the key to this planned society was, not only to utilize an understanding of groups, but also to educate members of the population about their psychological potential so that they would understand themselves and others. It was only through this self-education that individual consciousness could be overcome and a 'new order' of group consciousness begin to emerge. In his view, democracies could not choose to ignore the psychological power of the group, painfully learnt in the struggle against Nazism.[21]

On the international stage, British mental hygienists promoted such thinking in two arenas. The first was in defeated Germany where British psychologists and psychiatrists were called upon to psychologically assess the minds of Nazis and to advise on postwar reconstruction, de-Nazification, and reeducation.[22] This experience helped to confirm their ideas about the importance of culture in shaping the individual psyche, but also of the need for psychology to develop an ethical dimension. Accepting that the Nazi mind was not a product of innate racial difference, there did seem to be a genuinely important role for psychologists in helping to reform it. Future Tavistock Clinic psychiatrist H. V. Dicks was one of those employed. His bilingual skills had already been put to use during the war in studies of enemy morale through interviewing German prisoners of war. At the end of the war he was taken on by the Control Commission in the British Zone of occupation to conduct screening of high-level German personnel to select any with potential as 'democrats'. He discovered that those who were dedicated Nazis and 'near Nazis', rather than simply Nazi because of the situation, had a markedly different and 'immature' personality structure compared to the normal German (he suggested that less than 35% of the *Wehrmacht* were active carriers of the ideology).[23] However, it was also clear that the German culture had fostered an unusually high proportion of authoritarian personalities and that the only way to break away from this would be to rear a new generation who would bring up their own children in a less authoritarian manner.[24] Such experience was undoubtedly a factor in pushing Dicks to search for an ethical basis for mental health:

> I believe that "mental health" is an emerging goal and value for humanity of a kind comparable to the notions of "finding God", "Salvation", "perfection", or "progress" which have inspired various eras of our history, as master-values which at the same time implied a way of life.[25]

The same was the case in the careers of J. R. Rees, who undertook a psychological study of the captured Nazi Rudolph Hess for the British government and went on to be the leading figure in the World Federation of Mental Health and Director of the Tavistock Institute, and Freudian, Roger Money-Kyrle, again involved in post-war psychological assessment of the Nazis, and another who examined the possibility of an ethical dimension in the psychology of the future.[26]

The second international arena in which the new psychological ideas had a practical impact was the post-war international organisations designed to establish a new world order. Mental hygienists had established an international movement already in the interwar years.[27] And in the 1930s, a number of British psychologists and psychiatrists had attempted to utilize their knowledge as a tool to assist the peace movement.[28] European mental hygiene groups had held several Congresses during the period, and an international movement had been instigated under the auspices of Clifford Beers' American Association for Mental Hygiene, meeting in Washington in 1930 and less successfully in Paris in 1937. In 1935 a letter on the subject of mental hygiene and peace was addressed to world statesmen by 339 leading psychiatrists from around the world.[29] These movements came together in 1948 in an International Congress on Mental Health in London, marking the formation of a new World Federation of Mental Health.[30] In its early years, no doubt helped by the fact that its first meeting was in London, British mental hygienists had a very high profile. J. R. Rees was President of the Congress and

H. V. Dicks and Professor J. C. Flugel of UCL were all members of the Preparatory Commission given the task of constructing a statement on world mental health aims for the new international agencies UNESCO and the World Health Organisation. The statement reflected the new vision of mental health which had emerged out of the War. It carried into the international arena the hope that mental health could provide a new value system which would overcome national and ideological divisions:

> The pursuit of mental health cannot but be a part of a system of values. In this Statement, values associated with Western civilisation are, perhaps, implicit in much that is said. Indeed, the very effort to reach a high degree of mental health is, in some respect, an expression of Western cultural achievement. But this by no means implies that mental health as understood in Western countries is in any sense necessarily at variance with the sense in which it is understood in other countries. On the contrary, it may be that here might be found a basis for common human aspiration.[31]

Part of the WFMH's aim was to encourage the development of mental health services throughout the world, but in line with the wartime shifts a much broader vision of mental health was also promoted: one in which the prospect of a third world war was to be prevented by fostering 'world citizenship'.[32] This was not a proposal for an end to national sovereignty, rather it was a vision of a new state of mind – a 'common humanity'.[33] World citizenship was seen as a prerequisite for mental health, since it was the only way to ease the growing anxiety and insecurity fostered by international tension; it was also, however, only possible once individuals had learnt to live at peace with themselves: 'No peace without mental health ... and at the same time no mental health without peace.'[34] This individual mental health was to be attained through the further development of those mental health services which had been encouraged in the West since the start of the nineteenth century. It was recognised that there would be problems translating these practices universally, but that the resistance in undeveloped countries could be exaggerated, and that there was a real hope that developmental problems encountered in the West could thereby be avoided in newly developing areas of the world.[35] It was also recognised that there were significant cultural differences which might stand in the way of universalised models of mental health: for instance, differences in family structure and in the pattern of life development. Nevertheless, there was an underlying pattern to development which could serve as a blueprint across cultures. In line with the broader wartime trends, the fostering of mental health could not stop at delivery of mental health services and the study of individual development: it had to embrace the whole organisation of society. As a consequence, the WFMH saw its role, not simply as a lobby group for mental health services, but also as providing psychological advice on social, political and cultural policy to bodies such as UNESCO, with plans for a United Nations Institute of the Human Sciences in 1947, whose remit was to include the psychological study of international relations, child development, national character, psychological security, and intergroup relations.[36]

The intellectual shifts had potentially profound implications for the boundaries between professional groups. With the compass of mental hygiene now extended to the whole of human society, it became very unclear where the boundary lines with the disciplines of psychology, sociology, anthropology, and even politics, now lay? The extension of boundaries came in both directions. Psychiatrists began to see the functioning of groups, the organisation of society, and patterns of culture as integral to their own work, while sociologists accepted that they had to integrate an understanding of the unconscious dimension to human nature into their analyses of society.[37] Professional boundaries shifted in two further, though less obvious ways. Firstly, the sort of subject matter that psychologists were now willing to consider broadened from human intellectual activitites to a study of everyday life: 'the trivial and the popular'.[38] In doing so, psychology stretched into former sociological territory, and it also broke down the boundaries beween the academic and the popular, the pathological and the normal. Secondly, the boundary between observer and observed began to break down. Under the influence of psychoanalysis, there was a growing awareness that the subjectivity, national character, and culture of the observer affected the process of observation, and also that there was an inter-relationship between observor and observed. Two shifts in practice resulted from these challenges to professional authority. Firstly, 'psy' professionals became much more introspective about themselves, their own prejudices, and the development of their professional boundaries.[39] And secondly, there was a shift in mental health strategy, away from paternalism, towards public education, self-understanding, and self-therapeutics.

This blurring of boundaries could have placed professional authority and status in danger. However there is little sign that this took place. There were calls for unification of disciplines and for greater interdisciplinary exchange, but this led to an era of fruitful exchange rather than disintegration of the professions. Institutional structures were generally firm enough, and status interests strong enough, to secure boundaries, and the field as a whole was strengthened by the new confidence about the scope of mental health as a political, social, and cultural, as well as a medical strategy. 'Mental hygiene', became a less persuasive term because of the broadening conceptualisation of mental health. The professions of psychiatry and psychology now had an outlet to address broader social questions through their own reshaped disciplines; as such, they were less inclined to seek the avenue of the mental hygiene movement. The voluntary sector within the mental hygiene movement struggled to find a voice as its role as a provider of care became less important in an era of welfare bureaucratisation and professionalisation. Its influence would increase when it shifted towards becoming the voice of the consumer and the advocate of the mentally ill and their families; however this had to wait until the 1970s.[40] Thus, though the changes brought about by the Second World War did greatly strengthen the case for the integration of a psychological dimension into the organisation and management of society – as the interwar mental hygienists had wanted – in some senses it ironically also marked the end of the felt need for such a movement, or at least in such a form.

The wartime shifts contained, if not the seeds of their own destruction, than at least some of the seeds which would foster an anti-psychiatric critique from the 1960s onwards. The problem of relativism had only temporarily been solved. It had been accepted that culture was key in shaping individual mental development, and in the desperate situation of war, and through the challenge of the Nazi regime and ideology, a counter vision of mental health had emerged, modelled on the ideal citizen of a planned, democratic society, supported by the bonds of family and nation. However, this ideal was itself going to be open to the challenge that it was merely culturally specific, a reflection of mid-century western values. As the faith of intellectuals in the superiority of capitalist democracy, the nation and the family unit waned, so too would their belief that mental health was an absolute category. The war had revealed the danger of innate human drives, and had consequently led to the acceptance of a regime for controlling these drives. There had been an acceptance of the need for 'social control', though a social control that stopped short at full repression, which was regarded as a dangerous totalitarian practice, storing up mental health problems and in turn political problems for the future; anti-psychiatry, would go a step further, aiming to destroy social control altogether and thereby unleash full or higher human development – even if it did not conform to accepted social norms or idealised western notions of 'mental health'. It would recognise and attempt to expose and subvert the relationship between dominant western values and a normative mental health. However, in practice it would tend to follow the wartime developments in its fascination with promoting a higher stage of mental growth, and paying far less attention to the increasingly neglected mentally ill and handicapped.

Flaws and contradictions in the postwar vision of spreading mental health both domestically and internationally were in fact evident from its conception. The WFMH's plans for a mental health based on 'world citizenship' met immediate criticism as a piece of western cultural imperialism, a problem highlighted at the International Congress in London by American anthropologist Margaret Mead, and by the difficulty of bringing the Soviets into the fold.[41] And plans for a 'psycho-catharsis' of the German people were modified as it was realised that any mental health strategy had to take into account the different pattern of culture in Germany, and had to emerge from within, rather than being imposed from above.[42] The way forward was to train German professionals and leave them the task of spreading the mental health message to other professionals and to the public at large.[43]

Domestically, there was an emerging critique of the loose way in which a normative concept of mental health had entered into social policy, effectively undermining individual rights and ceding legal and moral power to the medical professions.[44] And the work of figures such as Erich Fromm suggested that mental health, measured by a series of indicators such as levels of mental illness, alcoholism and suicides, actually remained worst in the most highly developed countries: the desire for an 'escape from freedom' which had led to the success of totalitarianism in the 1930s had not been solved in the affluence of liberal, post-war, western society.[45]

A second seed for the emergence of an anti-psychiatric critique was the blurring of professional boundaries. In reaching beyond mental illness the psychiatric profession opened itself to a critique from those who resented its intrusion, and questioned its expertise in the 'diagnosis of society'. The profession became polarised between those who wanted to confine it to a biomedical approach, and radicals who launched a sweeping critique about the order of society, and self-reflexively attacked their own profession for its role

Much of anti-psychiatry in England-Laing, USA-Szasz France-Faucault denied the existence of mental illness - ? mental health.

Before Anti-Psychiatry

in supporting an unnecessary and coercive system of order. The psychology of the wartime and post-war era had demonstrated and supported the importance of the social order, education, and the family in shaping the individual mind; the radical psychology of the sixties would also recognise this, but object to it, and attempt to destroy it. The anti-psychiatrists would adopt the therapeutic community as a tool for personal self-discovery and as an alternative to the asylum.[46] In doing so, however, they were again drawing on wartime developments of a very different ideological hue; drawing on a therapeutic tool which had emerged in the war, partly as a pragmatic solution to the management of group dynamics, but also instilled by a belief in the existence of 'mental health' – a mental health which was manifest in the development of the democratic citizen. In sum, in many respects anti-psychiatry drew on and developed wartime developments: the former invariably reacted against, but was nevertheless the child of, the latter.

Notes

1. Beers was the lay leader of the American mental hygiene movement. His career is assessed in N. Dain, *Clifford W. Beers: Advocate for the Insane* (Pittsburgh: University of Pittsburgh Press, 1980).

2. C. Unsworth, *The Politics of Mental Health Legislation* (Oxford: Oxford University Press, 1987)

3. For an analysis of the war's impact on psychology as tool for governing subjectivity: N. Rose, *Governing the Soul: The Shaping of the Private Self* (London: Routledge, 1989). Rose attributes considerable importance to the war, concentrating on the way it led to new psychological technologies for measuring and controlling the self, including the study of morale, attitudes, propaganda, and group therapy. This essay steers away from Rose's work on psychological management of subjectivity and instead explores the reconceptualisation of the scope, boundaries, and ethical and ideological underpinnings of the discipline of mental health.

4. E. Glover & M. Ginsberg, 'A Symposium on the Psychology of Peace and War', *British Journal of Medical Psychology*, xiv (1934), 274-93; Edward Glover, *War, Sadism and Pacificism: Further Essays on Group Psychology and War* 4th edn. (London: Allen & Unwin, 1946) (1st edn, 1933); William Brown, *War and Peace: Essays in Psychological Analysis* (London: Adam & Charles Black, 1939).

5. Evan Durbin, *The Politics of Democratic Socialism* (London: Routledge, 1940), p. 70.

6. Durbin was influenced by his close friend John Bowlby. He died

54

prematurely in 1946: Elizabeth Durbin, *New Jerusalems: The Labour Party and the Economics of Democratic Socialism* (London: Routledge & Kegan Paul, 1985); Stephen Brooke, 'Evan Durbin: Reassessing a Labour "Revisionist"', *Twentieth Century British History*, vii (1996), 40-1, 27-52; Jeffrey Holmes, *John Bowlby and Attachment Theory* (London: Routledge, 1993), pp. 22-5.

7. M. Ginsberg: 'National Character', *British Journal of Psychology*, xxxii (1942), 183-205.
8. 'The Psychology of Modern Germany', *British Journal of Psychology*, xxxiv (1944), 58, 43-59.
9. Julian Huxley, 'The Growth of a Group Mind in Britain under the Influence of War', *Hibbert Journal*, xxxix (1941), 337-50. The relationship between the two was, however, a matter of debate: Edward Glover criticised anthropologists for assuming that culture came prior to the individual mind, arguing that it was the unconscious which shaped culture in the first place: *War, Sadism and Pacificism*, p. 237. For a supporter of the anthropological stress on the prior importance of culture: T. H. Pear, 'Peace, War and Culture Patterns', *Bulletin of the John Rylands Library*, xxxi (1948), 120-47.
10. See for instance: D. W. Winnicott, 'Some Thoughts on the Meaning of Democracy', *Human Relations*, iii (1950), 175-86; R. Money-Kyrle, *Psychoanalysis and Politics: A Contribution to the Psychology of Politics and Morals* (London: Gerald Duckworth, 1951) and his earlier intervention 'Towards a Common Aim: A Psychoanalytic Contribution to Ethics', *British Journal of Medical Psychology*, xx (1944), 105-17; J. C. Flugel, *Man, Morals and Society: A Psycho-Analytical Study* (London: Penguin, 1962 (1st pub. 1945)); W. R. Bion, 'Psychiatry at a Time of Crisis', *British Journal of Medical Psychology*, xxi (1948), 281-9.
11. Michael Balfour, *Propaganda in War, 1939-1945: Organisation, Policies and Publics in Britain and Germany* (London: Routledge, 1979); Ian McLaine, *Ministry of Morale: Home Front Morale and the Ministry of Information in World War II* (London: George Allen & Unwin, 1979).
12. W. R. Bion, '"The War of Nerves": Civilian Reaction, Morale, and Prophylaxis', in E. Miller (ed.), *The Neuroses in War* (London: Macmillan, 1940), 180-200.
13. Glover, 'The Birth of Social Psychiatry', *Lancet*, 24 Aug. 1940, 239. For background on the Social Survey and Glover's involvement (though also the suspicion towards psychological experts within the Ministry of Information): Public Records Office, Kew, Ministry of Information Files 1/318.

14. J. R. Rees, *The Shaping of Psychiatry by the War* (London: Chapman & Hall, 1945), p. 51. More generally on the psychiatry and psychology in the armed forces: N. Rose, *Governing the Soul: The Shaping of the Private Self*, pp. 15-52.

15. British Library of Political and Economic Science, Evan Durbin Papers, 4/8

16. Jose Harris, 'Political Ideas and the Debate on State welfare, 1940-45', in H. Smith (ed.), *War and Social Change: British Society in the Second World War* (Manchester: Manchester University Press, 1986), pp. 233-63;

17. Denise Riley, *War in the Nursery: Theories of the Child and Mother* (London: Virago, 1983).

18. The centrality of family values is also evident in Richard Titmuss's influential study of wartime social policy: *Problems of Social Policy* (London: HMSO, 1950). For the way the welfare state settlement embraced traditional attitudes about gender in differentiating between men and women: E. Wilson, *Women and the Welfare State* (London: Tavistock, 1977); Rodney Lowe, *The Welfare State in Britain Since 1945* (Basingstoke: Macmillan, 1993), pp. 33-5.

19. Note also Durbin's continued interest in the intelligence of the population, and in a eugenic strategy to ensure this. On the background to this conference and the development of Durbin's later ideas on psychology and politics (unpublished): BLPES, Durbin Papers, 4/8.

20. Harris, 'Political Ideas and the Debate on State Welfare, 1940-45', pp. 240-3.

21. Karl Mannheim, *Diagnosis of Our Time: Wartime Essays of a Sociologist* (London: Routledge & Kegan Paul, 1943): quote from p. 79.

22. On one area of this work: David F. Smith, 'Juvenile Delinquency in the British Zone of Germany, 1945-51', *German History*, xii (1944), 39-63.

23. H. V. Dicks, 'Personality Traits and National Socialist Ideology', *Human Relations*, iii (1950), 152, 111-54.

24. R. Money-Kyrle, *Psychoanalysis and Politics: A Contribution to the Psychology of Politics and Morals* (London: Gerald Duckworth, 1951), pp. 13-15.

25. H. V. Dicks, 'In Search of Our Proper Ethic', *British Journal of Medical Psychology*, xxiii (1950), 3, 1-14.

26. R. Money-Kyrle, 'Social Conflict and the Challenge to Psychology', *British Journal of Medical Psychology*, xxi (1948), 215-21, an article which includes a discussion of work in Germany. The link is also discussed in the preface to his *Psychoanalysis and Politics*. Money-Kyrle

recognised that the study of the authoritarian German personality had
implications for the development of a 'humanist' society in Britain's
own welfare state, for it seemed to suggest that Germany's rapid moral
degeneration was closely tied to the emergence of a strong state
bureaucracy: *Psychoanalysis and Politics*, p. 15.

27. M. Thomson, 'Mental Hygiene as an International Movement', in
P. Weindling (ed.), *International Health Organisations and Movements,
1918-1939* (Cambridge: Cambridge University Press, 1995), pp.
283-304.

28. See the plans to set up a 'Psychologists' War Prevention Society' in
1937/8, and the establishment of a Psychological Section within the
Medical Peace Campaign, with support from William Brown,
Edward Glover, Ernest Jones, Hugh Crichton Miller, Emmanuel
Miller, J. R. Rees, and John Rickman: Contemporary Medical
Archive Centre (CMAC), Wellcome Institute for the History of
Medicine, PP/BOW/G.3/1. For a more independent line of attack,
see psychologist Ranyard West's work on the psychology of war and
his activities in the peace movement, for instance: *Psychology and
World Order* (Harmondsworth: Penguin, 1945). West's prewar and
postwar work can be traced in CMAC, Ranyard West papers. His
Psychology and World Order used a psychological model of human
behaviour to defend the need for a strict regime of international law
in the post-1945 world. He had adopted a similar position before the
war in his activities in the peace movement.

29. The letter was drafted by the Netherlands Medical Association:
'Mental Hygiene and Peace', *Mental Hygiene*, No. 15, October 1935,
pp. 113-5.

30. *International Congress on Mental Health, Volume IV. Proceedings of the
International Conference on Mental Hygiene* (London: H.K. Lewis,
1948).

31. 'Statement by the International Preparatory Commission of the
International Congress on Mental Health', *Human Relations*, ii
(1949), p. 67.

32. On the post-war boost to the world citizenship concept and its
inherent weaknesses: Derek Heater, *Citizenship: The Civic Ideal in
World History, Politics and Education* (London: Longman, 1990), pp.
139-60. Heater suggests that there was resistance to the idea of 'world
citizenship' at the UN: 'it was rarely used in the post-war decades ...
Fear that it denoted impractical idealism or an undermining of
national loyalty, or both, were powerful inhibiting factors among
educationists committed to the cause' (p. 152). Because of the rapid
descent into an era of cold war tension, the initial optimism which

surrounded international organisations such as the UN, UNESCO, WHO, and WFMH have attracted little consideration from historians. Typically, the UN gains just one brief (and critical) mention, after 430 pages, in a recent major history of the twentieth century: Eric Hobsbawm, *Age of Extremes: The Short Twentieth Century, 1914-1991* (London: Michael Joseph, 1994).

33. *Statement on Mental Health.*, p. 80
34. *Ibid.* p. 80.
35. *Ibid.* p. 68.
36. 'Proposal for the Establishment of a United Nations Institute of the Human Sciences', *Human Relations*, i (1948), 353-72.
37. K. Lewin, 'Frontiers in Group Dynamics', *Human Relations*, i (1947), 5, 5-41. For an overview history of the relationship between psychology and sociology: T. H. Pear, 'Relations between Psychology and Sociology', *Bulletin of the John Rylands Library*, xxxi (1948), 277-94; M. Ginsberg, 'What Can the Power of Social Sciences Do for Us?', *The Listener*, xxxix (1948), 822-3. For a psychologist enthusiastic about the broadening of scope and interdisciplinary exchange: T. H. Pear, 'Psychological Implications of the Culture Pattern Theory', *Bulletin of the John Rylands Library*, xxix (1945-6), 201-24; T.H. Pear, 'Personality in its Cultural Context', *Bulletin of the John Ryland Library*, xxx (1946-7), 71-90; T.H. Pear, 'Peace, War and Culture Patterns', *Bulletin of the John Rylands Library*, xxxi (1948), 120-47. And for an anthropologist working in the reverse direction: Ruth Benedict, 'The Study of Cultural Patterns in European Nations', *Transactions of the New York Academy of Sciences*, Series II, viii (1946), 274-9.
38. T. H. Pear, 'The Trivial and the Popular in Psychology', *British Journal of Psychology*, xxxi (1940), 115-28. T. H. Pear, 'Psychologists and Culture', *Bulletin of the John Rylands Library*, xxiii (1939), 417-31. T. H. Pear, *The Psychology of Conversation* (London: Nelson, 1939). Pear had been heavily influenced by an American article in the mid 1930s: Hadley Cantril, 'The Social Psychology of Everyday Life', *Psychological Bulletin*, xxxi (1934), 297-330. Mass Observation's work was the object of some controversy, its value defended by Pear but criticised by many academics as trivialising and non-professional in its use of lay observers.
39. T. H. Pear, 'The Psychology of the Psychologist', *Bulletin of the John Rylands Library*, xxv (1941), 101-20; T. H. Pear, 'The Social Status of the Psychologist and its Effect upon his Work', *Sociological Review*, xxiv (1942), 68-81.
40. Nick Crossley, 'Contesting Psychiatry: Mental Health Movements

and Pressure Groups in the Public Sphere in Post-War Britain', Paper presented to the British Sociological Association Annual Conference, 1997.

41. An awareness of the shortcomings is evident in *Annual Report of the World Federation of Mental Health, 1950,* p. 29. Note also that psychological work on group dynamics suggested that the larger the group the harder it would be to develop committment: Winnicott, *Human Relations* (1950). See also David Cohen, 'Psychiatric Imperialism', in *Forgotten Millions: The Treatment of the Mentally Ill – A Global Perspective* (London: Paladin, 1988), pp. 35-55.

42. 'Psycho-Catharsis was William Brown's term: 'The Psychology of Modern Germany', *British Journal of Psychology,* xxxiv (1944), 43-54. On the culture pattern of the Germans and the problem of psychological diagnoses of Hitler and the Nazis, see Pear: 'Psychological Implications of the Culture Pattern Theory', pp. 214-7.

43. J. R. Rees, 'Work for Mental Health in Germany', *Bulletin of the World Federation for Mental Health,* i (1949), 15-19. In this respect, note also the controversy regarding the lack of prosecution of psychiatrists and psychologists who had worked under the Nazis and had been involved in implementing eugenic policies: M. Burleigh, *Death and Deliverance: 'Euthanasia' in Germany 1900-1945* (Cambridge: Cambridge University Press, 1994), pp. 269-90.

44. Barbara Wootton, *Social Science and Social Pathology* (London: George Allen & Unwin, 1959).

45. *The Fear of Freedom* (London: Routledge & Kegan Paul, 1940); *The Sane Society* (London: Routledge & Kegan Paul, 1956).

46. On the therapeutic community: D. W. Millard, 'Maxwell Jones and the Therapeutic Community', *150 Years of British Psychiatry: Volume II. The Aftermath* (London: Athlone, 1996), pp. 581-604; N. Rose, *Governing the Soul,* pp. 40-52; P. Miller and N. Rose, 'The Tavistock Programme: The Government of Subjectivity and Social Life', *Sociology,* xxii (1988), 179-82.

4

Psychiatry and Society:
The Dutch Mental Hygiene Movement
1924-1960[1]

Leonie de Goei

Before the Second World War there would have been good reasons to compare the Dutch Mental Hygiene Movement [*Beweging voor Geestelijke Volksgezondheid*][2] with a seedling that was hardly viable. After the War it took this little moribund plant only a few years to grow into a full-blossomed tree. In this paper I will argue that the War gave a major impetus to this change. In 1945 mental hygienists claimed that substantial progress had been made in the understanding of psychiatric etiology and in the development of successful therapies. The war experience had confirmed and strengthened the importance of social factors. Mental disorders were caused by the environment rather than by biological predisposition. In this respect the mental hygienists of the forties and fifties paved the way for the anti-psychiatric critique of the sixties and seventies. Although the concept is hard to define, one of the central ideas that stand out in most descriptions of 'anti-psychiatry' is the conviction that society and the family are pathogenic. Why it was as yet to early to draw this ultimate conclusion in the fifties, I hope to demonstrate in the concluding part of this paper.

1

At the inaugural meeting of the first Dutch mental hygiene organization, established in 1924, leading Dutch psychiatrists stated that the mental health of the Dutch population was seriously at risk:

> Heavy demands are made on those who are to safeguard our level of civilization and on the working strength of our race. ... The number of mentally unstable and disabled individuals is increasing and ... will in the end outgrow the bearing capacity of the able-bodied population.[3]

The founders of this *Nederlandsche Vereeniging ter bevordering der Geestelijke Volksgezondheid* [Association for the Advancement of Mental Hygiene] believed that modernization had a pathogenetic effect. In their eyes, and those of many medical colleagues, modern society made people nervous. The human nervous system could not cope with the complexity of a newly emerging urbanized, industrial society. Moreover, modern medicine had produced a 'modern counterselection' by alleviating the struggle for life. The 'unfit' survived and reproduced themselves much faster than the 'fit' and this would have a negative effect on the quality of the future population.[4] There was another 'fact' that aggravated this situation in the eyes of contemporary psychiatrists. In the first decades of this century the asylum, then the major domain of psychiatry, was going through both an economic and therapeutic crisis. While nursing costs increased year after year, the number of recovered and discharged patients did not grow, or hardly at all. In the pre-War years established academic psychiatry believed that the causes of mental illness were to be found mainly in the individual's hereditary predisposition. This implied that a successful therapy was inconceivable. The mental hospitals that were originally designed to provide the insane with medical treatment had degenerated into storage rooms overcrowded with chronic patients. Even psychiatrists themselves spoke of 'uncommonly poor results', referring not only to the effect of care, but also to the therapeutic capacities of their profession.[5]

Mental Hygiene offered opportunities to break away from this undesirable situation and bring about a transformation of psychiatry. Since hereditary transmission was assumed to play a decisive role in the development of mental illness, the founders of the Association believed that heredity studies and eugenics would provide the necessary theories and practical knowledge.[6] However, during the thirties this approach turned out to be a failure. Both sterilization in cases of hereditary mental illness and pre-marital medical examinations met with objections of principle in religious quarters. Besides, even the proponents of the eugenic body of thought had little faith in the scientific merits or practical effects of such methods. Likewise, positive eugenic measures such as propaganda among the intelligentsia to bless their families with many children, yielded few visible results.[7]

Meanwhile in 1927 another Mental Hygiene organisation had been set up, the *Nederlandsche Vereeniging ter bevordering van Consultatiebureaux voor Moeilijke Kinderen* [Netherlands Association for the Advancement of Child Guidance Clinics], that advocated a totally different prevention strategy. This strategy was based on the psychoanalytic assumption that sick and healthy, normal and abnormal, were merely stages along a continuum. This was in sharp contrast to the traditional model of disease that had made a fundamental distinction between health and disease. The new model implied that early intervention, aimed at the patient and his or her immediate environment (i.e. the family) could prevent mild mental problems from degenerating into severe disorders of a chronic nature. During the pre-War years psychoanalysis was far from prominent in Dutch psychiatry and the practical application of this strategy was undertaken only in a handful of Child Guidance Clinics.[8]

Establishment versus newcomers, eugenics versus psychoanalysis, pathology versus normality, that is how the differences between the two mental hygiene organizations can be summed up. Apart from this dissention about the basic theoretical and practical tenets the Mental Hygiene Movement was limited in its striking power by the various denominational interests. In the thirties the pillarization of the Dutch society was in its heyday. Apart from the two aforementioned non-denominational organisations a Catholic, two Protestant and a Jewish Mental Hygiene Association had been established.[9]

With these differences in mind it was not surprising that difficulties arose when, as a channel for funds, an umbrella organization had to be created. Although the *Nationale Federatie voor de Geestelijke Volksgezondheid* [National Federation for Mental Health] was established in 1934, the pursuit of an independent policy was seriously frustrated by the various denominational interests. Up until the Second World War, the National Federation did little more than distribute money, an amount of NLG 25,000, among the member organizations. The money came from the so called *Prophylaxefonds* [Prophylaxis Fund][10], not directly from the government. National government authorities felt little if at all inclined to become involved with this newly emerging, much-troubled field of activities, especially during the economic slump of the thirties.[11]

2

In August 1945, barely three months after liberation, the Minister of Social Affairs sent a formal request for advice to the National Federation for Mental Health. He wished to be informed about the measures that should be taken to promote public mental health and the role to be played by the national government. The major recommendation to the Minister was to provide national government funding to mental hygiene promotion. The advice was accepted. 'After the War we could pretty well get as much money as we wanted', said one of the prominent mental hygienists looking back on those years.[12]

The Movement had been able to secure this kind of support because of developments which, having started before 1940, had gained momentum as a result of the War. Significant alterations were made in the setup of the Movement between 1940 and 1945 that made it into a strong, united organization, at least during the first post-War years when religious segregation had not yet flared up with renewed intensity. Despite the scarcity of paper, the Movement managed to put out an independent journal as early as October 1945, which was later to be known as the *Maandblad voor de Geestelijke Volksgezondheid* [Mental Hygiene Monthly].[13] In addition, the War gave a major impetus to the establishment of services. At the outbreak of the War, seven Child Guidance Clinics (CGCs) were in existence. The War created favourable conditions to establish services for the treatment and prevention of adults with mild mental disorders as well. Schemes that, before the War, had failed or had been difficult to get off the ground, could now be implemented by referring to the 'pressure of the times' and the increasing number of mental disorders that would be the result. In 1940 the first Institute for Medical Psychology (IMP) was established, modelled in part after the London Tavistock Clinic. Starting the same year, the National Health Council, the highest government advisory authority in the field of public health, made the explicit suggestion to establish Marital and Family Guidance Centres. In both types of facilities, 'severe and pathological cases' were explicitly excluded from treatment. They provided treatment only for incipient cases, light disorders or marital and family problems experienced by generally normal, healthy adults. The prevention objective of the Mental Hygiene Movement was now embodied in services for children as well as services for adults.[14]

However, the reorganization of the Movement and the realization of its prevention objectives are not sufficient to explain why mental health had become such a prominent issue on the agenda of policymakers after 1945. Most significantly, the war provided the Movement with convincing arguments to legitimize itself and its pursuits. It was very successful in getting its message across that mental health was an issue of national interest with first-class priority. The arguments focused on two elements: the seriousness and scope of mental health problems and the understanding of the nature and treatment possibilities of those problems.

In October 1945 the Mental Hygiene Monthly reported on the mental health situation of the Dutch population as follows:

> Unprecedented brutalization [...] has been the result of this horrible and ruthless war. In practically every domain of spiritual life disintegration can be clearly demonstrated. If ever there has been a time when public mental health might be considered in serious danger, it is certainly now. Today, as the smoke clouds of the battlefield are slowly lifting and we can begin to see the full scope of the ravages, our eyes discern the sorely battered look of our spiritual lives that surely must have been healthy before. Families are broken and disrupted, schools are out of order, labour is shattered, manners have become vulgarized, morality has sunk alarmingly, crime has surfaced everywhere and openly shows its shameless face without any embarrassment. In short, spiritual life in our beloved country has fallen seriously ill.[15]

This diagnosis was shared by many others in the newly liberated country of the Netherlands. The war had produced a moral crisis - a conclusion on which contemporaries of highly diverse political beliefs, varying from left to right, were in complete agreement.[16] The Federation argued in its report to the Minister that young people had become 'spiritually uprooted' as a result of the war. Manifestations were seen in the strong increase of juvenile delinquency and child neglect. A large group of children had come into existence whose development was in jeopardy: Jewish foster children, children whose parents had been interned, and children who had returned from the East Indies. The Federation urged the Minister to take measures to help these children without delay. If not, future generations would inevitably have to pay for the consequences in the form of increasing community expenses. As for adults, the Federation pointed out that the mental hospitals were greatly understaffed and underfunded, something which was now getting all the more urgent as an increasing number of severe disorders was observed in response to the tensions of war and occupation. Also, the Federation believed there were an 'alarmingly' great number of adults who 'had lost their balance or were not themselves'. The labourers who had returned from abroad would not, or at least not immediately, be capable of 'normal adaptation to work'. Furthermore, many family problems were thought to have emerged as a result of a prolonged absence of fathers and husbands. Serious adjustment problems were to be expected among former prisoners of war, the demobilized military from the East Indies or those who had fought with the Allied forces, those who had gone underground and those who had returned from the concentration camps. The Federation warned that without early intervention the difficulties of these people would grow from neuroses into chronic problems – and, consequently, social inadequacy.[17]

The Dutch mental hygienists stressed that the War had had serious adverse effects on mental health but also that the War had broadened the mental hygiene horizon. New theories emerged while older ones were confirmed. One of the main new insights was that mental disorders were far more widespread than they were thought to be before the War. This was especially believed to be true of the less severe or 'mild' disorders such as neuroses, adjustment disorders, and marital or family problems. 'It is not just a matter of a group of psychotic and oligophrenic patients, but something which concerns the entire population,' the National Federation stated in its 1945 Annual Report. Mental illness could justifiably be presented as a popular disease, i.e. a disease that, through its sheer scope, created serious social problems.[18]

The Dutch mental hygienists also claimed that the War had generated ideas that made it possible to address these problems, both in theory and in practice. The War experience confirmed and strengthened the importance of situational factors, both in etiology and in therapy. The idea that hereditary transmission played a major role in the development of mental illness was dealt a damaging blow. American and British army psychiatrists abandoned the idea in view of their front-line experience.[19] Their Dutch colleagues followed suit: the environment rather than predisposition was the most significant factor in the etiology of mental disorders. At the Movement's first great manifestation, the *National Congress on Mental Health* of 1947, this notion had gained such total acceptance that it was even thought necessary to put the question: is psychopathic behaviour determined exclusively by environmental factors or is some 'biological predisposition' active as well?[20]

Similarly, the therapeutic experience acquired from military psychiatry was found to be extremely useful for civil psychiatry. Lack of time and staff had compelled army psychiatrists to start treating several patients at a time. However, the Dutch mental hygienists stressed that the main benefit of group treatment was not that it became possible to treat several patients simultaneously. Far more importantly, as one of the Movements leading spokesmen pointed out in 1946: it was only now that, based on these experiences with group treatment, 'the psychopathological and psychological conclusions could be drawn from the notion that man is a social being'.[21]

Another idea that was reinforced by the War concerned the importance of prevention by early treatment in society. Mental hygienists now generally believed that early treatment could prevent mild mental problems from progressing into severe disorders for which admission to a mental institution would be indicated. Prevention could not only forestall unnecessary individual suffering, it could also save the community the costs associated with a loss of labour power, as well as the considerably higher costs of hospitalization. Naturally this strategy offered great attraction to policymakers and government officials who had been trying to cut back on expenses of costly institutionalization from the twenties onward. The attraction was not least due to the fact that, in contrast to prevention by means of eugenics, this strategy was a highly feasible one: The aim of prevention was now realized in services for mildly disturbed children as well as adults.

3

So far so good. Then came the *International Congress on Mental Health*. A splendid congress: if the pendulum swing between hope and despair that is so typical of the history of psychiatry has ever seen a moment when professional capacities were viewed with optimism, it must have been in London in 1948.

The fervour displayed at home by the Dutch Movement extended beyond the national borders. As many as 80 Dutch participants in the congress embarked for the City of London, still heavily marked by the violence of war. In terms of size, the Dutch delegation came second only to the Americans, while the Dutch also made disproportionately great contributions in other respects. Three of the 12 keynote speakers came from the Netherlands and the *International Preparatory Committee* had two Dutchmen among its members. In addition it was a Dutchman, H.C. Rümke (about whom more later), who was elected *Chairman of the Executive Board* of the *World Federation for Mental Health*, which was founded during the congress.[22]

It will come as no surprise that the ideas formulated in London became widely accepted in the Dutch Movement after 1948. The core ideas can be summarized as follows: First, there is absolute and direct interdependence between the expressions of the human spirit and the social structures that surround the individual. Secondly, both the unhealthy behaviour of the human individual and the damaging effects of social structures can be modified - in other words, man and his environment are 'makeable'. Thirdly, the *Mental Hygiene Movement* aims to achieve more than curing and preventing mental ill-health: it wishes to have a positive impact on inter-individual relations and on the relations between man and his environment, i.e. it intends to promote mental health. This turn toward a positive approach became manifest in the Movement's new name: *Mental Health* replaced *Mental Hygiene*.[23]

For all the optimism expressed by this concept of Mental Health, what I should like to discuss here are the essential questions that were raised within the Movement by the London body of ideas: How was mental health to be defined? Which criteria should be applied? What should be the scientific basis of the Movement? After all, the problems involved here were greater than - and different from - 'psychiatric problems', on that issue agreement was complete.[24]

In the Dutch Movement, *Mental Health* was defined in terms of the qualities and capacities that could be attributed to an ideal, healthy human individual. The same option had been chosen in London and would later be chosen in WFMH and WHO circles. It involved:

> the best possible development of the individual personality; harmonious satisfaction of the individual's instinctual, emotional and spiritual needs without this being achieved at the expense of society; self-acceptance and being at peace with oneself; the ability to establish good and productive relations with other people; the ability to comply with life's and society's normal demands and responsibilities; the ability to accept reality; the ability to adjust to changing conditions.[25]

Next, these criteria of individual mental health were used to derive the criteria that should be met by society if it was to be 'in good mental health'. A mentally healthy community, then, was a community that enabled its members to develop their personalities as widely as possible and to achieve the greatest possible harmony with their environment.[26]

It was explicitly stated that the criteria of mental health were not objective standards. Health, it was unanimously believed, was a relative or subjective concept and its perceptions varied with culture, time, social class and cherished values.[27] How would it be possible for the Movement to achieve its goal, i.e. the promotion of mental health, if a generally accepted definition of 'health' was lacking and objective criteria of mental health could not be defined?

During the fifties this issue was addressed from a pragmatic point of view. Was it really necessary for actual practice to have a solid definition of mental health? Naturally the Movement should be prevented from losing itself in an endless and boundless task, but that could also be done without an exact standard. Major spokesmen of the Movement argued that a 'useful working definition' would be sufficient: we should know 'by approximation what we are talking about'.[28] Armed with this working definition people set to work. But it goes without saying that this was not the end of the matter. More about that later.

Let us first look at the question of the Movement's theoretical foundation. Which scientific discipline should provide the knowledge that the Movement needed to realize its goals? Although psychiatry had usurped this domain or at least been the first to explore it scientifically, it had become obvious that this was a task for other disciplines as well. Psychiatry would continue to provide a major scientific basis, but its scope would have to be limited to a specific field, namely pathology.

H.C. Rümke was one of those who clearly expressed this generally accepted idea. Psychiatry, and medicine in general, exercised authority over 'purely medical' matters, i.e. illness. Rümke called this the domain of 'mental hygiene', where psychiatrists would continue to be the undisputed leaders, even if they needed the assistance of other disciplines. In Rümke's view, the field of mental hygiene should be distinguished from the quest for 'a better society', the domain of 'mental health', in which the psychiatrist would undoubtedly play a useful, but not a leading role. For as he put it: 'Again and again we observe how psychiatrists absorb current ideas and pass them on in their own idiosyncratic ways, sometimes even making it seem as if they are the ones who set the direction.' But, 'the world view or philosophy of life of psychiatry have never been able to point the way to innermost understanding.' The psychiatrist and the psychologist certainly had a task here, but they could not 'point the way'. Their task was merely to serve, since neither of them was an expert in normative matters. Based on their scientific professionalism, psychiatrists and psychologists might be able to help release specific forces, but they could not direct them. In Rümke's view the 'pioneers', those who gave direction in this domain, were the philosophers, theologians, philosophers of culture and sociologists.[29]

Psychiatry had a task to perform when people were ill, but what exactly was 'ill' and where was the line dividing it from 'healthy'? At this point the question of the definition of health and illness resurfaced in spite of all pragmatism. Rümke was one of the more outspoken exponents of those who were not yet ready to abandon the idea that there was a universal truth that was valid for everybody, as he wrote in 1951, even if the concept of health itself was personally defined.[30] Remarkably, however, Rümke did not attempt to establish a definition of mental health either. He, too, believed that it would be too difficult to establish objective criteria; he was satisfied if it could be roughly identified what the phrase 'mental health' meant. His definitions of the concept were inspired by the same body of ideas that was current in WFMH circles.[31] What Rümke was out to find, however, was the answer to the question of how health could be distinguished from illness.

Rümke was an adherent of the medical model. In his view illness was a condition defined by the physical, it had a biological basis. This may seem strange because Rümke also advocated that psychiatry should be based on the humanities as well as on science. He was one of the major proponents of the phenomenological and anthropological tradition in Dutch psychiatry and occupied a leading position in the *Utrechtse School*, the very influential circle of phenomenologically oriented psychologists, educationalists, psychiatrists, criminologists and lawyers.[32] According to Rümke, illness and health were different states of being, each with their own characteristics and laws. This conception differed from the generally held idea that health and illness were merely positions along a single continuum. Rümke opposed the idea of a smooth transition from the one into the other.[33] Did his views imply that the Movement should abandon its prevention strategy based, after all, on the psychoanalytic assumption that there were at least no qualitative differences between health and illness? Or that it should retrace its steps and limit its activities to the pathological, i.e. physically demonstrable disease? No, it did not. For Rümke made room for a new concept that could be situated in between health and illness: 'psychological disturbances in healthy individuals'. The symptoms that health and illness had in common and which appeared to invalidate a distinction between health and illness were merely mental disturbances in healthy individuals, not manifestations of disease. He believed it would be wrong to assume that 'any unusual behaviour, any unusual inner experience, any ill feeling, any inability to make inner or outer adjustments' was equal to illness. The same applied to social phenomena, such as the deterioration of morality in populations or groups, collective psychological infections, fluctuations in sexual morals and behaviour, psychological instabilities, tensions and whimsicality resulting from 'religious torment' and age-related crises. All these cases, according to Rümke, were the results of a normal life struggle rather than illness.[34]

It was this concept of 'psychological disturbances in healthy individuals' that would be used by Rümke's disciple Trimbos to proclaim a mental health science as the Movement's own scientific foundation. In 1959, the psychiatrist C. Trimbos published his thesis entitled *Geestelijke gezondheidsleer en geestelijke gezondheidszorg* [Mental Health Science and Mental Health Care].[35] Trimbos proclaimed a non-medical branch of psychiatry, i.e. mental health science, in which sociology and social psychology deserved a special place as its founding disciplines. The autonomy of mental health science, Trimbos argued, stemmed from 'our greatly enhanced understanding of the nature of mental ill-health in our times.' Trimbos followed in Rümke's footsteps; indeed, he argued that it was only Rümke's conception of 'mental disturbances in healthy individuals' that had opened up the perspective of a scientific discipline of mental health. This grey area, the border region between health and illness, had many inhabitants who could also be characterized as 'the victims of our times'. In contrast with mental illness that could be shown to have a physical basis, no medical-biological pathogenesis could be demonstrated in their disturbances. They were disorders whose etiology was of a socio-cultural nature.[36]

Trimbos stated that the next question that urgently needed to be answered was: What exactly is the relation between mental disorders and socio-cultural factors? Following Kretschmer, Trimbos made a distinction between sociogenic and socioplastic conditions in the development of mental disorders. Sociogenesis meant that a direct causal relationship existed between social factors and the emergence of mental disorder in the individual. Socioplasticity was defined by Trimbos as the colouring, moulding or manifestation of latent mental disorders as a result of social influences.[37] At this stage Trimbos made an important statement: Truly sociogenic factors were very rare. In his view, the ideas of contemporaries such as Horney, Fromm and others who attributed direct sociogenic meaning to the impact of the modern era were in truth related to socioplasticity. As far as Trimbos was concerned, it would be equally

71

fitting to say that the 'social inequities' attributed by Fromm to a sick society were socioplastic factors. After all:

> In our view, nearly all spheres that affect the human individual, e.g. school, the youth movement, the local community, leisure activities, socio-economic relations, relations based on cultural background and persuasion, labour relations [...] only have socioplastic significance in the development of mental disturbances in the individual. [...] Socioplastic factors can only make their disturbing effects felt if the individual has been disturbed or predisposed as a result of genetic make-up or other causal factors.[38]

'Truly sociogenic' factors were very rare or non-existent. Social factors had an effect only if a potential disturbance was involved. Thus it turned out that individual temperament and predisposition played a decisive role after all. This means that Trimbos did not draw the ultimate conclusion from the idea that mental disorders might be caused by social factors, i.e. that society has a pathogenic effect. And hence he did not argue for changes, let alone a revolution, in the existing social structures. I would like to argue that he was not in a position to do so for various reasons.

Firstly: The discourse presented by the Dutch Mental Hygiene Movement was not a revolutionary one. On the contrary, the intention of the mental hygienists was to deal with the consequences of modernisation and social change as best they could, rather than to establish a new society. Essentially, the Movement wished to preserve certain values or restore them when lost, values that are best defined as the virtues of a bourgeois middle class. Trimbos was no exception. In his thesis he complained:

> Of course, never before have so many people had access to, for example, the musical heritage of our civilization; concert series are fully booked everywhere, gramophone records are produced by the billions. But is it right to say that there is a musical culture if self-practice and the patience and prolonged preparations that should go with it, are missing? [...] What hollowness in many vis-a-vis the riches of their own civilization.'[39]

He also sided with the 'contemporary social sciences' (and against people like Fromm) in assuming the position that 'any community is normal to the extent that it functions and individual pathology only refers to the individual who fails to adapt to his community's way of life.[40]

Secondly: Even if the Movement's discourse might be

characterized as progressive in other respects (such as the idea of the makeability of society, the desire to let everyone share in the accomplishments of mental hygiene), the contemporary political and socio-economic relations were by no means conducive to a radical point of view. During the fifties, when post-War reconstruction was in its heyday, the all-including watchword was: working together to rebuild Dutch society. Occasionally, during the first few years following the war, voices could be heard arguing in favour of social change, but later the ranks closed and pre-War denominational pillarization was restored in all its glory. The Cold War made left-wing, progressive or radical look similar to communist or red, a colour that was part of the Movement's banner only in an extremely faded, social democratic hue. During the fifties, the social democrats did not undertake any revolutionary experiments, either. Long gone were the days of Troelstra, who preached socialist revolution in the Netherlands in 1918. In the decade between 1948 and 1958 the Social Democrats accepted government responsibility in four successive cabinets with the Roman Catholics.

Nevertheless, the seeds of change definitely began to sprout as early as the fifties. Trimbos may not have come to the conclusion that society *as such* or the family *in general* were pathogenic and had to be fundamentally changed in order to prevent mental illness. But he, and many of his fellow catholic mental hygienists did start a crusade within their own ranks. Starting from mental hygiene theories they tried to create room within the rigid sexual morals prescribed by the catholic church doctrine which, in their view, fostered so many neuroses among catholic families. Their crusade would eventually result in revolutionary changes within the Dutch catholic church and community.[41]

In conclusion: After the Second World War, the Dutch Mental Hygiene Movement advocated a social model of disease. The environment rather than the genetic makeup of the individual was pinpointed as the most significant factor in the etiology of mental illness. In this respect the mental hygienists sowed the seed for the anti-psychiatric critique of the sixties and seventies.[42] However, in the fifties two of the leading figures in the Movement restricted the concept of sociogenesis in two ways. Rümke stated that social factors played a significant role in the causation of psychological disturbances only in healthy persons, e.g. disorders whose etiology was not of a medical-biological nature. Secondly, Trimbos came to the conclusion that social factors did not cause mental illness, they only had a socioplastic significance. Thus the mental hygienists of the fifties did not, as the anti-psychiatrists of the sixties and seventies would do, proclaim that our modern capitalist society was sick and caused all mental illnesses (including the severe ones like schizophrenia) and that only fundamental and revolutionary social and economic change could prevent people from being afflicted by them. The social and economic relations of the fifties were not conducive to such radicalism and neither was the conservative character of the mental hygiene discourse. But things would change. As Gemma Blok describes in her paper elsewhere in this volume, Dutch psychiatry took another course during the seventies and embraced the idea that a simultaneous renewal of the psychiatric profession and of the Dutch society was what was needed. Not very surprisingly, Trimbos was one of those in the Netherlands who reported cautiously, if favourably, on the enterprises of anti-psychiatry.

Notes

1. If not stated otherwise, the information used in this paper is based on my PhD study on the Dutch Mental Hygiene Movement in the twentieth century which will be published in 1999.
2. Although the concept of Mental Hygiene was officially abandoned in favour of Mental Health in 1948 (see p. 68). Mental Hygiene remained very much in use afterwards. Both terms can thus be found concurrently in this paper. The Dutch concept 'Geestelijke Volksgezondheid' translates into Mental Hygiene as well as Mental Health and Public Mental Health.
3. 'Bevordering der Geestelijke Volksgezondheid', *Nederlandsch Tijdschrift voor Geneeskunde*, 68, (1924), 2677-9, p. 2677.
4. A. Kerkhoven and J. Vijselaar 'De zorg voor zenuwlijders rond 1900', in G. Hutschemaekers and C. Hrachovec (eds) *Heer en Heelmeesters. Negentig jaar zorg voor zenuwlijders in het Christelijk Sanatorium*, (Nijmegen: SUN, 1993), 27-58, p. 29-30; J. Noordman, *Om de kwaliteit van het nageslacht. Eugenetica in Nederland 1900-1950* (Nijmegen: Sun, 1989), 74-86.
5. W.H. Cox, 'Nog eens de kosten van onze krankzinnigenverpleeging', *Psychiatrische en Neurologische Bladen* 14 (1910) 230-44, p. 242. On the history of the Dutch asylum in the nineteenth and first decades of the twentieth century see J. Vijselaar, *Krankzinnigen gesticht: psychiatrische inrichtingen in Nederland, 1880-1910* (Haarlem: Fibula van Dishoeck, 1982) and H. Binneveld, *Filantropie, repressie en medische zorg: geschiedenis van de inrichtingspsychiatrie* (Deventer: Van Loghum Slaterus, 1985).

6. 'Wetenschappelijke Berichten: Nederlandsche vereeniging ter bevordering der geestelijke gezondheidszorg', *Nieuwe Rotterdamsche Courant*, 2-6-1924; *Nederlandsch Tijdschrift voor Geneeskunde* 68 (1924), p. 2678; Joh. van der Spek, *Geestelijke Volksgezondheid, een nieuwe taak voor de kerk* (Utrecht: Nederlandsche Hervormde Vereeniging voor Geestelijke Volksgezondheid, 1936), 18.

7. J. Noordman, *Om de kwaliteit van het nageslacht. Eugenetica in Nederland 1900-1950* (Nijmegen: Sun, 1989).

8. For the differences between the psychodynamic or psychoanalytic and the traditional bio-medical model of disease see G. Grob, *The Mad Among Us. A History of the Care of America's Mentally Ill* (New York: The Free Press, 1994), 142; G. Verwey, 'Freud en de psychiatrie rond 1900', *Nederlands Tijdschrift voor Geneeskunde*, 139 (1995), 2187-90. For the introduction and development of the Child Guidance Clinics [*Medisch-Opvoedkundige Bureaus*] in the Netherlands, see A.J. Heerma van Voss 'Het ambulante leven van Mej. mr dr E.C. Lekkerkerker', *Maandblad Geestelijke volksgezondheid*, 40 (1985), 1275-96; T. van der Grinten, *De vorming van de ambulante geestelijke gezondheidszorg. Een historisch beleidsonderzoek* (Baarn: Ambo, 1987), Chapter 3 (I); A. van der Wurff, 'Aspecten van medicalisering en normalisering bij de opkomst van het medisch-opvoedkundig werk in Nederland in het begin van de twintigste eeuw', *Pedagogisch Tijdschrift*, 15 (1990) 102-10. For the history of the psychoanalytic movement in the Netherlands, see I. Bulhof, *Freud en Nederland* (Baarn: Ambo, 1983) and C. Brinkgreve, *Psychoanalyse in Nederland* (Amsterdam: Uitgeverij De Arbeiderspers, 1984).

9. For the organizational development of the Dutch Mental Hygiene Movement before the Second World War, see Van der Grinten *De vorming*, Chapters 6-8 (I).

10. The resources of the 'Prophylaxefonds' came out of the premiums paid according to the 'Ziektewet' [Sickness Act] of 1931. The 'Prophylaxefonds' was officially independent but used by the Government to finance services aimed at the prevention of diseases. See T. van der Grinten, *De Vorming*, p. 98.

11. Heerma van Voss, *Het Ambulante Leven*, 1285-7; Van der Grinten, *De Vorming*, Chapters 9-10 (I); L. de Goei, 'E.C. Lekkerkerker in de oorlogsjaren', *Maandblad Geestelijke Volksgezondheid*, 45 (1990), 384-98, p. 387.

12. Heerma van Voss, *Het Ambulante Leven*, 1291-3; Van der Grinten, *De vorming van*, chapter 2 (II).

13. Heerma van Voss, *Het Ambulante Leven*, 1289-90; Van der Grinten, *De vorming*, Chapter 2 (II); De Goei, *E.C. Lekkerkerker*, 388-90, 393-6.

14. See Van der Grinten, *De vorming*, Chapters 4 and 5 (I) and Chapter 6 (II); R. Rigter, *Met Raad en Daad. De geschiedenis van de Gezondheidsraad 1902-1985* (Rotterdam: Erasmus Publishing, 1992), 177-80; C. Brinkgreve, J. Onland and A. de Swaan, *Sociologie van de psychotherapie 1. De opkomst van het psychotherapeutisch bedrijf* (Utrecht/Antwerpen: Uitgeverij Het Spectrum, 1979), Chapter 1.

15. *Mededeelingen van de Nationale Federatie voor Geestelijke Volksgezondheid*, 1 (1945), 3.

16. H. de Liagre Böhl, 'Zedeloosheidsbestrijding in 1945. Een motor van wederopbouw', in H. Galesloot and M. Schrevel (eds), *In fatsoen hersteld. Zedelijkheid en wederopbouw na de oorlog* (Amsterdam: SUA, 1987), 15-28. De Liagre Böhl has pointed out that the concept of 'moral crisis' was used by the political, social and cultural elites to blur the post-war problems in political and labour relations. For a discussion on the relation between mental health problems and the War, see G. Hutschemaekers, *Neurose in Nederland* (Nijmegen: SUN, 1990), and L. de Goei, 'Psychiatrie en de Tweede Wereldoorlog: een verkenning te Zeist', in Hutschemaekers and Hrachovec, *Heer en Heelmeesters*, 197-216.

17. Nationale Federatie voor de Geestelijke Volksgezondheid (NFGV), *Advies uitgebracht aan de Minister van Sociale Zaken betreffende maatregelen welke in de eerstkomende tijd ter bevordering van de geestelijke gezondheid moeten worden genomen* (Amsterdam: NFGV, 1945); NFGV, *Annual Report*, 1943-1944, 1945; NFGV, *Report on present-day psychological problems*, 1947.

18. NFGV, *Annual Report*, 1945; A. Querido, 'Groepsselectie en behandeling', *Tijdschrift voor Sociale Geneeskunde*, 24 (1946), 160-2; H.C. Rümke, 'De bestrijding van de neurose als volksziekte', *Tijdschrift voor Sociale Geneeskunde*, 24 (1946), 330-3.

19. G. Grob, *The Mad Among Us*, 191-7; H. Binneveld, *Om de geest van Jan Soldaat: beknopte geschiedenis van de militaire psychiatrie*, (Rotterdam: Erasmus Publishing, 1995), 209, 220-1.

20. 'Nationaal Congres voor de Geestelijke Volksgezondheid', *Maanblad voor de Geestelijke Volksgezondheid*, 3 (1947), 195-254, p. 208.

21. A. Querido, 'Groepsbehandeling en groepsselectie', 160-1.

22. E.C. Lekkerkerker, 'Het derde Internationale congres voor geestelijke hygiëne. Algemene indrukken', *Maandblad voor de Geestelijke Volksgezondheid*, 3 (1948), 355-61, p. 357; A. Querido, *Doorgaand verkeer. Autobiografische fragmenten*, (Lochum/Poperinge: De Tijdstroom, 1980), 186-7. See also *International Congress on Mental Health, Volume IV. Proceedings of the International Conference on Mental Hygiene* (London: H.K.

Lewis & Co. Ltd, New York: Columbia University Press, 1948).

23. A. Querido, 'De IPC. Een proeve van internationale en meerzijdige samenwerking', *Maandblad voor de Geestelijke Volksgezondheid*, 3 (1948), 387-93; A. Querido, 'Naschrift' *Maandblad voor de Geestelijke Volksgezondheid*, 5 (1950), 270-1, p. 70; H.C. Rümke 'Psychiatrie en maatschappij', *Nederlandsch Tijdschrift voor de Psychologie en haar grensgebieden*, 6 (1951), 1-22, p. 6-7. See also *Proceedings Volume IV*.

24. E.C. Lekkerkerker, 'Het derde Internationale congres voor geestelijke hygiëne. Algemeene indrukken', p. 360; H.C. Rümke, 'Naar aanleiding van de derde "Annual-Meeting" van de W.F.M.H.' *Maandblad voor de Geestelijke Volksgezondheid*, 6 (1951), 52-7, p. 52, 53.

25. E.C. Lekkerkerker, 'Wat is geestelijke volksgezondheid?', *Maandblad voor de Geestelijke Volksgezondheid*, 9 (1954), 33-50, p. 39.

26. H.C. Rümke, 'Psychiatrie en Maatschappij', 6-7; A. Querido, 'Openbare gezondheidszorg en geestelijke gezondheidszorg', *Maandblad voor de Geestelijke Volksgezondheid*, 6 (1951), 321-6, p. 323.

27. See, e.g., H.C. Rümke, 'Psychiatrie en Maatschappij' and E.C. Lekkerkerker, 'Wat is Geestelijke Volksgezondheid'.

28. H.M.M. Fortmann, *Een nieuwe opdracht. Poging tot een historische plaatsbepaling en tot taakomschrijving van de geestelijke gezondheidszorg in het bijzonder voor het katholieke volksdeel in ons land* (Utrecht/Antwerpen: Uitgeverij Het Spectrum, 1955), p. 11.

29. H.C. Rümke, 'Psychiatrie en Maatschappij'.

30. *Ibid.*, p. 8-9.

31. J.A. van Belzen, *Zicht op synthese? H.C. Rümke's streven naar integratie in psychiatrie en geestelijke gezondheidszorg*, PhD Dissertation, Utrecht 1988, p. 31-7.

32. J.A. van Belzen, *Zicht op synthese*, p. 66, 74-5, 79, 86, 88. Rümke's interest in the scientific approach grew in his later career. See, on the *Utrechtse School*, I. Weijers, *Terug naar het behouden huis. Romanschrijvers en wetenschappers in de jaren vijftig* (Amsterdam: SUA, 1991).

33. J.A. van Belzen, *Zicht op synthese*, p. 36-7.

34. J.A. van Belzen, *Zicht op synthese*, p. 43-4, 65.

35. C.J.B.J. Trimbos, *Geestelijke Gezondheidsleer en Geestelijke Gezondheidszorg* (Utrecht/Antwerpen: Uitgeverij Het Spectrum, 1959).

36. C.J.B.J. Trimbos, *Geestelijke Gezondheidsleer*, 'Inleiding' and chapters 3 and 4.

37. C.J.B.J. Trimbos, *Geestelijke Gezondheidsleer*, chapter 5.

38. *Idem*, p. 131-2.

39. *Idem*, p. 18-19.
40. *Idem*, p. 75-6.
41. R. Abma, 'De katholieken en het psy-complex', *Grafiet*, 1 (1981-1982), 156-97; J.C. Pols, 'Genezen van de moraal. Over katholieken en de geestelijke gezondheidszorg in Nederland 1930-1950', *Kennis en Methode*, 12 (1988), 4-19; R.H.J. ter Meulen, *Ziel en Zaligheid. De receptie van de psychologie en van de psychoanalyse onder de katholieken in Nederland 1900-1965* (Nijmegen/Baarn: Ambo, 1988); H. Westhoff, *Geestelijke Bevrijders. Nederlandse katholieken en hun beweging voor geestelijke volksgezondheid in de twintigste eeuw* (Nijmegen: Valkhof Pers, 1996).
42. There is another clear lineage between mental hygiene and anti-psychiatry in the Netherlands which I want to point out briefly. One of the basic assumptions of the mental hygienists was that 'modernisation' had an adverse effect on mental health. This 'anti-modernist' critique of culture can also be traced in the discourse of the Dutch anti-psychiatric and counterculture movement. As Ido Weijers has convincingly demonstrated, even the most radical proponents of Dutch anti-psychiatry were anti-modernists. They opposed large-scale plans and a more rational mental health care system, they wanted to improve the care for the mentally handicapped but they did not want assessments to be made of such improvements in terms of functionality or efficiency. In this urge to change and preserve at the same time, they continued in Weijers view the philosophical tradition of the generation of intellectuals before them, the *grands seigneurs* of the *Utrechtse School*. I. Weijers, 'De slag om Dennendal. Een terugblik op de jaren vijftig vanuit de jaren zeventig', in P. Luykx and P. Slot (eds), *Een stille revolutie? Cultuur en mentaliteit in de lange jaren vijftig* (Hilversum: Verloren, 1977), 45-65.

5

'They Used to Call it Psychiatry':
Aspects of the Development and
Impact of Psychopharmacology

E. M. Tansey

Introduction

'They used to call it psychiatry' is the somewhat ironical title
offered by the noted Canadian psychiatrist Thomas Ban for a
hypothetical personal history of the subject. In an interview with
David Healy, Ban, a pioneer in the field, suggested that whilst
psychopharmacology had been responsible, and laudably so, for
'dragging psychiatry into the modern world', he reflected that in the
process, psychiatry had become a laboratory focused research
activity, with too little emphasis on making the results relevant to
clinical conditions.[1] This paper is an attempt to accrue evidence to
examine that suggestion, by looking at the development, and role of
psychopharmacology, as a distinct discipline, especially in the
context of contemporary scientific knowledge about brain
chemistry and pharmacology. It is not my intention to provide a
catalogue of psychopharmacology but to illustrate early trends in
the discovery and therapeutic implementation of some named
drugs, concentrating on British experiences and looking particularly
at events in the 1950s, many of which were to have long-standing
consequences. The main features of the paper will be the fortuitous
discovery and introduction into clinical practice of chlorpromazine,
and the discovery of the tricyclic antidepressants, including a short
discussion on British legislation on drug safety and efficacy. I also
include an assessment of the role of industrially-based laboratories
in research and development, viewed especially in the context of
contemporary advances in neurochemistry and neuropharmacology,
in an attempt to determine what, if any, influences such knowledge
had on therapeutic programmes. Finally, I examine how the

discipline of 'psychopharmacology' was created and established during the 1950s, with a survey of various indices of professionalisation, recognising some of the tensions and conflicts between the clinicians and scientists who constituted that community. Thus I am approaching psychiatry from a somewhat tangential viewpoint, and hope this paper will provide the opportunity for a synergistic and creative dialogue that will approach some of these questions, and enrich our understanding of the modern history of psychopharmacology. In so doing, I hope to contribute relevant material to an assessment of post-war psychiatric practice.

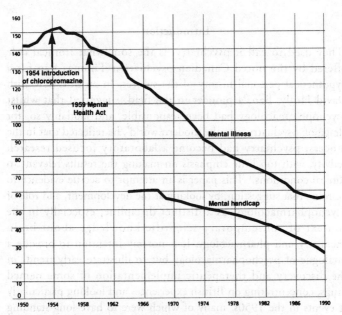

Source: DoH and Health and Personal Social Services Statistics for England.

Figure 1.
Resident in-patients in mental illness/handicap hospitals, England, 1950–1990. Reproduced with permission, from statistics compiled by the Office of Health Economics.*

Chlorpromazine

'Chlorpromazine is the result of one of those fateful accidents which has had a profound influence on the history of medicine'.[2]

The history of modern psychopharmacology is usually dated from the introduction of chlorpromazine in the early 1950s, one account even claiming 'if one defines psychopharmacology precisely as the utilisation of drugs in restoring or maintaining mental health and for exploring the mind, then everyone is agreed: the drug is chlorpromazine'.[3] I'm going to look briefly at the development of chlorpromazine, and its impact, especially by examining how its success drove the clinical, scientific and industrial communities to inaugurate further pharmacological therapies for psychiatric use.

The introduction of chlorpromazine had an almost immediate effect. Figure 1 (left) is taken from the Office of Health Economics in Britain, and shows the number of in-patients in mental illness/handicap hospitals and units in England for the period between 1950 and 1990. There is a steep decline in such in-patients, associated with both the introduction of chlorpromazine in 1954 and other major tranquillisers in subsequent years, and the Mental Health Act of 1959. By 1990, the last year for which full statistics are available, there were 50% as many psychiatric in-patient beds as there were in 1954. The strength of the causal relationship between that decline and the introduction of either chlorpromazine and/or more benign social therapies such as open-door, and more relaxed discharge, policies, has been questioned by some contemporary practitioners and also by later historians.[4] Government figures reflect a similar situation in the United States. 'In 1956, for the first time in 175 years, the numbers of patients in the United States psychiatric hospitals began to decline. Each year since, despite a steady increase in the admission rate, there has been a substantial decrease in the resident population of mental hospitals to an all time low of less than 350,000 patients at the end of 1970'. It can of course be argued that the introduction of the drug, which calmed disturbed patients, in itself created the climate that allowed patients to leave in-patient care for local day-care centres, etc.[5] However, it is undeniable that chlorpromazine had a powerful impact, which also coincided with the widespread post-war therapeutic optimism in Britain, amply illustrated for example, by the public recognition of the role that penicillin had played during the conflict.

81

The story of the paths, direct and indirect, leading to the psychiatric use of chlorpromazine is well-known, although not uncontroversial, and will be only briefly re-iterated.[6] It starts with the accidental discovery of histamine as a natural constituent of the animal body by Henry Dale, and increasing evidence of its role in pathological conditions such as asthma, allergy, and anaphylactic shock.[7] Those findings had a number of therapeutic implications and work on anti-histamine drugs to counteract these actions was initiated in a number of academic institutes and pharmaceutical companies. In 1927, Daniel Bovet, who was later awarded the Nobel Prize for his work on anti-histamines, and A. M. Staub, of the Institut Pasteur in Paris, first discovered a synthetic compound with anti-histamine properties, which stimulated further searches for such drugs. Just after the second world war, Paul Charpentier of Rhône-Poulenc, working on anti-protozoal and anti-helmintic compounds, synthesised a series of phenothiazine derivatives, one of which, later known as chlorpromazine, was shown to have strong anti-histamine properties. This factor made it worthy of further investigations, as a possible commercially viable drug and laboratory studies suggested that it might have a previously unknown effect on the central nervous system, these results coinciding with reports that allergic patients taking anti-histamine compounds experienced drowsiness. This 'drowsiness' effect was utilised therapeutically by a French surgeon Henri Laborit who used chlorpromazine to potentiate anaesthesia, and reported that it induced 'detachment' in his patients.[8] Laborit's paper attracted the attention of psychiatrists, especially Jean Delay and Pierre Deniker, who started investigating the potential of the drug in calming manic patients, for which there was then no known, reliable, medication.[9] Their ultimately successful results spread rapidly, as Caldwell has reported: 'By May [1953] the atmosphere in the disturbed wards of mental hospitals in Paris was transformed. Physical restraints were a thing of the past!'[10] Intrigued and inspired, psychiatrists across Europe rushed to try the new drug, and Rhône-Poulenc salesmen carried reprints of the resultant scientific and medical reports as publicity material. One recipient of such material was Heinz Lehmann, a Francophone psychiatrist in Montreal, whose colleagues were all monoglot English speakers. Lehmann accepted the French articles and read them with mounting incredulity: 'It was very strange, they made statements such as this is a sedative that produces something like a "chemical lobotomy" – somehow it was different from other sedatives. I really didn't believe this'.[11] His subsequent trials of the new drug accelerated its introduction into North America.[12]

The story of the introduction of chlorpromazine reveals a number of interesting features: the drug was not discovered as part of a focused search for psychiatric therapies, but was a chance find in a search for anti-infective agents, which was then found to have powerful anti-histamine properties. These desirable qualities ensured that the drug was used clinically for allergic patients and investigated further subsequent laboratory and clinical reports revealing other effects, notably 'drowsiness', initially utilised by a surgeon, whose subsequent reports of the drug's effects were picked up by psychiatrists. Thus it was at this point, fairly late in the drug's developmental history, that chlorpromazine was introduced into psychiatric practice.

There was however, little or no knowledge about its mode of action as a tranquilliser, as the drug had been principally investigated as an anti-histamine. Indeed, at that time there was little known about the chemistry and pharmacology of the central nervous system, and to assist the understanding of drug development let us consider the state of such knowledge in the early 1950s.

Neuropharmacology in the Early 1950s

The most startling work on the role of endogenous chemicals in the nervous system was that for which Sir Henry Dale from London and Otto Loewi from Graz in Austria shared the Nobel Prize for Physiology or Medicine in 1936. Their work, and that of their colleagues, demonstrated that nerve cells pass their messages from one to the other and to their target cells (such as a muscle or gland cell) by means of specific chemical substances (neurotransmitters).[13] In particular Dale and his team had shown that acetylcholine acted as a neurotransmitter at a number of sites in the nervous system, and there was then strong evidence that a substance very like adrenaline (later shown to be noradrenaline) was also a neurotransmitter. But there was little evidence that these chemical mechanisms operated in the brain, as Dale and Loewi's work had been in the autonomic nervous system, that part of the nervous system that controls the routine functions of the body, such as breathing, digestion, or in the peripheral nervous system, the nerves that transmit messages to skeletal muscle. A few clinicians attempted to utilise this new knowledge therapeutically, although it has proved difficult to trace individual case reports, and there may well have been many more, unrecorded, attempts. An early example was the neurologist Sir Russell Brain's experimental treatment programme for patients with myasthenia gravis, using an acetylcholinesterase inhibitor, and potentiator of acetylcholine.[14] Shorter also mentions the administration of acetylcholine to schizophrenic patients in the 1930s by an Italian psychiatrist, although the practice seems not to have been widespread.[15] Experimental work on the role of chemicals in the central nervous system was only just beginning to get off the ground in the 1950s, and discussion of the possibility of pharmacological therapies for psychiatric disease are usually absent from immediate post-war textbooks of psychiatry.[16]

Increasingly throughout the 1950s research attention was paid to the chemistry of the central nervous system. To some extent this was fuelled by the success of the psychoactive drugs, but was largely independent.[17] A number of approaches were taken, including attempts to locate chemicals such as acetylcholine and noradrenaline in precise areas of the brain, experiments to assess the effect of applying such chemicals to nervous tissue, and general examinations of brain preparations to determine its chemical constituents. In many ways the latter approach was the most interesting, revealing during the 1950s two chemical substances that were to play important parts in the later development of psychoactive drugs.[18] These were chemically related substances, both amines: serotonin, (also known as enteramine or 5HT, 5-hydroxytryptamine) and dopamine. Serotonin was first isolated by two independent groups: the Italian pharmacologist Vittorio Erspamer discovered it in the salivary glands of *Octopus vulgaris* and originally named it enteramine;[19] an American group of investigators lead by Irvine Page found, in serum, a substance that caused vasoconstriction, and called it serotonin.[20] Soon both substances were found to be identical, the chemical name of the compound 5-hydroxytryptamine providing yet another name, 5HT, and in 1953 the British pharmacologist John Gaddum also discovered that its actions could be antagonised by lysergic acid diethylamide (LSD).[21] Other significant work on the neurochemistry of the brain done in that decade and of relevance to the development of psychopharmacology was the discovery by Arvid Carlsson of dopamine, a precursor of noradrenaline, as an active, endogenous constituent of normal brain tissue.[22] All this basic work was undertaken in academic laboratories at the University of Bari and the Stazione Zoologica, Naples (Erspamer); the Cleveland Clinic, Ohio (Page and Twarog); the University of Edinburgh (Gaddum) and the University of Lund (Carlsson), and its direct relevance to therapeutic strategies was not immediately recognised, although work on the chemistry and pharmacology of dopamine and 5HT was to lead, in later years, to some carefully designed powerful psychoactive drugs. Work on 5HT, in particular, has penetrated into popular culture and public awareness, and 5HT, often referred to as 'the mood chemical' is the major known substrate of drugs such as Prozac and Ecstasy, and also mediates the mechanism whereby LSD causes psychedic experiences.[23] During the 1950s industrial research was principally directed towards finding compounds similar to those already shown to be effective, rather than towards understanding the underlying modes of action of such therapies. This was largely due to the serendipitous mechanisms by which the earliest effective drugs had been discovered.[24]

Psychopharmacology: Industry and Drug Development

Unlike contemporary developments in other therapeutic areas, those in psychopharmacology were almost entirely industry-driven.[25] The processes by which new drugs are discovered can be classified in a number of ways. For example, effective drugs can be found, either by empirical searches for new compounds, or by the systematic testing of established medicines for new effects. This latter route is often taken by scientists working in drug companies who have access to a wide range of compounds they can investigate for novel therapeutic effects, regardless of the mechanisms by which they caused their effects. Drugs can also be specifically designed, a process that relies on knowledge of the underlying pathological mechanisms and/or the molecular biology of other effective medicines and their receptor sites. By and large all these approaches have been used in the discovery of psychoactive compounds, the latter two approaches being predominantly the perogative of industrial concerns, especially in the past 20–30 years.

In the early years however, empirical studies were the major route for drug discoveries. In the U.K. two pharmaceutical companies were particularly important in the development of psychoactive drugs in the late 1940s and early 1950s, May & Baker and Geigy. In the early 1950s in the U.K. May & Baker were in a particularly unique position in the public eye for a pharmaceutical company. The success of their antibiotic M & B 693 had been a national triumph, especially after Winston Churchill's successful treatment with it during the war became widely known, and the company had a close commercial relationship with Rhône-Poulenc, the French company that had developed chlorpromazine.[26] That success encouraged further company research into psychoactive drugs, and over the next few years, tranquillisers, hypnotics and anti-depressants all emerged from their laboratories.[27] As the British partner in the enterprise, May & Baker benefited directly from this research, and marketed all the products in Britain, chlorpromazine being sold under the registered trade-name of 'Largactil'. Contemporary company information on Largactil indicates a broad range of applications: in general medicine, as a supplement to prolong the action of analgesics, especially in intractable pain; to treat nausea and vomiting; to relieve pruritus and the accompanying distress, *particularly when there is an important psychological factor* (my emphasis); in the management of senility and fever; and as a treatment for minor degrees of psychoneuroses. Specific psychiatric indicators were either as the sole treatment for manic, agitated or confused patients, or as a constituent of a sedative regime for prolonged sleep treatment.[28] By the 1970s Largactil had become part of the lexicon of constraint, as used by an acute feminist observer, 'As far as the woman is concerned, psychiatry is an extraordinary confidence trick: the unsuspecting creature seeks aid because she feels unhappy, anxious and confused, and psychology persuades her to seek the cause in *herself* ... If all else fails, Largactil, shock treatment, hypnosis and other forms of 'therapy' will buttress the claim of society'.[29]

In contrast to May & Baker, the Geigy Company was a Swiss-based firm with a small British commercial outlet situated just outside Manchester. In 1949 these very modest premises comprised a packing room for the dispatch of products from the parent company, and secretarial facilities.[30] Two scientific staff constituted the 'Pharmaceutical Laboratories Geigy Limited' in Britain, and they enjoyed a broad remit to re-examine company drugs already on the market, or to investigate compounds still in development. Geigy, like many companies at the time, were interested in anti-histamines, a focus further defined by Rhône-Poulenc's discovery of the phenothiazines. This commercial rivalry stimulated a search through Geigy's old samples and discarded chemicals in Switzerland to reveal a compound similar in molecular shape to phenothiazine. Subsequent laboratory work in the U.K., including a self experimentation trial,[31] suggested that this drug too had psychoactive properties, and that a clinical trial might be profitable, especially for schizophrenia. The results of that trial however were disastrous for the Geigy company, and for the Münsterlingen

Hospital where the trial was conducted. Many patients deteriorated rapidly and formerly well-controlled schizophrenics became increasingly agitated and manic.[32] The trial was stopped. Over the next few months, scientists in Switzerland and in Britain tried to understand what had happened. Despite the apparent failure of the drug to treat schizophrenia it had demonstrated remarkable effects on mood, and the idea arose that if the drug caused an unwanted elevation of mood in schizophrenics, might it not produce a similar, wanted, effect in depressed patients? A further such trial was undertaken, with spectacularly successful results, patients, their relatives and staff all remarking on a 'miracle cure'.[33] The company named the compound imipramine, and marketed it under the trade-name of Tofranil, the first, and for many years, the most frequently, prescribed of the tricyclic antidepressants.[34]

Although the biological mechanism of these drugs was still unknown this was not regarded as a high research priority. Geigy scientists, encouraged by the success of imipramine, started to examine related compounds for similar therapeutic efficacy, thus repeating the search strategy that had successfully uncovered the psychoactive properties of imipramine. A compound called clomipramine was one of the results.[35] This drug got into wide circulation as an antidepressive, but psychiatrists, now more familiar with, and confident about, experimenting with drug therapies, used it experimentally to treat other conditions. Once again, a new drug seemed to be particularly effective in an unexpected area: in this case for the treatment of obsessive-compulsive disorder (OCD), and pushed by Geigy U.K.'s then Medical Director, George Beaumont, the drug was successfully re-marketed as a specific treatment for OCD therapy.[36]

There is however, an exception to this account of industry-lead innovation. It concerns lithium, which in 1949 was discovered by the Australian psychiatrist J.F. Cade to have a quietening effect on manic patients, but his resultant paper seems not to have attracted much attention. Lithium salts of course, were not a patentable commodity, and no big drug company got involved in investigating, or promoting them further, and there was also concern that the salts were too toxic for routine therapeutic administration.[37] It was to be many years before this useful treatment for maniacal patients became widely available, due largely to the efforts of a Danish psychiatrist, Mogens Schou, in whose own family ran manic-depressive illness. Schou carried out one of the first placebo-controlled, double blind clinical trials in psychiatry, using patients and members of his own family, including himself. His report alerted the wider psychiatric community to the possibilities of lithium, but it was not until 1970 that the drug was approved by the Food and Drug Administration of the United States. Why the delay? There was, according to Shorter, a strongly 'entrenched therapeutic nihilism' in the United States, and especially in Britain.[38] This could be overcome, as demonstrated by the sales of chlorpromazine, by a well co-ordinated publicity campaign orchestrated by a powerful industrial advocate, but lithium, with no such support, was promoted almost by word of mouth alone, by reports in the scientific and medical press.[39]

Psychopharmacology – the Making of a Profession

Academic scientists, industrial scientists, and clinicians from a variety of different practical and theoretical backgrounds were associated with the development of new drugs and assessing their clinical and scientific impact. These activities increasingly lead to the definition of psychopharmacology as a distinct discipline, with a heritage that included pharmacology, chemistry and psychology, as well as psychiatry. What were the pressures that lead to the professionalisation of that discipline and to individuals identifying themselves as 'psychopharmacologists'? Obviously a number of standard indices can be examined to support and illustrate that growth such as the numbers of specialist articles published, the creation of specialised journals, societies, meetings etc. An immediate assessment of the phenomenal interest in the subject is provided by a bibliographic survey of the field compiled by the National Library of Medicine.[40] This recorded 2500 articles on aspects of psychopharmacology published between January 1952 and December 1956. These articles did not include papers on the chemistry and physiology of drugs, unless they were reports of side-effects. The indexes were prepared using standard bibliographic abstracting tools (*Index Medicus, Excerpta Medica, Chemical Abstracts*) and by examining individual issues of eleven relevant medical journals.[41] There were then no specialist publications devoted to the subject until *Psychopharmacologia* was published by Springer-Verlag in 1959 (in 1976 this became *Psychopharmacology*), and in the same year the United States Public Health Service started *Psychopharmacological Bulletin*. Other specialist journals were started somewhat later (see Table 1).

Table 1

1962 Neuropharmacology	1986 Human Psychopharmacology: Human and Experimental
1968 Pharmacopsychiatry	1987 Journal of Psychopharmacology
1969 Advances in Biochemical Psychopharmacology	1987 Neuropsychopharmacology
1974 Psychoneuroendocrinology	1989 Journal of Neuropsychiatry and Clinical Neurosciences
1976 Clinical Neuropharmacology	1990 European Neuropsychopharmacology
1977 Progress in Neuropsycho-pharmacology & Biological Psychiatry	1990 Lithium
1981 Journal of Clinical Psychopharmacology	1990 Behavioral Pharmacology
1983 Psychopharmacology [not the Journal started in 1959]	1991 Advances in Neuropsychology and Psychopharmacology

The creation of the first professional organisation in psychopharmacology was, somewhat unusually for academic societies, also influenced by industry. Two precursor meetings can be recognised. The first was a Rhône-Poulenc sponsored conference held in Paris in 1955, the 'International Colloquium on chlorpromazine and neuroleptic drugs in psychiatric practice', which was the first international meeting held on the subject.[42] The attendees were predominantly clinicians and provided a timely opportunity for psychiatrists from around the world to meet, to discuss the impact and possibilities of the new pharmacological therapies.[43] Two years later a somewhat similar international meeting on psychotropic drugs was held in Milan, stimulated by Italian pharmacologists keen to develop a scientific exchange with clinical colleagues. This meeting was principally attended by pharmacologists and other basic scientists from universities and industry, with few clinicians present, despite the organisers' original intention. During this meeting a pharmacologist, Corneille Radouco-Thomas, and a psychiatrist, Wolfgang de Boor, suggested founding a society for psychopharmacology which would embrace both scientific and clinical communities. This became the CINP, the Collegium Internationale Neuropsychopharmacologium, which held its inaugural meeting, attended by about 30 people in 1958, under the presidency of Ernst Rothlin, the Director of Sandoz.[44] One participant at that conference, Hannah Steinberg, recalls that the subject already attracted representatives from a wide range of disciplines and nationalities: an early administrative issue was that of electing an organising committee that adequately represented that diversity.[45] Equally diverse was the extent of scientific issues addressed, and in addition to papers on individual drugs and chemicals, the programme included sessions on therapies for schizophrenia, assessment techniques for different methodologies, and discussions about the use of psychoactive drugs in basic medical research.

Many national societies were founded in the wake, and often in the image, of the CINP, including those of Germany, Austria, Switzerland, the United States and a Central European Society.[46] In Britain however, it was not until 1974 that the British Association for Psychopharmacology (BAP) was started, accompanied by considerable controversy. The initial proposal to establish a society to further 'clinical and experimental research' and to evaluate new drugs came from clinicians as a letter in three medical journals in March 1974.[47] Twice in the short letter the authors address their proposal to 'members of the profession' seemingly indicating medical personnel only. The absence of a letter in a main-stream scientific journal, such as *Nature*, was used in later disputes as evidence of an attempt to exclude basic scientists from the proposed society. Several interested parties met in April of that year, and the idea was further developed: the Academy, as it was to be called, would principally meet in exotic places and membership would be strictly limited to two hundred. It was to be an exclusive elite with a deliberately strong clinical bias. There was increasing hostility to these ideas from basic scientists and some clinicians and a 'Gang of Five' sought widespread support from psychopharmacologists throughout Britain, threatening at one point to publish a letter in *Nature* denouncing the Academy.[48] Two further stormy meetings were held in November 1974, inter-connected arguments being presented as to what the Society should do, and who should belong to it. Ultimately a compromise was reached, the title 'Academy' being dropped in favour of 'Association' and the restriction on numbers of members was lifted, although many members believe that the trauma caused damage that blighted the BAP's early years.[49]

Psychopharmacology – Towards the End of Psychiatry?

The third meeting of the CINP, held in Munich in 1962 attracted 200 delegates. The occasion was used to hold a session, under the chairmanship of Heinz Lehmann, entitled 'Ten years of psychopharmacology: critical assessment of the present and future', with reflective contributions from France, Italy, Norway, Switzerland, Japan, Denmark, Austria, the USA, Germany and Hungary. It also provides a convenient point at which to end the present survey, and to make some assessment of the first decade of modern psychopharmacology.

This brief survey raises a number of questions and comments that have relevance to a larger historical study of post-war psychiatry, and some are listed here in the hope of promoting discussion which may contextualise this work as part of that larger history, and point to possible routes for further research.

Anti-Psychiatry

One question addressed more fully elsewhere in this volume is the relationship of psychopharmacology to anti-psychiatry. The use of drugs in psychiatric practice may well have fuelled anti-psychiatry rhetoric in Britain, but there was nothing like the movement that arose during the late 1960s and 1970s in the Netherlands, and there was, and is, no British equivalent to van Praag, the Dutch psychiatrist who was so reviled by the anti-psychiatry movement.[50] Why is that? Did British psychiatrists, and more significantly, their patients, have more confidence in drug therapy than their Dutch counterparts?[51] Or was there contemporary anti-medical protest in Britain, but directed elsewhere? There are good grounds for exploring the latter suggestion and protest against animal experimentation may well have provided a more potent 'anti-medical/anti-science' focus for British protesters than did psychiatric practice. Britain has a particularly long history of anti-vivisectionist protest, and during the 1970s when anti-psychiatry protest became prominent elsewhere, anti-vivisectionist protest was on the rise in Britain.[52]

Professionalisation

The introduction of psychoactive drugs generated, as the emergence of other new therapies frequently does in other areas, reluctance on the part of some practitioners to accept the new techniques. An interesting illustration of the contemporary reluctance of some practitioners to acknowledge new drug therapies is provided by an address on psychiatric research given to the Annual General Meeting of the Mental Health Research Fund in 1959 by David Stafford-Clark. There is no mention of pharmacological developments, although EEG studies, genetics, neurophysiology and psychosomatic approaches are discussed as possible lines of future research.[53] The introduction of psychopharmacology not only stimulated professional schism, but also accentuated differences between scientific and medical personnel in debates about who was a 'psychopharmacologist'. These were particularly pronounced in Britain, and delayed and disrupted the formation of a representative professional Society.

Drug Safety and Efficacy

The development of drugs for psychiatric patients coincided with, and further stimulated, concerns about drug safety in Britain. Legislation about the safety and efficacy of medicines in Britain really came to the fore in the early 1960s, stimulated to a very large extent, although not exclusively, by the thalidomide tragedy. Before then legislation had been passed in a rather piecemeal fashion. The Dangerous Drugs Act 1951, and the Therapeutic Substances Act 1956 were passed as consolidating legislation, and in late 1959 the Interim Report of an Interdepartmental Committee on Drug Addiction, chaired by Sir Russell Brain, recommended that any drug 'which had an action on the central nervous system and was liable to produce physical or psychological deterioration should be confined to supply on prescription', subject to the advice of an independent expert body. Chlorpromazine was specifically recognised as being possibly 'injurious to health' because of reports of adverse reactions, principally jaundice.[54] It was not until the passing of the Safety of Medicines Act 1968, which established the Medicines Commission, that Britain acquired a unified legislative framework for medical drug control. Many of the early workers in the field rapidly recognised the need for properly controlled clinical trials of these new remedies.[55] A number of additional problems and difficulties were recognised as psychoactive agents were increasingly used, for more patients, and for long term therapy. These included dosage levels (especially for long term maintenance), patient compliance (as patients felt better they omitted their medication, thus falling ill again), and the placebo effect,[56] and it was also recognized that symptomatic improvements, however desirable, were not necessarily matched by an understanding and thus a successful treatment of the underlying disease mechanisms.[57]

By the mid-1960s, a decade after the introduction of chlorpromazine, several pharmacological therapies for asychiatric disease were well established, and the development of others seen as a *desideratum* of industrialists, academic practitioners and even patients. Psychopharmacology had a notable impact on psychiatric practice and organisation, and not only spanned distinctions between commercial, clinical and scientific personnel, but also created new divisions and allegiances within those communities. Although Thomas Ban's plaintive comment "[T]hey used to call it psychiatry" is perhaps over-sensationalist, it is clear that the introduction of drug therapies permeated and changed every aspect of psychiatric practice, from patient care to professional allegiances.

Acknowledgements

I am most grateful to Mrs. Wendy Kutner and Dr. Daphne Christie for assistance in the preparation of this paper, and to the Wellcome Trust for financial support.

Notes

* Office of Health Economics 'Section 3. Hospital Services', *Compendium of Health Statistics* (8th edn) (London: Office of Health Economics, 1992) Figure 3.7, p. 23. The Mental Health Act, 1959 sought to view "mental disorder as a matter for treatment and not custodianship" see A Special Correspondent, 'The Mental Health Act, 1959, a Practitioners' Guide', *British Medical Journal*, ii (1959), 1478–80, p. 1479.

1. T. A. Ban, 'They Used to Call it Psychiatry', in D. Healy (ed.), *The Psychopharmacologists* (London: Altman, 1996), 587–620, p. 620.

2. F. J. Ayd, 'Chlorpromazine: Ten Years' Experience', in P. B. Bradley, F. Flugel, and P. H. Hoch (eds), *Neuro-psychopharmacology*, Vol. 3. Proceedings of the third meeting of the Collegium Internationale Neuro-psychopharmacologicum (Amsterdam: Elsevier Pub., 1964), 572–4, p. 572.

3. A. E. Caldwell, *Origins of Psychopharmacology: from CPZ to LSD* (Springfield: Charles C. Thomas, 1970). There is of course an earlier and lengthy history of the use of psychoactive drugs for social, religious and also medical reasons. Sporadic attempts, from the mid-nineteenth century onwards, to use drugs for the treatment of psychiatric disorders include Freud's suggestion of cocaine therapy, but the introduction of chlorpromazine heralds a clear line of

directed research and implementation. For succinct accounts of earlier attempts and later specific drug developments, see R. Byck, 'Drugs and the Treatment of Psychiatric Disorders', in L. S. Goodman and A. Gilman (eds), *Pharmacological Basis of Therapeutics*, 5th edn (New York: Macmillan, 1975), 152–200, p. 153, p. 157, p. 167–8, p. 174, p. 181, p. 184 and p. 189, and A. Hordern, 'Psychopharmacology: Some Historical Considerations', in C. R. B. Joyce (ed.), *Psychopharmacology, Dimensions and Perspectives* (London: Tavistock, 1968), 95–148.

4. For a contemporary comment, see e.g. H. E. Lehmann, 'Foreword' to T. Ban, *Psychopharmacology* (Baltimore: Williams & Wilkins Co., 1969), v–vi.

5. F. J. Ayd, 'Preface' to *The Future of Pharmacotherapy: New Drug Delivery Systems*, F. J. Ayd (ed.), (Baltimore: International Drug Therapy Newsletter, 1973), p. 7.

6. This summary account is principally derived from J. Swazey, *Chlorpromazine in Psychiatry: a Study of Therapeutic Innovation* (Cambridge, Mass.: MIT Press, 1974), and A. E. Caldwell, *Origins of Psychopharmacology: from CPZ to LSD* (Springfield: Charles C. Thomas, 1970). The different emphases, and attributions of credit, of these two books is specifically commented upon by one of the major players in the story, Pierre Deniker; see note 9 below for further details.

7. For a review of Dale's work on histamine, see H. H. Dale, 'The Pharmacology of Histamine; with a Brief Survey of Evidence for its Occurrence, Liberation and Participation in Natural Reactions', *Annals of the New York Academy of Sciences*, l (1950), 1017–28; E. M. Tansey, 'Henry Dale and the Microcirculation', in L. H. Smaje (ed.), *Aspects of the History of the Microcirculation, International Journal of Microcirculation*, xiv (Basel: S. Karger, 1994), 95-103.

8. H. Laborit, P. Huguenard and R. Alluaume, 'Un Nouveau Stabilisateur Végétatif (Le 4560 RP)', *Presse Médicale*, lx (1952), 206–8.

9. Laborit's significance and the allocation of credit for the discovery of the significance of chlorpromazine is one of the controversial features of this story. Pierre Deniker has written 'In a book entitled *From CPZ to LSD* (sic) Miss Caldwel (sic) (1970) presented the surgeon Laborit as the main, if not the only originator of the psychiatric applications of CPZ. The physicians of Hôpital Ste-Anne had robbed him of the credit for these applications using methods customary in "the academic jungle" of our old Europe...' – Deniker further suggests that American outrage at this apparent bias led to a Committee of the

American Academy of Sciences commissioning Dr Swazey to make 'a thorough enquiry'. P. Deniker, 'Discovery of the Clinical use of Neuroleptics', in M. J. Parnham and J. Bruinvels (eds), *Discoveries in Pharmacology, Vol 1: Psycho- and Neuropharmacology* (Amsterdam: Elsevier, 1983), 163–80. Preliminary searches through the published literature have revealed no support for Deniker's assertions.

10. A. E. Caldwell, *op. cit.*, note 6 above, p. 72.

11. H. Lehmann, 'Psychopharmacotherapy' in D. Healy (ed.), *The Psychopharmacologists* (London: Altman, 1996), 159–86, p. 159. The effect of a 'chemical' versus a surgical lobotomy particularly concerned Walter Freeman, a leading advocate of the surgical approach in the United States, who considered that, as far as improvement in ward environment was concerned, there was little to choose between drugs and surgery, but that only a lobotomy could produce a basic change in personality; see E. S. Valenstein, *Great and Desperate Cures: the Rise and Decline of Psychosurgery and Other Radical Treatments for Mental Illness* (New York: Basic Books Inc., 1986), especially '"A Living Fossil": the Decline of Lobotomy and the Final Years of Walter Freeman', 268–83.

12. J. Swazey, *op. cit.*, note 6 above, especially 'The Chlorpromazine Migration, 1952–54', 142–57.

13. U. S. von Euler, 'Historical Perspective: Growth and Impact of the Concept of Chemical Neurotransmission', in L. Stjärne, P. Hedqvist, H. Lagercrantz, and Å. Wennmalm (eds), *Chemical Transmission 75 Years* (London: Academic Press, 1981), 3–12; W.S. Feldberg, 'Henry Hallett Dale 1875–1968', *Biographical Memoirs of Fellows of the Royal Society of London*, xvi (1970), 77–174.

14. Sir Russell Brain to Sir Henry Dale, 12th March 1935, explaining that he wished to use physostigmine, an acetylcholinesterase inhibitor, for selected myasthenia gravis patients, as a result of Dale's work on acetylcholine. NIMR Archives, file 435/2 Sir Russell Brain. This approach remains the first line of treatment for myasthenic patients. C. Herrmann, 'Myasthenia Gravis', in R. E. Rakel (ed.), *Conn's Current Therapy 1991* (Philadelphia: W. B. Saunders Company, 1991), 857– 63.

15. E. Shorter, *A History of Psychiatry: from the Era of the Asylum to the Age of Prozac* (New York: John Wiley, 1996), p. 396 cites the work of A. M. Fiamberti, 'Sul Meccanismo di'azione Terapeutica della "Burrasca Vascolare" Provate con Derivati della Collina', *Giornale di Psichiatria e di Neuropatrologica*, lxvii (1939), 270–80. I have not been able to track down a copy of this paper.

16. As yet, a systematic survey of psychiatric textbooks has not been

undertaken. One such book, published in the year of chlorpromazine's introduction, attempts to extrapolate from findings in the autonomic nervous system to the central nervous system, and suggests that the work 'seems to have great potentialities for neurology and clinical medicine', E. Gellhorn, *Physiological Foundations of Neurology and Psychiatry*, especially 'Neurohumours and Neuropharmacology of the Autonomic Nervous System' (Minneapolis: University of Minnesota Press, 1953), 231–68.

17. The papers in A. E. Caldwell, *Psychopharmaca: a Bibliography of Psychopharmacology 1952–57*, compiled for the Psychopharmacology Service Center, National Institute of Mental Health, National Institutes of Health. Public Health Service Publication 581, United States Government Printing Office (1958) show a wide range of action of chlorpromazine and other known psychoactive drugs.

18. H. McIlwain, *Biochemistry and the Central Nervous System*, 2nd edn (London: J. A. Churchill, 1959) provides a snapshot of contemporary knowledge about brain chemistry. Henry McIlwain's own copy of this book is heavily annotated in preparation of the third edition, the sections on the catecholamines (adrenaline, noradrenaline and dopamine) and serotonin, being particularly marked, in contrast say, to the section on acetylcholine, emphasising a surge of new work on these chemicals. I am grateful to Dr Malcolm Segal for the gift of this book. By the time the third edition appeared in 1966 these sections had been enormously extended.

19. V. Erspamer and B. Asero, 'Identification of Enteramine, the Specific Hormone of the Enterochromaffin Cell System, as 5-Hydroxytryptamine', *Nature*, clxix (1952), 800–1; V. Erspamer, 'Pharmacology of Indolealkylamines', *Pharmacological Reviews*, vi (1954), 425–87. Further details of Erspamer's work, including a description of the first isolation of enteramine, using 30,000 pairs of *Octopus* salivary glands, are in E. M. Tansey, 'Neurotransmitters in the Cephalopod Brain: a Review', *Comparative Biochemistry and Physiology*, lxivc (1979), 173–82.

20. B. M. Twarog and I. H. Page, 'Serotonin Content of Some Mammalian Tissues and Urine and a Method of its Determination', *American Journal of Physiology*, cixxv (1953), 157–61.

21. Biographical vignettes of Erspamer, Page and Gaddum, and extracts of their papers are given in B. Holmstedt and G. Liljestrand (eds), *Readings in Pharmacology* (Oxford: Pergamon Press, 1963), 222–7. Betty Twarog's role is best described in her own account: B. Twarog, 'Serotonin: a History', *Comparative Biochemistry and Physiology*, xciC (1988), 21–4.

22. A. Carlsson, M. Lindqvist, T. Magnusson, and B. Waldeck, 'On the Presence of 3-Hydroxy-Tryptamine in Brain', *Science*, cxxxvii (1958), 471.

23. It is not feasible, nor desirable, to provide lengthy accounts of the psychiatric drug developments that are dependent on work on the metabolism and functions of dopamine and 5HT. Major drug groups such as the benzamides (e.g. sulpiride) have emerged from work on dopamine receptors, although originally designed as therapies for gastrointestinal disorders, see e.g. P. Jenner and C. D. Marsden, 'The Substituted Benzamides – a Novel Class of Dopamine Antagonists', *Life Sciences*, xxv (1979), 479–86; B. M. Angist, 'The Neurobiologically Active Benzamides and Related Compounds: Some Historical Aspects', in J. Rotrosen and M. Stanley (eds), *The Benzamides: Pharmacology, Neurobiology and Clinical Aspects* (New York: Raven Press, 1982), 1–6. A very readable account of the relevant 5HT brain chemistry, including a description of his own 'acid trip' is S. Snyder, *Drugs and the Brain* (2nd edn) (New York: Scientific American Librarian, 1996). The pharmacology of 5HT was discussed at the very first meeting of the CINP in 1957, see H. Steinberg, 'Bridging the Gap: Psychology, Pharmacology and After', in D. Healy (ed.), *The Psychopharmacologists* (London: Altman, 1996), 215–37.

24. The 1950s saw the discovery, all by serendipity, of other psychotropic agents in addition to those mentioned here, including reserpine, and the monoamine oxidase inhibitors (MAOIs); M. Weatherall, *In Search of a Cure: a History of Pharmaceutical Discovery* provides concise details of the history of these drugs, especially 'Drugs and the Mind' (Oxford: Oxford University Press, 1990), 251–68. Personal accounts by some of those involved in these discoveries are given in F. J. Ayd and B. Blackwell, *Discoveries in Biological Psychiatry* (Philadelphia: Lippincott, 1970).

25. An example of non-industry-driven research is the way Henry Dale's work on acetylcholine was taken up by the clinical community, see note 14 above. Other examples, including the academic discovery of therapeutic antitoxins, penicillin and the sulphonamides are given in Weatherall, *op. cit.* note 24 above, *passim*.

26. See R. Lovell, *Churchill's Doctor: a Biography of Lord Moran* (London: Royal Society of Medicine, 1992), p. 246.

27. J. Slinn, *A History of May & Baker, 1834–1984* (Cambridge: Hobsons Ltd., 1984), 158–9. E. Shorter suggests that chlorpromazine sold well in Britain 'because the firm of May & Baker was flogging it', Shorter, *op. cit.*, note 15 above, p. 258.

28. May & Baker, *Concise Information on 'Largactil'*, Company information leaflet (*c.*1954); May & Baker, *'Largactil' Bulletin no. 1. – Intractable Pain*, Company information leaflet (*c.*1954). Towards the end of the 1950s, Largactil was still marketed broadly for a variety of different conditions, see e.g. May & Baker *Established Uses of 'Largactil' in Geriatrics*, Company information leaflet (*c.*1957).

29. G. Greer, *The Female Eunuch* (London: Paladin, 1970), 90.

30. Much of the detail about the early Geigy laboratories and the discovery of imipramine comes from A. Broadhurst, 'Before and after Imipramine', in D. Healy (ed.), *The Psychopharmacologists* (London: Altman, 1996), 111–34. The name frequently associated with the discovery of imipramine is that of Roland Kuhn, then a staff psychiatrist at the Münsterlingen Hospital, and for a more detailed account of his role, see Shorter, *op. cit.* note 15 above, 258–61.

31. 'Volunteering came with the job' commented Broadhurst, describing the first trial in which he over-dosed, because of a mis-extrapolation of the human dose from animal data. See Broadhurst, *op. cit.* note 30 above, 115–6.

32. The definition of 'schizophrenia' at the time may well have included patients who would now be classified as 'manic-depressives'. However, Broadhurst (*op. cit.*, note 30 above) believes that a very high proportion of the treated patients would still be defined as schizophrenics using modern diagnostic criteria.

33. E. Shorter, *op. cit.*, note 15 above, p. 261.

34. A useful summary of the pharmacology of the tricyclic antidepressants, and some of the relevant pharmaceutical developments is provided by T. Ban, 'Tricyclic Antidepressants', in T. Ban (ed.), *Psychopharmacology* (Baltimore: Williams & Wilkins Co., 1969), 270–89.

35. Much of this account of clomipramine, its development and uses, is taken from G. Beaumont and P. Healy, 'The Place of Clomipramine in the History of Psychopharmacology', *Journal of Psychopharmacology*, vii (1993), 378–88.

36. Benzodiazepines, first discovered in 1947, provide yet a further illustration of almost accidental discovery in an industrial lab, this time that of Hoffman-la-Roche in New Jersey; see W. Haefely, 'Alleviation of Anxiety – the Benzodiazepine Saga', in M. J. Parnham and J. Bruniels (eds), *Discoveries in Pharmacology, Vol 1: Psycho- and Neuro-Pharmacology* (Amsterdam: Elsevier, 1983), 269–306.

37. J. F. Cade, 'Lithium Salts in the Treatment of Psychotic Excitement', *Medical Journal of Australia*, ii (1949), 349–52, a later comment is *idem*, 'The Story of Lithium', in F. J. Ayd and B. Blackwell (eds),

Discoveries in Biological Psychiatry (Philadelphia: Lippincott, 1970), 218–29.

38. E. Shorter, *op. cit.* note 15 above, (1996) 255–8.
39. M. Schou (1968), 'Lithium in Psychiatry – a Review', in D. H. Efron, J. O. Cole, J. Levine, and J. R. Wittenborn (eds), *Psychopharmacology: a Review of Progress, 1957–1967,* Public Health Service Publication (Washington: Government Printing Office, 1836), 701–18.
40. A. E. Caldwell, *op. cit.,* note 17 above.
41. These were: *AMA Archives of Neurology and Psychiatry; American Journal of Psychiatry; Annals of the New York Academy of Sciences; British Medical Journal; Diseases of the Nervous System; Encephale; International Record of Medicine; Journal of Clinical and Experimental Psychopathology; Journal of Mental Science; Journal of Nervous and Mental Disease; Psychiatric Quarterly.*
42. An earlier meeting was held in December 1954 in the United States, a symposium organised jointly by the section on medical sciences of the American Association for the Advancement of Science and the American Psychiatric Association. However, those attending, and the focus of the meeting, were entirely American, and it is not therefore regarded as a forerunner of the CINP. The proceedings of the American meeting are published as N. S. Kline, *Psychopharmacology* (Washington: American Association for the Advancement of Science, 1956).
43. This was the first important post-war psychiatric conference with German participants, and it allowed German psychiatrists, handicapped by post-war travel restrictions, to meet each other, see H. Hippius, 'The founding of the CINP and the discovery of clozapine', in D. Healy (ed.), *The Psychopharmacologists* (London: Altman, 1996), 187–213, p. 191–2.
44. Details of the founding of the CINP are primarily taken from Hippius (*op. cit.,* note 43 above).
45. Hannah Steinberg trained as a psychologist before completing a doctorate in pharmacology, and she became Reader in Psychopharmacology in the University of London in 1962, probably the first use of such a title in Europe. This account is principally taken from H. Steinberg, *op. cit.* note 23 above, p. 223.
46. D. Healy, 'One Hundred Years of Psychopharmacology', *Journal of Psychopharmacology,* vii (1993), 207–14.
47. See e.g. S. Brandon, A. Coppen, M. Hamilton, M. Holden, A. Hordern, N. Imlah, A. Jenner, D. Shaw, and D. Wheatley, 'British Academy of Psychopharmacology', *British Medical Journal,* i (1974), 391.

48. Details of the opposition to the Academy are given by Ian Stolerman, one of the 'Gang of Five', along with Philip Bradley, Tim Crow, Channi Kumar and Malcolm Lader, in I. Stolerman, 'Origin of the BAP', *Journal of Psychopharmacology,* ix (1995), 287–8. This account, submitted as a 'Letter to the Editor' was written in response to a series of interviews in the *Journal of Psychopharmacology* by David Healy with some founder members of the BAP. Stolerman believed that these interviews 'reflected the views of only one group involved in the founding of the society', thus his letter. Another member of the 'Gang of Five', Malcolm Lader, was later interviewed by Healy, and his account has also been used to develop the current brief account of the controversy surrounding the founding of the BAP, M. Lader, 'Psychopharmacology: Clinical and Social', in D. Healy (ed.), *The Psychopharmacologists* (London: Altman, 1996), 463–81, p. 472. This issue is also analysed by the participants in a Wellcome Trust Witness Seminar, E. M. Tansey, D. A. Christie, and L. A. Reynolds (eds), *Wellcome Witnesses to Twentieth Century Medicine. Volume 2* (London: The Wellcome Trust, forthcoming).

49. I. Stolerman, *op. cit.*, note 48 above, p. 288.

50. Herman van Praag began research in psychopharmacology in the early 1960s, and was the focus, towards the end of that decade, of much hostility from the Dutch anti-psychiatry movement, his lectures being picketed and he and his family receiving death threats. He moved to the United States during the 1980s, recently returning to Holland, see H. M. van Praag, *Make-Believes in Psychiatry or the Perils of Progress* (New York: Brunner-Mazel, 1993), especially 'Second Domain of Concern: the Brain and Behaviour Miracle', 5–8; *idem* 'Psychiatry and the March of Folly', in D. Healy (ed.), *The Psychopharmacologists* (London: Altman, 1996), 353–79.

51. There is, for example, no explicit mention of the use of drugs in David Cooper's *Psychiatry and Anti-psychiatry* (London: Paladin, 1967). But see the comment by Germaine Greer, note 29 above.

52. There is no good historical account of animal experimentation and anti-vivisection activities in twentieth -century Britain. The reader is referred to R. D. French, *Antivivisection and Medical Science in Victorian Society* (Princeton: Princeton University Press, 1975) and the essays in N. A. Rupke (ed.), *Vivisection in Historical Perspective* (London: Croom Helm, 1987) for material relating to the origin and early history of anti-vivisectionism, especially in Britain.

53. Some of these tensions are elaborated by Shorter, *op. cit.*, note 15 above, see especially 'The Second Biological Psychiatry', 239–87. See D. Stafford-Clark, 'The Foundations of Research in Psychiatry',

British Medical Journal, ii (1959), 1199–1204.

54. See Anon, 'In Parliament: CNS Drugs', *The Chemist and Druggist*, clxxii (1959), 527. For a useful summary see E. M. Tansey and L. A. Reynolds (eds), 'The Committee on Safety of Drugs', in E. M. Tansey and P. P. Catterall (eds), 'Technology Transfer in Britain: The Case of Monoclonal Antibodies', *Wellcome Witnesses to Twentieth Century Medicine. Volume 1* (London: The Wellcome Trust, 1997), 103–33, p. 103–7.

55. E.g. F. Frayhan, 'Ten Years of Clinical Psychopharmacology: Hopes and Frustrations', in P. B. Bradley, F. Flugel, and P. H. Hoch (eds), *Neuro-psychopharmacology*, Vol. 3. Proceedings of the third meeting of the Collegium Internationale Neuro-psychopharmacologicum, (Amsterdam: Elsevier, 1964), 559–62.

56. F. J. Ayd, *op. cit.*, note 2 above.

57. See for example C. L. Cazullo, 'Ten years of Psychopharmacology: Critical Assessment of Experimental and Clinical Data', in P. B. Bradley, F. Flugel, and P. H. Hoch (eds), *Neuro-psychopharmacology*, Vol. 3. Proceedings of the third meeting of the Collegium Internationale Neuro-psychopharmacologicum (Amsterdam: Elsevier, 1964), 534–43.

6

LSD and the Dualism between Medical and Social Theories of Mental Illness

Stephen Snelders

Introduction

Let the men of the world and the ignorants, curious to know extraordinary enjoyments, be very well aware then that they will not find in LSD anything miraculous, absolutely nothing than an exaggeration of the ordinary. The brain and the organism on which LSD acts will show only their ordinary, individual characteristics, increased it is true in number and force, but always true to their nature. Man will not escape the destiny of his physical and moral temperament: LSD will be for the familiar impressions and thoughts of man a magnifying mirror, but a mirror that does not distort.[1]

In this quotation from Baudelaire's *Artificial paradises* I have changed the word 'hashish' into 'LSD'. As Baudelaire formulates his position (and this position is echoed by modern investigators into the effects of hallucinogens[2]), a hallucinogenic substance merely shows the user what is in him or her.

We can extrapolate this effect and say that the reaction toward the LSD-experience, either of the user himself or of outside observers, doesn't say much about LSD itself, but very much about the person in question. Looking at material from my own research into the relationship between the use of LSD and developments within Dutch psychiatry in the period from 1950 to 1974[3], I wondered if we could not get some clues on the way mental health care developed by studying, firstly, the reaction within this profession to the LSD-experience, and secondly, traceable influences of the use of LSD on developments within mental health care.

In this paper I will investigate the role of LSD in the development of two concepts of the origin and nature of mental illness in the 1970s which were often interpreted as antithetical, the

103

biomedical and the social. I will describe what they had to do with LSD, and will try to analyze and explain it.

In this way, a subject which was only of slight concern in the discussion between the biomedical and social concepts of medical illness itself, LSD, can perhaps give us some insights into essential elements of origin and content of these concepts.

An Example of the Clash between the Biomedical and Social Theories

The clash between biomedical and social theories of mental illness was given new impetus with the rise of anti-psychiatry. The word 'anti-psychiatry' was, as we know, used for the first time by the South African psychiatrist David Cooper in 1967 in his book *Psychiatry and Antipsychiatry*. The word quickly became a concept with which were designated all kinds of different ideas and people, who in some way were critical of psychiatry as it existed, despite great differences in mutual opinions and methods among these 'anti-psychiatrists'. This is not the place to get into these differences. I will only notice that, schematically, antipsychiatrists opposed the medical model of mental illness. In this model a person who arrives (in whatever way) at a doctor is diagnosed by him and can be classified as a patient, suffering from certain phenomena which constitute an illness. He or she is then treated according to the medical system, i.e. further diagnosis, prognosis and therapy.

An important element among 'antipsychiatrists' in their critique of this medical model is that the phenomena that constitute the so-called disease are not to be treated in isolation of the social factors that caused them. Social and economic status, gender, race, education etc. are factors which contribute or even cause the illness: this is the 'social' model of mental illness. Not the patient is ill, but society itself – it is society that makes the patient ill. A psychiatry that does not acknowledge these social factors is guilty of continuing existing power relations in society – what's more, psychiatry is one of the existing powers in (an oppressive) society. For many, but not all, antipsychiatrists mental illness itself became only a label that psychiatry puts on unadjusted behaviour – a behaviour that is however, healthy from the point of view of the individual. He who adjusts his behaviour to what is expected in society, in the family, etc., he is the one who is really mentally ill.[4]

For the purpose of this paper this sketchy definition of the medical and social models of mental illness, and their association with traditional psychiatry and anti-psychiatry respectively, must suffice (although their relationships were of course much more complex). How did the conflict between these models express itself in the Netherlands?

In 1975 a Dutch book was published on *Antipsychiatry* by Kees Trimbos, one of the founders of Dutch social psychiatry. A second, revised and enlarged edition, appeared in 1978. In his review of antipsychiatrists, Trimbos put one portrait of a Dutchman: Jan Foudraine.[5] In his review of Dutch critics of anti-psychiatry, it struck him that the number of publications were small – this although Foudraine's work *Who is made of wood...*, first published in 1971, had been a bestseller among the lay public. The book had sold in a short time 50,000 copies.[6]

Trimbos came to the conclusion that in the Dutch discussion, the central problem was mainly the conflict between the medical and the social model.[7] The idea that mental illnesses were mainly of social origin was vehemently attacked by the founder of biological psychiatry, Herman van Praag. In his inaugural lecture as professor of psychiatry at the State University of Utrecht in 1978, he held an oration in which he attacked what he considered to be the 'scientific foundation' of anti-psychiatry: the labelling theory.

Van Praag's Critique of Anti-psychiatry

I take Van Praag's lecture, and the resulting 'discussion' with the sociologist Paul Schnabel, as a starting point of my discussion of the relationship between the LSD-experience and the biomedical and social theories. As mentioned, Van Praag considered the 'labelling'-, or 'societal reaction'-theory, as the scientific foundation of anti-psychiatry. In his analysis, there was a dichotomy between 'traditional' psychiatrists, who considered deviant behaviour to be symptomatic of an 'abnormal', 'ailing' process within organism and personality[8], and anti-psychiatry, that denied or minimalized the importance of the existence of ailing processes within organism and personality, and sought the causes for deviant behaviour outside of the individual. The individual transgresses the norms and rules of society and is therefore classified as 'ill'.[9]

This position, presented in contrast to the more 'balanced' position of the traditional psychiatrist (who 'recognizes the pathogenetic significance' of 'societal and relational factors', while the anti-psychiatrist looks at the proces of illness as a 'mystification', and at interactional processes as the 'essence'[10]), was strongly disliked by Van Praag. He remarked that no one questioned the right of the surgeon to operate. There was no anti-surgery. There was however an anti-psychiatry, but was there any empirical evidence on which it was justly based?[11] Van Praag set out to answer this question in the negative. The labelling-theory, a sociological thesis that stated that deviant behaviour was chiefly caused by labelling, that labelling itself was chiefly caused by social and economic factors (not so much by deranged behaviour), and that this deviant role was the most important role in a psychiatric patient's possible repertoire of roles[12] – this labelling theory was according to Van Praag not empirically founded. He cited a number of, mainly American, studies, to defend his case. Although he gave the labelling-theory credit for its sensitizing function (to be seen as abnormal or ill can contribute to abnormal behaviour[13]), it went too far in denying the possible causes of deviance within the individual mind itself.[14]

Van Praag's lecture, published as a small booklet, provoked the wrath of the sociologist Paul Schnabel, who worked at the National Centre for Public Mental Health in Utrecht. In the *Maandblad Geestelijke Volksgezondheid*, he published a sharp polemic against Van Praag's critique on anti-psychiatry and the sociological labelling-theory.[15] To start with, Schnabel accused Van Praag of more or less plagiarizing the works of the American Walter R. Gove. He counted that 36 of the 50 pages in the book of Van Praag were taken from Gove – but less shaded than the original. He thought that Van Praag hadn't read the works of the anti-psychiatrists that were mentioned in his bibliography. Just like Gove, Van Praag simplified the labelling-theory.[16]

Only in the last two pages of his article did Schnabel come to the crux of the matter, as far as I am concerned: that the labelling-theory was not the scientific foundation of anti-psychiatry. Anti-psychiatrists were, according to Schnabel, eclectics. The importance of the movement had nothing to do with its scientific status, but everything with the legitimacy of psychiatry. Anti-psychiatry questioned its scientific, medical and moral character.[17]

In the same edition of the *Maandblad Geestelijke Volksgezondheid*, Van Praag replied to Schnabel's critique; i.e., he stated that one can defend oneself only with much difficulties against whole and half untruths and insinuations. In his opinion, Schnabel provided no arguments; he did not discuss, he slandered.[18] But Van Praag had become the bogey-man of the reform movements in Dutch mental health care.

What has this discussion to do with LSD? Van Praag was the founder of the Interdisciplinary Society of Biological Psychiatry in 1966. The sociologist Schnabel was connected with the reform movements in mental health care. Both movements had a different angle for looking at the 'mentally ill'. In both movements, the same drug, LSD, played a different role.

Biological Psychiatry and LSD

One of the few pages from Van Praag's lecture that was, according to Schabel, original work, was the section on biochemical research. It is also a key section, because biochemical research was Van Praag's forte. In this section a main difference between himself and the anti-psychiatrists was formulated by Van Praag as follows: anti-psychiatrists thought that there were no essential differences between the mentally 'ill' and 'normal' individuals, no different psychological or biological characteristics. For a medical and biological researcher like Van Praag however, there were no psychological functions without a cerebral 'substratum', i.e. a cerebral compound of functions. Empirical research showed, according to Van Praag, that in schizophrenic psychoses and in depressions abnormal functioning of the central nervous system and genetic dispositions played a role.[19]

Biological psychiatry had grown out of the biochemical research of psychiatric syndromes. Here hallucinogens had played an important role. We can already see this in an interesting Dutch precursor of biological psychiatry, Herman de Jong. De Jong and his research associates discovered in the 1920s that a catatonic state could be produced in animals by the use of bulbocapnine.[20] He went on to study the effects of other chemical substances, but also of electrical and neuro-surgical methods. All these methods and procedures could, concluded De Jong, probably together with psychogenic factors, result in catatonic states. He went so far as to see a possible cause of schizophrenia in a damaged liver.[21]

Among the substances that De Jong used were cannabis indica and mescaline. He gave mescaline to mice, a cat, a monkey, pigeons and frogs.[22] His conclusion is interesting:

> it seems that mescaline is capable of producing a psychophysiological parallelism consisting of hallucinations, autonomic phenomena, and the psychomotor symptoms of experimental catatonia. It may be of interest to note that in dementia praecox [i.e., schizophrenia] the same groups of syndromes may occur. Of course, we do not assume that mescaline is capable of producing an experimental schizophrenia, but we think that we may be entitled to state that there is a marked

similarity in the principle of the triad of groups of symptoms occurring in both.[23]

The interpretation of the mescaline experience by De Jong ('hallucinations, autonomic phenomena, psychomotor symptoms of experimental catatonia') led him to, as well as sprung forth from, a biochemical line of research. In his work a drug (mescaline) was seen from a point of view dictated by two factors: the assumption that psychological functions were rooted in the material, and therefore possible objects of medical research (compare the position of Van Praag, *supra*); and that the mescaline-experience was a sign of a distorted brain. It was, or looked suspiciously like, some sort of psychosis.

A flourishing of this kind of research in the second half of the 1950s was triggered by research with another hallucinogen: LSD. Important was the hypothesis of the American researchers Woolley and Shaw, published in 1954. Comparing schizophrenic states of consciousness with those triggered by LSD in an 'experimental psychosis' they wrote that naturally occurring psychic states such as schizophrenia might well be pictured as resulting from a deficiency of serotonin in the brain, brought about not by drugs, but by failure of the metabolic processes which normally synthesize or destroy them.[24] This hypothesis turned out soon to be too simple, but gave rise to comparable research. 'It was the first proof that it could be done, that one could lay down something of the relationship between brain and behaviour, between deranged brain and deranged behaviour', said Van Praag.[25] This, together with other developments within psychopharmacology, the discovery of neuroleptics and antidepressiva, stimulated biological psychiatric research.

As psychopharmacology itself, biological psychiatry was based on some sort of assumptions of what constitutes 'mental health'. The interpretation of the effects of LSD gives clues to what these assumptions were. Although Van Praag thought the comparison between schizophrenia and LSD-psychosis rather superficial and the differences as more important,[26] he did classify LSD among the category of 'psychodysleptics'. 'Psychodysleptics are compounds that disorganize the psyche in such a way that grave psychopathological processes result.'[27] (We will see that in anti-psychiatry there existed a different interpretation.) The research in psychodysleptics was according to Van Praag not only interesting for the psychopathologist, because 'model psychoses' could be created by their use, but also for the neurobiochemist and the neurophysiologist. The questions about the influence of psychodysleptics on brain metabolism, on the working of neurons and neurotransmitters, could give insight in the relation between material processes in the brain, and psychopathological syndromes.[28]

We can see now that Van Praag had the same assumptions as De Jong: that psychological functions were rooted in the material, and therefore possible objects of medical research; and that the hallucinogenic experience was a sign of a distorted brain. It was, or looked suspiciously like, a psychosis. Van Praag's summary of the effects of LSD are stated in a rather negative sounding medical language: disturbances in visual observation, phenomena of depersonalisation, loosening up or even dissolution of the ego, infantilisation.[29]

In biological psychiatry, the effects of LSD were put in a medical context where they closely resembled psychotic phenomena. This made it possible for biochemical researchers to start up a line of investigation, wherein the material effects of LSD in the brain should give more insight in the material processes that accompanied psychopathological syndromes. In this way, LSD gave ammunition for biomedical models of mental illness. It is, however, interesting that the same drug also gave ammunition for very different, social models of mental illness.

Anti-psychiatry and LSD

I will only concern myself here with evidence that links anti-psychiatry, as defined above, with LSD. More than with biological psychiatry, essentially a movement within psychiatry that derived its impetus from developments in psychopharmacology, we now step over the boundaries of strict psychiatry.

Anti-psychiatry took its place at the end of the 1960s (as mentioned, the word was used for the first time in 1967) among the movements, groups and individuals that were designated by another term with no fixed meaning. This was the *counterculture*, that coalition of people who were in some way or another in revolt against western society: radical students, hippies, bikers, Maoists etc. One of the earliest self-reflective texts to arise out of this movement, Jeff Nuttall's *Bomb Culture* (1968), lists in its description of the countercultural 'Underground' in various countries also R. D. Laing and his 'anti-psychiatric' therapeutic community Kingsley Hall.[30] The case of Laing is interesting, because he was probably the most famous anti-psychiatrist, whose works were avidly read, in the Netherlands too, by the lay public. The interest for anti-psychiatric works was very great under a lay audience: it suited the taste of the times. We have already seen that Foudraine was a bestseller.

Laing's work *The Politics of Experience and The Bird of Paradise*, first published in 1967 was one of the classic texts of the sixties. It was also primarily meant for the lay public. Laing's view that schizophrenia could be a stage in a natural healing process, a journey towards a state that was more sane than that of the so-called sane in an insane society, was from 1964–1965 on not presented before his professional colleagues or medical students, but before a lay audience.[31] *The Politics of Experience* is based on a series of lectures and articles, that partly appeared in journals as *The Journal of Existentialism, Peace News, The New Left Review*, and *The Psychedelic Review*. *The Bird of Paradise* is more literary in character: in fact it looks like the ravings of a disordered mind, or the description of a dream ... or a LSD-trip. That there was wide speculation about possible psychedelic experiences of Laing was mentioned by Trimbos.[32]

What was Laing's connection with LSD? We know that he had contacts with the group surrounding 'LSD-guru' Timothy Leary in Millbrook, New York. Leary tells us so himself in two of his books.[33] Both Laing and Leary were involved in the Sigma-project of Alexander Trocchi. Trocchi inspired a number of intellectuals and artists from different countries with this project, wherein art should inform the people that every act should be the result of creative behaviour. Intellectuals and artist would work together in a cultural revolt, based on an exchange of ideas and the development of forms of interaction aimed at the stimulation of self-consciousness. This revolt would bring an end to contemporary society.[34]

Another important figure within the Sigma-movement was a Dutch friend of Trocchi and Leary, the writer and poet Simon Vinkenoog. Vinkenoog was also the most well-known or notorious (depending on your viewpoint) advocate of the benefits of the use of LSD in the Netherlands.

Vinkenoog wrote a review of *The Politics of Experience* in the Dutch undergroundpaper *Witte Krant/Papieren Tijger* in 1967, that was published at the Sigma-centre in Amsterdam. His conclusion from this book, mirroring his own preoccupations, was: we are a race of gods, and have nothing to be afraid of.[35] In the same issue there was an editorial comment on the 'Dialectics of Liberation' congress in London, that stated that Laing was an advocate of limited biochemical warfare in the revolutionary struggle; namely, by putting LSD in the drinking water.[36]

I don't know if Laing seriously entertained such thoughts in

1967 (it was not in the published version of his lecture on the congress.[37] His colleague Cooper did advise *not* giving LSD to Che Guevara, because it would weaken his fighting capabilities[38]), but it illustrates how firmly their branch of anti-psychiatry, counterculture and LSD were interconnected.[39] I have the following hypothesis: through the medium of underground literature and magazines, Laing's ideas became commonplace among the youthful counterculture, including the Dutch variation. I emphasize the medium of the underground press, because I do not think that everybody read Laing, as little as they read Marx, Mao or Leary.[40] But I have not done any research in this matter.

What was the influence of LSD-experiences on Laing's model of mental illness, or what did he take from LSD-experiences which mirrored and deepened his understanding of mental illness? At the First International Congress of Social Psychiatry in London in 1964, Laing delivered a paper on 'transcendental experience in relation to religion and psychosis'. This paper was printed in 1965 in *The Psychedelic Review*, the magazine of the Leary-group, and republished in *The Politics of Experience*. LSD or other drugs are not mentioned in the paper, but in the whole context of the volumes of the *Psychedelic Review* it was clear that the transcendental experience referred to that state, in which you could get by taking LSD, or alternatively by doing mystical exercises, or by whatever other possible means. That was what the magazine was all about.

In his paper on the transcendental experience, Laing stated that we were living in a age 'in which the ground is shifting and the foundations are shaking'.[41] We are all searching for firm foundations on which we can live, to survive the catastrophe. If we are to find this, we have to transcend our way of experiencing the world, i.e. the way most people experience the world. Laing names this mode of experiencing *egoic*. These people 'experience the world and themselves in terms of a consistent identity, a me-here over against a you-there, within a framework of certain ground structures of space and time, shared with other members of their society.'[42] This egoic experience means that we have abdicated a large part of our world: our inner world, the ecstacy of our childhood. The transcending of this experience, the transcendental experience in which we recognize the egoic experience as an illusion, is the well-fount of all religions.

So far there is no difference between the views of Laing and those of Leary. The specific angle that interests Laing however are psychotic experiences. The psychotic also transcends our common, that is communal horizon, and enters a world with no fixed meaning, no anchors. He goes mad, but that does not mean necessarily that he becomes ill. His madness is as little 'true' madness as our sanity is 'true' sanity. In his inner world he can find illumination, can encounter the archetypal mediators of divine power, can he die and be reborn in a new world, with a new meaning. This is *possible* for some psychotics, according to Laing – it is by no means certain that it will happen.[43]

There is clearly an intimate connection between this views of Laing and the viewpoints of Leary and his collaborators Alpert and Metzner. They thought that our psychological problems are caused by the fact that we have a limited experience of ourselves, that we identify ourselves with the social roles that we have to adopt, instead of transcending all these social constructs (most easily, by ingesting LSD) and experiencing the timeless, divine world that we really are.[44]

The development in Laing's thought in *The Politics of Experience* was named his 'psychedelic' model of madness by his critics Siegler, Osmond and Mann. They described it as follows, quoting Laing himself: 'Schizophrenia is 'itself a natural way of healing our own appalling state of alienation called normality …'. 'Madness … is potentially liberation and renewal as well as enslavement and existential death … It is not an illness to be treated, but a 'voyage'. Socially, madness may be a form in which 'often through quite ordinary people, the light begins to break through the cracks in our all-too-closed minds.'[45]

The role of the medical team in schizophrenia in this model was to limit itself to guide the inner voyages of the schizophrenic, in the same way that one used guides in psychedelic sessions. This guiding task should not be limited to doctors; indeed, Siegler, Osmond and Mann asked whether doctors are at all capable for such a task, and if ex-patients and theologians are not better qualified.[46]

Psychedelic and Psychotic Experiences

We now see that both Van Praag and Laing started out with a comparison of the LSD-experience with (schizophrenic) psychosis, but that their conclusions from this point of view were radically different. For Van Praag, it meant that it gave clues for investigating biomedical hypotheses of mental illness; for Laing, it took him beyond the horizons of psychiatry into transcendental religion.

Neither Van Praag nor Laing seem, however, to have been schizophrenics themselves. None of their comparisons was based on their own experiences. But is schizophrenia (if it is more than just one of the many terms in medical classification going in and out of fashion) comparable to a psychedelic LSD-experience? Osmond clearly thought otherwise: and he has something to say on the matter, since he coined the word psychedelic and entered history as the man who turned Aldous Huxley on. Osmond started out himself in the early 1950s with the idea of a psychedelic experience as an experimental psychosis, and formulated together with Smythies one of the earliest biomedical hypotheses on the origin of schizophrenia. During the fifties, he became part of the network around Huxley, dedicated to making a better world by spreading psychedelics among an elite of politicians, scientists, intellectuals and artists. He had now moved on to a radically different view of the similarities between psychotic and psychedelic experienc: psychedelic voyages were voluntary, only took six or eight hours, and gave people a clearer vison of the world, clearer perceptions, a sense of identification with the transcendental Self. Psychotic experiences were involuntary, could take ten to twenty years, blurred the vision of the world, dissolved the integrity of the psychotic and gave him a feeling of insignificance and smallness.[47]

Counterculture and Anti-psychiatry

Be this at it may, Laing's view of a special position of the schizophrenic in society as one who transcended, however shattered, its boundaries on a voyage to a possible state of 'metanoia', superhealth, without conforming himself to the rat-race of capitalism; this view was very appealing to the newly risen counterculture. It was the same audience which was very interested in the work of Foudraine, with his stance against one of the pillars of society, the psychiatric profession. Trimbos noted that a similar positive view of the madman was a characteristic of Romanticism, and he quoted the 19th century Romantic German psychiatrist Ideler: '[In mental hospitals] we almost never meet those dull, soulless, unimportant persons from the everyday world ... Every madman is a representative of a ruling basic thought, the hero of a shocking drama, its catastrophes written in his heart's blood.'[48]

I would like to suggest that for an analysis of the reform movements within psychiatry and the mental health care in the 1960s and 1970s, we should give special attention to the nurses. There is of course a tendency to concentrate on the reforming psychiatrists themselves, but they were dependent for their reforms on the cooperation of their staff, the nurses. Foudraine made it clear in *Who is made of wood...* that not only the institutional environment or the patients themselves made it difficult for him in his attempts to change his department of the mental hospital Chestnut Lodge in a 'life school', but also the incomprehension of the nurses[49] – and they have to do the work of keeping the hospital running. Foudraine demanded in his reforms a high degree of devotion from the personnel. The same thing happened on his return to the Netherlands, when he was *chef de clinique* of Veluweland in Ederveen[50] (in 1966–1968) – a clinic, by the way, where the founding director Willy Arendsen Hein had made LSD-treatment an integral part of the program.

I think, but more comprehensive research in this matter is necessary, that the position of the nurses changed at the end of the 1960s and the beginning of the 1970s with the spread of the counterculture (as defined above) among youth, and the subsequent rise of a new generation of nurses that was very influenced by this counterculture. And we must not forget, as I have tried to argue elsewhere[51], that the use of LSD with its direct and indirect effects was an integral part of this counterculture. The look and the clothes of the sixties with their wild and flowing lines and their bright colours – that become suddenly 'right' when taking a trip – pop music with its psychedelic sound effects and its references to trip experiences (the Beatles from 1965 on at the head) – the transcendence of old and square, rigid ways of communication and etiquette – the mellow acceptance of things as they are, which is just what you have to do if you want to have a good trip – and at the same time the rage against a society where you have to conform to a rat-race of careering and to meaningless tasks – this was what the counterculture found in LSD and what LSD gave to the counterculture. And this had its impact on the new generation of nurses. We can see this in at least one mental hospital: Dennendal.

Dennendal

Carel Muller, psychological director of the Dennendal Clinic for mentally handicapped, tried from 1969 on to make an end to the medical model in the clinic, influenced by the psychology of Maslow and by the gentle, anti-authoritarian and anarchist Kabouter-movement that succeeded Provo. He was also very interested in Laing's ideas about the inner voyage and the role of the doctor as guide, although he thought that mainly appropriate to clinical psychiatry.[52] In Dennendal, patients became residents, their living units smaller, the use of medication was limited, the clinic changed into a living community where people could be themselves.

The conflict that arose between the staff of Dennendal, that at a certain moment made itself independent into a 'New Dennendal', and the directors and medical authorities resulted in the evacuation of the clinic by the police in 1974.[53]

What bothered the right-wing part of the Netherlands was that the staff of the clinic no longer seemed to consist of nurses in white robes, but of long-haired hippies. Hippies meant drugs, as was made clear in 1971 in the largest Dutch daily, the right-wing *Telegraaf*: a horror story of long hair, hippy clothes, refusers of military service, and Kabouters who created an alternative society, all this in the 'penetrating smell of hashish'.[54]

This was not totally off the mark, although what one made of it depended on one's political views. One of the nurses of Dennendal described to me the conflict that took place among the staff of Dennendal. There were two generations. A new generation had risen, people who were educated at social academies (hot-houses of countercultural thought), people who were much younger than the old nurses that were sometimes married and had lived for ten or fifteen years on the terrain of the clinic. The older people took their favourite drug, alcohol, at the local café in Den Dolder. Patients sometimes came there, but were not very welcome. The new generation created its own café, on the grounds of the clinic: the tea garden, decorated in quasi-oriental hippy style, where tea could not only be drunk (tea), but also smoked (marijuana and hashish).[55]

This was before the change in Dutch drug laws in 1976, which decriminalized limited possession for own use of marijuana and hashish. It was also enough for the press to create the impression that the whole personnel went stoned about its duties, although this is certainly far too exaggerated. But it does show that there was a new species of nurses with new attitudes, influenced by the counterculture and a different drug use. Without this generation, it is hard to see how Muller could have effected his reforms. He himself, also long haired, was very tolerant and created a scandal by smoking a joint at a social gathering.[56]

As an example of the way part of the nurses were interconnected with the Dutch countercultural scene, there is in the archives of New Dennendal a letter of Ton de Bakker to Carel Muller, dated 23 March 1971. De Bakker was a member of the working party on drugs of the Moksha centre in Haarlem, an alternative drug crisis centre. He wrote the letter to tell Muller to keep up the good work, and made the interesting remark: 'we have a fairly large number of friends who are working there with you on the Hoeve.'[57] An enemy of Muller, the director of the nursing staff W. André, wrote in the same month in a critical report: 'About seven or eight months it was a usual practice that drugs within Dennendal were propagated as a new elixir of life.'[58]

From the archive of New Dennendal it becomes clear, however, that the new young nurses did not form a homogeneous group. As everywhere in the counterculture, there were different groups, the macrobiotics, the political radicals, and also a psychedelic group. The nurse Hans Bogers remembers that the last group did not manifest itself very much, consisting more of a few individuals but was influential in the sense that the use of hashish and marihuana became something quite normal when off-duty. A few of these individuals went even further and took LSD on duty, without Muller knowing it. By being 'zonked out', under the influence of LSD, they wanted to get a deeper contact with the patients, tried to get a non-verbal communication going.[59]

Leading characters from the Dutch psychedelic movement who were very regularly on LSD and therefore in very sensitive mental state, report that on a visit of solidarity to Dennendal they had indeed a feeling of a deep psychic report with the mentally handicapped. There was however no systematic exploration in this field, it seems to have been very individualistic and spontaneous.[60]

It would be interesting to trace the influence of LSD and the counterculture on the nurses in other mental hospitals in the early 'seventies.[61]

Conclusions

I have tried to examine the role of LSD within biomedical and social theories of mental illness, as exemplified by representatives of biological psychiatry and anti-psychiatry. Both started out with a comparison of the LSD-experience with mental states beyond 'normal' sanity. For biological psychiatry, the way LSD created an experimental psychosis gave clues for its research in pathogenesis, the biochemical causes of mental illness. This reflected the adherence to a medical model of psychiatry, and was stimulated by the revolutionary developments in psychopharmacology in the 1950s.

Social developments outside of psychiatry, the rise of the counterculture and a non-medical use of LSD aimed at transcendental experiences, were in two ways influential on anti-psychiatry. It made a certain way of looking at the LSD-experience and at schizophrenic psychosis, as a supernormal state of mental health, a part of the ideas of anti-psychiatry; and it contributed to the rise of a new generation of nurses, that was essential for effecting reforms within the mental health care.

·There is of course still a lot to be done on this subject. I hope to have contributed to future research. But concerning LSD: as Baudelaire immediately would have recognized, it gave people in the mental health care just what they wanted, by mirroring what they had already wanted to think.

Notes

1. Charles Baudelaire, *Les paradis artificiels* (Paris: Conard, 1928), 17-18.
2. E.g., the American psychologist Richard Yensen spoke of the effect of LSD as magnifying the intentions of the user at the XIIth International Congress of the International Transpersonal Association, Prague 25-27 June 1992.
3. The results of this research should be published in 1998 as my Ph.D.-thesis under the title 'LSD and Psychiatry in the Netherlands'.
4. In the discussions at the workshop, the participants did not succeed in arriving at a conclusive definition of anti-psychiatry. I did like, however, these two attempts: 'anti-psychiatry is the carnavalesque celebration of the inversion of medical authority and legitimicy' (Colin Jones); and 'anti-psychiatry is the moment an internal reform of psychiatry explodes in revolt' (Roy Porter). The problem remains that it was hard to point out any genuine anti-psychiatrist proud of the label, with the exception of David Cooper.
5. On Foudraine, see, in this volume, Gemma Blok, '"Messiah of the Schizophrenics": Jan Foudraine and Anti-psychiatry in Holland'.
6. Kees Trimbos, *Anti-psychiatrie. Een overzicht* (2nd edn) (Deventer: Van Loghum Slaterus, 1978), 123; Jan Foudraine, *Wie is van hout... Een gang door de psychiatrie* (Bilthoven: Ambo, 1971).
7. Trimbos, *Anti-psychiatrie* 120 ff.
8. 'All kind of factors have an influence on our behaviour: psychological, societal, genetic, acquired physical and so on. They have this influence however not directly, but mediated by changes in cerebral functions, changes that in principle can be measured.' H. M. van Praag, *Over de wetenschappelijke fundaties van de anti-psychiatrie* (Assen/Amsterdam: Van Gorcum, 1978), 12-13.
9. *Ibid.*
10. *Ibid.*, 13.
11. *Ibid.*, 14.
12. *Ibid.*, 16.
13. *Ibid.*, 54.
14. *Ibid.*, 53-59.
15. Paul Schnabel, 'Een antiwetenschappelijke aanval op de anti-

psychiatrie. Over de Utrechtse oratie van prof. dr. H. M. van Praag'
MGV, xxxiii, (1978), 429-41.

16. *Ibid.*, 430-9.

17. *Ibid.*, 439-40.

18. H. M. van Praag, 'Over wetenschappelijke discussie gesproken' *MGV* xxxiii (1978), 442-5.

19. Van Praag, *Over wetenschappelijke fundaties* 25-30.

20. Bulbocapnine is the psychotoxic principle from **Corydalis cava** (in Dutch de 'pijpbloem'), which was used in the Middle Ages against certain forms of madness. H. M. van Praag, *Psychofarmaca. Een leidraad voor de praktiserend medicus* (Assen: Van Gorcum, 1966), 179-80.

21. H. de Jong en H. Baruk, *La catatonie expérimentale par la bulbocapnine. Etude physiologique et clinique* (Paris: Masson 1930); Herman Holland de Jong, *Experimental Catatonia. A General Reaction-Form of the Central Nervous System and Its Implications for Human Pathology* (Baltimore: Williams & Wilkins 1945).

22. De Jong, *Experimental catatonia* 52-6.

23. *Ibid.*, 56-7.

24. D. W. Woolley and E. Shaw, 'Some neurophysiological aspects of serotonin', *British Medical Journal* (1954), 122-6; H. M. van Praag, *Een kritisch onderzoek naar de betekenis van monoamineoxydaseremming als therapeutisch principe bij de behandeling van depressies* (Nijmegen: Gebr. Janssen, 1962), 26.

25. Interview with Van Praag, April 1997.

26. Van Praag, *Kritisch onderzoek* 26.

27. Van Praag, *Psychofarmaca* 179.

28. *Ibid.*, 181-183.

29. *Ibid.*, 189.

30. Jeff Nuttall, *Bomb Culture* (London: MacGibbon & Kee, 1968) 207, 208, 217ff.

31. Peter Sedgwick, *Psycho Politics* (London: Pluto Press, 1982) 93-94.

32. Trimbos, *Anti-psychiatrie* 99. For the relationship of Laing with LSD, see also the biography by his son: Adrian Charles Laing, *R. D. Laing: A Biography* (London; Chester Springs: Peter Owen, 1994); and Clancy Sigal, *Zone of the Interior* (New York: Thomas Y. Crowell, 1976), in which Laing figures as Dr. Willy Last. I am obliged to Roy Porter for pointing this author out. Too late for consideration in this paper arrived Antonio Melechi, 'Drugs of Liberation: From Psychiatry to Psychedelia', *Psychedelia Britannica: Hallucinogenic Drugs in Britain*, edited by Antonio Melechi (London: Turnaround, 1997), 21-52.

33. Timothy Leary, *The Politics of Ecstacy* (Berkeley: Ronin, 1990), 112-

114; Timothy Leary, *Flashbacks. A Personal and Cultural History of an Era* (New York: G. P. Putnam's Sons, 1990), 194. See also Sedgwick, *Psycho Politics* 105-106.

34. Trocchi's ideas in Alexander Trocchi, 'De onzichtbare opstand van een miljoen geesten', and 'Sigma. Een tactische blauwdruk' *Randstad* nr. 11-12 (1966), 17-44. Contact between Trocchi, Laing and Leary: Greil Marcus, *Lipstick traces. A Secret History of the Twentieth Century* (London: Secker & Warburg, 1989), 387. Sigma: Nuttall, *Bomb Culture* 190-191.

35. *Witte Krant/Papieren Tijger* nr. 5 (1967), 3.

36. *Ibid.*

37. R. D. Laing, 'The Obvious' in: *The Dialectics of Liberation*, edited by David Cooper (Harmondsworth: Penguin, 1968), 13-33.

38. Allen Ginsberg, 'Consciousness and practical action', *Counterculture*, edited by Joseph Berke (London: Peter Owen, 1969) 170-181.

39. See also Hans Geluk, 'The inner space of Ronald Laing', *Moksha. Een psychedelisch bulletin* nr. 5 (1968), 2.

40. Carel Muller, the reformist director of the clinic for mentally deficient Dennendal in Den Dolder, was in a telephone conversation with me in December 1996 of the same opinion.

41. R. D. Laing, *The Politics of Experience and The Bird of Paradise* (Harmondsworth: Penguin, 1985), 108.

42. *Ibid.*, 113.

43. *Ibid.*, 108-119.

44. For their most influential formulation of this position, see Timothy Leary, Ralph Metzner and Richard Alpert, *The Psychedelic Experience. A Manual Based on the Tibetan Book of the Dead* (New York: Carol, 1990).

45. Miriam Siegler, Humphrey Osmond and Harriet Mann, 'Laing's Models of Madness', *Laing and Anti-Psychiatry*, edited by Robert Boyers and Robert Orrill (Harmondsworth: Penguin, 1973), 112. The authors analyse *The Politics of Experience* and discover three different models of schizophrenia that Laing uses in the course of his different papers. They call them the psychoanalytical, the conspirational, and the psychedelic models.

46. *Ibid.*, 113, 115.

47. *Ibid.*, 115-121. Laing's associate Joseph Berke made the point that 'psychotics' (if there existed such a category) primarily had auditive hallucinations, while people on psychedelic drugs had visionary hallucinations (eidetic images). Andrew Rossabi, '"Anti-Psychiatry". An Interview with Dr Joseph Berke', *ibid.*, 214. Research seems to show that 'When LSD or mescaline is administered to

schizophrenics, their responses vary as greatly as that of normal people. Apparently they can distinguish psychedelic drug effects from their own hallucinations and illusions.' Lester Grinspoon and James B. Bakalar, *Psychedelic Drugs Reconsidered* (New York: Basic Books, 1980), 249.

48. Trimbos, *Anti-psychiatrie* 98.
49. Foudraine, *Wie* 144ff.
50. Interview with Marijke Pik-Mes, secretary on Veluweland, March 1997.
51. Stephen Snelders, 'Het gebruik van psychedelische middelen in Nederland in de jaren zestig. Een hoofdstuk uit de sociale geschiedenis van druggebruik', *Tijdschrift voor Sociale Geschiedenis* xxi (1995), 37-60.
52. Interview, Muller.
53. See, in this volume, Ido Weijers on Dennendal; and also the history of Dennendal, based mainly on 'official' sources: J. J. Dankers and A. A. M. van der Linden, *Om het geluk van de zwakzinnige. De geschiedenis van Dennendal, 1969-1994* (Den Dolder: Stichting Dennendal, 1994).
54. *Ibid.*, 39.
55. Interview with Hans Bogers, September 1996.
56. Archive Nieuw Dennendal (at the International Institute of Social History in Amsterdam) map 46, letter College van Regenten Willem Arntz Hoeve to Carel Muller d.d. 14 April 1971.
57. *Ibid.*
58. *Ibid.*
59. Interviews Bogers and Muller.
60. Interviews with Hans Plomp and Hans Geluk, June 1996.
61. At the workshop, both Joost Vijselaar and Gemma Blok gave as their opinion that the case of Dennendal is exceptional and cannot be generalized to other Dutch clinics or hospitals.

7

R. D. Laing in Scotland:
Facts and Fictions of the 'Rumpus Room'
and Interpersonal Psychiatry

Jonathan Andrews

The appearance since 1994 of three biographies of R. D. Laing –
namely those by Laing's son, Adrian,[1] by Daniel Burston[2] and by
John Clay[3] – as well as a fascinating volume of conversations
between Laing and Bob Mullan,[4] and Zbigniew Kotowicz's[5] critique
of his work in the context of the anti-psychiatry movement, testifies
to a resurgence of interest in Laing's life and work. There has been a
veritable open season on Laing since his death in 1989 at a time
when his reputation whether as psychiatrist, anti-psychiatrist, family
man or guru, was well on the wane.

My own especial interest in Laing is not remarkable, but is
relatively personal and long-standing. It was aroused when I read
some of his books in the early 1980s, and heightened when I lived
(as lodger-cum-baby-sitter) for two years in the Hampstead
household of John Heaton and Barbara Latham, a psychiatrist and
psychotherapist who were colleagues and friends of Ronnie's. Both
were and are members of the Philadelphia Association (PA).
Heaton, in particular, was one of Laing's intimate circle in London,
and was much quoted by Laing's biographers. Subsequently, during
1991-6, I spent five years myself in Glasgow, where Laing was born,
researching patient histories at Gartnavel (Glasgow) Royal Hospital,
the first mental hospital where Laing worked and where his interest
in schizophrenia and the family took off.

The following account is mostly confined to Laing's early career
during 1953-57, when Laing was a Registrar and Senior Registrar in
Glasgow, but particularly the period 1953-55 when he was at
Gartnavel – i.e. I concentrate on the pre-famous Laing, the context
of Glasgow psychiatry in the 50s and what Laing made of it then
and subsequently. In doing so, I must acknowledge my debt to

another former Gartnavel Registrar, Isobel Hunter Brown, who came to the Hospital in 1956,[6] just a year or so after Laing left it (for the post of Senior Registrar at Glasgow's Southern General Hospital).[7]

In particular in his autobiography,[8] but also in various works and conversations published before and since, Laing depicted 50s Glasgow psychiatry as impersonal and depersonalising. He pointed to the emphasis amongst Glasgow psychiatrists on somatic models of mental illness, and on physical treatments such as ECT and insulin coma therapy. He claimed that his fellow doctors not only did not talk to patients, but actually were discouraged from doing so by senior colleagues. In this context, Laing portrayed himself as a considerable innovator, if not a pioneer. He described how his initial fascination with neurology and his concern with blending a neurological and psychiatric approach were replaced by increasing unease at the psychiatry of his day, and by a growing espousal of psychological and psychotherapeutic approaches, by 'the talking cure', and by armchair psychiatry. In place of the impersonal, Laing offered the 'interpersonal'.[9] In this sense, Laing emerges from his own writings and conversations about his Glasgow years as somewhat isolated from the contemporary modern mainstream of Glasgow psychiatry, and the mainstream of Glasgow psychiatry as somewhat detached from him. It is the validity of this portrayal that I want to question here.

Laing joined Gartnavel Royal as Registrar in 1953. He commenced his duties on 3 November, taking the place of John L. Cameron (more of whom, later).[10] Gartnavel was Laing's first encounter with a mental hospital, and with chronic, long stay patients. Previously Laing had dealt only with recent psychiatric cases during his time in the army, in Netley and Catterrick. By contrast, at Gartnavel, as Laing himself put it, he encountered 'patients who had been "in" for ten, thirty, sixty years: since the nineteenth century'.[11] Some of the staff (the nursing staff especially) had been in for that long too. Patient numbers at Gartnavel were mounting throughout the 1950s, the Hospital's population topping the 900 mark for the first time in its history at the end of 1953 (the month after Laing's arrival)[12] and reaching a peak of 979 patients in mid-1956.[13] The attitude of Angus MacNiven, Gartnavel's Physician-Superintendent, to admissions was, by his own confession, that it would be wrong to turn applicants away if they and their families wanted relief. Those on his staff during the 50s recall him occasionally arriving by car at Gartnavel with a new patient in the back, while a contemporary manager recounted how MacNiven once phoned him to suggest easing overcrowding by installing double bunk-beds at the Hospital.[14] An acute shortage of medical staff was afflicting the Hospital at this time, staff:patient ratios were widening throughout 1950-56, and doctors were needing to see more and more patients on ward rounds and were able to spend less and less time with them. Evidently, not all of MacNiven's colleagues fully agreed with his liberal attitude towards admissions. Patrick McGrath, junior house officer at Gartnavel during 1946-7, recalled an occasion when, having objected to a patient's admission because the Hospital was overcrowded, MacNiven took his ironic suggestion to place the patient in the doctors' common room seriously.[15] More especially, MacNiven's staff were worried about the effect overcrowding was having on patients' medical care. In 1953, overcrowding in the East House had got so bad that in one ward designed for 15 patients there were over 40 queuing for the toilets.[16] Given such conditions it is scarcely surprising that psychiatry at Gartnavel, as at many other contemporary mental hospitals, had become somewhat routine. In January 1956, MacNiven's deputy, James McHarg, expressed his 'growing' concern 'over the impossibility, with our existing medical staff establishment, of giving to patients the degree of personal attention that some of them require and expect'.[17] This, at the very least, implies that there was some validity in Laing's depiction of psychiatry in Glasgow as impersonal and depersonalising – if more by default, than intention. Nevertheless, it is prudent to point out that the vast majority of patients at Gartnavel were still short-stay cases, discharged on average after seven to eight months, in accordance with the high-turnover admissions' policy that many large mental hospitals were pursuing contemporaneously. Indeed, Laing and the work he became involved in, orchestrating the careful selection of some of the most chronic schizophrenic patients for a famous group therapy[18] experiment in what became euphemistically known as Gartnavel's 'Rumpus Room', misrepresented the typical patient who came in and went out of Gartnavel in the 50s. Despite the conspicuous presence of '"lost souls" in the wards of Gartnavel, Stobhill and the Southern General in Glasgow'[19], such patients comprised only a small portion of all of those who came through these hospitals' gates.

This is not to deny the importance of Laing's and his colleagues' endeavours in Gartnavel's refractory ward itself. There is scant evidence to contradict Laing's portrayal of conditions there when he arrived. Here was, as Laing put it, 'the end of the line', the ward 'overcrowded', the nurses 'harassed and overworked', and the patients unoccupied, 'self-absorbed' and highly disturbed.[20] Here (according to Clay) 'most patients' had received ECT and insulin 'to no avail' and 'several had had lobotomies'.[21] In this specific context, there is no doubting the innovatory nature of what Laing and co. went on to do. It occurred to Laing that some of the behaviour he was witnessing in patients was environmentally conditioned, that they might be reacting negatively to their milieu, or actually acting up, reserving their most florid symptoms for doctors and staff. The Rumpus Room was envisaged as a means to test these kinds of hypotheses. Nevertheless, what I am and shall be arguing is 1) that what Kotowicz calls Laing's 'distinctly different approach' was broadly shared by a number of other psychiatrists in the Hospital, and was very sympathetically received by a wide variety of people in Glasgow's mental health department; 2) that work on schizophrenia and group therapy at Gartnavel pre-dated Laing's arrival and was to continue for years after his departure; and 3) that work incorporating psychotherapeutic models into mainstream psychiatry, including group therapy work and general concerns with staff:patient interrelations, was in wider currency both beyond and within Glasgow than Laing was apt to admit.

The collaborative nature of Laing's work at Gartnavel itself suggests that the treatment regime may not have been as attached to the organic model of mental illness, and Laing's colleagues in Glasgow not as dubious about, or uninvolved with, psychological approaches to mental illness as Laing would later like to have it. Laing described how it was mostly the more senior amongst his colleagues who expressed doubts about treatments such as ECT, insulin and the new sedative drugs (the latter, in fact, were not introduced to Gartnavel until late in 1955, after Laing had left the Hospital).[22] By contrast, younger ambitious men were more amenable to such novelties. If one wanted to make Professor of Psychiatry, according to Laing, one had to get on board the modern therapeutic wagon.[23] Laing depicted the reservations of more senior psychiatrists less as a result of any countervailing ideas about treatment, *per se,* than as the innate conservatism of the older generation.

To some extent, this view is endorsed by the contemporary record. Similar points have been made by other historians, for example by Grob and Valenstein.[24] And yet it also represents an over-simplification. There is little doubt that ECT was standard issue at Gartnavel as Laing alleged. This is suggested, *inter alia,* by the fact that it was suspended for just '2 weeks' or so when, in July 1956, Dr Stevens, the anaesthetist, was on holiday, only to be 'carried on again' as regularly as normal when Stevens returned.[25] After talking about ECT at Gartnavel in conversation with Mullan, Laing described a Rio de Janeiro hospital where ECT was administered without medication to control its convulsive side-effects, without patients' consent and sometimes without their knowledge.[26] Yet, this story itself, presenting an extreme case, suggests how Laing's broad recollections of psychiatry in the 50s were apt occasionally to tar everything with the same brush. For, unlike Brazilian patients, Gartnavel patients did not receive ECT without medication or consent – although later generations have generally been prepared to concede that dosages were excessive, while just how informed consent was in the 50s remains a vexed subject. And patients were carefully selected for such treatment. Amongst the 17 chronic male and female patients from Gartnavel's refractory wards who provided the clinical material for Freeman, Cameron and McGhie's 1958 book *Chronic Schizophrenia*, the average amounts of physical treatment administered was 'three injections of Cardiazol, seven electro-shocks, and forty insulin-induced comas per patient'.[27] The average length of stay of these patients was eight to nine years. Insulin therapy, as is recalled by Cairns Aitken, a medical student at Gartnavel during 1955 (who went on to become Professor of Rehabilitation Studies, Dean of the Medical Faculty, and then Vice-Principal at Edinburgh), 'was administered every morning to a group of about a dozen patients gathered in a large summer house behind the west wing', patients being revived by tube-feeding with glucose a few hours after the start of coma.[28] Management Minutes confirm[29] that the Insulin Unit had 12 beds, as well as rooms set aside for electro-therapy in 1955, and the relatively routine way such therapies were administered. Concurrently, overcrowding was continuing to hamper the pursuit of these 'modern treatments', a room in an in-patient ward having to be temporarily commandeered during the day for the administration of out-patient ECT, which was given four times weekly to up to 16 patients.

Yet even these patients received a combination of psychological and physical treatments. For example, a special occupational therapy group was also formed for patients receiving insulin therapy in this year.[30] Years before Laing's arrival, contemporary clinicians at Gartnavel and elsewhere were beginning to voice doubts about where precisely and in what degree the efficacy of insulin and electro-convulsive treatments lay. Freeman himself summarised the 'psychological hypotheses' about insulin and the reactions to it in a study of 40 cases published in 1949.[31] He concluded that 'neither psychological or physiological hypotheses alone can explain the mode of action of insulin shock'. Moreover, he emphasised that while some patients certainly experienced heightened fear, anxiety or libido, in other cases the treatment failed 'to influence mental mechanisms' at all, agreeing with Schatner that the treatment could not alleviate patients' fundamental pathology. Furthermore, insulin treatment did not endure for long after Laing's departure. As Cairns Aitken later recalled, more and more research was published during the 50s demonstrating its ineffectiveness and indicating that efficacy lay instead in the interpersonal relationships between staff and patients and amongst patients themselves.[32] In an equally forthright paper of 1953, following on from the work of Alexander[33] in the States, Freeman and Cameron collaborated in a clinical experiment on ECT which came to similar conclusions.[34] *Inter alia*, it highlighted the frequency of anxiety amongst patients after ECT and the need for psychotherapeutic intervention (see below).

Both the aforementioned therapeutic experiments were more about blending than replacing physical treatments with psychotherapeutic treatment. Yet, as Laing himself emphasised, it was well-known amongst MacNiven's colleagues that Gartnavel's chief was far from convinced about the benefits of widespread (let alone exclusive) employment of physical treatments, including the new shipments of largactil. Quite to the contrary, he encouraged juniors to use such sparingly, in small doses, with a mind to selectivity of patients' mental conditions. Freeman spoke of MacNiven going about his ward round with a jocular cynicism as to drug therapies, asking nurses 'what poisons' patients were on now.[35] And MacNiven's reports to the Board, while accepting the 'undoubted value' of the new tranquilizers, underlined that patients' improvements must also be due to 'factors other than chemical'.[36] Despite his own recollected excitement at opening the first shipments of largactil as a junior at Gartnavel in the '50s, Cairns Aitken's first paper was very much in the Gartnavel mould about the dangers of chemical restraint.[37] As far as what Thomas Freeman referred to as a personal 'preference for a psychotherapeutic approach', MacNiven had laid his cards on the table much earlier than this. Most conspicuously, this was when, in 1938, along with David Yellowlees, he established the Lansdowne Clinic for Functional Nervous Disorders close by the Hospital.

What then of Laing's and others' specific portrayal of the experimental therapy conducted with schizophrenics in Gartnavel. The results of the Rumpus Room experiment with schizophrenics were published jointly by Cameron, Laing and McGhie, in the *Lancet* in 1955, under the title 'Patient and nurse effects of environmental changes in the care of chronic schizophrenics'.[38] This short paper explained how the project had emerged out of a growing recognition of the possibility of more hopeful prognoses for chronic schizophrenics, that the condition was 'not necessarily a consequence of an inexorable process' and that the hospital environment itself was implicated in the 'enforced inactivity' of such patients. It emphasised how the project emerged from a six week period when (not just Laing, but) 'one of us' was spending 'an hour or two every day' in the female refractory ward, which housed 65 patients. It underlined also how the project had sprung from a desire to give 'patients and nurses the opportunity to develop interpersonal relationships of a reasonably enduring nature'. It described how the 11 schizophrenic patients selected, aged between 22 and 63, had 'all ... been in the same ward for over four years' without remission. Nurses presented daily reports and sociograms, and the project was discussed in weekly meetings. After an initial period of 'settling down', positive changes were reported in both patients and nurses. While problems of the project were addressed, such as perceptions of patients and nurses as being given preferential treatment, it was confidently concluded that the experiment witnessed positive changes in patients being more socialised and interested and losing features of their psychoses, as well as in nurses themselves feeling more involved with and related to patients. Initially no term seems to have been adopted by the doctors for the experiment. The term 'Rumpus Room' was actually applied by the nurses to the scheme, encapsulating their initially intensely mixed feelings and insecurities about it. As they grew more comfortable with it, and once the Matron made money available for trips out of the room, it was alleged, 'the term ... fell into disuse'. Nevertheless, despite the use in subsequent publications by Freeman, Cameron and McGhie of the phrase 'treatment centre', it was the 'Rumpus Room' label that stuck and that is still used by current staff at Gartnavel Royal in referring back.

Laing's more recent retrospective accounts of this are, not surprisingly, given the conversational and biographical way they were divulged, very personal. He emphasised the effect that his relationship with one particular elderly woman patient, a pious spinster, had on him: how she, in a role-reversal that was later to become quite emblematic of the Laingian brand of psychiatry, became his 'mentor'.[39] This lady was then in the female refractory ward at Gartnavel, diagnosed with periodic mania, and had been hospitalised for over 20 years. Subsequently, Laing described in rather heroic, Pinelian terms, although not without humour and self-irony, the way in which he (and nobody else) elected to spend 1-2 hours a day sitting with over 50 or 60 (his accounts vary) female patients in the refractory ward. Here, initially, with women patients fighting each other to grope or undress him, kiss him and sit on his lap, as Laing put it, 'I had to fight for my life'. Laing also described how MacNiven and the Matron gave him 'permission to try out an experiment in the management of a few of these chronic patients'.[40] This seems of interest, incidentally, in that it indicates the importance of the Matron's role by this time (as head of the female nursing department), in approving (or disapproving) of therapeutic initiatives that involved doctors working with female patients. Laing was later to claim talking to Mullan that 'the nurses ran the whole thing', and that doctors were little more than overseers, ensuring that 'morale' was sustained[41] – one of many examples of how his recollections verged from egotism to startling humility and perspicacity.

It is obvious that not even Laing's retrospective account and the published results of the Rumpus Room experiment tally in full. Laing's account is noteworthy in part for the rather minimal role he assigns MacNiven. In conversation with Mullan later, Laing described MacNiven in just a couple of sentences, as 'an old-style conservative psychiatrist', portraying himself as 'a conservative revolutionary'.[42] Laing said little about MacNiven's role in facilitating the Rumpus Room project, beyond the fact that he allowed it. Yet what emerges from the Minutes of Gartnavel's Board of Management, from MacNiven's own reports to the Board and from the testimonies of other contemporaries, is that MacNiven was a stronger advocate of this experiment and of group therapy in general at Gartnavel than Laing implies. MacNiven described the earlier group therapy experiments with schizophrenics at considerable length in a report of 1953 to the Hospital's Board of Management.[43] In a subsequent report, he gave the new Rumpus Room experiment a positive recommendation to the Board, referring to its results as 'very interesting'. MacNiven proceeded, having fanned the Board's interest and gained their approval in principle, to distinguish Laing as the project's principal exponent and to invite him to come before the Board himself and describe it.

This Laing did accordingly, although, frustratingly, his oral account was not transcribed in the minutes. Even if the Board of Management rarely vetoed therapeutic initiatives at the Hospital, administrative problems with therapeutic group experiments experienced elsewhere underline the fact that gaining the confidence and approval of hospital administrators was not insignificant. The Board echoed MacNiven's assessment of the project as highly 'interesting', and were sufficiently concerned to ask Laing to come and report to them regularly on its progress. Unfortunately, again, Laing was to leave the Hospital just a few months later.

Laing's appearance before the Board appears to have been considerably more than a mere formality. Above and beyond having given Laing 'permission' to conduct this experiment, MacNiven offered active encouragement and support. And this seems typical of MacNiven's general readiness to smooth the way of his juniors in the Hospital and in their wider careers: to be, if not an initiator, then a profound facilitator of therapeutic initiatives. Cairns Aitken regarded MacNiven as 'supportive of any new treatment', and opined that whereas 'he relied on others for its introduction', MacNiven's liberal and encouraging attitude created a welcome climate for innovation.[44] Patrick McGrath plainly agreed, observing that MacNiven 'showed great trust in us, the new boys, and let us "do our own thing"'.[45] This included letting juniors admit and discharge 'our own patients, experiment with medication', and try out psychotherapy at the Lansdowne, or child psychiatry at the Notre Dame Child Guidance Clinic. Far from a place of impersonal routine, McGrath found Gartnavel to be a place where 'vitality ... permeated every aspect of the work, from meals in the doctors' mess to formal case conferences'. Medical and nursing staff alike have all expressed their peculiar debt to MacNiven's approach to clinical management. And MacNiven's influence clearly went even deeper than this. Aitken recollected how the Senior Registrar, Ronnie Stewart, 'modelled his behaviour, including his Highland accent, on ... MacNiven'.[46] Laing was evidently less impressed, or impressionable. Perhaps, he was less disposed to concede his debt to his former chief and also less authentically indebted than his colleagues, given that his subsequent career gravitated so far away from the mental hospital.

Further to qualify my argument here, it should be said that Laing's account of MacNiven was nevertheless relatively candid and self-reflexive. Indeed, Laing's view that his own stress on therapeutic groups and talking to patients chimed with psychiatrists like

MacNiven, who regarded patients 'as people under their care and protection' and were antipathetic to the 'new wave of [organic] psychiatry', seems an incisive and convincing one – sufficiently generous and true to MacNiven's qualities, and humble about the secrets of his own success.[47] MacNiven was certainly an old-style Superintendent, distinguished as much for his eccentricities and the folklore they generated – such as his riding about the hospital grounds on a white horse, greyhound at his side, and umbrella and newspaper in his hands – as for his contributions to psychiatry. Yet he was clearly also an inspiring, as well as an accommodating, leader.[48]

A more important issue is the extent to which Laing also minimised the role of outside influences. Laing and his colleagues at Gartnavel were far from the only people interested in therapeutic community approaches to mental illness at this time. Such approaches had already enjoyed considerable currency in the States, and also, in particular, through the work of the Edinburgh trained, South African M.D., Maxwell Jones, in two British institutions. In conversation with Mullan, Laing conceded that he was aware of Maxwell Jones' 'idea of the therapeutic community and of opening the doors'.[49] Yet, Laing was generally at pains to emphasise the relative isolation of the Glasgow project from other British and American initiatives in the same area. This itself had the obvious effect and intent of identifying his primacy or originality, Laing also claiming that 'I had already opened the doors ... at Gartnavel'. While 'it was no big deal', Laing was careful to point out that 'we never published it'[50] – implying that, if he had, Gartnavel may have been the first mental hospital to adopt this innovation. In fact, Laing's recall seems to have been imperfect. It was Jones' work at Dingleton Hospital on the Scottish borders which he mentioned, and yet Jones did not practice there until 1962. The doors had been opened at Dingleton (and at a few other British mental hospitals) in the 1940s, before Jones' arrival there. It was Jones' (and others') influential work during and soon after the war in early experimental communities at the (Belmont) Effort Syndrome Unit, attached to Mill Hill Emergency Hospital, Surrey, and at the Ex-POW Unit at the Southern Hospital, Dartford, Kent; and subsequent work at the Industrial Neurosis Unit at Belmont Hospital (where Jones practised between 1947 and 1959), that Laing and other Glasgow colleagues must have known about by the '50s. Jones was penning articles on group therapy from 1942, but it was the book Jones co-authored on *Therapeutic Communities*, which came out in 1952, the year before Laing began at Gartnavel, that was the first major crystallisation of the therapeutic group approach at Belmont.[51] Like Laing, Jones had made a transition from a preoccupation and growing disenchantment with organic psychiatry (writing early articles on insulin treatment of schizophrenia) to social psychiatry and psychotherapy.

More importantly, if Laing was aware of Maxwell Jones' work in the 50s at Gartnavel, the Consultant, Thomas Freeman, must have been even more familiar with it. Freeman had been Senior Registrar at Belmont for two years during 1948-50 and was one of the contributors to Jones' *Therapeutic Communities*, writing Chapter V on inpatient psychotherapy in the Belmont Unit.[52] Freeman's chapter was mostly confined to a survey of the problems in the psychotherapeutic treatment of neurotics, and actually regarded the more severe of such cases, in whom there was 'a suspicion of schizophrenia', as not amenable to psychotherapy. It underlined the limitations rather than the efficacy of psychotherapy in such a context, and admitted to considerable ignorance about the patient community. Yet Freeman adopted a number of positive perspectives regarding psychoanalysis within a hospital setting which seem pertinent to subsequent group therapy work at Gartnavel. For example, he gave a qualified advocacy to relying more on psychological methods in treating neuroses than on physical methods such as insulin. He expressed familiarity and acceptance of Fromm-Reichmann's stress on the therapist becoming part of the therapeutic community. Likewise, he echoed Chasel's viewpoint as to the importance of the psychiatrist having personal responsibility for his patients and their environment, *in loco parentis*, and the need for a different kind of psychoanalytic approach to the norm. Freeman also emphasised the crucial nature of the nurse-patient relationship, stressing not just the inevitability, but the need, of the nurse being drawn into the therapeutic relationship. While the therapeutic community was little discussed directly by Freeman, the book as a whole was centrally devoted to an exploration of therapeutic communities, and the history of the various experiments at Belmont, Mill Hill and Dartford. And Freeman was plainly highly conversant with and deeply influenced by such models. (Hunter-Brown also went on to work with Jones after less than 18 months at Gartnavel).

Laing was in general careful to emphasise his own and others' unawareness at Gartnavel of kindred work around contemporaneously, including Russell Barton's, *Institutional Neurosis*, and Goffman's *Asylums*.[53] On the other hand, the article

Cameron, Laing and McGhie published in the *Lancet* in 1955 demonstrates that they were at the very least inspired by E. C. Adams' conviction regarding therapeutic communities: 'that the most important therapeutic element in the environment is the people in it'. [54] There were clearly many similar ideas floating around at the time. By the mid-1950s at least, Cameron, Freeman and McGhie were certainly aware of Rosen and Chasen's work (of the late 40s) on resistance in therapeutic groups of chronic psychotics. [55] Both McGhie and Freeman were also familiar with work on schizophrenia and psychoanalysis by Wilfred Ruprecht Bion, K. R. Eissler, and H. Rosenfeld, published during 1951-4. [56] Eissler and Rosenfeld had emphasised the benefits of a psychoanalytic approach to schizophrenia. [57] Laing himself confessed to Mullan that he 'got imbued with Bion's work theoretically and did Bionesque groups in Glasgow', and 'all these analytic group techniques before going to the Tavistock'; although it seems to have been at the Glasgow Department of Psychological Medicine and then later in London, rather than at Gartnavel, that Bion's influence on Laing really took root. [58] Contrariwise, he showed scant respect for Rosenfeld when later encountering him at the London Institute of Psychoanalysis. [59]

Earlier and more significantly than this, there was also the work of Tom (T. C.) Main, Siegmund Heinz Foulkes and others using small group therapy units at Northfield Hospital in Birmingham, some of which came out in publications from the Menninger Clinic in the mid- '40s. [60] During the war, and before he had worked at Belmont, Freeman had spent about five months at Northfield observing Main's work. (Main went on to be Medical Director at the Cassel Hospital from 1946). [61] This experimental work with therapeutic communities was already attracting considerable attention at the time, and Freeman has openly confided that it had much in common with the group therapy that he and others subsequently conducted at Gartnavel. [62] Freeman encountered Foulkes whilst working at Northfields, but was apparently less directly influenced by him. Bion had also worked at Northfield before Freeman arrived.

Laing was equally bold-faced about primacy in taking credit over and above his three Gartnavel colleagues for the real initiative in the work with schizophrenia at Gartnavel. There is no doubting that it was Laing who – with Cameron's assistance – devised the Rumpus Room experiment itself, and none of his colleagues would or have disputed this. Freeman has always conceded that he had nothing to do with it until Laing had left Gartnavel. Yet, even if Laing was (or later became) the most charismatic figure amongst them all, and even if the Rumpus Room experiment was essentially his own invention, group work with schizophrenics as a whole was very much a collective effort, and this and other analogous work had a significant pre-history at Gartnavel. About a year before Laing's arrival, Cameron and Freeman were already doing research on therapeutic groups. Their first collaborative project, begun circa 1952, focused on involutional melancholia. In January 1953, Freeman and Cameron presented jointly with John D. Sutherland, Medical Director at the Tavistock, on group therapy in involutional melancholia at a British Psychological Society Symposium in Edinburgh devoted to the subject of group therapy.[63] Cameron and Freeman continued to conduct and present the findings of this research in a series of papers and published articles during 1953-55, also combining with Ronnie Stewart, Gartnavel's Senior Consultant.[64] While this work was not with schizophrenics, it shared much in common with the basic premises, methodologies and orientations of that work. The work began with a small carefully selected group of chronic inpatients, most of whom were elderly and all of whom were female and had been unsuccessfully treated by electro-shock therapy. Subsequently, it broadened out by seeking, with limited success, to involve additional inpatients and those who had become out-patients. It emphasised the importance of interpersonal roles, of inter-patient and patient-staff relationships, and the need for nursing staff to be 'integrated with the therapy'. It also pointed to the problems of resentment, attention-seeking and anti-group attitudes amongst patients; of relapse when patients left the hospital, and to problems if the therapist was not relieved of administrative duties. All of these findings were to be reiterated to varying degrees in the therapeutic work with schizophrenics. This is hardly surprising when this work mostly involved the same personnel and actually proceeded in partial parallel with that on schizophrenia.

Nonetheless, this work on melancholia also hinted at the rather divergent concerns of Freeman and his colleagues to those of Laing, a divergence that was to emerge more clearly as time went on. More than environmental considerations with regard to melancholia, they were concerned with problems with the super-ego amongst patients, and with prognosis. They highlighted the importance of external socio-psychiatric and external psychological factors, but also concluded that 'the explanation for the illness must be sought in [patients] themselves and not in the environment'.[65] On the one hand, their work was critical of ECT as a specific, because it 'does not alter the basic unconscious patterns' and also because of the problems it created in arousing anxiety and fear amongst patients.[66] Yet it did not advocate replacing ECT with group psychotherapy, rather accepting that it was a useful 'adjunct to psychotherapy' and might actually break down the 'defences which were holding unconscious aggressive drives in check'.[67] Laing was by contrast more disposed to see ECT as nugatory and the environment as a more fundamental factor.

As Esterson and Cameron expressed it in a 1958 article they jointly authored, an increasing incentive was being felt by therapists and psychiatrists at this time to study schizophrenia. This had institutional pertinence, for with 'so many different psychotherapeutic schools ... struggling for supremacy', the schizophrenic was important 'as a kind of test subject'. Also, because schizophrenia had been neglected and regarded as incurable, it was being seen 'as a tremendous challenge'.[68] Laing, Freeman *et alia* were all clearly inspired by the new centrality that chronic schizophrenia was beginning to assume in psychiatry. According to Freeman, before Laing's arrival, Glasgow psychiatrists were already familiar with claims made since the end of the war 'that the most disturbing symptoms of the severe mental disorders' were actually a product of 'custodial care of the chronically ill'.[69] And, as Freeman tells it, it was Ferguson Rodger who got MacNiven to agree to sponsor 'a study, with the aid of the nursing staff' with the explicit aim 'to investigate these claims'. The grant for research into schizophrenia in 1953 had already been obtained when Laing arrived in November. Significantly, it was procured from the same body which had already funded Freeman and Cameron's work with involutional melancholia – the Scottish Hospitals Endowment Research Trust.[70] (Laing's involvement simply arose as an adjunct to his role as Registrar). Moreover, the project had the names of Cameron, Freeman and McGhie on it first and foremost. To quote directly from management minutes, the research was to be undertaken 'over a 3 year period on Group Therapy in Schizophrenic Patients' and 'would be under the direction of Professor Ferguson T. Rodger and was to be carried out at Gartnavel by Dr. J. L. Cameron and Dr. Thomas Freeman'.[71] Cameron was in fact to be the main researcher on the project. Indeed, it was because Cameron was to work full-time on this research that he was obliged to resign his post as Registrar, as well as to quit his sessions at the Lansdowne, and that Laing was appointed in his stead.[72] While Cameron was appointed research psychiatrist (or assistant) on the project, Andrew McGhie was appointed concurrently as research psychologist.

Originally, also, the project was being managed and discussed in two different groupings. When MacNiven first reported on it to the Board of Management in 1954, Laing's name was not even mentioned, and it was Cameron and Ferguson Rodger who presided over one group, and Freeman over the other.[73] As Freeman later recounted, it was 'through a series of publications describing the results of the clinical research' associated with this project (and not only the article that Laing co-wrote), that 'Gartnavel came to be recognised as pioneering aspects of ... the therapeutic community approach to mental disorders'. [74] According to Freeman, Laing – whom he portrayed, with deliberate understatement, as someone 'who was later to achieve some notoriety for his anti-psychiatry views' – simply arrived at the hospital 'about this time', and 'for a time ... collaborated with ... Cameron and ... McGhie in group work which demonstrated the important role nurses play in the treatment of mental illnesses'. Freeman emphasised then, and not without justification, that Laing's contribution was far from the original, instigating one, and was brief and fleeting. Indeed, as Freeman remarked, 'the academic work continued' after Laing left in 1955 for the Southern General.

Amongst all of those Glasgow psychiatrists Laing described, he was most negative of all about Ferguson T. Rodger. And yet Rodger seems to have given this and other Gartnavel group therapy projects every encouragement. He was himself a major instigator of the research money for Cameron and McGhie, and was initially a director of the research – even if, like MacNiven, he tended ultimately to take a back seat. Both Rodger and MacNiven were thanked by Cameron, Laing and McGhie in their *Lancet* article on the Rumpus Room experiment 'for advice, assistance, and support in carrying out this work'.[75] Rodger, like MacNiven, continued to be thanked in subsequent research completed by Cameron, Freeman and McGhie in the 50s. In a 1966 article reflecting back on psychiatry's recent history, Rodger was far from negligent towards the contributions made by 'ideas about group dynamics and group therapy', and expressed pride at the 'psychoanalytically oriented staff' at Glasgow.[76] Furthermore, as Burston suggests, Rodger's earlier admiration for Laing's work at Gartnavel led him to act very much as Laing's patron, supporting his application for the Senior Registrar's job at the Southern General and later bringing him to the attention of J. D. Sutherland, the Medical Director of the Tavistock Clinic (1947-68).[77] Rather than at Gartnavel, Laing's somewhat critical attitude to Rodger, if not to Glasgow psychiatry in general, was more acutely formed whilst under the latter's wing in Glasgow's Southern General, where Laing was forbidden to conduct another Rumpus Room experiment, and was upbraided for being opinionated and for interviewing patients from an armchair 'in front of his desk', or getting 'too close to them'.[78]

It is an even more striking feature of Laing's various accounts of his Glasgow days that so little mention is made of his colleagues, Cameron, Freeman or McGhie. And yet all went on to rather impressive careers, and all sustained a vigorous interest in psychological or psychotherapeutic approaches to mental illness. Freeman, a Belfast medical graduate, was a Lecturer in Psychotherapy at Glasgow's Department of Psychological Medicine (based at the Southern General) and was Consultant Psychiatrist at Gartnavel for 13 years, from 1952-65, serving concurrently, during 1958-65, as Medical Director of the Lansdowne Clinic. His time in Glasgow was divided more or less equally between work at Gartnavel and at Ferguson-Rodger's Department at the Southern. He had begun his career as Assistant at Queen's University's Physiological Department (1942-3), before serving during the War (c1943-7) as a Major in the RAMC. Freeman's training as a psychiatrist began in 1945, he working at Northfields Hospital, Birmingham, from August 1945 to January 1946. He moved on in quick succession subsequently to the post of Registrar at St. Ebb's Hospital, Epsom (1947-8), Senior Registrar at Belmont Hospital, Sutton (1948-50) and Senior Registrar at London's Tavistock Centre (1950-52). Subsequent to leaving Gartnavel, during the mid-60s he was a Visiting Professor at the University of Otago's Medical School in New Zealand, where he made a number of influential contributions on schizophrenia, group psychotherapy and psychoanalysis in the mental hospital, as well as publishing on community care and the training of mental nurses.[79] During the mid-60s, Freeman was also Consultant Psychiatrist to the Royal Dundee Liff Hospital. He finished his career as Consultant Psychiatrist to Holywell Hospital in Antrim, N. Ireland and to the Anna Freud Centre. He is currently retired and living in N. Ireland. Freeman published widely in psychiatry and psychotherapy – his interest in schizophrenia (if not quite in group therapy) proving as deep and as long-lasting as Laing's own. Cameron, a post-war Glasgow medical graduate, had started his career at Killearn Hospital as a resident in the Neurosurgical Unit (1950) and then as Senior House Officer in the Psychiatric Unit (1951-2). He served as

Registrar at Gartnavel Royal during 1952-3, after passing his DPM (1952), before becoming the Research Assistant at the University's Department of Psychological Medicine.[80] While Cameron may not have had the charisma of Laing, he did go on from Gartnavel to establish a distinguished career in the United States, becoming a member of staff (1955) and then Director of Chestnut Lodge Sanatorium in Rockville, Maryland. And Laing himself conceded that the work being done at the Chestnut Lodge was not only already coming out in the 50s, but was an influence on his own approach. McGhie, another Glasgow graduate (in the arts), took a first job as Clinical Psychologist at the Department of Clinical Psychology at Crichton Royal Institution, Dumfries (1951-3). Employed as Research Psychologist at Glasgow's Department of Psychological Medicine during 1953-5, he became Senior Clinical Psychologist at Gartnavel Royal from 1955. He went on subsequently to become Principal Psychologist and then Director of the Department of Clinical Psychology at the Royal Dundee Liff Hospital and Lecturer in Clinical Psychology at Queen's College, Dundee. Aitken described McGhie as 'a sensible clinical psychologist', who was latterly to emigrate to Canada 'where he flourished in an academic career'.[81] The career resumés of these men hardly bespeak of psychiatrists detached from therapeutic initiatives elsewhere, or who contributed to an impersonal and depersonalising regime at Gartnavel.

In conversation with Mullan about the 1955 *Lancet* paper, Laing complained that his wasn't 'the first name on' this paper, 'though I did all the work for it'.[82] This seems a trifle begrudging. It was relatively standard in jointly written medical papers for authors to be classed in alphabetical order rather than order of merit. Even if Laing wrote up all, or most, of the results of the experiment, clearly it was not his alone. Furthermore, it has been to Laing that most of the limelight for therapeutic community work at Gartnavel has subsequently accrued. Freeman, Cameron and McGhie might all have been justifiably piqued at the lowering of their profile in this as time went on. While the Rumpus Room experiment itself carried on for around a year after Laing's departure, his former colleagues all continued to work on schizophrenia and group therapy for years, as MacNiven's periodic reports and their own publications during 1955-60 testify. In February 1956, for example, Freeman and McGhie were granted leave to visit the Hampstead Child Therapy Clinic having been asked to give a talk on chronic schizophrenia. In August of the same year, Cameron, Freeman and McGhie published an article which discussed two group psychotherapeutic experiments with six male and six female chronic schizophrenics at Glasgow Royal.[83] While devoting considerable attention to communication, regression and withdrawal in schizophrenia, this paper also highlighted the significance of the project workers, and of interpersonal relationships between them and the patient. Further articles between 1957 and 1960 further exploited the Gartnavel research project.[84] In 1958, Cameron also collaborated as supervisor with Aaron Esterson as therapist, in the psychotherapy of a schizophrenic woman at Glasgow's Southern General. (Esterson later jointly authored the classic *Sanity, Madness and the Family* with Laing).[85] Subsequently, as Freeman retrospectively related, work on therapeutic groups was carried on at Gartnavel following the arrival of Drs James Chapman, James Davie and W. T. McClatchey, the latter succeeding McHarg as Deputy-Superintendent in 1960, and a further grant was obtained in 1963 permitting C. E. Gathercole to be employed as research psychologist.

More significant than these events, no doubt, in fuelling Laing's resentment, as John Clay's biography suggests, was the book that Cameron, Freeman and McGhie published as *Chronic Schizophrenia* (1958), soon after Laing left Gartnavel, in which they exploited material from the Rumpus Room experiment.[86] Furthermore, they did this without consulting him, a fact that must have stuck firmly in his craw. The authors were careful to attribute due merit to Laing in their introduction. They explained that the 'treatment centre' experiment had been 'originated' by Laing and summarised the work he had done there.[87] But, by now, the project had moved on, and Laing's approach was absorbed and re-articulated by his erstwhile colleagues as the second of 'three methods' they had been employing in 'the study of chronic schizophrenic patients in a group setting'.[88] Indeed, they modified Laing's approach, to the extent that the treatment centre now became in part 'a proving ground for therapeutic measures developed from our observations in the groups', while through weekly meetings 'a two-way channel of communication was gradually established between the group sessions and the treatment centre'.[89] The first method employed had entailed the original project of group psychotherapy for two groups, one male, one female, meeting for an hour on four days a week. The third involved Freeman, Cameron or McGhie 'spending several hours per day in the female refractory ward', sitting in the same seat, interacting with patients verbally, and then discussing events in the ward at weekly staff meetings. Laing may also have been piqued that the main conclusions that were arrived at in this book concerned the endorsement of the psychoanalytic view that the schizophrenic process was an ego disorder, and the implications for a therapeutic community appeared as a secondary concern. Yet the authors were still at pains to echo Stanton and Schwartz[90] as to the need to address not only patients' verbalisations, but their total social environment. They were also emphatic regarding the importance of the relationship between nurse and patient, of the nurse being continuously involved in the patient's environment, supporting appeals by Stanton and Schwartz and Maxwell Jones for a broadening of the function of the mental nurse.

The gulf only widened between Laing and his former colleagues as time went on, and this itself must have jaundiced accounts of the past to some degree. Cameron, who died a few years before Laing, had continued whilst at Chestnut Lodge to visit and combine with his colleagues back in Scotland on occasion and to publish on the psycho-analytic treatment of the psychoses, although his published output somewhat dried up in later years.[91] But Freeman and McGhie moved increasingly away from group experiments with schizophrenics, to examine the endogenous mental processes of schizophrenia. McGhie especially became preoccupied as a clinical psychologist with cognitive dysfunction, speech disorders, attention span and distraction in schizophrenia, authoring and collaborating with Chapman and Lawson in a series of articles on these subjects.[92] Freeman continued to spotlight schizophrenia in his work between the 1960s and 80s, producing a welter of books and articles – a few of which were jointly written and researched with Cameron and McGhie and more than a few of which continued to preach the benefits of group therapeutic approaches.[93] Yet most of his work focused more broadly around the areas of psychosis, psychopathology and psychoanalysis, and more specifically on such subjects as diagnosis, narcissism and defensive processes in schizophrenia.[94] While, as Freeman observed in 1960, ego-psychology, in particular that of Federn (1953) and Freud (1923), had been a strong influence from 'the outset of our work with chronic schizophrenia', this tended to become much more centre-frame from the mid-50s, at the expense of an environmental focus.[95]

Beside his own evident dissatisfaction that Cameron's name and not his own, was first on the *Lancet* article, Laing said little more about Cameron in his autobiography and various conversations than that Cameron had offered buns made by some of the Rumpus Room patients round the doctors' common room, only to have them suspiciously shunned by most. It was a story that Laing adeptly deployed in his autobiography to highlight negative mind-sets amongst Glasgow psychiatrists towards patients and towards schizophrenia, as well as the demoralising effect that a mental hospital might have on interpersonal relations.[96] And yet, as Laing might have emphasised, Cameron could clearly not be counted amongst this group. Beside this episode, Laing merely mentioned that Cameron had been a POW when in the army, had gone to Chestnut Lodge in America and was now dead.[97] Yet, Laing failed to detail that he had known Cameron well as a medical student before arriving at Gartnavel. Moreover, according to Freeman, Cameron (as a war veteran and 6 or 7 years Laing's senior), had very much taken Laing under his wing (or 'fathered' him) at medical school, being impressed by Laing's erudition and his philosophical bent.[98] Freeman suggests that it was partly as a natural result of this that Laing attached himself to Cameron and to the schizophrenia project on his arrival at Gartnavel. Despite the impression conveyed by Laing's own writings, furthermore, it had been Cameron not Laing who had initiated the practice of the therapist sitting in the midst of the patients in the refractory ward. And Laing's brevity and occasional inaccuracy with regard to Cameron and others in the Glasgow Clinic are echoed in the various biographical accounts.

Virtually all of Laing's recent biographers mentioned the story about 'Ian [Iain=John in Scotland] Cameron' and the buns. Burston said almost nothing about others involved in the work at Gartnavel, except that the experiment was 'reluctantly allowed' 'thanks to MacNiven's support'.[99] Clay, remarked that Laing 'was given permission with others to initiate this', and that Cameron, McGhie and Freeman were all 'collaborators' on the project.[100] Adrian Laing emphasised how his father 'persuaded ... Cameron and McGhie to participate' in the Rumpus Room experiment, but skipped more quickly than any of his other biographers over Laing's time at Gartnavel and in Glasgow.[101] Kotowicz emphasised how the concerns expressed in the *Lancet* paper – especially with the constructed nature and 'mutual' breaking down of barriers between staff and patients, and the development of interpersonal relationships – were 'typical of Laing's later writings'.[102] And yet they are also concerns that are evident in the work of both Cameron and Freeman before and after Laing's arrival at Gartnavel. The centrality of the 'interpersonal' to mid-twentieth century psychiatry had, in general terms, been emphasised by figures such as Meyer, and by journals such as *Psychiatry* since the late 1930s. Despite going through three name changes since its establishment in 1938, the latter journal has always retained the term 'interpersonal' in its title.[103] Similarly, early Bleulerian recognition of the importance of psychosocial influences on the psychoses was another important bridge towards more environmentally-led interpretations of schizophrenia and the deployment of therapeutic group approaches in the 40s and 50s. This is in spite of the fact that Cameron, McGhie and Freeman seldom referred explicitly to Bleulerian models in their early work on schizophrenia.[104]

Possibly, Freeman's narrative of these events minimised Laing's role in the schizophrenia projects – although not as much as Laing's treatment of Freeman's contribution did the opposite. If Freeman and others have felt to different degrees misrepresented by Laing's accounts of his Glasgow years, there may be an inevitable element of bias and self-defence in their own recollections of events. Quite naturally those who have spent longer in Glasgow psychiatry have had more reason to identify, if not over-identify, with it. On the other hand, in some respects they know, or knew, it better than Laing. Furthermore, Freeman *et alia* have always tended to recognise the importance of Laing's contribution at Gartnavel. Freeman would certainly not accept the charge of prejudice, and has convincingly asserted that the very assimilation of the Rumpus Room approach is a clear sign that they recognised it as an important observational and therapeutic method.[105] However tediously clichéd it may sound – the real truth about where credit should be apportioned may lie somewhere between the two extremes.

Laing's, Freeman's and indeed most other accounts of what happened in the 50s have, of course, been largely written or recounted long after the fact, often 30 years or more, and it is possible that their recollection were unclear. Laing's memories about the time were sometimes vague, inconsistent, or eliptically expressed. Even his accounts of how many patients were in the Rumpus Room and the female refractory ward differed. Often such represent minor rather than fundamental slips, and one is generally impressed more by the credibility and equity of Laing's portrait of Gartnavel and Glasgow psychiatry, than by its distortions and prejudices. Yet there were evident differences of agenda being expressed through such distortions. Laing's version of events was probably coloured by a growing concern at self-vindication – for Laing had been treated increasingly unsympathetically by the media and the psychiatric and academic community as time went on, his theories as rather flawed and old-hat. In interviews, as in print, Laing regularly complained that he was misquoted and went to some lengths to put the record straight – and yet in his own courting of media attention and of counter-culture status, and the casual, conversational, provocative way he liked to express himself, Laing was himself responsible for a good deal of the confusion in the record.

Some of Laing's biographers may have relied too much on Laing's own account of his time in Glasgow. Burston goes too far perhaps in attributing all the credit for the Rumpus Room experiment to Laing (given the fact that this was but one constituent of a broad programme of research at Gartnavel). Nevertheless, it should be stressed that, despite the collaborative nature of the project, there were clearly crucial differences between those involved with it. These emerged more starkly after Laing left Gartnavel, and when all of those 11 patients who had been released back into the community as a result of the Rumpus Room experiment were back in the Hospital within a year or so. According to Burston, 'most of Laing's colleagues argued that this corroborated the theory that schizophrenia is an insidious and incurable disease; improvements are only temporary'. Laing by contrast argued that their relapse or return was an indication that 'there was something radically wrong with the social contexts "out there"', and that their 'families were the source of the problem' – the abnormal context of the mental hospital providing more empathy for them than that offered by the 'normal' world. According to Burston, also, 'Laing's position did not please his colleagues' and 'intensified his growing estrangement from the psychiatric profession'.[106] To some extent, the continuation of work on schizophrenia and group therapy at Gartnavel long after Laing left seems to belie the force of these views. Indeed, the conclusions of Freeman, Cameron and McGhie's *Chronic Schizophrenia* (1958) hardly gave grounds for rejecting the significance of environmental factors in schizophrenia. This seems to be more the exaggerated gloss that Laing and Burston imposed on the historical record. It was from the 60s that Laing's real and growing differences with his former Glasgow colleagues over interpretations of schizophrenia and group therapy in mental hospitals were more forcibly expressed – although Laing had evidently never valued the ego-psychology approach Freeman followed.[107] As Laing later recounted, the real point was that he now increasingly believed that therapeutic community projects in large institutions were not the way forward, but that one needed to work in smaller groups and get closer to the roots of the problem in the community and the family itself – i.e. one needed to leave the asylum. With his characteristic mix of disarming, no-nonsense honesty and back-handed self-promotion, Laing by the 1980s was conceding quite openly to interviewers that if his own writings, as well as those by Cooper, Ssasz and 'other critics of psychiatry ... had never existed, the practice of psychiatry in Gartnavel and Woodilee would be exactly the same'.[108]

Notes

1. Adrian Laing, *R.D. Laing. A Biography* (London & Chester Springs PA: Peter Owen, 1994).

2. Daniel Burston, *The Wing of Madness. The Life and Work of R. D. Laing* (Cambridge, Mass. & London: Harvard University Press, 1996).

3. John Clay, *R. D. Laing. A Divided Self. A Biography* (London: Hodder and Stoughton, 1996).

4. Bob Mullan, *Mad To Be Normal. Conversations with R. D. Laing* (London: Free Association Books, 1995).

5. Zbigniew Kotowicz, *R. D. Laing and the Paths of Anti-Psychiatry* (London: Routledge, 1997).

6. Greater Glasgow Health Board Archives (henceforth *GGHB*), *13/1/2, 177, 178 & 220/56*, 6 July & 7 Sept. 1956.

7. Hunter-Brown is currently working on a book about Laing, Gartnavel and Glasgow psychiatry in the twentieth century. Her advice has been invaluable to me in preparing this paper.

8. R. D. Laing, *Wisdom, Madness and Folly. The Making of a Psychiatrist* (New York *etc.*: McGraw-Hill Book Co., 1985), 114, 125, 133, 137, 142-3, 146.

9. *Ibid.*, 104, 117-8, 123, 146.

10. *GGHB13/1/2, 260/53.*

11. *op. cit.* ref. 8 above, 112.

12. *GGHB13/1/2, 280/53*, 11 Dec. 1953.

13. *GGHB13/1/2, 177/56*, 6 July 1956.

14. Douglas Smith, in unpublished reminiscences on Gartnavel Royal Hospital, in possession of Rev. Derek Haley.

15. McGrath, in Rev. Derek Haley (ed.), *Reflections on the Occasion of the 150th Anniversary of Gartnavel Royal Hospital 1843-93* (Glasgow; Gartnavel Royal Hospital, 1993), 22.

16. *GGHB13/1/2, 86/53*, 10 April 1953.

17. *GGHB13/1/2, 5/56*, 6 Jan. 1956.

18. I am using the term group therapy rather loosely here to embrace all forms of therapy that took place with patients in large groups, including milieu therapy, occupational therapy and the nexus of

approaches known as therapeutic community. The term was commonly employed in this way by clinicians at Gartnavel Royal, as well as by many other contemporary psychiatrists and psychoanalysts. It is not therefore used merely to connote group therapy in the narrower psychoanalytic sense, as a forum for patients to articulate in groups with a therapeutic goal in mind, presided over by one or more therapists.

19. Adrian Laing, *op. cit.*, ref. 1 above, 60.

20. Laing, *op. cit.*, ref. 8 above, 114; Burston, *op. cit.*, ref. 2 above, 16-17. See, also, P. Mezan, 'After Freud and Jung, now comes R. D. Laing', *Esquire* (Jan., 1972), 168.

21. Clay, *op. cit.*, ref. 3 above, 54.

22. Cairns Aitken, in *op. cit.*, ref. 15 above, 31.

23. Mullan, *op. cit.*, ref. 4 above, 108.

24. Gerald N. Grob, *The Mad Among Us. A History of the Care of America's Mentally Ill* (Cambridge, Mass.: Harvard University Press, 1994), 200-201; Elliot S. Valenstein, *Great and Desperate Cures. The Rise and Decline of Psychosurgery and Other Radical Treatments for Mental Illness* (New York: Basic Books, 1986); Andrew Scull, 'Somatic Treatments and the Historiography of Psychiatry', *History of Psychiatry*, 5, 1, 17 (March, 1994), 1-12, p. 9.

25. *GGHB13/1/2, 177/56*, 6 July 1956, PS rept. 'Owing to the impossibility of getting an anaesthetist to take the place of Dr. Stevens, who was on holiday, the electric convulsive therapy had to be suspended for the last 2 weeks of the month, but this treatment is now being carried on again'.

26. Mullan, *op. cit.*, ref. 4 above, 108.

27. John L. Cameron, Thomas Freeman and Andrew McGhie, *Chronic Schizophrenia* (London: Tavistock, 1958), 43.

28. Cairns Aitken, in Haley, *op. cit.*, ref. 15 above, 32.

29. *GGHB13/10/11*, 6 Dec. 1955.

30. *Ibid.*

31. T. Freeman, 'Some Observations on Insulin Shock Therapy', *British Journal of Medical Psychology*, 22 (1949), 183-8, pp. 183, 184, 188; M. Schatner & F. J. O'Neill, 'Some Observations on the Treatment of Dementia Praecox with Hypoglycemia', *Psychiaric Quarterly*, 12 (1938), 5-41.

32. T. Freeman, in Haley, *op. cit.*, ref. 15 above, 27.

33. L. Alexander, *American Journal of Psychiatry*, 107 (1950), 241.

34. T. Freeman and J. L. Cameron, 'Anxiety after Electroshock Therapy in Involutional Melancholia', *British Journal of Medical Psychology*, 26 (1953), 245-61.

35. Cairns Aitken in Haley, *op. cit.*, ref. 15 above, 32.

36. E.g. *GGHB13/1/2, 262/56*, 2 Nov. 1956.

37. Author's own transcript of a taped private interview with Cairns Aitken (1992).

38. *Lancet*, ii (1955), 1384-6.

39. Laing, *op. cit.*, ref. 8 above, 113.

40. *Ibid.*

41. Mullan, *op. cit.*, ref. 4 above, 108.

42. *Ibid.*, 107.

43. See *GGHB13/1/2, 42/54, 181/54, 191/54, 148/55*; 5 Feb., 2 July 1954, & 6 May 1955; *GGHB13/10/1*, 6 Dec. 1955.

44. Aitken, in Haley, *op. cit.*, ref. 15 above, 33

45. McGrath, in *ibid.*, 22.

46. Op. cit., ref. 37 above.

47. Mullan, *op. cit.*, ref. 4 above, 107.

48. See e.g. McKendrick, in Haley, *op. cit.*, ref. 15 above, 14.

49. Mullan, *op. cit.*, ref. 4 above, 106-7.

50. *Ibid.*, 107.

51. Maxwell Jones *et al*, *Social Psychiatry: A Study of Therapeutic Communities* (London: Tavistock, 1952). See, also, *idem*, 'Group Psychotherapy', *BMJ*, ii (1942), 276-8; *idem*, 'Group Treatment, With Particular Reference to Group Projective Methods', *American Journal of Psychiatry*, 101 (1944), 292-9; D. W. Millar, 'Maxwell Jones and the Therapeutic Community', in G. E. Berrios and H. Freeman (eds), *150 Years of British Psychiatry. Volume II. The Aftermath* (London: Gaskell, 1995), 581-604.

52. Thomas Freeman, 'Some Problems of Inpatient Psychotherapy in a Neurosis Unit', in Maxwell Jones *et al.*, *Social Psychiatry* (1952), chap. 5, pp. 69-84.

53. Mullan, *op. cit.*, ref. 4 above, pp. 106-9.

54. *Lancet*, ii (31 Dec. 1955), 1384.

55. Irving M. Rosen and Mignon Chasen, 'Study of Resistance and its Manifestations in Therapeutic Groups of Chronic Psychotic Patients', *Psychiatry*, 12 (1949), 279-83. Cameron, Freeman and McGhie cited this 1949 article in their 1956 article on chronic schizophrenia, 'Clinical Observations on Chronic Schizophrenia', *Psychiatry*, 19 (Aug. 1956), 271-81, p. 275.

56. They cited this work in an article published in that year; Thomas Freeman and Andrew McGhie, 'The Relevance of Genetic Psychology for the Psychopathology of Schizophrenia", *British Journal of Medical Psychology*, 30 (1957), 176-87, p. 187.

57. K. Eissler, 'Remarks on the Psychoanalysis of Schizophrenia',

International Journal of Psycho-analysis, 32 (1951); H. Rosenfeld, 'The Psycho-analytic Approach to Acute and Chronic Schizophrenia', *ibid.*, 35 (1954).

58. Mullan, *op. cit.*, ref. 4 above, 147, 150, 161-2; W. R. Bion, 'Notes on the Theory of Schizophrenia', *International Journal of Psycho-Analysis*, 35 (1954).

59. Mullan, *op. cit.*, ref. 4 above, 287.

60. E.g. S. H. Foulkes, 'Principles and Practice of Group Therapy', *Bulletin of the Menninger Clinic*, 10 (1946), 85-9; *idem, Introduction to Group-Analytic Psychotherapy* (London: Heinemann, 1948); Millar, *op. cit.*, ref. 51 above, 586-8. *idem*, with Elwyn James Anthony, *Group Psychotherapy: The Psycho-analytic Approach* (London: Penguin Books, 1957).

61. Freeman, private communication with the author. See, also, The Cassel Hospital for Functional Nervous Disorders, Ham Common, Richmond, Surrey, *Medical and General Reports and Accounts for the year ended 31st December, 1946* (Ham, Surrey: Cassel Hospital, 1947); *idem, ibid. for the year ended 31st December, 1947* (Ham, Surrey: Cassel Hospital, 1948); *idem, ibid. for the period 1st January to 4th July, 1948* (1949); *idem, Annual Reports for the year 1st April 1950 to 31st March 1951* (1951).

62. Freeman, private communication with the author.

63. John D. Sutherland, Thomas Freeman and J. L. Cameron, 'A Preliminary Report on Group Psychotherapy in Involutional Melancholia', delivered at a Symposium on Group Therapy at the Scottish Branch meeting of the British Psychological Society, 31 Jan. 1953; announcement of meeting.

64. E.g. Thomas Freeman, 'Involutional Melancholics who Fail with Electro-Shock Therapy: Some General Observations and a Provisional Report of their Response to Group Psychotherapy', delivered at a meeting of the BPS, 27 May 1953; announcement of meeting. According to a Gartnavel Board of Management minute, the latter paper was to be given jointly by Freeman and Cameron; see *GGHB13/12. 142/53*, 5 June 1953. See, also, Freeman and Cameron, (1953), *op. cit.*, ref. 34 above; John L. Cameron, Thomas Freeman and Ronald A. Y. Stewart, 'Prognosis in Involutional Depression', *Journal of Mental Science*, 100 (April, 1954), 478-90; John L. Cameron and Thomas Freeman, 'Observations on Treatment of Involutional Depression by Group Psychotherapy', *British Journal of Medical Psychology*, 28 (1955), 244-38.

65. Cameron, Freeman and Stewart (1954), *op. cit.*, ref. 64, 488.

66. *Ibid.*, 489.

67. *Ibid.*
68. Cameron and Esterson, 'Psychotherapy with a Schizophrenic Woman', *Psychiatric Quarterly*, 32 (1958), 304-17.
69. Freeman in Haley, *op. cit.*, ref. 15 above, 26.
70. *Ibid.*; Cameron, Laing and McGhie (1955), *op. cit.*, ref. 38 above; and Freeman, Cameron and McGhie (1958), *op. cit.*, ref. 27 above, ix.
71. See *GGHB13/1/2, 215/53* & *240/53*, 4 Sept. & 2 Oct. 1953.
72. See, e.g., *GGHB13/1/2, 206/53* and *215/53*, 4 Sept. 1953, where Dr J. L. Cameron is said to have resigned as Registrar of 30 Sept. 1953, and also to have relinquished his Lansdowne duties. The PS then states that Cameron would be employed for the next 3 years on research financed by the Advisory Committee on Medical Research of the Dept. of Health for Scotland, in which work he would still be associated with Gartnavel. The Regional Board was to be asked to advertise a.s.a.p. for a successor.
73. *GGHB13/1/2, 240/53*, 2 Oct. 1953.
74. Freeman, in Haley, *op. cit.*, ref. 15 above, 27.
75. Cameron, Laing and McGhie, *op. cit.*, ref. 38 above, 1386.
76. Ferguson T. Rodger, 'The Role of the Psychiatrist', *British Journal of Psychiatry*, 112 (1966), 1-8, p. 2.
77. Burston, *op. cit.*, ref. 2 above, 42.
78. See *ibid.*, 58; Laing, *op. cit.*, ref. 8 above, 142-3.
79. Freeman, 'The Role of Psychoanalysis in the Mental Hospital', *New Zealand Medical Journal*, 65 (1966), 972-75; *idem*, 'A Clinical Approach to Research in Schizophrenia', *ibid.*, 66 (1967), 722-25; *idem*, 'Group Psychotherapy in a Mental Hospital', *ibid.*, 726-30; *idem*, 'The Ambulant Patient and Community Care', *ibid.*, 730-33; *idem*, 'The Psychiatrist and the Training of Nurses', *ibid.*, 758-62.
80. Cameron was, along with a number of others – including the theologian Professor Henderson; Archie Craig; the Jewish quasi-Jungian psychotherapist, Karl Abenheimer and Joe Schorstein, a Jewish psychiatrist, and the Heidegerian, John McQuarrie – one of the members of a monthly study group that Laing, as he expressed it, 'was the instigator of' when at the Glasgow University Department of Psychological Medicine after he left Gartnavel. At this study group, which rotated between members' houses, members presented papers to each other, Laing himself presenting a paper called the 'Ontology of Human Relationships' which was the germ of *The Divided Self.*
81. Aitken, in Haley, *op. cit.*, ref. 15 above, 30.
82. Mullan, *op. cit.*, ref. 4 above, 106.

83. *GGHB13/1/2*, 24 Feb. 1956; Cameron, Freeman and McGhie (1956), *op. cit.* ref. 55. McGhie presented a paper at the British Psychological Association in the same month on 'the role of the mental nurse'; *GGHB13/1/2, 183/56*.

84. Freeman, McGhie and Cameron, 'The State of the Ego in Chronic Schizophrenia', *British Journal of Medical Psychology*, 30 (1957), 9-18; Freeman and McGhie, 'The Relevance of Genetic Psychology for the Psychopathology of Schizophrenia', *ibid.*, 30 (1957), 176-87; Freeman, 'Clinical and Theoretical Notes on Chronic Schizophrenia', *ibid.*, 33 (1960), 33-43.

85. Cameron and Esterson, *op. cit.*, ref. 68 above; Laing and Esterson, *Sanity, Madness and the Family* (London: Tavistock, 1964).

86. Clay, *op. cit.*, ref. 3 above, 58-9; Cameron, Freeman and McGhie (1958), *op. cit.*, ref. 27 above.

87. Cameron, Freeman and McGhie (1958), *op. cit.*, ref. 27, 6-7.

88. *Ibid.*, 2-3.

89. *Ibid.*, 6.

90. Alfred H. Stanton and Morris S. Schwartz, *The Mental Hospital: A Study of Institutional Participation in Psychiatric Illness and Treatment* (London: Basic Books, 1954).

91. John L. Cameron, 'Patient, Therapist and Administrator: Clinical and Theoretical Considerations of a Conflictual Situation', *British Journal of Medical Psychology*, 36 (1963), 13-25; Thomas Freeman, John L. Cameron and Andrew McGhie, *Studies on Psychosis. Descriptive, Psycho-Analytic, and Psychological Aspects* (London: Tavistock, 1965), where chapter 10, 197-230, 'The Psycho-Analytic Treatment of the Psychoses', is by Cameron; John L. Cameron, 'Symbolism in the Treatment of Schizophrenia', *British Journal of Medical Psychology*, 43 (1970), 257-63.

92. Andrew McGhie, 'A Comparative Study of the Mother-Child Relationship in Schizophrenia. I. The Interview II. Psychological Testing', *British Journal of Medical Psychology*, 34 (1961), 195-221; James Chapman and Andrew McGhie, 'A Comparative Study of Disordered Attention in Schizophrenia', *Journal of Mental Science*, 108 (1962), 487-500; *idem*, 'An Approach to the Psychotherapy of Cognitive Dysfunction in Schizophrenia', *British Journal of Medical Psychology*, 36 (1963), 253-60; Andrew McGhie, 'Disturbances in Selective Attention in Schizophrenia', *Proceedings of the Royal Society of Medicine*, 57 (1964), 419-22; James Chapman and Andrew McGhie, 'Echopraxia in Schizophrenia', *British Journal of Psychiatry*, 110 (1964), 365-74; J. S. Lawson, Andrew McGhie and James Chapman, 'Perception of Speech in Schizophrenia', *ibid.*, 110

(1964), 375-80; Andrew McGhie, James Chapman and J. S. Lawson, 'The Effect of Distraction on Schizophrenic Performance. (1) Perception and Immediate Memory (2) Psychomotor Ability, *ibid.*, 111 (1965), 383-90 and 391-8; J. S. Lawson, Andrew McGhie and James Chapman, 'Distractibility in Schizophrenia and Organic Cerebral Disease', *ibid.*, 113 (1967), 527-35. Their work represented a collaboration between the Royal Dundee Liff Hospital and St Andrews University's Dept. of Psychiatry. Lawson was Medical Research Council Research Assistant and then Lecturer in Clinical Psychology at the Dundee Liff and at St. Andrews' Dept. of Psychiatry, while Chapman was Research Assistant and then Senior Registrar at the same Dept of Psychiatry and at Queen's College, Dundee. McGhie also collaborated with S.M. Russell on 'The Subjective Assessment of Normal Sleep Patterns', *Journal of Mental Science*, 108 (1962), 642-54.

93. E.g. Thomas Freeman, 'Group Psychotherapy in a Mental Hospital', *New Zealand Medical Journal*, 66 (1967), 726-30; *idem*, with Cameron and McGhie (1965), *op. cit.*, ref. 91. Freeman was also concerned with promoting group approaches in the teaching of medicine; *idem*, 'L'Enseignement de la Médecine Psychosomatique et de la Psychothérapie aux Médecins Practiciens par Discussions de Groupe', *Revue de Médecine Psychosomatique et de Psychologie Médicale*, 6 (1964), 391-5.

94. Thomas Freeman, e.g. 'A Psycho-Analytic Approach to the Diagnosis of Schizophrenia Reactions', *Journal of Mental Science*, 108 (1962), 286-99; *idem*, 'The Concept of Narcissism in Schizophrenic States', *International Journal of Psychoanalysis*, 44 (1963), 293-303; *idem*, 'Narcissism and Defensive Processes in Schizophrenic States', *ibid.*, 43 (1962), 415-25; 'Some Aspects of Pathological Narcissism', *Journal of the American Psychoanalytic Association*, 12 (1964), 540-61; Psychoanalysis and the Psychotherapy of Psychoses', *Anglo-German Medical Review*, 2 (1965), 780-6; 'Preservation – the Clinical Symptoms – in Chronic Schizophrenia and Organic Dementia', *British Journal of Psychiatry*, 112 (1966), 27-32. For other books he authored, see Thomas Freeman, *Psychopathology of the Psychoses* (London: Tavistock, 1969); *idem*, *A Psychoanalytic Study of the Psychoses* (New York: International Universities Press, 1973); *idem*, *Childhood Psychopathology and Adult Psychoses* (New York: International Universities Press, 1976). See, also, Clifford Yorke, with Thomas Freeman and Stanley Wiseberg, *Development and Psychopathology: Studies in Psychoanalytic Psychiatry* (New Haven: London: Yale University Press, 1989).

95. Freeman (1960), *op. cit.*, ref. 84 above, 33.

96. See Laing, *op. cit., ref. 8 above*, 116; Burston, *op. cit.*, ref. 2 above, 37-8.

97. Laing, *op. cit., ref. 8 above*, 116; Mullan, *op. cit.*, ref. 4 above, 146-7.

98. Freeman, private communication with the author.

99. Burston, *op. cit.*, ref. 2 above, 37-8.

100. Clay, *op. cit.*, ref. 3 above, 55-6.

101. Adrian Laing, *op. cit.*, ref. 1 above, 57.

102. Kotowicz, *op. cit.*, ref. 5 above, 72.

103. *Psychiatry: Journal of the Biology and the Pathology of Interpersonal Relations* (1938-47); *Psychiatry: Journal for the Operational Statement of Interpersonal Relations* (1948-9); *Psychiatry: Journal for the Study of Interpersonal Processes* (1950-1985); *Psychiatry: Interpersonal and Biological Processes* (1986-).

104. Eugen Paul Blueler, *Dementia Praecox or, The Group of Schizophrenias* (1911), translated by Joseph Zinkin (New York: International Universities Press, 1950). For one explicit reference to this work, see Freeman, Cameron & McGhie (1958), *op. cit.*, ref. 27 above, 147. See, also, Bleuler, *The Theory of Schizophrenic Negativism*, translated by William A. White (New York: The Journal of Nervous and Mental Disease Publishing Co., 1912); *idem, Textbook of Psychiatry*, authorized English ed. by A. A. Brill (New York: Dover, 1951).

105. Freeman, private communication with the author.

106. Burston, *op. cit.*, ref. 2 above, 38.

107. See Laing, *Self and Others* (London: Tavistock, 1961); *idem, op. cit.*, ref. 90; Freeman, private communication with the author.

108. *Inside Out*, 1 (1984), 'R. D. Laing – A Return from the Radical Trip'.

8

"Messiah of the Schizophrenics"
Jan Foudraine and Anti-Psychiatry in Holland

Gemma Blok

In the spring of 1971, many a bookseller in Holland was surprised by the large amount of people asking for a book written by a Dutch psychiatrist, Jan Foudraine (1929). It bore the intriguing title *Wie is van hout...* (*Who is made of wood...*)[1], and within weeks the first print run was completely sold out. New printings quickly followed and after some time, *Wie is van hout...* even drove the another very popular book at the time, *Soldaat van Oranje* (*Soldier of Orange*), away from the number one position in the bestseller list. What was happening here? Why was a scientific book suddenly more popular than the heroic adventure story of two Dutch soldiers in World War II, who put their lives on the line for queen, country and swooning pretty girls? By 1979, almost 200,000 copies of Foudraine's book had been sold. It had become one of the biggest Dutch bestsellers of the seventies and was translated into English and German.[2]

What was happening, a little later in Holland than in America or England, was 'anti-psychiatry'.[3] During the sixties and seventies, psychiatry was suddenly attacked from the inside as well as from the outside, as a result of the urge felt by people in society as well as in mental health care to create a more human, democratic and tolerant world. Psychiatrists such as Laing, Szasz, Cooper and Foudraine voiced criticism of psychiatry, which was enthusiastically picked up by the media, by the various professions working in mental health care, and by many people in society.

Solidarity with the 'Mentally Ill'
First of all, criticism was directed at the poor situation in which many psychiatric patients spent their lives. Isolated from society, they wasted away in huge hospitals which were often old and badly

kept. The patronising and authoritarian climate in these asylums, the critics argued, robbed people of their personality and self-esteem, so that they became passive and scared to leave the hospital. Therefore, mental hospitals should be abolished and the patients integrated back into society. Moreover, the psychiatric treatment many patients received was criticized. Therapeutic methods such as electroconvulsive therapy (ECT) and psychopharmaceuticals were labelled inhuman. Many critics argued that psychiatric patients did not suffer from a biological illness or a brain disorder. Instead, the state they were in was caused by their social environment. They were victims of the intolerance, stress and lack of real communication in modern society and in their own families. Therefore, patients should be listened to in an environment where they could relax and be themselves, instead of being humiliated and medicalised in 'total institutions'.

Furthermore, the right of psychiatry to exist at all was called into question. Why should a group of doctors be given the power to define normality? Some stated that psychiatry was not a science at all, but an instrument for social control, paid for by the state. According to this point of view, people with non-conformist ideas or behaviour were 'labelled' insane and put in institutions until they were willing to conform again. Finally, madness gradually came to be romanticized. The so-called mentally ill were thought to be more in touch with their real selves and less hypocritical than most 'normal' people. They were rebels in a world full of spiritually dead, intolerant zombies, and since they were punished for their rebellion, they became the martyrs of modern society.

The seeds for all this solidarity and identification with the mentally ill had been planted during the forties and fifties. In 1941 for example, philosopher Erich Fromm had written that schizophrenic disorders were the most extreme expression of the loneliness and alienation which were so typical for man in modern western capitalist, individualistic society.[4] And in 1959, the American publicist Seymour Krim stated that the mentally ill were actually victims of modern life, which was 'brain-trying' and 'anxiety-loaded'. They 'only acted out what other less passionate people feel, but do not express', he thought.[5] However, it was not until the sixties that such notions became popular. The critical and anti-authoritarian climate in western society was strong. Parents, universities, religious leaders, employers, judges and politicians were all faced with the fact that their authority was no longer a matter of course. It was only logical that psychiatry should come under fire as well.

Furthermore, issues concerning deviance and tolerance were topical at the time. Marginalised groups in society, such as homosexuals, women and Afro-Americans, started to emancipate and conformism came to be a dirty word. Doubtless the increasing individualism in society and the growing interest in psychological literature and psychotherapy also proved a great influence on anti-psychiatry.

In Holland, anti-psychiatry gave rise to several action groups and critical magazines, protests against ECT, medication and isolation, and to therapeutic experiments in psychiatric hospitals.[6] Moreover, during the beginning of the seventies a huge conflict evolved around Dennendal, an institution for the mentally handicapped. This conflict had many parallels with anti-psychiatry, since the humanisation and democratisation of care was at stake here as well. Ido Weijers describes the Dennendal-affair in the next chapter.

This article will focus on *Wie is van hout...*, the book written by Holland's most famous anti-psychiatrist Jan Foudraine. This subject was chosen not only because the book became a major bestseller, but also because the reactions it evoked perfectly illustrate what I believe to be the essence of anti-psychiatry. Firstly the fact that psychiatry, which had long been able to operate in a relatively isolated fashion, now came to be forced to interact with society and justify its theories and methods to a critical audience. Secondly, the 'projection' onto psychiatry of ideas and feelings which were topical in Western society roughly between 1965 and 1975. And finally, the important role of the press in mobilising the public attention surrounding psychiatry.

Human Dignity

The cover of *Wie is van hout...*, which was published in may of 1971, promised that Foudraine had a radically anti-psychiatric message. '"Mentally ill" are the loudspeakers through which the ills of our time sound loudest', it read. 'Therefore it will not benefit our society to put them away somewhere in an institution.' In the introduction, Foudraine directly addressed anti-authoritarian sentiments by stating that it was 'about time psychiatry was stripped of its mysterious and magical properties, that the psychiatrist came off his pedestal and that the layman, too, learned to think about what psychiatrists are wrestling with.'[7] Finally, the motto on page one suggested that the author was a brave non-conformist:

Two roads diverged in a wood, and I
I took the one less travelled by,
And that has made all the difference.　　　　(Robert Frost)

The book, which is full of references to Szasz, Scheff, Laing, Fromm, Goffman and other critical authors, starts off with Foudraine's experiences as an assistant-psychiatrist during the 1950s. He was deeply disappointed by the lack of 'human dignity' in psychiatric practice. There was hardly any emotional contact in the often patronising relationship between doctor and patient, Foudraine thought. In his view, Dutch psychiatry was still dominated by the tradition of Kraepelin, a 'rather obsessional German professor' whose emphasis on diagnosis, prognosis and clinical observation had led to the cold and impersonal climate within psychiatry. The doctors wore white coats, observed their patient's behaviour without listening to them, and regarded the mentally ill as 'broken down radios producing strange sounds', as one of Foudraine's teachers put it. The title of Foudraine's book is a variaton on a patient demonstration by Kraepelin. The patient cries out: 'I'm made of wood, I'm made of wood!' Foudraine explains to the reader that this is not the senseless babble of a crazy person, but a symbolic way for the patient to express that he feels treated like an insensitive piece of wood. There is reason in the so-called madness. So, Foudraine asks rhetorically, who is made of wood: the patient or the doctor?[8]

However, Foudraine does recognise the fact that some psychiatrists did sit down with patients to try an empathic and psychotherapeutic approach. But even they did not enter into an emotional relationship with their patients. If their psychotherapeutic measures did not help quickly enough, the patient was still labelled schizophrenic, given ECT and gradually forgotten about. Freudian psychoanalysis, which did not draw such a clear line between the sick and the healthy, and which explained psychiatric problems in a psychodynamic way, was a lot more appealing to Foudraine. Unfortunately, Freud had been pessimistic about the possibilities of psychoanalysis with psychotic patients, whereas Foudraine suspected that their afflictions probably had a strong psychodynamic and sociogenetic basis as well.

So, he directed his attention to the writings of American neo-Freudians like Harry Stack Sullivan, Frieda Fromm-Reichman and John Rosen. In spite of Freud's pessimism, they had applied psychoanalytic theory to schizophrenia. Fromm-Reichman for example is the one who coined the term 'schizophrenogenic mother.' John Rosen attached a lot of importance to the role of the parents as well, especially the mother. As a result of family-interaction, he thought, psychotic patients had withdrawn into a dreamlike state. The therapist had to break through the regression and autism and get the patients to 'wake up'.

Inspired, Foudraine selected the most hopeless patient in the clinic for an experiment in 'direct analysis'. Karel was a 'defect-schizophrenic' who never laughed, cried, or spoke. For months, Foudraine tried to establish contact by going for walks with him, inviting him to his room and telling him about his own life. But the man refused to be drawn. Foudraine describes how he would seize Karel by the shoulders and give him a good shaking: 'he should and he would respond to my appeal for contact; I refused to accept his total rejection of me'.[9]

Then one day the dramatic breakthrough came about. A bird was singing outside and Foudraine, standing by the window, said: 'do you hear that bird, Karel?' He looked outside expecting no reply but suddenly, at his back he heard Karel say: 'I hear it all right. It makes me sad. It's scalding under the sand.' From that moment on, therapy flourished and Foudraine and Karel talked in depth about the patient's weak father, oversolicitous and dominant mother and catholic upbringing, all of which together had apparently caused his insecurity and fear of sex and human relationships. After some months, the psychosis lifted and the triumphant Foudraine was forever 'lost to classical clinical psychiatry'.

A couple of years later, in 1960, he left for America to work in the Chestnut Lodge. This upper-class psychoanalytic clinic near Washington was the homebase of his heroes, Sullivan, Fromm-Reichman and Rosen. But once again Foudraine was disappointed. The therapeutic setting was completely wrong, he thought. The structure of the clinic was rigidly hierarchic and both patients and staff were caught in a web of hospitalism. Foudraine spent a couple of years transforming his ward into a therapeutic community, or a 'school for life', as he called it. Psychiatrists were to be called 'teachers', nurses 'assistants-teachers' and patients 'students'. In the future these schools should replace the traditional asylums.

Back from America, Foudraine felt in his own words like the 'messiah of the schizophrenics' and more or less expected to become the centre of attention in Holland.[10] But his Dutch collegues did not seem interested at all. Frustrated, Foudraine sat down and wrote *Wie is van hout...* This book certainly brought him the attention he had wished for.

Holland as a Guide for the World

To explain why Foudraine's book became a bestseller and caused such commotion, it is necessary to give a rough sketch of both Dutch society and Dutch psychiatry. Both were rapidly changing during the 1960's, and these changes formed the breeding ground for Foudraine's ideas. Perhaps the feeling of entering a new era was more pronounced in Holland than in, for example, America or England. Life in Holland between 1965 and 1975 changed very quickly and thoroughly compared to other countries in the western world.[11] Industrialisation and urbanisation didn't really get well under way until after 1945.[12] Moreover, the influence of religion, which had always been very strong in the Netherlands, diminished quickly during the sixties and seventies. On top of this the nuclear family, the 'corner-stone of society' which had been held in high regard in Holland longer than elsewhere, started to show signs of wear.[13] Children revolted against their parents, the pill was introduced giving people more sexual freedom, the birth-rates were falling and feminists fought for women's rights.

Around 1970, Amsterdam had become the 'magical centre' of the world, attracting a stream of hippies. Homosexuals, who became increasingly tolerated in Holland, assembled in Amsterdam as well. On all fronts, authorities were criticized and like everywhere in the western world the conflicts concentrated around the universities. The number of students had risen spectacularly from 28,000 in 1950 to 103,000 in 1970.[14] For a long time, higher education had been a privilege of the rich. Now, people from the lower classes gained access to the universities as well. This development was crucial to the anti-authoritarian spirit of the sixties.

Another important role in the revolution of morals and power was taken by the press.[15] For a long time, Dutch journalism had been dominated by the standards of objectivity and restraint. Those in power did not have a lot to fear from the press. In the course of the sixties however, journalists became the voices of Dutch counter-culture; in particular the journalists of the *Volkskrant (Journal of the People)*. A new draft of young journalists was given a wide berth, and they used it to attack the 'bourgeois' authorities and to stimulate public debate about new topics such as conformism and tolerance, women's rights, education and healthcare. In the favourite pub of the *Volkskrant*-journalists, heated discussions and emotional scenes often took place. 'A lot of us were still wrestling with ourselves and the world, with our education and background', as one of them later recalled.[16]

A favourite topic for the progressive press was the actions of the Provo's (Provocateurs), the 'core' of Dutch counter-culture. This group of young people ridiculed and provoked the police, and the whole of bourgeois Holland, with playful gestures. They hoped to thus expose the 'real face' behind the benign attitude of those in power. In 1968, the Provo movement was transformed into an organisation called the Kabouters (Hobgoblins). They too preached a playful anarchism, but they didn't leave it at that: they wanted to be more active in reforming society. In 1970, they proclaimed the Oranje Vrijstaat (Orange Free state), a symbolic state within Dutch state which was supposed to become an example of a better kind of society.

According to the Kabouters a lot was wrong with the western world. Following the ideas of philosophers like Erich Fromm and Herbert Marcuse, they believed capitalism had alienated people from their inner selves, from their real needs, and from each other.[17] It had transformed both the proletariat and the bourgeoisie into 'one big grey mass of assholes, of addicted consumers'.[18] The existing democracy was just an illusion, they thought. In reality, the individual freedom western man had created for himself was so lonely and scary that most people were inclined to imitate others, or follow authoritarian leaders. This tendency to conform led to a loss of personality, and thus the large mass of people had turned into manipulable zombies.

Such ideas fell on fertile soil amongst two rapidly growing, partly overlapping groups in Dutch society: academics who studied social or behavioural sciences, and people working in the expanding field of welfare. A lot of social and political unrest during the sixties and seventies was started by them.[19] Politics was influenced by social criticism as well. In 1970 an influential report was published by the Wiardi Beckman Foundation, the scientific research-institue of the Partij van den Arbeid (the Dutch Labour Party).[20] This report, called *Verbeter de mensen, verander de wereld (Improve the people, change the world)*, stated that it was high time to turn 'prosperity into well-being'. Since the technological and social evolution of society had led to alienation and materialism, politicians had to busy themselves with the solution to this problem. Creating equal opportunity for everybody was one part of the solution. But along with politics, 'mental health care is one of the roads towards general well-being too', the authors of the report stated. 'It is time for a revolution, which will work seriously on the third ideal of the French Revolution: from paternalism to fraternity.' In 1973, when the Partij van den Arbeid gained power in government, its prime-minister Joop den Uyl voiced the optimism even more strongly. Dutch society, he pronounced, would be completely transformed to achieve an 'equal division of income, knowledge and power.' This would result in a better world, making Holland a political and moral 'guide for the world'.[21]

Renewal and Doubt in Dutch Psychiatry

Dutch psychiatry at this point was rapidly changing.[22] During the 1950's, new psychopharmaceuticals had caused a revolution in treatment. This apparently made the growing variety of therapeutic interventions more possible. Besides, psychiatrists gradually recognized that the development of psychiatric problems could be attributed to social interactions and other dynamics in human relationships. As a result of these developments, sociotherapy, group psychotherapy, behavioural therapy and individual psychotherapy became more popular. Mental health care then demanded new professions to become more involved, such as psychologists and social workers. Furthermore, the possibilities and demand for psychiatric treatment outside of the asylums rapidly increased. In Amsterdam for example, the number of people who undertook individual therapy at the Instituut voor Medische Psychotherapie (Institute for Medical Psychotherapy) rose from 150 in 1960 to 2500 in 1976.[23]

Besides, the number of child guidance clinics, institutions for psychiatric after-care and agencies for 'Questions about Life and Family' was also growing. Therapeutic communities were evolving as well. One of them, set up in 1968 for the treatment of adolescents, was strongly influenced by anti-psychiatric ideas. The founder of this community, psychiatrist Jan van de Lande, was inspired by David Cooper's Villa[21] experiment and was a huge fan of Laing as well, a large portrait of whom decorated a wall in the community building.

Around 1970, psychiatry was undergoing something of a shift in identity, maybe even a crisis. As a result of the new professions working in mental health care, psychiatrists no longer held the monopoly. Many of them started to move away from the traditional medical perspective and adopted a more 'psycho-social' outlook. Within the Dutch Association for Psychiatry and Neurology, a discussion had started during the sixties around the question whether those two disciplines should remain so closely associated. Eventually, the Association was split in 1974. (More information about this can be found in chapter 11, by Saskia Wolters and Harry Oosterhuis.)

At the same time it became increasingly clear to many psychiatrists that the traditional mental hospitals were outdated. In 1966 the critique was voiced sharply by a medical director of a large asylum: 'We encapsulate our patients in our care without any distinction; care which we, completely out of place, call "therapy". Everything we do with our patients we call therapy: work-therapy, sociotherapy, singing-therapy, fishing-therapy… and therefore, without wanting to, we damage our patients by treating them as patients only… by dehumanising them.'[24] Steps were taken to create community care, sheltered accomodation and part-time treatment, but it was as yet a rather slow process and a lot of hospitals were still stuck with a large army of chronic patients and a shortage of nursing staff.

On top of this, trainee psychiatric nurses started to protest against their one-sided, medically oriented education, their lack of say in the treatment and the clinical atmosphere in the mental hospitals.[25] Last but not least, patients made their voices heard. In 1971, the Cliëntenbond (Clients' Association) was founded. The confused atmosphere in mental health care became very clear at a conference called 'Te gek om los te lopen' ('Too crazy to be true'), which was held in November of 1970. It was organised by the National Federation for Mental Health to bring together psychiatrists, related professions, nurses, patients and interested citizens to discuss the future of mental health care.

Jan Foudraine, one of the speakers, had invited a couple of Kabouters to the conference as well.[26] They had recently taken up an active interest in psychiatry. Within the Oranje Vrijstaat, a department for mental health care had been set up. Its members formulated ideas for 'alternative clinics' and read the works of, amongst others, R. D. Laing and Timothy Leary.

Tragically though, the first time the psychiatric establishment reached out to the clients of and workers in mental health care, showing a slightly vulnerable face, it became a traumatic experience. 'The blow hit so hard that one can assume psychiatry will never be the same again after these two emotional days', wrote the Volkskrant.[27] A mass of people working in psychiatric institutions, armed with angry banners, appeared to be intensely frustrated. They felt their work consisted of patching up 'mental wrecks', only to send them back to the 'front' and see them back again soon; because after all, 'the real cause of their problems lies in society'.[28] They strongly criticized the lack of humanity in psychiatry. At some point during the conference there was an embarrasing incident when a patient went up on stage to tell his story, got a bit emotional and asked for help. When he got no response, a young woman started crying and broke the awkward silence by shouting: 'Here is one of the persons you all claim to be experts on, and now you don't know what to say!'

In the course of the two days, the audience got more and more excited and at one point the plan came up to force the Ministry of Defence to hand over 10 million guilders to psychiatry by going on a strike. This proposal was out-voted because most people did not want to harm the patients. Foudraine probably made himself very popular with the audience by stating that psychiatrists earned a ridiculously high income.[29] In short, the conference became an emotional chaos and Kees Trimbos, a professor in social psychiatry, concluded afterwards that it had 'shown the psychiatric establishment in an unexpected and slightly rough manner that the things we have felt and talked about for years, but within our own quarters, have now become a public matter'.[30]

Barely recovered from this shock, another trauma awaited the psychiatric world. A conflict evolved around Dennendal, an institution for the care of mentally handicapped patients. Medical director Carel Muller, a good friend and ideological follower of the Kabouters, tried to create a more human and democratic form of treatment. However, tension between Muller and his superiors grew. In the spring of 1971, the media got wind of the conflict and a conservative newspaper started a big offensive against Dennendal, accusing the personnel of drug use at work and the neglect of patients. Progressive newspapers started to write in favour of Muller and gradually the conflict achieved widespread national attention. One was either 'for' or 'against' Dennendal, which itself became a symbol of the new society some wanted and others feared.

In short, Foudraine's timing could not have been better. In Dutch society, anti-authoritarian sentiments and urge for change were strong. Many felt that knowledge and power should be democratized, and that people should become more tolerant of difference and communicate more. Moreover, religion and traditional family-values had been criticized. At the same time, mental health care was in a ferment. The 'psycho-social' model grew in importance, bringing with it a large number of social scientists working in the field. Together with psychiatric nurses, they uttered strong feelings of discontent with the methods of psychiatry. Psychiatrists were at this time a bit doubtful about the future of the mental hospitals and about the relationship between the medical and the social 'model' in psychiatry. The stage was set. When *Wie is van hout...* was published in may of 1971, it became the focal point for a lot of pre-existing feelings of unrest.

Democrat or Demagogue?

As soon as the book was in the stores, a veritable media-circus broke loose. Numerous interviews with Foudraine and reviews of his book appeared in magazines, newspapers, and on radio and television.[31] 'Psychiatry is on a slippery slope', one inciting headline concluded. Most journalists seem to have been very eager for the message Foudraine had to tell, and he got the opportunity to repeat it many times. Madness has a lot to do with everyone, he emphasized. 'Everybody knows very well that they dream the weirdest things, and that those dreams mean something... and then when a person stands before us who is constantly dreaming, all day long, we pull up a wall, because we are afraid.' Inspired journalists turned their reviews of the book into emotional pleas for human contact. 'We should all start listening to our psychotic fellow human beings', one of them wrote passionately, 'who show us the ills of this society: the alienation in family, church and neighbourhood, and the dehumanisation to which this society has contributed'.[32]

Another journalist thought Foudraine's book refreshing because it counterbalanced the 'paralyzing feeling of powerlessness' in society. 'As individuals we feel like we run into walls all the time', she wrote. 'We are prisoners of the system, and we have to wait and see if our guards will be willing to give us some fresh air.'[33]

Meanwhile, Foudraine's basic assumptions – that schizophrenia is caused by the family, chronic schizophrenia does not exist and mental illness does not have a biological basis – hardly met with any criticism. Many fully agreed with Foudraine that 'the family has long been a taboo in society', and that the medical world had long been scared to acknowledge the 'fact' that 'parents can ill-treat their children so horribly'. Some writers positioned Foudraine in an evolution of society towards more humanity. 'Finally, the middle-ages are disappearing from the hospitals as well', they wrote, but 'we still have to learn a lot, learn how to really encounter each other emotionally'. The comparison with Freud was sometimes made: didn't he have to fight a smug psychiatric establishment as well before he found recognition?

Of course, there was some criticism. Some remarked that Foudraine's ideas weren't really all that new. Others thought it strange that Foudraine gave no credit in his book to some of his more progressive Dutch colleagues working in therapeutic communities. But on the whole, the press was very positive. One of the things journalists appreciated most in his book was the fact that Foudraine made complicated scientific knowledge understandable and accessible to the public: 'Laymen, who also have a lot to do with psychiatry, can now form their own opinion, and are thus able to enter the discussion.'

However, this fact stongly displeased some of Foudraine's colleagues. They attacked him in pamphlets, newspapers and scientific journals.[34] One was amazed by the fact that otherwise intelligent minds were able to take the 'unscientific and comical prose' of people like Laing and Foudraine seriously.[35] Others called Foudraine unscientific as well, a 'quarrelmonger' who 'pretends nobody has used his brain during the last 30 years'. A Belgian professor of psychiatry thought that Foudraine, like Laing, had shown a 'very serious example of wrong ethics. It is very indecent to sweet-talk the crowd, because the crowd, for its lack of knowledge, education and experience, and thus inabiliy to utter criticism, is very easy to influence. What difference is there, then, with demagogy?'[36]

Democracy or demagogy, this is one of the central themes in the discussion about the book. Some of the critics had very patronising points of view. One stated for example that people only bought Foudraine's book because they were greedy for juicy stories about other people's misery. Others claimed that Foudraine cashed in on the spirit of the times, with its 'pre-occupation with relationships', 'anti-authoritarian sentiment' and 'trifling club-chat of pseudo-revolutionaries'.[37] But democracy had finally caught up with psychiatry. As the well-known Dutch psychiatrist Jongerius put it: psychiatry was being punished for the fact that 'it had rendered itself guilty of pretending to have the answer to all questions of life, and had combined this with a complacent isolation from society'.[38]

In spite of what Foudraine would later suggest, several of his colleagues did give *Wie is van hout...* a fair chance or were even supportive.[39] It was appreciated that Foudraine focused on the doctor–patient relationship as an essential element in psychiatry, stressing the impact psychiatrists' assumptions and attitudes have on their patients' lives. Foudraine's emphasis on the importance of social factors in the development of psychiatric problems was valued as well. However, both the fiercely critical and the mildly positive psychiatrists regretted the fact that Foudraine had polarised the discussion about the 'medical' and 'social' model. According to Foudraine, there were only two kinds of psychiatrists: the natural scientific and the psychotherapeutic ones. 'And if there one thing I don't want to do, it is to reconcile those two', he said. This uncompromising attitude met with little sympathy.

Swami Deva Amrito

And then of course there were the tens of thousands of other people who read Foudraine's book. Who were they? It seems likely that a lot of newspaper-readers probably bought it because it got such good reviews and because certain themes, like the evolution of civilization and humanity in western society and the democratisation of knowledge, were appealing at the time. Many buyers were probably social scientists, psychiatric nurses, welfare workers and psychologists working in mental health care, who were not happy with their position as subordinates to the doctor, and who recognised their own criticism on psychiatry and the medical model in the book.

According to some psychiatrists, a struggle for power was going on in the mental hospitals between the psychiatrists and the social scientists.[40] The publication of Foudraine's book probably dropped more fuel on the fire. At the same time, nurses aspired to a more therapeutic rather than just a caring task. Foudraine held the opinion that the therapeutic potential of psychiatric nurses was much undervalued, so finally a psychiatrist had joined their camp.

In all likelihood, many readers were young people and students who appreciated an all-out attack on an authoritarian institution like psychiatry, on positivist science, and on the 'happy family'. Finally, *Wie is van hout...* was probably widely read amongst patients and their families. Just like a lot of highschool students and other young people, they bombarded Foudraine with letters and phonecalls, telling him their stories and asking for advice.[41]

In 1978, Jan Foudraine became a disciple of Baghwan Shree Rajneesh. The bestseller-success of his book had confused him a lot, he later explained. The dream had turned into a nightmare. He was very disappointed by the supposed lack of recognition his book received amongst his colleagues. Besides, his relationship with the press was not as good as it used to be. In 1972 for example, journalist Heerma van Voss had called him a 'fibber' in one of his articles. He accused Foudraine of being dishonest about one of the case-histories in the book, and of trying to make psychotherapy with psychotic patients look much more successful than it actually was.[42]

During the 1980s, Foudraine became Baghwan's 'personal ambassador' in Holland and popularized his ideas by writing books. The press continued to follow his actions with interest. Remarkably,

Foudraine gradually developed some reactionary ideas. In 1988, he stated that democracy should be abolished and that 'we have to make mankind healthy again, because it is very ill. By genetically preventing the births of all the blind, crippled, hereditary tainted and mentally handicapped people, we have to diminish it by 25 percent.' He caused quite a stir with his views on homosexuality, which he derided as unnatural. Once he angrily shouted during an interview that 'Pricks should be put in vaginas! They just don't belong in an anus!'[43] Apparently, Foudraine no longer led the way to a more human and tolerant society.

Epilogue

This article has attempted to situate the phenomenon called anti-psychiatry in the context of developments in mental health care, the media and society as a whole. Jan Foudraine's bestseller and the reactions it evoked were used as a case-study. His book, and the enthusiastic reactions of the press, triggered a process during which ·certain pre-existing feelings and ideas topical in society were 'projected' onto psychiatry. Such as the strive for democratization of knowledge and power; the call for a more human and tolerant world; and the longing for more communication between people to fight the 'alienation' in modern society.

The Dutch psychiatric world reacted confused and divided to all the sudden attention, which added fuel to a pre-existing struggle for power between social scientists and psychiatrists, and polarized the discussion about the medical and social model in psychiatry.

More research will be necessary to assess the effect anti-psychiatry had on mental health care. But for now I think it is possible to conclude that research into anti-psychiatry can be used to shed more light on the history of the sixties and seventies. For anti-psychiatry was a mirror of western society at the time, as seen in the interest in Che Guevara or the fascination with eastern philosophy.

Notes

1. J. Foudraine, *Wie is van Hout... Een Gang Door de Psychiatrie* (Bilthoven: Ambo, 1971); the English translation is called *Not Made of Wood* (London: Quartet Books, 1974).

2. J. Jansen van Galen, *Het Ik-tijdperk (Haagse Post*-special, 22 December 1979), 55-63.

3. On anti-psychiatry, see for example N. Dain, 'Psychiatry and Anti-Psychiatry in the United States', in R. Porter and M.S. Micale (eds), *Discovering the History of Psychiatry* (Oxford: Oxford University Press,

1994), 415-45; D. Ingleby, *Critical Psychiatry* (Harmondsworth: Penguin, 1981); J. Postel and D. Allen, 'History and Anti-Psychiatry in France', in Porter and Micale, *Discovering*, 384-415; D. Tantam, 'The Anti-Psychiatry Movement', in G.E. Berrios and H. Freeman (eds), *150 Years of British Psychiatry* (London: Gaskell, 1991), 333-51; K. Trimbos, *Anti-psychiatrie: een overzicht* (Deventer: Van Loghum Slaterus, 1975).

4. E. Fromm, *De Angst Voor Vrijheid* (Utrecht: Bijleveld, 1962), p. 22 (translation from *Fear of Freedom* [New York: Farrar and Rinehart, 1941]).

5. S. Krim, 'The Insanity Bit', in B. Kaplan (ed), *The Inner World of Mental Illness. A Series of First-Person Accounts of What it Was Like* (New York: Harper and Row, 1964), 62-80.

6. B. Fox, B. van Herk, R. Esselink and R. Rijkschroeff, *Psychiatrische Tegenbeweging in Nederland* (Amsterdam: Van Gennep, 1983); S. van 't Hof, *'Een Ambt, Hoog en Subtiel...' Psychiaters over Psychiatrie 1971-1996* (Utrecht: NVvP, 1996), 11-36.

7. J. Foudraine, *Not Made of Wood* (London 1974), xv.

8. This anecdote cannot be found in Kraepelin's clinical lessons; Foudraine has made it up himself, as a 'variation' on a patient-demonstration by Kraepelin as told by Laing in *The Divided Self.*

9. Foudraine, *Not Made of Wood*, 17-20.

10. Interview with Foudraine by 'Bibeb' in *Vrij Nederland*, 28 November 1981.

11. M. van Rossem, E. Jonker and L. Kooijmans, *Een tevreden natie. Nederland van 1945 tot nu* (Baarn: Tirion, 1993), p. 7.

12. J. Kennedy, *Nieuw Babylon in Aanbouw. Nederland in de jaren zestig* (Amsterdam: Boom, 1995), 23-45; H. Rigthart, *De eindeloze jaren Zestig. Geschiedenis van een Generatieconflict* (Amsterdam: Arbeiderspers, 1995), 52-59.

13. D. Damsma, *Het Hollandse huisgezin 1560 – heden* (Utrecht: Kosmos, 1993); Kennedy, *Babylon*, 101-103; P. Luykx and P. Slot (eds), *Een Stille Revolutie? Cultuur en Mentaliteit in de Lange Jaren Vijftig* (Hilversum: Verloren, 1997), p. 137.

14. Kennedy, *Babylon*, p. 168.

15. J. Jansen van Galen and H. Spiering, *Rare Jaren. Nederland en de Haagse Post 1914-1990* (Amsterdam: Nijgh en van Ditmar, 1993); F. van Vree, *De Metamorfose van een Dagblad. Een Journalistieke Geschiedenis van De Volkskrant* (Amsterdam: Meulenhoff, 1996), p. 107.

16. Vree, *Volkskrant*, 112.

17. C. Tasman, *Louter Kabouter. Kroniek van een Beweging 1969-1974* (Amsterdam: Babylon-De Geus, 1996), 51-3.

18. Kennedy, *Babylon*, 133.

19. H. van Goor, 'Pressiegroepen en Sociale Verandering', in: L. Rademaker (ed), *Sociale Problemen* 1 (Utrecht: Het Spectrum, 1978), 151-74.

20. J. van den Bergh, E. Dekker, W.J. Sengers and J.A. Weijel, *Verbeter de Mensen, Verander de Wereld. Een Verkenning van het Welzijnsvraagstuk Vanuit de Geestelijke Gezondheidszorg* (Deventer: Kluwer, 1970).

21. Kennedy, *Babylon*, 77-9; Van Rossem, *Tevreden Natie*, 89-129.

22. On Dutch psychiatry during the 1950's, 1960's and 1970's, see for example G. Blok, 'Onze Kleine Wereld, 1945-1965', and J. Vijselaar, 'Vrijheid, Gelijkheid en Broederschap: een Franse Revolutie in de Psychiatrie', in J. Vijselaar (ed), *Gesticht in de duinen. De geschiedenis van de provinciale psychiatrische ziekenhuizen van Noord-Holland van 1849 tot 1994* (Hilversum: Verloren, 1997), 166-238; Van 't Hof, 'Een ambt, hoog en subtiel...'; J. Dankers and J. van der Linden, *Van regenten en patiënten. De geschiedenis van de Willem Arntsz Stichting: Huis en Hoeve, Van der Hoeven Kliniek en Dennendal* (Amsterdam: Boom, 1996); A. Kerkhoven, *Beeld van de psychiatrie 1800-1970* (Zwolle: Waanders, 1996).

23. C. Brinkgreve, J. Onland and A. de Swaan (eds.), *Sociologie van de psychotherapie deel 1. De opkomst van het psychotherapeutisch bedrijf* (Utrecht: Het Spectrum, 1979), p. 147.

24. J.P. de Smet, 'De plaats van de psychiatrische inrichting in het totaal van de geestelijke gezondheidszorg', *Voordrachtenreeks* 1966, p. 259.

25. Fox a.o., *Tegenbeweging*.

26. Tasman, *Louter Kabouter*, p. 284.

27. Ferd. Rondagh, 'Crisis in de Geestelijke Gezondheidszorg', *De Volkskrant*, 3 October 1970.

28. M. Aalders, 'Te gek om los te lopen', *De Haagse Post*, 25 November 1970; G. van den Berg, 'Procesbeschrijving seminar', *Maandblad voor Geestelijke Volksgezondheid (MGv)* January 1970.

29. N. Verwey, *Oude kost en revolutie. Kritische beschouwingen over Jan Foudraine's 'Wie is van hout...'* (Franeker: Wever, 1972), p. 21.

30. K. Trimbos, 'Enige korte reflecties', *MGv* December 1970.

31. B. Bos, interview with Jan Foudraine, in: G. Bruijn, *Dat wordt me te gek. Psychiatrie kritisch bekeken* (Amsterdam: Contact, 1972); G. Bomans, 'De Psychiatrie op de Helling', *Avenue* February 1972; B. van Garrel, 'Een Psychopaat is Helemaal Niet Gek', *Haagse Post* 15 June 1971; P. van der Eijk, 'Visie van een Psychiater op het "gek-zijn"', *De Tijd*, 31 July 1971; H. Elzerman, 'Psychiater Jan Foudraine: Ik Geloof dat de tTijd voor Mijn Boek Rijp was', *Trouw* 24 December 1971; A.J. Heerma van Voss, 'Jan Foudraine, Vervolgd. Analyse van een Bestseller', *Haagse Post* 5, 1972; N. Noordzij, 'Gran-

dioze kijk op psychiatrie en psychiater', *De Telegraaf* 19 June 1971; M. de Vreede, 'De Onverwachte Bestseller van Psychiater Foudraine: "Het gaat niet om psychopathen of schizofrenen, maar om mensen met problemen"', *Het Parool* 9 October 1971; W. Woltz, 'Veel Gezinnen Hebben een Rubber Muur om Zich Heen', *Nieuwe Rotterdamse Courant* 24 July 1971.

Review of *Wie is van hout...?* by an anonymous reporter, *De Waarheid. Volksdagblad voor Nederland* 5 June 1971.

J. Fortuyn, 'Hoevelen Zijn van Hout en Hoevelen Zijn Hoger', *De Groene Amsterdammer* 30 October 1971.

For example, J. Huijts, 'actualia', *MGv* 9 July 1971; A. Poslavsky, '50,000 maal "Wie is van Hout" en de Anti-Psychiatrische Beweging. Enkele aantekeningen', *Tijdschrift voor Psychiatrie (TvP)* 14 (1972), 366-79; H. Rooymans, 'Alternatieve psychiatrie', *TvP* 14 (1972), 389-408; N. Verbeek, *Psychiatrie in Holle en Bolle Spiegels* (Nijkerk: Callenbach, 1975); Verwey, *Kritische Beschouwingen.*

Rooymans, 'Alternatieve Psychiatrie'.

Verbeek, *Holle en Bolle Spiegels.*

Rooymans, 'Alternatieve psychiatrie', and Poslavsky, '50,000 maal wie is van Hout'.

J. Jongerius, 'Psychiatrie en Publiciteit', *MGv* 197?

R. van den Hoofdakker, 'Wie is van rede', in: R. van den Hoofdakker, *Een Pil voor Doornroosje. Essays over een Wetenschappelijke psychiatrie* (Amsterdam: Van Gennep, 1976); J. Marlet, 'Over het boek van Jan Foudraine', *Streven* January 1972; Trimbos, *Anti-Psychiatrie.*

P. Idenburg, 'Er woedde een machtsstrijd binnen het APZ', *Het Ziekenhuis* 23/24, 21 December 1995, 36-9.

Swami Deva Amrito/J. Foudraine, *Oorspronkelijk Gezicht. Een gang naar Huis* (Baarn: Amboboeken, 1979).

A.J. Heerma van Voss, 'Foudraine als Jokkebrok', *Haagse Post* 23 February 1972; A.J. Heerma van Voss, 'Swami Jokkebrok en de weggewaaide pagina', *Studenten Weekblad Propria Cures* no.14/15, 25 December 1980, 19-23.

E. Etty, 'Het Testament van Jan Foudraine', *Nieuwe Rotterdamse Courant*, 2 July 1988.

9

The Dennendal Experiment, 1969–1974
The Legacy of a Tolerant Educative Culture[1]

Ido Weijers

In reflections on Dutch culture in the first decades after World War II, one element is usually lacking that may be considered characteristic of the period. This is a typically Dutch, tolerant, educative perspective on social and cultural questions. It is the proposition of this article that it was this perspective, in particular, that enabled Dutch society to develop to a level of maturity which meant it was ready for the social and cultural changes and experiments of the sixties.

Maturity is not used here in the sense in which Jamison and Eyerman, for instance, use it to argue that 'partisan' intellectuals like Hannah Arendt, Herbert Marcuse and Erich Fromm sowed the cultural seeds for the sixties in America in the fifties. Jamison and Eyerman argue that the movements of the sixties built on the body of ideas that had been raised in the previous decade by these lone wolves in *The Human Condition* (1958), *Eros and Civilization* (1955) and *The Sane Society* (1955).[2] However, in the Dutch context it was not the writings of certain critical intellectuals in the margins of society that provided this cultural link between the two periods. On the contrary, in the Netherlands it involved the collective development of ideas, which emerged in the forties and became widely accepted and further developed in many circles in the fifties. This tolerant, educative perspective may first of all be seen as the cultural legacy of the so-called Breakthrough, the intellectual movement that tried to break through the segregated cultural and political relations in the Netherlands after World War II. At a political level, this movement had little success.[3] At a cultural level however, that is in fields like education, mental health care, social work and criminal justice, its influence was great.

169

After the war a broad Dutch intellectual elite emerged, that began to lead and to give substance to what may be designated as a new 'politics of the personal' or a 'personalist' culture. Their 'personalism' stressed above all the inviolable dignity of persons. These intellectuals were not primarily interested in political influence; they were suspicious of systems, including the market economy and the state, because these systems are not ultimately focused on the dignity of persons. They were interested in cultural influence and change. Their personalism focused, in particular, on marginal and deprived persons, using their condition as an index of the health and justice of society. Convinced of the need for cultural and moral renewal, this elite focused its attention on the help that the Dutch population needed, in its view, to modernize personal life. Modernization required careful guidance in the opinion of this elite. Community spirit and personal responsibility were its key terms.[4]

The School of Utrecht emerged as part of this post-war movement in the broad field of criminal justice, forensic psychiatry and child welfare. This paternalistic, tolerant, educative perspective was central to this influential circle, whose renowned key figures included: Willem Pompe, the scholar in criminal law, the criminologist Ger Kempe and the younger forensic psychiatrist Pieter Baan.[5] Under their influence the main theme of post-war Dutch criminal law until well into the seventies was accommodation, not the efficient confinement of criminals, mentally disturbed and juvenile offenders. Priority was to be given to accommodation and confinement avoided where possible as that meant social exclusion. There was also an interest in the creation of alternative forms of special treatment.[6] Around 1950 the situation in the Netherlands was much the same as in England and Wales, but twenty years later the situation had changed completely. In the seventies half of all sentences were very short (less than one month) in the Netherlands, while in England and Wales the very short sentences had decreased to less than one-fifth of the total. At the other extreme, long prison sentences (12 months or more) had decreased in the Netherlands to less than 5 percent, while in England and Wales this category had increased to almost one third of the total.[7] (The mid-seventies, however, was a turning point. Since then there has been a slow rise in longer sentences with a clear acceleration at the end of the eighties. The Netherlands is now up with the leaders when it comes to capacity and use of prisons.) Every comparative research study of European systems of criminal justice mentions this explicit educative and tolerant approach in the

Netherlands from the beginning of the fifties (and the reverse trends after 1975).[8]

Little or no attention has been paid so far to this element in Dutch studies of the first decades after the war. Recent studies of the sixties mostly postulate an overpowering conflict between generations, which overlooks the strikingly tolerant and educative climate which was characteristic of the first post-war decades.[9] For that reason the point of view which James Kennedy adopts in *Nieuw Babylon in Aanbouw* is very interesting. Kennedy states that the generation-gap that is recorded everywhere in the West as the main cause of the social and cultural changes and experiments of the sixties, turns out to be less significant in the Netherlands. According to Kennedy, the Netherlands owes its tolerant and progressive climate to a heterogeneous group of cautious authorities, who were so concerned about keeping developments under control, that they allowed behaviour that in other countries would not have been tolerated. The point on which the Netherlands differed from other countries was the aversion of the Dutch authorities to conflict, harsh confrontation and violence.[10]

This view does not, however, give adequate recognition to the ambiguity of Dutch post-war culture. In the post-war Netherlands there were not only members of the old guard who seemed willing in retrospect to adapt, but also autonomous, modern-thinking and authoritative intellectuals. The Breakthrough elite took a leading part in a number of fields in post-war Dutch culture. It was this elite, in particular, with modern *grand seigneurs* like Buytendijk, Rümke, Pompe and Langeveld, that articulated the typically educative perspective of the fifties to the seventies. These personalist intellectuals developed into our national educators, and were considered by many, including many in political circles, as spiritual and cultural guides.[11] Their pupils then went on to develop this tolerant, educative perspective in various fields of personal and community life, from Han Fortmann to Pieter Baan and from Peter Hoefnagels to Kees Trimbos.

James Farrell is right in arguing that 'for too long, the fifties have been the "happy days" of popular culture and the "unhappy daze" of historians'.[12] This not only holds for the historical reception of post-war culture in the United States, but surely also for the reception of the 'silent' fifties and the 'revolutionary' sixties in Western Europe. Recent revisions of the fifties viewed the period as showing a precarious balance between tradition and renewal.[13] This idea, however, can easily put paid to any further discussion. More interesting and fruitful are the stories that really try to clarify the pre-revolutionary character of some aspects of post-war culture and to make sense of cultural continuities. James Farrell's *The Spirit of the Sixties* is an inspiring example and the same holds, for instance, for Peter Clecak's *America's Quest for the Ideal Self.* Clecak pointed to the intriguing combination of the ideal of personal fulfilment and social justice, both emerging from the fifties and radicalized in the sixties.[14] Farrell draws attention to the personalist roots of American radicalism of the sixties. For the Dutch, the personalism of the Dutch Breakthrough movement seems of similar importance. The Dennendal Experiment provides a good, concrete illustration of this proposition. In this typical high point and subsequent nadir of Dutch flower-power, in this grand finale of Dutch counterculture, something of that tolerant, educative perspective developed in the preceding decades is revealed. This article will demonstrate how far the flowers of the counterculture, that were in full bloom here for some years in the field of mental health care, were the (unintended) results of what an older generation had sowed.

Kind-heartedness[15]

Dennendal was and is an institution for mentally retarded people. Dennendal is autonomous now, but in the sixties and seventies it was a (new) part of the psychiatric institution Willem Arntsz Hoeve in Den Dolder. Here, at the beginning of the seventies, the personnel led by the director, psychologist Carel Muller, created an alternative caring culture of extremely informal manners, a relaxed but inspired attitude to work, and, above all, an attitude of 'being yourself'. As an experiment Dennendal found itself at the end of 1973 in escalating conflict with the administration of the coordinating foundation. However, the point of this chapter is to describe this alternative approach, interpret its emergence within Dutch mental health care and illustrate the cultural continuity from the tolerant, educative climate of the fifties. Dennendal came to stand for an ideal: it meant anti-conventions, anti-smugness and anti-hierarchy. Muller and his fellow workers demanded the realization of their ideas for the further development of the institution, the so-called *verdunning* or dilution. Dilution meant, strictly speaking, that people from outside the institution would live together among inmates in houses of their own in the grounds of the institution. However, the dilution ideal of Dennendal was, at the same time, much broader and more embracing.

In order to view the idea of dilution in the right perspective, that

172

is in the perspective that raised so much enthusiasm and impassioned solidarity at the time, both within and far beyond mental health care circles, at least two dimensions must be distinguished. First, the 'therapeutic' dimension, that has directly to do with the location of Dennendal within Dutch care services for mentally retarded people and within general mental health care of that time. Second, the dimension that I will refer to by the term 'accommodation', the dimension that has to do with ideas about residence in an institution, notions about the meaning of the space in which people with (and also people without) handicap live and about the quality of life. Bases for these ideas could, of course, be found in notions about the treatment and care of people with mental handicaps and other needy people. At the same time, however, these ideas went much further and expressed a broader cultural dissatisfaction. They articulated counterimages with a much more wide-reaching cultural impact.

As for the location of Dennendal within the care services for mentally handicapped people, the basic assumption of Muller and his staff was the principle that mentally handicapped people need our help, but that apart from that, their being different is a positive rather than a negative fact. The mentally handicapped person is authentic; he does not hide his feelings and expresses himself directly.[16] In this sense he is not only an object of care but also an *example*. According to this viewpoint, mentally handicapped people need to be approached as much as possible as autonomous people, as people who do, indeed, need help, guiding and coaching, but who also have specific potential of their own. Their personal potential and interests had to be appreciated positively and stimulated, so a series of initiatives were taken. The use of medicines which were considered to produce dependency and repress the personality was reduced. Purely technical nursing, which degraded the residents to numbers, to occupiers of beds, was also reduced as far as possible in favour of personal treatment. The residents got more freedom to go where they wanted within the grounds of the institution, and the group leaders let themselves be guided, where possible, by the residents' wishes for individual and group activities. They did not only get freedom but also more responsibility, for their own room, for some activities in the living unit, or outside in the garden or the workshop. The point of departure was that care should, as far as possible, take on the character of normal living, in a kind of family relationship with freedom and responsibility where and whenever possible.

The Dennendal Experiment, 1969-1974

Dennendal stood for a new approach toward the mentally handicapped person, in which his limitations were recognised just as his strong point, that is his authenticity, was valued. The significance of (limited) mental abilities was considered to be relative. The handicapped person was dependent above all on appreciation and confirmation. For this reason the guidance and the daily environment as a whole had to provide first of all for sufficient appreciation of the conduct and initiatives of the residents. The therapeutic approach at Dennendal actually amounted to 'non-therapy': specialist therapists with their tests, special programs and medicines were barred. All kinds of special professionals had to make way for the general humanizing and self-development approach, or what they themselves called 'kind-heartedness'. The mentally handicapped person needed only to be enabled to be himself, that was the crux of the therapy of Dennendal. As a matter of fact, that goal did not only relate to the mentally handicapped residents but also to their carers. 'To become yourself and to use your full potential was the task everyone had to set himself'.[17]

On that point Dennendal fitted in completely with the countermovement in mental health care at the time. 'Ever met a normal man?' was the critical slogan that accompanied many 'happenings'. Let people with deviant behaviour be themselves, appreciate their peculiarities and do not try to change them into 'normal' people at the expense of their personality. These and similar ideas inspired innumerable people to go along the road of the alternative culture. The alternative approach also implied a new attitude on the part of the care workers and a different environment for deviant people, less focused on achieving normality. This was a new relaxed culture, where performance, conventional norms and efficiency would no longer be dominant, but authenticity, kind-heartedness and a relaxed atmosphere.

Dilution meant much more than a certain kind of integration. In this respect Dennendal did not fit in with the ideas of many followers of radical anti-psychiatry, that the residents should leave the asylum and enter society. The workers at Dennendal found society unsuited, lacking sufficient understanding of the mentally handicapped person, and they feared that he would be pushed aside and abandoned to his fate. In that sense dilution meant 'internal-integration', which implied, first and foremost, an extension of the group of kind-hearted people. The point was not that 'normal' people would live among them, but *unconventional* people with whom the mentally handicapped people would feel at ease and appreciated, and vice versa. Dilution was a denominator for a kind-hearted culture, a criticism of the social relations in and outside the institution. It implied a typical countercultural vision of a social alternative, a new world that would be created within the shell of the old .

Here we arrive directly at the other dimension of the idea of dilution, concerning the living environment. Dilution implied explicit notions about an optimal environment for mentally retarded people. Muller and his staff were convinced, that the usual living arrangements in groups of sixty to eighty people in huge wards and in uniform clothing (just like their attendants) could not be a stimulating, but only a negative, pathogenic environment. This approach reduced the residents to mere numbers, without a place of their own, without anything of their own, anything that confirmed their presence and their identity. The institution itself had to be changed. Uniform clothing was abandoned, residents and care staff had to arrange their accommodation within the walls of the institution as much as possible according to their personal ideas and tastes. The huge wards were divided into smaller units. The white hospital walls were painted in lively colours. The rooms were furnished less uniformly, were made more comfortable and cosy with personal things, drawings and photographs. The residents were housed in small groups, where possible, with a living room, kitchen, bathroom and a private bedroom, like a family

This approach was applied to the whole arrangement of the institution, the accessibility of its grounds and the organization of its facilities. Muller and his staff abhorred modern design, efficient and separate staff offices, buildings for different activities, and big, neat canteens, bedrooms and recreation rooms. They feared barriers and anonymity for the residents and for themselves. They longed for kind-hearted individuality and authenticity.

Not Ill, Only Different

Traditionally, care for mentally retarded people had been charity-based in the Netherlands, that is undifferentiated care for dependent people on a religious basis.[18] Mentally retarded people were also treated in psychiatric institutions, but *specialist* medical involvement in this field only emerged around the end of the nineteenth century, mainly via the inspectorate.[19] The rise of specialist medical involvement implied the emergence of a clinical model, in which dependency and mentally inadequate functioning was seen as something in the individual, that could be diagnosed by clinically trained professionals. The popularity of this model rested primarily on a biological approach, which viewed mental handicaps as organic damage or deformity. Mental retardation was an illness or disorder, the doctor was the appropriate expert, and the psychiatric hospital was the proper place for the treatment or nursing of persons suffering from this illness. The medical, clinical approach only became dominant in the Netherlands after World War II. Confinement of mentally handicapped people on a large scale only came into being here after 1945.[20] There were two decisive causes for this late change of approach: new material wealth and a greatly increased trust in medical treatment. Regarding the first cause, around 1960 there had been a turning point in government policy in the field of health care and the liberalization that followed made it much easier to build institutions.[21] Subsequently, the introduction of the Social Security Act in 1965, and the Exceptional Medical Expenses Act three years later, made residence in an institution possible for many more people as subsidies were made available to everybody.

Without doubt these measures were important for the rapid growth of institutions in the sixties, but the growth had actually begun a long time before that. That had to do with the second factor, the increased prestige of medical knowledge in the field of mental retardation in the middle of the fifties. Important progress had been made, especially on prevention, and promising new steps in medical treatment were expected. The treatment of Down's syndrome and successes with the use of diets and vitamin cures had increased the authority of the doctor and encouraged the belief in treatment and cure. A modern approach to mental retardation meant medical treatment. That was the idea after the war in the Netherlands and this belief, in turn, stimulated the growth of institutions. To be modern meant that one could send one's child to an institution with confidence.

Medication and hygiene came first in this approach and the white-coat culture of the hospital, with the psychiatrist at the top of the knowledge pyramid, followed by the psychologist and the remedial educationalist as his assistants, and the nurse, the physiotherapist, the speech therapist and the teacher at the bottom of the hierarchy. In the fifties belief in this approach led to considerable expansion of bed capacity, due to accelerated building of new institutions and modernization of existing institutions.

The curious thing about the post-war development of this sector is that the same model and this whole medical approach was in crisis within two decades. By the end of the sixties the seemingly inviolable authority of the doctor-psychiatrist in this field was being debated on many sides, and many were enthusiastically looking for alternatives to the huge institutions. The *fall of the medical-clinical* model is the most important point in the relation between the fifties and the sixties. How can this rapid downfall of the clinical model be explained? A combination of factors was involved, of which the first is the most important. That is the turnaround in medical thinking itself.

Around 1970 the relevance of the clinical model for mental retardation began to be doubted by the doctors themselves. There was renewed interest in the influence of the environment on illness and disorders. The emergence of social medicine also occurred in this period. Some doctors came to the conclusion that the huge hospital institutionalized its inhabitants and could even make many of them ill. However, the decisive fact seems to have been that more and more doctors began to realize that their knowledge was *actually* of little importance for real care in this field. The doctor was supposed to make the diagnoses, but the psychologists had appropriated the major part of this activity with their extensive testing apparatus. The doctor was supposed to diagnose psychiatric problems, but they turned out to be present only in a minority of cases. The psychologists and remedial educationalists were better equipped for specific treatment and activities meanwhile, and the nurses and many group leaders were sufficiently educated to provide hygienic care. Diagnostically the psychiatrist continued to pull the strings for a long time, employing DSM III-codes, but therapeutically he had become *marginalized* in this field. In the area of prenatal care and treatment of newborn babies the doctor remained the authority, but he appeared to have little to offer in the area of general care and treatment.

At this point his 'assistants', the psychologist and the remedial educationalist, came into the picture. Both had a long tradition of involvement with mental retardation. The educationalists had many years' experience with special education. Individual attention, furthering personal development and opportunities for stimulation and learning rather than treatment had always set the tone here. For the psychologists too, the key question was not whether they were dealing with an ill or a healthy person. They started from the assumption of a sliding scale of mental powers, from very low to very high, in which the change from normal to abnormal had become diffuse and an approach in terms of illness or health was actually irrelevant. Furthermore, more and more people among both groups of experts began to realise the importance of the *lifeworld.* More or less familiar with the principles of the phenomenological eye, they began to realize the negative consequences of life on a hospital ward, as a number without a place of one's own, without anything on which to base a personal identity. An individualizing approach proved to have positive consequences, so here and there these experts brought alternative accents to the fore within the medical regime.

While in the forties and fifties the clinical model seemed unassailable and the belief in the asylum as a hospital for the mentally handicapped person got stronger, an intellectual vacuum came into being in the following decade. From this intellectual vacuum new experts emerged here and there, from among the former 'assistants', the behavioural scientists. However, their approach was still far from clear, and what they had to do exactly, and how far their intellectual authority would reach, was also far from clear. Where they became the new executives, they had to fight for their intellectual authority and legitimacy. While some psychiatrists had begun to doubt their own authority in this field and had begun to retreat into the background, this certainly did not happen everywhere.

The Dennendal experiment has to be seen in this context. While institutional growth in this sector could no longer be stopped, at the same time doubts were growing about the intellectual authority of those who were supposed to be competent in this field, and who were supposed to manage the institutions on the basis of their competence. These doubts also created a *hierarchical vacuum,* which, in turn, led to a concentration of alternative energy, in which not only was alternative expertise and authority claimed, but in some cases every form of specific knowledge, expertise and authority was rejected. In the most extreme view only 'real empirical knowledge' counted, and who had more right to speak in that respect than the lowest in the hierarchy, the group leaders and the other people who cared for the residents on a daily basis? The most radical answer to the intellectual crisis in this field and to the hierarchical vacuum resulting from it was to delegate all responsibility to the lowest level. That is what happened at Dennendal.

The staff at Willem Arntsz Hoeve were clearly aware that a new basis for care for the mentally handicapped was needed within their walls and so, in 1969, the medical director, psychiatrist Poslavsky, deliberately appointed a *psychologist* as the new director. This was Carel Muller who had been associated with the institution for some years. Muller had had encouraging results with his approach which focused on the individual person's potential for development. He was the first director of Willem Arntsz Hoeve who had a background in the behavioural sciences rather than a medical background. Muller was, in fact, given the opportunity to dismantle the hospital model within an institution which was still completely dominated by modern, large-scale nursing of the sick. The large psychiatric and geriatric departments were nowhere near being ready to see medical-clinical thinking in relative terms, so Dennendal had a spearhead role within Willem Arntsz Hoeve.

Many saw Carel Muller's approach and the conflicts which he and his staff ended up in over the course of time as variations on a general problem in psychiatry. Dennendal was claimed to be part of the attack on the authoritarian, professional-managerial bulwark of medical-psychiatric authority within the mental health services.[22] Dennendal did, indeed, fit into this movement in broad terms. However, Dennendal was able to develop into a model for the countermovement in the whole field of mental health services due to the unique situation which existed at that time in care services for the mentally handicapped. Against the background of the professional and hierarchical vacuum at the point where care was being delivered, alternatives were given a greater chance here than elsewhere. In other fields, while psychiatrists were subjected to criticism, they could not be pushed aside. It was in the field of care for the mentally handicapped that it became possible to break through the hegemony of the medical-clinical model, which had only been achieved a few decades earlier at the expense of charitable care which had scarcely any medical basis. It was precisely in this area that the progress made in the fifties was undone by a countermovement, which was even recognised within the medical world itself.

Change in order to Care and Conserve

The legacy of post-war personalism can easily be traced in the approach of Muller and his staff. The inheritance of the Breakthrough movement and personalism, both of which were critical of culture, did not only affect the social compartmentalism of Dutch society and the cultural ossification associated with it. The criticism of parochialism implied a longing for a new common spirit, a '*mesure comune*', a new authentic, internalised community life. The dominance of commerce and hankering for material gain was rejected. People wanted a fairer distribution of resources and opportunities, but not equality, because people simply are not equal. People were striving for optimal development of each person's individual potential but pulled out all the stops to resist commercialism and individualism. There was a fear of consolidation, dislike of rapid technological innovation imposed from above and a fear that this would lead to the loss of humane personal relationships. The earlier perspective, labelled as tolerant and educative, articulated this so called 'post-materialist' critique of culture.

To put it simple and concisely: the care for the masses which had occupied the old guard of the seigneurale elite became an aversion to petty bourgeois norms and values among the young people of the post-elitist age. This inheritance made a vital contribution to the link between the forties-fifties and the sixties, and to the relatively smooth relationship between the older generation who had become adults during or before the war, and the younger generation who grew up after the war. Carel Muller, born in 1937, came from a typical Breakthrough background, from which it was natural for him in 1957 to go and study psychology in Utrecht, under Buytendijk, Van Lennep, Langeveld, Rümke and Linschoten, in short under the Utrecht phenomenologists, the intellectual vanguard of the Breakthrough movement. The key ideas of this circle fell on good ground with him. He lapped them up as it were, especially the ideas about personal experience of space, the emphasis on the existential significance of people's daily living environment, the surroundings in which people live and work or where people are forced to reside.

This body of ideas can be seen at a very elementary, practical level in Muller's approach, as he realised that life on a large ward reduced the patients to numbers who were unable to take any initiative for themselves. From this background he started to develop a series of initiatives to enable the residents to make their stay at Dennendal as personal as possible. The way Dennendal was run and the concept of dilution clearly involved additional existential meaning for him. He regarded Dennendal as a real community. However, the relationship between Muller's approach and the Utrecht School is even more fundamental than that, as will become clear if we take another look at the dilution ideal. That ideal actually did not only imply a strong belief in the possibility of *change*, on the part of both the workers and the mentally handicapped patients, who all had the opportunity to shake off the commercial, materialistic, performance-oriented attitudes which characterised the world outside the institution in exchange for kind-heartedness. Dilution also meant an equally strong longing for *conservation*.

Dennendal was also setting an example in the field of mental health care in that respect. In the spate of experiments, 'happenings', occupations, blackbooks and plans to democratise and improve the care services, the emphasis in this sector was overwhelmingly on 'change ... to conserve'. The alternative movement in the field of mental health care in the Netherlands, even that which associated itself with 'antipsychiatry', was not modernistic; at least its alternatives were, without exception, anti-technological. They did not believe in doing things on a large scale, they did not hold system management dear, they resisted the desire of the mental health world to organise services following plans and calculation. This conservation-inspired vision was a characteristic of Dennendal from the beginning to the end. Dennendal was geared, first and foremost, to improving what was there, without judging improvement primarily in terms of social functioning and efficiency. The aim was not mastery over things, but people had a keen eye for what things meant to the people involved. Innovative in principle, but also concerned about social rationalisation being implemented too far and too quickly; open to experiment but also surprisingly anti-modernistic: in that fundamental philosophical viewpoint Carel Muller showed himself to be a typical pupil of the personalism of the Utrecht School.

Notes

1. See for an extended version of this article 'De slag om Dennendal. Een terugblik op de jaren vijftig vanuit de jaren zeventig', in Paul Luykx and Pim Slot (eds) (1997), *Een stille revolutie. Cultuur en mentaliteit in de lange jaren vijftig*, 45-65.

2. Andrew Jamison and Ron Eyerman, *Seeds of the Sixties* (Berkeley: University of California Press, 1994).

3. See Jan Bank, *Opkomst en ondergang van de Nederlandse Volksbeweging*, (Deventer: Kluwer, 1978).

4. Dutch personalism seems to bear striking resemblances with American postwar personalism. See James J. Farrell, *The Spirit of the Sixties. The Making of Postwar Radicalism* (New York: Routledge, 1997).

5. See Ido Weijers, *Terug naar het behouden huis. Romanschrijvers en wetenschappers in de jaren vijftig* (Amsterdam: Sua, 1991).

6. See Ido Weijers, 'De misdadiger. Toerekeningsvatbaarheid en behandeling', in Jeroen Jansz & Peter van Drunen (eds), *Met zachte hand: opkomst en verbreiding van het psychologisch perspectief* (Utrecht: Lemma, 1996), 187-204.

7. Erhard Blankenburg and Freek Bruinsma, *Dutch Legal Culture,*

(Deventer, Boston: Kluwer, 1994), 52.

8. See Frans Koenraadt, 'Forensic Mental Hospitals According to Dutch Standards', *Criminal Behaviour and Mental Health* (1993), 322-34.

9. See D. Downes, *Contrasts in Tolerance* (Oxford: Oxford University Press, 1988); Vincenzo Ruggiero, Mick Ryan and Joe Sim (eds), *Western European Penal Systems* (London: Sage, 1995); Christopher Harding et al (eds), *Criminal Justice in Europe* (Oxford: Clarendon Press, 1995).

10. James C. Kennedy, *Nieuw Babylon in aanbouw. Nederland in de jaren zestig* (Amsterdam: Boom, 1995), 145-6.

11. See Ido Weijers, 'Filosofie en Wederopbouw', *Krisis* (1990), 64-71.

12. James J. Farrell, *The Spirit of the Sixties*, 17.

13. See for instance Hans Righart and Piet de Rooy, 'In Holland staat een huis. Weerzin en vertedering over "de jaren vijftig"', in *Een stille revolutie*, 18.

14. Peter Clecak, *America's Quest for the Ideal Self. Dissent and Fulfillment in the 60s and 70s* (New York/Oxford: Oxford University Press, 1983).

15. This paragraph is a revision of articles that Evelien Tonkens and I have written for *Maandblad Geestelijke volksgezondheid* ('De actualiteit van Dennendal' (1994), 1111-1118) and for *Comenius* ('Een sterk plekbesef. Dennendal revisited' (1996), 185-198). The content of this part is based partly on an long interview we had with Carel Muller on 1 June 1995. Evelien Tonkens will publish her dissertation on Dennendal and the self development regime in 1998.

16. See Arend Jan Heerma van Voss, 'De voorbeeldige zwakzinnige. Over de alternatieve zwakzinnigenzorg van Carel Muller, Otto Haspers en Kay Okma', *De haas en de jager. Psychische stukken* (Amsterdam: Meulenhoff, 1993), 54-73.

17. These were the words of Barto Smit, a member of the Dennendal-staff, in Winnie Meyering et al., *Nieuw Dennendal. Een goede buurt gesloopt* (Baarn: In den Toren, 1975), 60.

18. See Annemieke Klijn, *Tussen caritas en psychiatrie. Lotgevallen van zwakzinnigen in Limburg 1879-1952* (Hilversum: Verloren, 1995).

19. See Evelien Tonkens and Ido Weijers, 'De geschiedenis van de zorg voor mensen met een verstandelijke handicap', in G.H. van Gemert & R.B. Minderaa (eds), *Zorg voor mensen met een verstandelijke handicap* (Assen: Van Gorcum, 1997), 15-32.

20. See B. Bouwens and J. Hoek, *Enkel den mensch ...Assisië, negentig jaren zorgen voor zorg* (Biezenmortel, 1994); P.A.T. Dickmann, *Maria Roepaan 1951-1986* (Ottersum, 1986); A.F. Manning, *Groesbeekse Tehuizen 1929-1989* (Zeist: Kerckebosch, 1989); and F.G. Kluit, *Herlevend verleden. Het verhaal van honderd jaar zorg van verstandelijk*

gehandicapte mensen op 's Heerenloo-Lozenoord 1891-1991 (Ermelo, 1991).

21. See P. Juffermans, *Staat en gezondheidszorg in Nederland* (Nijmegen: Sun, 1982).
22. See for instance Rozemarijn Esselink *et al.*, *Psychiatrische tegenbeweging in Nederland* (Amsterdam: Van Gennep, 1983), chapter 2.

10

Enemies Within:
Postwar Bethlem and the Maudsley Hospital

Keir Waddington

Apparently much is *known* about the Bethlem Royal Hospital and its alter-ego, Bedlam.[1] It can boast to being the oldest mental hospital in England, while the term 'Bedlam' has entered into common English usage. As the Hospital's archivist Patricia Allderidge explained in 1985: 'historians of psychiatry actually do not want to know about Bethlem as a historical fact because Bethlem as a reach-me down cliché is far more useful'.[2] The basic outlines of the Hospital's story are common currency in the history of psychiatry. Founded in 1247 as the Priory of St. Mary of Bethlehem by Simon fitzMary to provide hospitality for the Bishop of Bethlehem, Bethlem was first described as a hospice in 1329. From the early fifteenth century it had started to admit a small number of lunatics. Bethlem's function of housing the insane grew, surviving the Henrican reformation when the Hospital was refounded and attached to Bridewell, the House of Correction. It was a link that persisted until the creation of the National Health Service (NHS) in 1948 when Bethlem swapped its association with Bridewell for a 'partnership' with the London County Council's (LCC) young and energetic Maudsley Hospital.[3] From the mid-seventeenth to the early-nineteenth century Bethlem reached the apotheosis of its fame. Anyone interested in the history of psychiatry, and especially those influenced by the anti-psychiatry movement, *knows* that during the eighteenth century Bedlam was more than a metaphor for madness. It was one of the sights of London, allegedly admitting an estimated 96,000 visitors a year until 1770.[4] It is common knowledge that the staff were fraudulent and that the Governors were unaware of what was happening, incapable as they were of running the Hospital despite their best

intentions. Images are created of an institution that did not even to
pretend to care for its patients. Evidence from the 1815 Select
Committee on Madhouses has been used to show that Bethlem
represented the very worst in the treatment of the insane. In the
history of psychiatry, Bethlem has all too eagerly been shown as the
London twin of the Hôpital Général in Paris, the villain of the piece
in Foucault's *Madness and Civilisation*.[5] These *facts* have been
repeated so often that a historical image has been created of an
institution that has come to symbolise all that was mad and bad in
the management of the insane. This is all that has been needed to be
known about the Hospital at least until the revisionist view put
forward by Jonathan Andrews's thesis, 'Bedlam Revisited', and the
recently published *History of Bethlem*.[6]

Few histories of psychiatry take Bethlem's story beyond 1815 to
show that the Hospital became the subject of a further damaging
inquiry in 1851.[7] Neither do they mention that in Charles Hood,
the first resident physician superintendent, Bethlem found its John
Conolly, nor that from 1852 onwards the Hospital was transformed
into a semi-private institution for the educated middle classes in a
'presumably curable condition'.[8] So great was the transformation
that Vicki Hayward, a young probationary nurse working in the
Hospital in the late-1920s, could reflect that 'entering the wards was
rather like stepping into a hotel reception'.[9] In the first half of the
twentieth century, Bethlem had an environment that rivalled any
'first class hotel': a marked contrast to the conditions found in many
asylums, and on a par with private mental institutions like
Ticehurst.[10] When Bethlem moved to Monks Orchard, Beckenham
in 1930, these high standards were maintained in a new hospital
that was widely seen to be in the vanguard of mental hospital
design. While the Maudsley had to send its patients across the road
to King's College Hospital for x-rays, Bethlem used the most up-to-
date equipment.[11] Although the Hospital failed to promote research
and often spent too much in comparison on ferns and pianos, it did
acquire a pioneering spirit. It was one of the first psychiatric
institutions in England to admit patients on a voluntary basis over
forty years before the 1930 Mental Treatment Act encouraged this
category, while in the Hospital for Nervous Diseases Bethlem
provided one the first, albeit short-lived, psychiatric outpatient's
department in London.[12]

All this has been ignored. For historians, Bethlem in the
twentieth century does not seem worthy of interest.[13] Even the link
between the name Bedlam and the institution had begun to lose its

potency by the 1930s. While many may not be aware that Bethlem was 750 years old in 1997, they readily associate the term Bedlam with chaos or refer to the January sales as 'utter Bedlam'. Perhaps this is not surprising. Twentieth-century Bethlem tried to withdraw itself from the 'public eye'.[14] It might even be said that the Hospital no longer exists. The NHS saw Bethlem merging with the Maudsley to create a new institution, the 'Bethlem Royal Hospital and the Maudsley Hospital', locally known as the Joint Hospital. In 1991 the corporate name was changed to 'The Maudsley'. In many ways the merger marked a turning point in Bethlem's history. From 1948 onwards, Bethlem became part of a triumvirate, linked to the Maudsley and the Institute of Psychiatry, part of England's only psychiatric teaching hospital. Bethlem in effect was now finally incorporated into the psychiatric establishment. At the time, however, so many changes were taking place in the health service that the merger attracted little attention. Contemporaries did not seem to consider that the institution created out of the merger would have an important bearing on the development of postwar British psychiatry, given its role in the training of psychiatrists.

How had this situation come to exist? What was Bethlem's position in the new hospital, and how did it react to the changes facing postwar psychiatry? The story is one of institutional survival, where the provision of sherry and the size of the dairy herd became symbols of what the Hospital's Governors were trying to maintain. It is very much a story 'from above'. In the discussions surrounding the merger it was not considered important to consult the nurses, the patients, or their families. The staff emerge as a dissatisfied group only after the Joint Hospital had been established. Even for Bethlem's Governors the Joint Hospital was not the institution they had anticipated. At one level it was able successfully to adapt to the postwar developments in psychiatry and the NHS; on another problems existed. It is these aspects that this chapter addresses. It looks at the nature of the merger and its aftermath from Bethlem's perspective, leaving behind the usual story of Bethlem in order to analyse the period between 1944 and 1970.

Rebirth: The NHS and the Merger with the Maudsley

The history of the merger did not start with wartime debates on reconstruction in which plans for a national health service were central to the proposed collectivist welfare system. Initially the inclusion of mental hospitals within the new service was not envisaged, but even when this decision was reversed in the 1944

White Paper, Bethlem paid little attention.[15] The Hospital's Governors at first believed that the proposed legislation would not affect them, while county and borough asylums made no attempt to resist as they were already managed at a local authority level. Opposition to the NHS came from the voluntary hospital sector, of which Bethlem was on the margins. In 1944, Bethlem was far too preoccupied in repairing its extensive war damage after three German V-1 rockets had landed in the Hospital's grounds.[16] At the time, with some Governors suggesting that Bethlem might have to close given the extent of the repairs, returning the Hospital to normal seemed more important than any outside concerns. It was only in 1946, after most of the wards had been reopened, that the Governors began to alter their earlier assessment. Now any national health service was seen as a threat that would remove the Hospital's charitable status, appropriate its endowments, and replace the personal style of administration with anonymous control within a regional board. This was clearly intolerable. The Governors feared being placed on the same footing as the county and borough asylums, and a decision was made to resist the NHS.[17] Bethlem allied itself with the opinion expressed by the British Hospitals Association, which feared the 'mass murder of the hospitals'.[18]

There was still room for manoeuvre, however. After fresh negotiations, Aneurin Bevan, Labour's Minister of Health, held out an olive branch to win over the influential teaching hospitals.[19] In the final drafting of the 1946 National Health Service Act, provisions were included that allowed teaching hospitals a limited form of autonomy through the appointment of boards of governors with control over endowments.[20] No other type of hospital was offered these advantages and teaching hospitals were won over. At Bethlem, Bevan's concessions presented an opportunity for the Hospital to maintain its independence as since 1924 it had been a recognised school of the University of London. There was just one problem. In the postwar reorganisation of the University after the 1944 Goodenough Report, Bethlem's teaching status had been withdrawn.[21] This was the final recognition that the school had been unable to attract students since the mid-1930s given the Hospital's distance from London after its move to Beckenham. Students and lecturers had instead favoured the more dynamic school at the Maudsley, which had also been recognised in 1924 but offered better opportunities in terms of facilities, research, and jobs. Whereas Bethlem declined, the Maudsley rose under Edward Mapother and Aubrey Lewis who understood the importance of teaching and research.[22] It was therefore no surprise that the Goodenough Report felt that the Maudsley occupied 'a special place in psychiatric work'. With the University of London having to approve one postgraduate psychiatric teaching hospital, it chose the Maudsley, renaming the school the Institute of Psychiatry in 1948.[23] Stripped of its teaching status, Bethlem was in danger of being absorbed into the 'general health service of the country'. The Governors, however, wanted Bethlem to 'occupy a position commensurate with its dignity'. The only way that Gerald Coke, the confident and newly appointed treasurer, could see of securing this was to regain the Hospital's teaching status.[24] Bethlem therefore put aside its rivalry and wooed the Maudsley, negotiating a merger that it anticipated would at least secure a degree of independence within the NHS.

Historically it was not such a radical step. Bethlem had been linked to Bridewell since 1547, although from the mid-nineteenth century it had become the dominant partner. Similarities even existed between Bethlem and the Maudsley: both were small institutions aiming to treat early, recoverable patients on a voluntary basis. In 1946, Bethlem's Governors hoped to swap Bridewell for the Maudsley. They expected a repeat of its history in which the Hospital would end up the dominant partner. Sir Bracewell Smith, Lord Mayor of London, expressed the hopes behind the merger at Bethlem's 700th anniversary celebrations in 1947. He referred to 'a new era' and felt that in the new institution 'an entity' would be created that would 'be capable of leading the world in psychiatric teaching'.[25]

In May 1947 the Hospital's senior administrators presented the Governors with their proposal to merge with the Maudsley. Although Coke made a good show of consultation, promising that no move would be made before the NHS's appointed day in July 1948, the Governors were in reality presented with a *fait accompli*. The removal of the old administrative guard during the war (by death rather than by revolution) meant that such a 'partnership', as the Governors viewed it, was more acceptable. Seeing a way to save the Hospital, they conveniently forgot their previous antagonism to the Maudsley and wholeheartedly agreed.[26] This was a formal recognition of a situation that was gaining acceptance outside Bethlem. Aubrey Lewis and the Ministry of Health had already been approached by Coke before May. The aggressively sceptical Lewis was sympathetic from the start. During the war he had come to the conclusion that the Maudsley needed to establish links with other psychiatric institutions. At the time Lewis had been uncertain about which presented the best opportunities, but when he visited Bethlem in the spring of 1947 he felt that it had the most 'up-to-date buildings of any mental hospital...'.[27] Lewis was probably being more mercenary than Coke. Between 1940 and 1945 the Maudsley had been evacuated to Belmont Hospital, Surrey, and Mill Hill and on its return to Denmark Hill problems quickly emerged. Different practices had been followed at the two sites, dividing the staff between those interested in psychotherapy and those committed to physical treatment. Tensions developed. Many who had been at Belmont became dissatisfied with Lewis's style of management and vision for the Maudsley, and resigned.[28] The Maudsley, like many public asylums, was also experiencing 'major difficulties' after the war. Accommodation was cramped and urgent work was needed to modernise the Hospital.[29] With Lewis concerned to promote teaching and research and 'help his pupils in their careers', the merger offered a unique opportunity.[30] Bethlem promised 'the proper sort of surrounds for mentally sick people', a thoroughly modern hospital, and something more fundamental: the accumulated wealth of seven centuries and an annual endowed income of over £36,000.[31] Such a dowry left the Maudsley 'goggle-eyed' and reduced opposition . For Lewis, Bethlem was a financial prize with the merger representing access to much needed funds to stimulate research and teaching.[32] In 1979, Sir Denis Hill summed up the situation: 'The one, Royal Bethlem, was very old and very rich. The other, Maudsley, was very young and very poor'.[33] With the passing of the 1946 Act Bethlem needed the Maudsley's teaching status to survive on what it felt were its own terms; the Maudsley needed the accommodation and Bethlem's wealth to create the type of institution Lewis was striving for. It was to be a marriage of convenience.

Once Bethlem's Governors had made their decision, negotiations with the LCC were started.[34] In a wave of enthusiasm on Bethlem's part, a Joint Committee was formed but no attempt was made to consult the junior staff or nurses. Bethlem was under-represented from the start, but with Coke as the chair of the Joint Committee it was anticipated that the Hospital would take the lead in the new institution.[35] The Joint Committee quickly became the broker between Bethlem, the LCC and the Maudsley. It had the difficult task of merging 'two so very different hospitals, the one rich in history and tradition, well endowed, beautifully sited, the other thrusting, somewhat brash, poor and ugly'.[36] Problems over the new name were dealt with diplomatically, although much time was wasted discussing the size of the dairy herd.[37] Planning took just over a year and it was Lewis who took the prominent role in shaping the new institution. While the Joint Committee was making decisions about the structure and staffing of the Joint Hospital, co-operation started at an informal level. Staff from each hospital were seconded to the other and Bethlem was persuaded to use its funds to establish joint research projects.[38] Less co-operation existed at an administrative level and a certain sadness began to permeate Bethlem's management in the final days before the merger. At the last meeting of Bethlem's House Committee, the Governors noted that the Hospital had been run with 'efficiency and courtesy'.[39] The hope was that this would continue.

The NHS and the Joint Hospital came into existence on the same day in July 1948. To the marriage of the two hospitals, Bethlem 'brought the fine buildings at Monks Orchard and the accumulated wealth of centuries'; the Maudsley 'the revivifying influence of a virile teaching hospital of international reputation'.[40] There was considerable optimism for the future.

Enemies Outside?
Anti-Psychiatry, Anti-Institutionalism, and NHS Spending Cuts

The creation of the Joint Hospital coincided with a sense of optimism among its staff, who felt that wartime experiences and the NHS brought a new spirit to psychiatry. They were confident that 'mental hospitals everywhere are undergoing at the present time a stimulating and exhilarating experience – a rethinking of the patient's needs and a replanning of the ways in which these may best be satisfied'.[41] For the patients this meant a relaxation of Bethlem's authoritarian nursing regime and an extra hour in bed. Although insulated from NHS administrative reforms by the Hospitals' privileged teaching status and so able to maintain its distance, the Joint Hospital did not stubbornly adhere to old methods. The new institution did incorporate the ideas beginning to permeate psychiatry, taking note of what was happening at other institutions like Fulbourn or Belmont. However, the Joint Hospital did not embrace them wholeheartedly. Only gradually were doors unlocked, units mixed, and multidisciplinary therapeutic teams established. Here it was the Maudsley and the Institute of Psychiatry that took the lead in the Joint Hospital. Differences did emerge over the type of treatment that should be adopted: a battle was fought over the value of physical treatments in the 1950s. However, the Joint

Hospital was more successful at combining different approaches than the Maudsley had been immediately after the war, and perhaps better than many other mental hospitals in the postwar period. If anything, the Joint Hospital was able to adopt a multidisciplinary approach. Here a larger hospital split between two sites became an advantage. Friction obviously existed, but the Joint Hospital remained a broad church able to incorporate treatments ranging from psychotherapy to neurosurgery.

Against this the development of a British anti-psychiatry 'movement' around R. D. Laing, David Cooper, and the media attracted little attention in the Joint Hospital at a formal level.[42] Within the Joint Hospital's broad church the new approaches that anti-psychiatry stimulated existed side-by-side with the same biological methods that it came to attack. This helped defuse the need for out-right criticism. At the same time, those running the institution were more concerned with the problems presented by the NHS. The fears expressed by the anti-psychiatry movement were not those of the Board of Governors or its successors. Consequently, few references were made to anti-psychiatric ideas in the Hospitals' committees or internal publications. Whereas outside critics and elements within the psychiatric profession increasingly came to view mental hospitals as inappropriate locations for treatment, the Joint Hospital was more concerned with expansion. This may have been true of many British mental hospitals at an institutional level. They were preoccupied with the day-to-day business of caring for the mentally ill. At the same time as criticism was being voiced about psychiatry and the nature of the asylum, Bethlem was establishing new institutional services for psychogeriatric patients, adolescents, drug addicts, mentally disturbed children, and those judged criminally insane. Local opinion failed to mobilise against Bethlem. It was not until 1976 that the local community expressed anxiety about the Hospital, but this was in response to plans for a medium secure unit and not about the institution itself.[43]

Anti-psychiatric debates did obviously have some effect, however. The encouragement anti-psychiatry gave to non-institutional services was given expression within the Joint Hospital's multidisciplinary approach. In 1960 the chair of the Board of Governors could confidently comment that 'it was difficult to see how more could be done for the community'.[44] However, most of these projects were organised through the Maudsley's District Service Centre and had little significance for Bethlem. Attacks on different treatments also had a limited impact. Criticism of ECT led not to an abandonment of the treatment, but to revised views as to how it should be administered.[45] Even in the 1990s ECT continued to be used at Bethlem as an emergency measure or after other treatments had failed.

For those running the Joint Hospital, the position of mental hospitals within the NHS and the shift in emphasis away from the funding of institutional services created greater problems than any external criticism of psychiatry. Here the difficulty was money. The NHS proved considerably more expensive than anticipated. One contemporary felt that administrators were in an 'Alice-in-Wonderland position: run as hard as they might they were always overtaken by costs'.[46] Mental healthcare in particular represented an under-funded 'Cinderella' service. The Ministry of Health itself admitted that mental hospitals received 'a smaller portion than was reasonable' between 1948 and 1954.[47] Faced with a crisis in funding and accommodation, 'many mental health planners became enthusiastic about forms of therapy permitting [a] more rapid turn-over of patients'.[48] Enoch Powell's 1962 *Hospital Plan* called for a 45 per cent reduction in mental hospital beds and suggested that community care should replace expensive mental hospitals.[49] Increasingly funding began to work against the provision of institutional services.

National constraints on funding restricted the income available to the Joint Hospital. From 1954 onwards, the main management committee started to complain that 'the overall allocation of Exchequer money to the Health Service was not sufficient to meet ... demands by the various hospital authorities'.[50] The Governors, however, refused to yield to pressure from the Ministry of Health to reduce spending, restrict growth, or de-institutionalise in favour of cheaper community projects encouraged by the anti-psychiatry movement. Services were not cut but expanded, albeit at a slower rate than desired. To achieve this, economies were made, salaries were reduced, recruitment was restricted, and overspending became a regular feature of the Joint Hospital's finances. Here Bethlem proved its worth. Lewis's idea of using Bethlem's endowed income became a means through which the Joint Hospital could overcome the problems presented by financial restrictions. Legal niceties were put aside and endowments were used to fund 'any deficiencies arising from the reduction of the Exchequer allocation'.[51] While the Governors tried to attract as much capital funding as possible, they worked with the knowledge that Bethlem's endowments could be used. Major projects like the District Services Centre at the

Maudsley, the Community Centre at Bethlem, and the Institute of Psychiatry's new building were possible only because the Governors were prepared to use endowed income to supplement Exchequer funds. Increasingly the Joint Hospital found itself in a position where this was necessary but the financial difficulties facing the Hospital only became worse in the 1980s.

Bethlem as part of the Joint Hospital was an anomaly. While other mental hospitals closed wards or closed entirely, the Joint Hospital expanded. All was not plain sailing, however. If outside pressures could be resisted or circumvented, the merger created its own problems. Until the early 1970s, hostility between the two parts of the same institution was only barely concealed. This conflict created more difficulties than any criticisms from outside or funding restrictions.

Enemies Within: A Troubled Institution?

In a confidential report in 1949, the merger was seen as providing complementary not duplicate services.[52] According to the first House Governor, Kenneth Johnson, the two hospitals were 'gradually fused together, so that [by 1953] they were more like two wards of one hospital than separate entities'.[53] This was the official view, but animosity began to emerge from the beginning.

Whereas Bethlem's management structure had been the model for the new institution, from the start the Hospital was assigned an inferior position. This created hostility between the two parts of the Joint Hospital.[54] On Lewis's suggestion, Bethlem's physician-superintendent, John Hamilton, was sent to America to study psychiatric practices there. This gave Lewis more room for manoeuvre in the planning of the joint medical administration. With Hamilton temporarily removed, Lewis was able to ensure that the medical administration of the new hospital matched the Maudsley's needs and adopted the structure he had tried to develop at Denmark Hill since 1945.[55] The post of physician-superintendent was abolished and Bethlem was swamped by a large medical staff, dominated by the Maudsley. At one point it was even suggested that those doctors who worked at Monks Orchard should be excluded from the Medical Committee.[56] Changes were made quickly. Of Bethlem's old medical staff, only Hamilton remained. Duncan Whittaker, Bethlem's senior assistant physician, resigned in protest over the lack of opportunity for anyone from Bethlem in the Joint Hospital.[57] No member of the Maudsley's staff lost their post.

Lewis also secured changes to the type of the patient admitted and treatments offered at Bethlem. He persuaded the Joint Committee to transfer all 'early and recoverable' cases to the Maudsley. This left Bethlem to provide a home for psychotic children, senile patients, chronic schizophrenics, those needing long-term treatment, and those suffering from organic mental illness. When Lewis considered the treatments offered at Bethlem, he felt they were old-fashioned and consequently had the 'ultra-violet, douche and other installations' removed to make room for pathological and psychological research.[58] Bethlem did, in some respects, mix Victorian ideas on treatment with more modern methods and had a highly paternalistic attitude that did not match the tenor of the times. Lewis on the other hand was striving to advance the institution along what he felt was the most modern lines. The two ideas clashed at Bethlem's expense. In the process Lewis had 'a tremendous stand-up fight with Matron ... who was against the beautiful, recently private Bethlem being occupied by these nasty old people'.[59] He was equally opposed by Coke who felt that there was a need to bear in mind that owing to the more congenial surroundings at Monks Orchard the type of patient to be sent there should so far as possible be those who could appreciate and derive most benefit from their surroundings.[60]

Coke was trying to defend Bethlem's traditional character, but in both cases Lewis won. Bethlem gradually became established as 'the place which caters for all the difficult patients whom other places won't take', promoting anxiety and concerns about the level of violence.[61]

It was not only in the medical administration that Bethlem held an inferior position. Although it was Bethlem that had appointed Johnson as House Governor, he had been the executive officer of the LCC's mental health service and was more sympathetic to the Maudsley.[62] Johnson was suspicious of management by committee and believed in 'a committee of one, the one being myself'.[63] He was autocratic and some of his decisions earned him the hostility of the medical staff. Under Johnson, Bethlem's role in the administration was eroded. He delegated the task of running Monks Orchard to his academic but inept assistant. Within five months of the merger, Coke had resigned as chair partly because he was unhappy with the new arrangements.[64] His resignation further weakened Bethlem's position. In 1951, meetings were transferred from Bridewell's offices to the Guildhall and the secretarial work was moved to Denmark Hill.[65] In addition, Bethlem's secretary was encouraged to resign and his post was combined with that of the House Governor's.[66] By 1955 no member of Bethlem's former medical or governing body was on the Board, which was dominated by representatives from the LCC, Maudsley and the Institute of Psychiatry. The Joint Hospital had Bethlem's administrative structure, not its administrators.

These changes generated considerable anxiety and resentment at Bethlem, with the Maudsley being viewed as arrogant and domineering. One of the main areas of bitterness was the large amount that was spent on Denmark Hill. In the 1949/50 estimates of the £81,200 allocated for capital projects, only 10 per cent of this was to be spent on Bethlem.[67] The imbalance remained until the 1970s. It was only in 1961 that the first new building was approved for Bethlem, but work was delayed because funds were urgently needed to finish projects at the Maudsley.[68] In 1970, Leslie Paine, Johnson's successor, admitted that since 1948 most of the Joint Hospital's income had been spent on the Maudsley.[69] Bethlem's staff and former Governors recognised that the Maudsley was being improved out of Bethlem's endowments. Few were prepared to consider that Monks Orchard provided a physical environment superior to the Maudsley's and so needed less attention. Spending on Denmark Hill was vital to raise standards with wards, which were, even in the late-1960s, still seen as a disgrace. This was not how it appeared at Bethlem.

The hope in 1947 that Bethlem would dominate the new institution quickly faded. The Maudsley did not prove to be another Bridewell. Bethlem was not at first considered an important part of the Joint Hospital's teaching or research. It was widely seen as an 'appendage of the Maudsley'.[70] Communications between the two sites were poor and Bethlem was felt to be a long way from the Institute of Psychiatry, and so undesirable. At Monks Orchard doctors felt separated from the Joint Hospital, although many were later to recall that Bethlem was a much happier place to work. Doctors at the Maudsley regarded being sent to Monks Orchard as being placed in the 'B' stream and an indication that Lewis was losing interest in a registrar. Lewis rarely visited Bethlem and an apocryphal story has it that on one occasion when he did his ulcer reacted badly, making him severely ill and discouraging him from returning. Dissatisfaction was present at all levels. According to Felix Post 'there was an exodus of staff from Bethlem, which became short staffed', providing opportunities for Lewis's protégés.[71] Lewis also became frustrated. In 1949, he admitted that the merger had been 'incompletely realised'. He noted that the residue of 'pre-July staff at Bethlem fear change and are in a suspicious or reluctant mood'.

However, he did not question his role in creating this situation.[72] Others were equally dissatisfied, with some leading figures resigning.[73] Such an atmosphere was not conducive to development. By the 1960s, the Joint Hospital had become a 'multifactorial pluralistic community' that was 'morbidly introspective'.[74]

All Change!

The Governors were not oblivious to these problems, but with the Maudsley in the dominant position any attempt to improve the situation was slow to emerge. It was only in 1962, after fourteen years of conflict, that an effort was made to redress the balance between the two institutions. Johnson's retirement presented an opportunity for change and the Governors appointed Paine in his place. Paine's job was to enhance communications between the two sites and promote greater harmony. An early measure to improve the bus service between Denmark Hill and Monks Orchard was, in many ways, symbolic of the greater level of co-operation Paine was trying encourage.[75] In this he was aided by Lewis's retirement. Lewis's successor, Denis Hill, was more sympathetic to Bethlem and equally sought to develop services at Monks Orchard. No immediate solutions were found, but under Paine and Hill a new attitude developed and morale improved. Although Paine failed to promote the tripartite organisation he wanted, he did bring Bethlem and the Maudsley closer together. Gradually the view emerged that Bethlem had its 'own particular and different contribution' to make to the Joint Hospital.[76] By 1971, the Governors had realised that there was a 'need to consider future major developments at the joint hospital (i.e. including Bethlem) and not merely on the Maudsley Hospital site'.[77] Staff at Monks Orchard continued to complain into the 1980s that Bethlem was often neglected, but the problems that had greeted the first twenty years of the Joint Hospital began to decline as co-operation increased.

The situation was to change in the 1980s. A rhetoric of co-operation came to replace the co-operation that had existed, with many doctors blaming the management for further financial cuts in the NHS. The morale built-up under Paine quickly dissipated; tension developed. Bethlem as part of the Joint Hospital had weathered the problems confronting postwar psychiatry, but faced its own difficulties. With these largely solved, new external dangers presented themselves that encouraged a split between staff and management; not Bethlem and the Maudsley. However, now the problem was no longer a question of enemies within, but of enemies outside in the shape of NHS reforms and further spending restrictions.[78]

Notes

1. For a history of Bethlem see Jonathan Andrews *et al.*, *History of Bethlem* (London: Routledge, 1997).

2. Patricia Allderidge, 'Bedlam: Fact or Fantasy?', in W. F. Bynum, Roy Porter & Michael Shepherd (eds), *Anatomy of Madness*. 3 vols (London: Tavistock, 1985), ii, 17-33, p. 18.

3. For the origins and foundation of the Maudsley see Patricia Allderidge, 'The Foundation of the Maudsley Hospital', in German Berrios & Hugh Freeman (eds), *150 Years of British Psychiatry* (London: Gaskell, 1991), 79-88.

4. See for instance, Robert Youngson & Ian Scott, *Medical Blunders* (London: Robinson, 1995), 286.

5. See Michel Foucault, *Madness and Civilisation* (London: Tavistock, 1965).

6. Jonathan Andrews, 'Bedlam Revisited: A History of the Bethlem Hospital c.1634-1770' (Unpublished Ph.D. Thesis, University of London, 1991); Andrews *et al.*, *History of Bethlem*.

7. Edward G. O'Donoghue, Bethlem's quirky chaplain, was the first to write sympathetically about the Hospital. In his *The Story of Bethlem Hospital from its Foundation in 1247* (London: T. Fisher Unwin, 1914) he brought Bethlem's history up to 1914, believing that from 1852 the Hospital was advanced 'from the grub to the chrysalis' (p. 353). However, even O'Donoghue devoted most of his attention to the period before 1815. A recent study by David Russell, *Scenes from Bedlam* (London: Baillière Tindall, 1996) does look at the period after 1815, but Russell focuses on the nursing staff and patients, rather than on the administration or treatments.

8. Bethlem Hospital Archives and Museum (hereafter BRH Archive), Bethlem Royal Hospital, Monks Orchard Road, Beckenham: Bethlem Subcommittee, 9 October 1930.

9. BRH Archive, *Inter Nos*, January 1980, 4.

10. *London Argus*, 15 October 1904, 27-28; see Charlotte Mackenzie, *Psychiatry for the Rich: A History of Ticehurst Private Asylum 1792-1917* (London: Routledge, 1992).

11. BRH Archive, Aubrey Lewis Papers, Box 10: Letter to the director of the British Postgraduate Medical Federation, 11 November 1946.

12. For the 1930 Mental Treatment Act see Clive Unsworth, *The Politics of Mental Health Legislation* (Oxford: Clarendon, 1987). The

Hospital for Nervous Diseases opened in 1918 only to close in 1928 as part of Bethlem's move to Monks Orchard in 1930. The Governors argued that the reason for the decision was because the department was not admitting the type of early recoverable patients initially aimed for, but the need to save money for the new hospital played an important part.

13. A few general histories make some reference to Bethlem: Kathleen Jones, *Asylums and After: A Revised History of the Mental Health Service, From the Early Eighteenth Century to the 1990s* (London: Athlone Press, 1993), notes that the Hospital was rebuilt in 1930 (p. 138); Edward Shorter, *A History of Psychiatry: From the Era of the Asylum to the Age of Prozac* (New York; Chichester: John Wiley & Sons, 1996), shows the use of hyoscyamine at Bethlem in the 1930s as symptomatic of general attitudes (p. 198).

14. *Daily Telegraph*, 15 October 1920, 5.

15. For the development of the National Health Service see: Brian Abel Smith, *The Hospitals 1800-1948* (London: Heinemann, 1964); H. Eckstein, *The English Health Service: Its Origins, Structure and Achievements* (Cambridge, Mass.: Harvard University Press, 1958); D. Fox, *Health, Politics and Health Politics* (Princeton: Princeton University Press, 1986); F. Honigsbaum, *Health, Happiness and Security: The Creation of the National Health Service* (London: Routledge, 1989); J. E. Pater, *Making of the National Health Service* (London: Kings Fund, 1981); Charles Webster, *Problems of Health Care: The National Health Service Before 1957* (London: HMSO, 1988).

16. BRH Archive, Physician Superintendent's Report, 9 August 1944.

17. BRH Archive, House Committee, 10 April 1946.

18. Cited in Frank Prochaska, *Philanthropy and the Hospitals of London: The King's Fund, 1897-1990* (Oxford: Clarendon Press, 1992), 159.

19. Geoffrey Rivett, *Development of the London Hospital System* (London: Oxford University Press & Kings Fund, 1986), 266.

20. *Public Assistance Journal*, 20 February 1948, 123.

21. See Negley Harte, *University of London, 1836-1986* (London: Athlone Press, 1986), 242-3; Rivett, *op. cit.*, 257-60; 282-4.

22. For Mapother see Allderidge, 'The Foundation of the Maudsley Hospital', in Berrios & Freeman, *op. cit.*, 79-88; Aubrey Lewis, 'Edward Mapother and the Making of the Maudsley Hospital', *British Journal of Psychiatry*, 115 (1969), 1349-66. More has been written on Lewis, see Michael Shepherd, 'Professor Aubrey Lewis', in P. H. Hock & J. Zubin (eds), *Comparative Epidemiology of the Mental Disorders* (New York: Crome & Stratton, 1961), ix-xiv; *idem*, 'From

Social Medicine to Social Psychiatry' in Charles E. Rosenberg (ed.), *Healing and History* (New York: Dawson, 1979), 191-204; *idem, A Representative Psychiatrist* (Cambridge; New York: Cambridge University Press, 1986).

23. *1949-50 Institute of Psychiatry Annual Report*, 2; London County Council records, Greater London Record Office (hereafter LCC), LCC Mental Hospital Committee,16 March 1948, LCC/MIN/606.

24. BRH Archive, General Committee, 13 May 1947.

25. BRH Archive, Anniversary Papers: Letter from Hewitt to the Lord Mayor, 24 June 1947.

26. BRH Archive, General Committee, 13 May 1947.

27. BRH Archive, Aubrey Lewis Papers, Box 5: Future of the Maudsley; General Committee, 13 May 1947.

28. LCC, Maudsley Subcommittee Papers, LCC/MIN/1238.

29. BRH Archive, Aubrey Lewis Papers, Box 10: Letter to the director of the British Postgraduate Medical Federation, 11 November 1946.

30. Contemporary Medical Archive Centre (hereafter CMAC), Wellcome Institute, London. Foulkes Papers, PP/SHF/B.11: Letter from Taylor, 24 October 1949; BRH Archive, Aubrey Lewis Papers, Box 10: Letter from Michael Shepherd, 3 April 1978.

31. *Lancet*, ii (1947), 24; BRH Archive, Statement of Accounts and Balance Sheet, 1947.

32. William Sargant, *The Unquiet Mind* (London: Heinemann, 1967), 141.

33. BRH Archive, Denis Hill, 'Origins of the Joint Hospital' (Unpublished Paper, 1979), 1.

34. BRH Archive, Aubrey Lewis Papers, Box 12: Letter from Lewis to Coke, 22 May 1947.

35. *Ibid.*, Letter from Coke to Lewis, 23 June 1947.

36. *Bethlem & Maudsley Gazette*, September 1962, 290.

37. Hill, *op. cit.*, 3.

38. BRH Archive, Physician Superintendent Weekly Reports, 14 January 1948; House Committee, 12 August 1947.

39. BRH Archive, House Committee, 30 June 1948.

40. *Bethlem & Maudsley Gazette*, May 1953, 15.

41. *Croydon Advertiser*, 7 November 1958, 6.

42. See chapters in this volume, and Digby Tantam, 'The Anti-psychiatric Movement' in Berrios & Freeman, *op. cit.*, 333-47.

43. *See Beckenham Journal & Kentish Times*, 23 September 1976, 1.

44. *Nursing Times*, 28 October 1960, 1344-5.

45. BRH Archive, Board of Governors Presented Papers: 6 January 1969, Appendix F.

46. Cited in Pauline Gregg, *The Welfare State* (London: George Harrap, 1967), 189.
47. Webster, *op. cit.*, 338.
48. *Ibid.*, 340.
49. Brian Watkin, *National Health Service: The First Phase, 1948-1974 and After* (London: Allen & Unwin, 1978), 62-3.
50. BRH Archive, Finance & General Purposes Committee, 29 March 1954.
51. *Ibid.*, 22 June 1970.
52. BRH Archive, Aubrey Lewis Papers, Box 5.
53. *Bethlem & Maudsley Gazette*, May 1953, 15.
54. BRH Archive, Court of Governors, 24 June 1948.
55. BRH Archive, Joint Committee, 14 August 1947.
56. BRH Archive, Charles Blacker Papers: Letter from Nevin to Blacker, 7 July 1948.
57. BRH Archive, Joint Committee, 4 December 1947; *Bethlem & Maudsley Gazette*, December 1966, 17.
58. BRH Archive, Aubrey Lewis Papers: Circular Letter, 21 June 1948.
59. Greg Wilkinson (ed.), *Talking About Psychiatry* (London: Gaskell, 1993), 169.
60. BRH Archive, Board of Governors, 26 July 1948.
61. BRH Archive, Working Party on Forensic Unit at Bethlem, 8 November 1974.
62. BRH Archive, Court of Governors, 28 February 1948.
63. BRH Archive, Charles Blacker Papers: Letter from Johnson to Blacker, 8 March 1949.
64. BRH Archive, Board of Governors, 1 November 1948; 6 December 1948.
65. *Ibid.*, 21 May 1951.
66. BRH Archive, Finance & General Purposes Committee, 21 May 1951.
67. BRH Archive, 1950 Estimate of Expenditure and Income.
68. BRH Archive, Board of Governors, 6 February 1961.
69. BRH Archive, Finance & General Purposes Committee Presented Papers: 2 November 1970, Appendix D.
70. Sargant, *op. cit.*, 141.
71. Wilkinson, *op. cit.*, 166.
72. BRH Archive, Aubrey Lewis Papers, Box 5: Confidential Memorandum, *c.* 1949.
73. William Sargant opposed Lewis's conception of the new hospital, wanting the Maudsley to mirror the more porous model of the West End Hospital for Nervous Diseases, Queen's Square. In 1949 he

resigned partly ostensibly over the new regulations controlling part-time appointments: See Sargant Papers, CMAC, PP/WWS/B.1/1.

74. *Bethlem & Maudsley Gazette*, June 1963, 54.
75. BRH Archive, Board of Governors Presented Papers: 5 July 1971, Appendix J/1.
76. *Bethlem & Maudsley Gazette*, Winter 1969, 2.
77. BRH Archive, Finance & General Purposes Committee Presented Papers: 20 September 1971, Appendix K.
78. See J. Mohan, *A National Health Service? Restructuring of Health Care in Britain Since 1979* (London: Macmillan, 1995).

Well done; The prediction of "Prince John" at the trial of Freeman N Y State 1843 re that psychiatrists as definers of mental illness (insanity) would, if accepted by society + the Courts would place them in the position of controlling life in American society.

11

The Changing Professional Identity of the Dutch Psychiatrist 1960–1997

a good summary

Harry Oosterhuis and Saskia Wolters[1]

From the second half of the nineteenth century on, the professional identity of psychiatrists in the Netherlands has been determined first and foremost by their status as physician. Because of their shared medical training, physicians and psychiatrists have always belonged to the same professional group. Today, however, Dutch psychiatrists tend to consider themselves no longer primarily as medical doctors. Last year the Dutch Association for Psychiatry issued a new professional profile in which the psychiatrist is described as a "bio-psycho-social generalist" in the area of mental health care. This new conception of professional identity – which is not undisputed – did not emerge out of the blue but is a result of substantial changes in the field of mental health care since the 1960s, including the growing input of other professional groups (such as psychologists, social workers, psychiatric nurses), the increased involvement of patients, and the broadening of the psychiatric domain outside of the confines of the hospital or institution.

Between the 1960s and the 1990s, psychiatry in the Netherlands suffered from an identity crisis. Major concerns about the relationship between neurology and psychiatry, the psychiatrist's professional training, and, more generally, the scientific character of psychiatry were raised continually. In this article, we will try to determine how since 1960 the cognitive orientation and the professional interests of Dutch psychiatry began to change and what role was played by the relevant professional organizations and by developments in Dutch mental health care at large. We will focus our discussion on the professional organization of psychiatrists, the relationship between neurology and psychiatry, and the growing significance of ambulatory mental health care, psychotherapy in particular.

The Professional Organization of Psychiatry

In contrast with the United States and England, where neurologists and psychiatrists parted ways early on, in the Netherlands these two medical specialists were represented by one professional organization, the Dutch Association for Psychiatry and Neurology (NVPN), for a long time, from 1895 to 1974.[2] In its early days, the NVPN focused much of its energy on scientific explanations for mental disorders. Although psychological approaches gained ground in Dutch psychiatry before the Second World War, mainly under the influence of psychoanalysis and phenomenology, it was in the brain and the central nervous system that the causes for mental illness were primarily sought. The handful of psychiatrists that were active in the Netherlands at the beginning of this century were also practicing neurologists and by and large they embraced a medical-scientific approach. In 1930, the umbrella organization of the Dutch medical world, the Royal Dutch Society for the Advancement of Medicine (KNMG) began listing medical specialists. Until 1972, it listed the combined field of neurological and mental illness as one specialty. Whether prospective specialists chose either neurology or psychiatry as their main field, in both cases they would be registered as "nerve specialist" and they were qualified to be active on each other's field of expertise. Up until 1984 neurology was a substantial and mandatory part of the Dutch psychiatrist's basic training.

The early 1960s marks the beginning of the official division between neurologists and psychiatrists in terms of their professional organization. In 1962 the NVPN created separate sections for neurology and psychiatry,[3] but this could not prevent the Association's ultimate demise: in 1974 it was split into the Dutch Association for Psychiatry (NVvP) and the Dutch Association for Neurology (NVvN).[4] Over the years, members of both sections had witnessed the two disciplines drift apart and it was widely considered desirable that psychiatrists and neurologists follow their own independent course with regard to professional training, scientific future, and the internal differentiation of their respective fields. In the years to follow, psychiatry evolved into a much more diversified, multidisciplinary field, partly as a result of the growth of a public, non-institutional mental health care system, whereas neurologists became more closely associated with a strictly scientific orientation. Their exclusively medical specialization had little to expect from the multicausal approach that was gaining ground in psychiatry.[5]

Although the division was regretted by some, especially when in the 1970s significant progress was made in the biological and neurological research of mental disorders, most psychiatrists considered the separation a step forward; having their own organization gave them something they seriously needed – more of a sense of professional identity. They felt they hardly benefited from neuropathology and some believed that psychiatry would be unable to develop into a separate discipline if a proportionally small group of neurologists continued to have a say in, for instance, basic psychiatric training requirements. The professional identity of the psychiatrist was changing as a result of the widening of his role in mental health care, which itself was a burgeoning field with a host of non-medical professionals playing an increasingly larger part. The new NVvP sought to extend its reach and lift psychiatry out of its strictly medical constellation by opening the Association to members of other professional communities who qualified as associate member because of their training or involvement in the area of mental health. Other medical specialists, physicians without one particular speciality, or those still in training but somehow connected to the field could now become a member of the Association as well. It was clear that the NVvP presented itself no longer exclusively as a medical organization of specialists, but as a broad interest group of people involved in mental health care. However, psychiatrists held the upper hand as far as their training and their interests as physicians were concerned.

The Training of Psychiatrists and the Relationship between Psychiatry and Neurology

From the 1950s on, the growing gap between neurology and psychiatry became noticeable in particular in the discussions about substantial changes in both content and length of the basic training period for psychiatrists. Although psychiatry as a medical specialty was already taught by 1896, only in 1930 the KNMG established a Specialists Registration Commission which decided that a "nerve specialist" should go through a training period of three years.[6] This period was extended with one year in 1950: two and a half years psychiatry and one year and a half of neurology for those who chose psychiatry as their main field, and the reverse for those with neurology as main field. By 1956 it also became mandatory that those who wanted to be psychiatrists work six months in an institution as part of their training.

To advise the NVPN on educating psychiatrists and neurologists, the KNMG established the "Consilium Neuro-psychiatricum" in

1958. Four years later, when the NVPN took the initiative to set up separate sections for psychiatrists and neurologists, this committee proposed to have separate training curricula as well, so as to provide more space for specialized education. It was suggested that the two and a half years of specialized training for Dutch neurologists and psychiatrists was far less than that of such specialists elsewhere. In 1964, therefore, the training period was again extended with one year, so that now psychiatrists and neurologists received a total of five years of education, of which three and a half years in their respective main fields. To educate psychiatrists, a broad basic approach was adopted. In addition to two years of clinical and polyclinical psychiatry, during which the candidate was familiarized with fields and techniques like clinical psychology, electroencephalography,[7] psychotherapy, and psychiatric research, it was also required to do six months of institutional psychiatry, six months social psychiatry, and six months child psychiatry.[8]

This new training curriculum, however, elicited various objections from both neurologists and psychiatrists. Although the two fields had increasingly grown apart during the 1950s and 1960s and although most 'nerve specialists' tended to be heavily specialized in either psychiatry or neurology (so that it made more sense to be certified as one or the other), the idea of the combined specialty was formally held up after all.[9] Neurologists continued to focus their attention on curing somatic disorders of the nervous system, wheras psychiatrists increasingly devoted their attention to neurotically and socially disabled patients for whom psychotherapeutic treatment seemed more appropriate than any strictly medical treatment. In this light, it is relevant that at the 1967 Spring Meeting of the NVPN, the Amsterdam professor and psychoanalist P.C. Kuiper argued in favor of a multicausal approach in psychiatry as opposed to the one-sided neurological focus on somatic medicine. Psychiatry should be concerned with somatic, psychological, and social aspects of mental disorders. 'In daily practice the double specialty has become a nuisance,' he argued, saying that it was no longer possible for anyone to have an overall view of the two specialties, let alone cover them. 'Neurology and psychiatry will only have a bright future as independent specialties.'[10] Kuiper felt that neurology obstructed the evolution of psychiatry toward an integral 'bio-psycho-social' discipline and that the required one year and a half of neurological training was hardly useful to a psychiatrist. A future social psychiatrist or psychotherapist would hardly ever benefit from having solid neurological knowledge.

Other objections against the new training curriculum for

psychiatry involved its proposed length of five years and its far-reaching differentiation: the various mandatory internships would result in dissipation of energy.[11] Furthermore, a practical issue was that the required portion of neurology caused long delays and waiting periods because there were few internships (or residencies) available. Finally, it was seen as a problem that the new proposal left no space for choice or individual emphasis.

The ensuing debate ultimately caused the introduction of the registration of neurology and psychiatry as separate specialties in 1972. This meant the end of the double specialty, as neurologists and psychiatrists were now no longer licensed to practice each other's field of expertise.[12] Based on EEC guidelines, psychiatric training was again limited to four years, one year of which was to be devoted to neurology. During the two-year basic training program a wide variety of aspects of psychiatry were addressed: the biological, neurological, psychological, and social dimension of psychiatric syndromes; social and non-institutional psychiatry; child psychiatry; clinical psychology; geriatric psychiatry; psychopharmacology; and various forms of psychotherapy. Mandatory internships were abolished and opportunities for individual choice were enlarged; the prospective psychiatrist would complete his training by doing one year of internships as desired.

During the second half of the 1970s, however, the precise content of psychiatric training was questioned once again, especially the relevance of the one year of neurology training. After it was proposed repeatedly that the mandatory year of neurology be replaced with a year of a more general somatic internship, Professors M. Romme and M. Richartz of the University of Maastricht proposed to devote more attention to issues of biological psychiatry instead of neurology.[13] They argued that 'biological psychiatry encompasses much more than just the diagnosis and treatment of organic (neurological) disorders in psychiatric patients.' They even worried that holding on to the mandatory neurology internship, rather than be an incentive, would pose an obstacle to Dutch clinical psychiatry in its attempt to garner more awareness of biological and somatic aspects in psychiatric patients.[14]

There were other Dutch psychiatrists who shared the views of Romme and Richartz. During the mid-seventies a number of them criticized the existing psychiatric training program in the leading Dutch journal for psychiatry, the *Tijdschrift voor Psychiatrie*.[15] Although there were differences of opinion on the exact content of psychiatric training, there was agreement on the impossibility of designing one all-embracing program. Psychiatry was seen as a specialty that is at once broad and general as well as narrow and specific. It should be desirable, therefore, to complement a more general basic training period with a period of specialization in one specific area of psychiatry.

In 1981, the discussion caused the NVvP to adopt new basic training standards. The new four-year program consisted of a two-year basic training period in clinical and polyclinical psychiatry, one year of residency (with a choice of either social psychiatry, child psychiatry, psychotherapy, or institutional psychiatry), and one year of neurology. If a candidate were to fail to succeed in finding an opening for his residency in neurology (these were scarce and there were long waiting periods), he was allowed to seek out another training option, preferably in internal medicine or child psychiatry, if, at least, he satisfied all requirements and asked for advance permission from the Specialists Registration Commission.[16]

This new curriculum included many of the suggestions of Romme, Richartz, and others, and it was clearly an attempt to bring a more integral approach to psychiatric training. In addition to a general clinical-psychiatric education, the candidate had to devote at least two hundred hours to psychotherapy, eighty hours to biological psychiatry, and forty hours to social psychiatry. There was also more freedom of choice. But one of the major complaints of previous decennia, the neurology requirement, was still not yet fully met. Although the amount of neurology as part of psychiatric training had gradually been reduced over the years, only in 1983 it was finally decided to abolish it as a mandatory part of the curriculum. The reasons for this, though, turned out to be practical rather than ideological: there was a great shortage of training opportunities in the neurology departments of the various Dutch general hospitals. When speculating on the reasons why a majority of the membership of the NVvP has hold on to neurology as part of psychiatric training for so long, it is probably associated with the concern for the medical status of their field. Despite the growing attention for psycho-social approaches, they held on to their professional identity as medical specialist. The board of the NVvP emphasized in 1982 that the medical character of the overall psychiatric training program had to be guarded. After the mandatory neurology segment was abolished, required training in somatic pathology was added to the basic standards[17]. Moreover, starting in 1984, the psychiatric training program was extended with six months, to include a mandatory segment of social psychiatry. The program now consisted of three years of clinical and polyclinical psychiatry (the so-called basic training period), six months of social psychiatry, and one year of various internships.[18]

In addition to the role of neurology in psychiatric training, one of the major issues that kept returning over the years was the question of a general versus a diversified training approach. During the 1960s most psychiatrists favored a generalist approach, as became clear in the training requirements of 1964 and 1972. By the end of the 1970s, however, there was a greater demand for specialized psychiatrists and there was a plea for more differentiation and individual choice within the psychiatric training program. However, this was not expressed in the 1981 training requirements. Even when the neurology segment was done away with, there was still little space for diversity. To this day, Dutch psychiatric training is basically generalist, with for the advanced candidate some opportunities to focus on developing sub-specialties while still in training.

Ambulatory Mental Health Care and Psychotherapy

The debates on the relationship between psychiatry and neurology and on the proper training of psychiatrists are best understood against the backdrop of developments in mental health care in the Netherlands, notably the growth of non-institutional, ambulatory care after 1945 and that of psychotherapy after 1960.

In the years following the Second World War, psychiatrists increasingly found themselves employed outside of the mental institution. Psychiatry not only became more integrated into general hospitals but psychiatrists also more and more focused on providing ambulatory mental health care. The Dutch mental health care system, which is basically government subsidized, developed an extensive psychiatric network that existed independently from mental institutions and hospitals. The ambulatory mental health care system, characterized by a mixture of preventive and curative medicine and by a multidisciplinary approach, evolved out of various, largely private and religious organizations which over time merged into one care system. In 1982, this process toward the integration and regionalization of the existing clinical and ambulatory facilities was completed with the establishment of so-called RIAGG centers, local or regional facilities for out-patient mental health care. In addition to these RIAGG centers, independent psychiatric practitioners and psychiatric polyclinics continued to provide similar services.[19]

The Dutch ambulatory mental health care system consists of a heterogeneous group of practitioners and facilities that offer a variety of approaches and methods of treatment. The roots of this situation go back to the 1920s and 1930s when many preventive and postcare services were set up, for example, the Social Psychiatric Services (SPD), aimed at the medical and social support of psychiatric patients who for various reasons were no longer or not yet eligible for admittance into hospital. The Medical Counselling Bureau (MOB), founded in 1928, was geared toward behavioral disorders and psychiatric problems of children. During the 1930s and 1940s, a number of facilities for adults were established, such as the Centers for Life and Family Issues (LGV) and the Catholic Bureaus for Marriage Counselling. The Institute for Medical Psychotherapy (IMP), founded in 1940, was initially aimed at providing short-term psychotherapeutic help to adults who suffered from war traumas. After the Second World War, psychotherapy gradually became available to the population at large, culminating in the 1970s in what has been called 'the marketplace of well-being and happiness,' where an army of psychotherapists is always ready to offer a wide variety of customized care.

The development of a broad network of ambulatory mental care facilities in the Netherlands went hand in hand with the rise of social, out-patient psychiatry, but it was also greatly stimulated by the pillarized political structure of Dutch society and by the influence of the Mental Health Movement that originated in the United States. Although the Dutch Association for Mental Health Care was established (in 1930) on a general, non-ideological basis, it was mainly the various confessional organizations (e.g. Catholic, Protestant, Reformed) that were responsible for providing the actual care. These organizations were also the first to combine their forces in the area of mental health care. The serious concern for the social devastation that resulted from the occupation and the liberation greatly enhanced the growth of out-patient mental health care in the post-war period. New areas of attention included the care for derailed youngsters, the recuperation of disrupted families, and the treatment of war victims. Influenced by the Mental Health Movement, the ambulatory mental health care organizations not only counted the prevention and curing of mental disorders and deviant behavior among their tasks, but they also considered it their role to improve the mental health of the population at large.

The organizations for mental health care not only directed their efforts at curing psychological disorders such as neuroses but also at various psycho-social problems in the realms of marriage, family, raising children, education, sexuality, labour, crime, and drug or alcohol addiction. The conviction that in many of these areas the medical, clinical-nosological model fell short caused a number of psychiatrists to argue in favour of a multidisciplinary and multicausal approach in psychiatry.[20] Influenced by phenomenology, the social sciences, and the growing importance of social work, they arrived at the view that humans are more than isolated subjects and that a patient's profile was not only determined by organic or psychological factors but also by aspects of his or her social context. In addition to the dominant institutional psychiatric model, the medical-somatic one, a more psychological and sociological approach of mental disorders gained ground. In a psycho-social approach, for example, mental problems were linked to drives and motives or the patient's social environment, whereas remedies were sought in psychological or behavioral therapies.

The rise of social-psychiatric approaches during the 1960s was acompanied by a growing attention for the psychotherapeutical aspects of psychiatry. Because there was an increasing demand for psychotherapy, the various forms of therapy shifted from the periphery to the center of mental health care in the Netherlands.[21] Personal growth and the unfolding of individual talents became more highly valued in Dutch society – which had become more affluent – and this new ideology contributed to the trend that relatively healthy people with some deficiency in their personality structure or development became an object of psychotherapeutic care. New institutes for psychotherapy were established in several Dutch cities during the 1960s and the number of clients could rise quickly because psychotherapy was covered for those on social security (from 1965 to 1976) or those receiving disablement benefits (from 1976 to 1980).[22]

The issue of psychotherapeutic competence was an important subject at meetings of the NVvP during the seventies. Psychiatrists had always been qualified to practice psychotherapy, even though it was never a specific area of attention in their training, nor was their therapeutic competence ever specifically tested.[23] During the mid-sixties, however, their monopoly came under attack. In 1966, the Dutch Society for Psychotherapy (NVP) decided to admit not only psychiatrists but also physicians and psychologists[24] as members. This meant that they could be trained as psychotherapists at an Institute for Multidisciplinary (formerly: Medical) Psychotherapy (IMP). As a consequence, it was no longer the sole right of psychiatrists, based on their medical training, to perform psychotherapy.

In the 1970s there was a confrontation between two groups that practised psychotherapy: those who were employed by the IMP (mainly psychiatrists and psychologists) and a group of independently established psychiatrists. The discussion converged around the issue whether psychotherapy was exclusively a medical-psychiatric discipline or a separate field of expertise, entirely independent from psychiatry. Psychiatrists who had their own practice tried to challenge the competition of other professional groups by arguing that only a medical specialist is capable of deciding what therapy is appropriate and then apply it. But the IMP therapists suggested that psychiatrists who had not been specifically trained as psychotherapists had no advantage whatsoever over therapists without medical training and that psychotherapy was most likely to be successful if an interdisciplinary teamwork approach was adopted. They argued that clinical psychologists were in fact better qualified than psychiatrists. The non-medical psychotherapists won their first victory in 1973 when a Government Commission on the Medical Profession (the De Vreeze-Commission), whose assignment it was to prepare new legislation for medical practice, asserted the right to apply therapy to psychiatrists as well as to therapists with no medical training.[25] Psychotherapeutical expertise was not necessarily identical with medical-psychiatric expertise.

Initially, the NVvP remained silent on the issue. It counted both IMP therapists and independent psychiatrists among its members, so it was difficult to express a univocal point of view. Moreover, the psychiatrists themselves were divided on the issue. Displeased with the entire situation, some of the independently established psychiatrists founded the Association of Dutch Psychiatrists (VNP) in 1977. The VNP considered psychotherapy to be an exclusively medical form of treatment.[26] One year later the NVvP made its view public in a discussion paper entitled 'Psychotherapy and Psychotherapist'. Although it claimed that psychotherapy was a medical treatment and that psychiatrists were qualified to practice it because of their medical training, it was also put forward that psychiatrists needed more psychotherapeutic training and that cooperation in multidisciplinary teams was an important step forward. The Consilium Psychiatricum subsequently suggested that five per cent of psychiatric training should be specifically reserved for training in psychotherapy, a proposal which became effective in 1981.[27]

Meanwhile, the government had become a player in the discussion – which, by then, was a heated one – about the fees, funding, and training standards of psychotherapy and about its demarcation from other forms of psycho-social services. In 1977, the General Director of Public Health set up a special study group for psychotherapy (the Verhagen Commission I). Like the De Vreeze-Commission, this commission viewed psychotherapy as a specialty that could also be practised by those without medical training, if at least they satisfied certain prescribed training requirements. Therapeutic expertise could be acquired by following a specifically designed training for which a background in various disciplines was allowed to serve as basis.[28] In addition to medicine (preferably psychiatry), two other preparatory studies were singled out as appropriate basic training: a degree in one of the behavioral sciences (preferably clinical psychology) or specific advanced training in the theory and practice of social work.[29] The training of psychotherapists had to consist of a general part, a specialization, and an internship at one of the psychotherapeutic institutes. The outcome of the government's involvement is that psychotherapeutic expertise was not seen as restricted to one professional group or one discipline. Although psychiatrists were forced to give up their monopoly and accept psychologists and social workers as their equals, the NVvP could still agree with the final report of the Verhagen Commission I. It made it possible for psychiatrists to reformulate the conditions of their training in such a way that they became officially qualified to perform psychotherapy.[30]

The Identity Crisis of the Dutch Psychiatrist

The discussions about the content of psychiatric training, the scientific character of psychiatry, and the proper qualifications for psychotherapy are signs of the sketchy professional profile of psychiatry. It is part of a more general dilemma that psychiatrists have had to face for a long time. There are several reasons why the professional identity of the psychiatrist has never been self-evident. First, from the nineteenth century various sciences and practices have contributed to the development of modern psychiatry; the delineation from other disciplines, such as medicine/neurology and (clinical) psychology but also philosophical anthropology, law, and criminology, has therefore been subject to debate and susceptible to fluctuation. Second, psychiatry is difficult to define as a science because its object and the objectives of the psychiatrist are not fixed. Contents, meanings, and names of psychiatric disorders have changed regularly. What counts as mental illness is largely a matter of definition and interpretation. While psychiatrists of the nineteenth century were preoccupied primarily with what was called 'madness' (meaning unpredictable and dangerous behaviour) and neurological disorders like epilepsy, dementia, and serious mental disorders like psychosis, the object of psychiatry in this century was extended to include various forms of maladjusted or non-conformist behavior, various psychological and neurotic symptoms, developmental disorders, disturbed relations and emotions, identity problems, existential problems, questions of life's meaningfulness, and the (dys)functioning of groups of people (within families, in the army, at school, at work). From the 1950s on, in the context of ambulatory mental health care, psychiatrists have been engaged not only in curing symptoms but also in the prevention of psychiatric disorders and the improvement of the general population's mental health.

This extension of the professional psychiatric domain caused an increase in the number of professional roles. Whereas at the beginning of the century the psychiatrist's professional horizon was limited to the confines of the mental institution, the university, and the independent practice, during this century psychiatrists found work in psychiatric clinics of general hospitals, in social and forensic psychiatry, in various non-institutional mental health care facilities, the army, the rehabilitation of prisoners, education, the care for drug and alcohol addicts, and in various managerial positions. The extension and differentiation of their professional roles contributed to changes in psychiatry's treatment practices and scientific concerns. If before 1900 psychiatry was largely geared toward the locking up and safeguarding of people (the asylum function), after the turn of the century psychiatrists were increasingly involved in evaluation (diagnosis and classification), treatment (including medical and pharmacological interventions and therapeutical manipulation), and the general support of patients.[31]

In terms of the explanation and treatment of psychiatric disorders, there was – and is – hardly any dominant paradigm or fixed cognitive basis in psychiatry. The world of psychiatry has been characterized by pluralism: diverging models, theories, and therapies replace each other or exist side by side. They are either philosophical-anthropological,[32] medical-scientific, psychological, social, or some combination of the last three mentioned. Since the second half of the nineteenth century, psychiatrists have relied on a scientific-medical basis, yet at the same time the scientific status of psychiatry – just like its medical basis – has never been undisputed. The early history of psychiatry shows that this medical emphasis is partly derived from a distinction between the psychological and the somatic. During the first part of the nineteenth century, the

214

pioneers of institutional psychiatry applied therapies having a moral and psychological basis (the 'traitement morale') rather than adopting a strictly medical treatment. From the beginning, psychiatry has been stuck with this duality, this pendulum of somatogenic and psychogenic approaches. On the one hand, psychiatry leans heavily on the model of scientific medicine in which (subjective) complaints are transformed into objective symptoms of an underlying somatic pathological process, thus excluding the psychological experience of the patient. On the other hand, psychiatric practice is geared toward actual psychological phenomena and realities, relying on an individual, hermeneutical, and normative approach.[33] Furthermore, the medical dimension of a psychiatrist's profession loses validity as soon as psychiatrists involve themselves with problems that have a social, ethical, or political basis. In recent years, psychiatrists have become more deeply involved in social-political or ethical issues, such as abortion, labour conditions and the medical examination of employees, drug addiction, sexual abuse, and euthanasia and assisted suicide.

Especially during the 1960s and 1970s, there was great confusion about the professional profile of the psychiatrist. At least three reasons for this uncertainty can be identified. First, the legitimacy of psychiatry as a medical science was questioned by the outside world as well as by some critical psychiatrists. People involved in social sciences, the antipsychiatry movement, and the client movement were extremely critical of institutional psychiatry in particular, because of its dominant medical regime involving forced institutionalization, stigmatizing, hospitalization, and 'inhuman' methods of treatment like electroshock and psychopharmaceuticals.[34]

Secondly, the social and behavioral sciences began to play an increasingly larger part in mental health care which broke down the psychiatrist's monopoly in this area as well as his sense of professional autonomy and expertise. Treatment of patients was increasingly coordinated by multidisciplinary teams that were horizontally and democratically structured and in which the psychiatrist was just one expert among others.[35] Psychiatrists responded to this new situation by exchanging their medical image with a more psycho-social one and by broadening their own field of expertise, making it more an integral – that is, a biological and psycho-social – specialty.[36] But in their cooperation with the other professional groups they reserved a central, leading, or managerial role for themselves, which in turn provoked the others to argue that the role of the psychiatrist as physician should only be limited.[37] A potential leadership role of the psychiatrist in the new democratically organized and multidisciplinary structure was not at all self-evident to the other parties involved.

Third, the rapid development of ambulatory mental health care obfuscated the borders of the psychiatric domain. The increase in the number of approaches and methods of treatment made psychiatry quite a versatile field, less medical and more psycho-social and psychotherapeutical. The internal contradictions of psychiatry as a profession came to light right after the split between neurology and psychiatry. During the seventies, for instance, there was clearly a polarization between the medical-biological and the psycho-social approach in psychiatry, while a conflict of interest between psychiatrists who performed psychotherapy in private practices and those psychiatrists who worked in IMP's in multidisciplinary teams became visible as well.

Revisionist historians and sociologists have often depicted psychiatrists as powerful agents of social control who successfully expanded their professional domain. However, we observe that especially from the 1960s psychiatrists have had difficulties in convincing other professional groups and the public that as physicians, they had an exclusive and scientific insight in the nature of mental disorders. To this day, the absence of a sharply delineated professional profile constitutes a dilemma for psychiatrists. Their medical status was always largely derived from the close ties with neurology but these were severed in the early 1970s.[38]

Psychiatrists continue to struggle with two uncertainties: How is their specialty related to, on the one hand, medical science, and the social and behavioral sciences on the other? And what is their relationship to members of the various other professional groups in mental health care? In the early 1980s, the NVvP held a survey among the over twelve hundred psychiatrists that were then active in the Netherlands about their professional role; the results showed that substantial competition was felt from other professional groups and that psychiatrists thought they were quite dependent on government policies.[39] Many psychiatrists believe that their influence has diminished over the years. Their professional association, the NVvP, is often trailing new professional and political trends, rather then setting the agenda, and tends to be quite cautious and conservative in an attempt to reconcile the sometimes conflicting views within its membership. The major innovations in psychiatry of the last twenty-five years – the growing significance of empirical research, the application of psychopharmaceuticals, and the increased awareness and rights of patients – were not the result of initiatives from within psychiatry but they were pushed by outside forces, including other professional groups (psychiatric nurses, empirical psychologists, pharmacologists, and biomedics), the client movement, and the government.[40]

The professional differentiation and bureaucratization of the mental health care system has strongly challenged psychiatrists – as represented in various organizations, commissions, and study groups – to develop a better and less ambiguous sense of their professional identity. In 1993, the NVvP established a special committee aimed at formulating a clear picture of the role of the psychiatrist in mental health care. The committee determined the knowledge and skills a psychiatrist should have and set the terms for cooperation with the other professional groups involved in mental care. Psychiatry was defined as a medical specialty concerned with 'mental illness' that uses a 'clinical-descriptive' method of diagnosis.[41] However, at the same time the committee distanced itself from this basic view by emphasizing that psychiatry is not only concerned with somatic aspects of mental illness but also with the psychological and social aspects and that psychiatry should embrace a multidimensional approach. As a generalist with medical, pharmacological, and psycho-social expertise, the psychiatrist ought to have a coordinating and leading role when treating patients in a multidisciplinary team.

Against the backdrop of the changes in Dutch mental health care since the 1960s, as discussed in this paper, it is not difficult to understand the professional dilemma of the psychiatrist. On the one hand, the psychiatrist seeks to hold on to his scientific status as medical specialist because that is what sets him apart from the other professionals involved in mental health care. But, on the other hand, the psychiatrist can have a central and leading role in mental health care only by appropriating at least some of the expertise of other professions and by claiming that he is more than just a medical specialist.

Notes

1. The authors are indebted to Prof. Mark M.W. Richartz for helpful comments on earlier drafts of this article.
2. The Dutch Association for Psychiatry was established in 1871, but in 1895, after more and more neurologists joined the Association, its name was changed into Dutch Association for Psychiatry and Neurology (NVPN). In addition to the NVPN, a second professional organization of psychiatrists was founded in 1919: the Dutch

Association of Institutional Psychiatrists (Its name was slightly altered in 1964). Whereas the NVPN presented itself primarily as a scientific organization, this second association was more geared toward the – material – interests of psychiatrists employed by mental hospitals.

3. There was one central board that served as representative body to the outside world, whereas the control over the decision process continued to be in the hands of the general assembly of the two sections.

4. The new NVvP, which aimed to look after all the interests – but especially the scientific ones – of Dutch psychiatry, consisted of members of the former NVPN and the members of the Dutch Association for Institutional Psychiatrists, which was discontinued on December 31, 1973. Between 1974 and 1982, the NVvP's membership grew from 850 to 1200. (Paul Schnabel, *De Psychiater in Beeld* (Utrecht: NcGv, 1982), 70-71.)

5. *Mededelingenblad van de Nederlandse Vereniging voor Psychiatrie en Neurologie,* xi (1969), 13-4.

6. This KNMG commission's role was to implement the decisions made by the Central Board involving the licensing and registration of medical specialists and it was also responsible for registering new specialists. Since 1961, the Central Board has been a semi-governmental, legislative body regarding all medical specialties. It decides which areas of medicine are acknowledged as medical specialty and it sets the standards for all medical training.

7. Electroencephalography researches electrophysical brain activity and possible cerebral aberrations.

8. Cf. M.S. Vos & H. van Berkenstijn, 'De Geschiedenis van de Opleiding tot Psychiater in Nederland', *Tijdschrift voor psychiatrie,* xxxv (1993), 22; *Mededelingenblad van de Nederlandse Vereniging voor Psychiatrie en Neurologie,* ii (1964), 10.

9. *Mededelingenblad van de Nederlandse Vereniging voor Psychiatrie en Neurologie,* xiii (1970), 6.

10. *Mededelingenblad van de Nederlandse Vereniging voor Psychiatrie en Neurologie,* ix (1968), 17, 21.

11. The plea for a shorter training period was related to an anticipated shortage of psychiatrists. (Sonja van 't Hof, *'Een Ambt Hoog en Subtiel...' Psychiaters over Psychiatrie 1971-1996* (Utrecht: Nederlandse Vereniging voor Psychiatrie, 1996), 68). During the 1960s, the NVPN was not only concerned with the quality of psychiatric training but also with the number of psychiatrists that had to be trained in order to meet the demand. It was estimated that the number of mental disorders who could be treated would go up,

yet hard quantitative data about society's need for psychiatrists were unavailable. (*Mededelingenblad van de Nederlandse Vereniging voor Psychiatrie en Neurologie*, vii (1967), 22-8.)

12. Cf. *Medisch Contact*, xxvii (1972), 123. In addition to this new situation, in which one would be registered as either neurologist or psychiatrist, the old option – of being listed as 'nerve specialist' – would remain open for ten more years. From 1972 to 1982, therefore, there were in fact three specialties: psychiatry, neurology, and the combined specialty of psychiatry and neurology.

13. Utrecht Professor Van Praag was denounced for his biological approach during the late seventies, but his approach regained some terrain in the 1980s with the comeback of electroshock and the increased use of psychopharmaceuticals (although there were still psychiatrists who warned against reductionism at the cost of psycho-social factors).

14. M. Romme & M. Richartz, 'Argumenten voor Voorgestelde Wijzigingen', *Tijdschrift voor Psychiatrie*, xx (1978), 463.

15. *Tijdschrift voor Psychiatrie*, xix (1977), 38, 41 83, 329.

16. *Medisch Contact*, xxxvi (1981), 766.

17. Vos & Van Berkestijn, 'De Geschiedenis van de Opleiding tot Psychiater in Nederland', 26-7.

18. *Medisch Contact*, xxxviii (1983), 1646.

19. T. van der Grinten, *De Vorming van de Ambulante Geestelijke Gezondheidszorg. Een historisch beleidsonderzoek* (Baarn: Ambo, 1987).

20. See for example: P.C. Kuiper, 'Geestelijke Gezondheidsleer en Gezondheidszorg', *Maandblad Geestelijke Volksgezondheid*, xv (1960), 77-83; *Maandblad Geestelijke Volksgezondheid*, (1971), 322.

21. P.J. Jongerius, 'Le Phenomene Hollandais, een Geschiedenis van het Psychotherapeutisch veld', in C.P. Breemer ter Stege, *Mental health care in the Netherlands* (Utrecht: NcGv, 1983), 127.

22. Health insurance covers psychotherapy done by independently established psychiatrists since 1959. After 1965, the IMPs saw an annual growth of twenty-five percent in the number of requests for psychotherapeutic treatment. In a period of ten years, there was a ninefold increase in the number or requests.

23. Right after the Second World War, when the somatic approach was dominant, there was an unsuccessful proposal to open up space for psychotherapy in the basic training curriculum.

24. From the 1960s on, the number of psychologists increased rapidly in the Netherlands and surpassed that of psychiatrists.

25. For the De Vreeze-Commission's report, see C. Dijkstra & H. van Donselaar, 'Psychotherapie in Nederland 1. Geschiedenis van de psychotherapie van 1900 tot nu', *De Psycholoog*, xxiii (1988), 1-7.

26. 'Functie van de psychiatrie', *Maandblad geestelijke volksgezondheid*, xxxiii (1978), 51; M. Valstar, 'De psychiater als psychotherapeut', *Maandblad Geestelijke Volksgezondheid*, xxxiv (1979), 573-4.

27. *Medisch Contact*, xxxvi (1981), 771.

28. W.J. de Waal, *De Geschiedenis van de Psychotherapie in Nederland* ('s-Hertogenbosch: De Nijvere Haas, 1992), 117.

29. H. Reijzer, *Naar een Nieuw Beroep, Psychotherapeut in Nederland* (Houten: Bohn Stafleu Van Loghum, 1993), 222.

30. Van 't Hof, *'Een ambt hoog en subtiel ...'*, 60.

31. Cf. P. Schnabel, *De Weerbarstige Geestesziekte. Naar een Nieuwe Sociologie van de Geestelijke Gezondheidszorg* (Nijmegen: SUN, 1995).

32. Until the 1960s, the theoretical foundation of psychiatry in the Netherlands was not only medically but also strongly philosophically oriented.

33. Cf. A. Mooj, *De Psychische Realiteit. Over Psychiatrie als Wetenschap* (Meppel: Boom, 1988), 11, 27.

34. In comparison to countries like Italy, England, and the United States, the antipsychiatry movement was less controversial in the Netherlands, partly because many of its ideas were integrated in the widespread system of ambulatory mental health care. There were surely some psychiatrists in the Netherlands who subscribed to the antipsychiatry movement's ideology (or parts thereof), but not everyone could agree with its alternative, romanticized point of view.

35. F. van den Boom, *De RIAGG en de Psychiater* (Utrecht: NcGv, 1987), 111.

36. A. Korzec & M. Korzec, 'Een Revolutie in de Gedachte van het Biologisch Denken', *Intermediair*, xxix (1993), 31-5.

37. The government more or less supported this view. A 1984 governmental paper on mental health care suggested that the RIAGGs devoted too much attention to minor psycho-social mental problems while not spending enough time on serious mental disorders. It was proposed to shift attention for minor mental problems to the basic care provided by family doctors, psychologists, and social workers, whereas the more serious cases would be treated by psychiatrists in RIAGGs, or in cooperation with polyclinics or out-patient facilities of general mental hospitals.

38. See F. Rouppe v.d. Voort, 'De Psychiater en de Ambulante Geestelijke Gezondheidszorg Anno 1980', *Metamedica*, lvii (1978), 202-208.

39. Paul Schnabel, *De Psychiater in Beeld* (Utrecht: NcGv, 1982).

40. Van 't Hof, *'Een amt Hoog en Subtiel...'*, 88.

41. W. van Tilburg, *Profielschets Psychiater* (Utrecht: Nederlandse Vereniging voor Psychiatrie, 1996), 10, 13.

*Good + also at times illogical ie
ideologically driven*

12

From the Asylum to the Community:
the Mental Patient in Postwar Britain

Peter Barham

In these pages I offer some reflections on the situation of the mental patient in the era of deinstitutionalization in post-war Britain. Starting from some research of my own, I proceed to a number of other sitings. The coverage is clearly not intended to be comprehensive, but hopefully it may help to stimulate further debate.[1]

The New Mental Patients of the 1980s and 1990s

At the end of the 1950s Erving Goffman was studying the 'moral careers' of long-stay asylum inmates.[2] In recent years, researchers have started to take an interest in the 'moral careers' of the younger generation of mental patients who have never been long-stay patients and throughout their illness careers have been beneficiaries of regimes of community care. The high-point in the population of mental hospitals in England and Wales had been achieved in 1954 with 148,100 patients, and it has declined at a fairly even rate ever since. By the end of the century, the majority of large Victorian asylums will have closed down. Though more people than in the past are admitted to in-patient psychiatric units, only a small minority stay there a long time or become permanent residents. In Britain these days, to acquire permanent tenure as a mental patient is more difficult than to acquire tenure in, say, a university. department: temporary, short-term contracts are the norm; ours is the era of the part-time psychotic.[3]

I shall start by summarising the conclusions of a study of the younger generation of mental patients which my colleagues and I undertook in a town in the north of England in the late 1980s.[4] The locality was economically depressed and described by a local psychiatrist as 'an unpromising place in which to be schizophrenically ill'. The subjects of the study all had a diagnosis of schizophrenia, most them had been hospitalized at least six times, and the average duration of their illness careers was sixteen years. All told, they are fairly representative of the population of people with long-term mental illness.

Though all of the subjects lived alone, most of them were able to forge some form of connection or life-line that kept them going and helped maintain the integrity of their life projects. Many of them were in contact with at least one relative who proved important in a variety of ways, both material and emotional. Some people derived a source of connection from looking after pets; and sometimes, to their surprise, after a succession of bad experiences with members of the public, subjects were able to develop a supportive connection with a sympathetic neighbour. But to a large extent these were moments of relief within a wider experience of disconnection and structural isolation. In the spheres of housing and employment in particular, our subjects generally found themselves powerless to influence their fates and felt they had to choice but to accept (and be grateful) for what was given to them. The poverty of lives led on welfare benefits enforced a competition over basic necessities that could prove detrimental to a person's health. Often, a visit to the cinema or a night out with friends, would mean a sandwich for dinner. Budgets were maintained under a tight rein, everything worked out to the last penny, with little scope for contingency, a new pair of boots or a coat for the winter.

Friendships were as vital as they were tenuous. Time and again participants reported a vicious circle in which lack of resources coupled with the burden of their psychiatric histories exacerbated such difficulties as they already had in making and sustaining friendships. Lack of resources also affected their mobility, and they repeatedly complained how difficult it was for them to find the wherewithal to escape from the sites of their daily lives. 'I'd love to see the ocean again', said Barry, 'even if it's only for a day'. And for those who did manage to escape, a holiday was always a tremendous boost in the trials that confronted them.

They all experienced difficulty in surmounting an identity as a 'mental patient'. Even where they might be said to have 'got better', their credibility was easily put in question. At best they had a precarious foothold in ordinary life in which their personhood was constantly on probation, and they were required to provide repeated demonstrations that they were normal and there was nothing untoward about them. And a relapse invariably meant that another

222

round of repair work had to be undertaken. Though they were several of them active strategists in their own care, and could in an important sense be said to be their own main carers, their potential as human beings capable of giving as much as receiving was generally disregarded. Philip identified a shared desire to make a mark, to achieve some form of recognition, when he spoke of the importance of being able 'to make a difference to something, affect something'.

Ben described how some people were able to 'react to him in his illness' and still treat and respect him as a person of worth who was not primarily defined by his illness. But this was very much the limiting case, and 'reacting to people in their illness' generally meant viewing them in their difference as denizens of an alien sphere of being. Disclosure of a psychiatric history incurred the risk of being made to feel 'less of a person'. Typical was Henry's experience at the Job Centre where he found staff to be 'nervy because they know you're schizophrenic, as though they feel "What's he going to do next?"' Indeed, it would appear that the term 'schizophrenia' is often freighted with such denigratory meaning that the perception of the person is distorted, in Henry's apt phrase, 'completely out of perspective', and people are brought 'to think all sorts from different corners'.

These psychiatric patients had apparently received little or no guidance in tackling the meanings of schizophrenia and negotiating the cultural burden which the diagnosis inflicted on them. They had as best they could to become their own guides and to try to 'put bits together to realise what it means'. The social world often appeared strange and threatening, assumptions and expectations that in the pre-mental hospital phase of their lives could have been taken for granted were unsettled, and they found themselves groping for answers as to what makes life worth living in a seemingly inauspicious set of structural conditions, itinerants in a strange country, equipped with only a very rudimentary map for guidance. Psychiatric services seemed at best to provide regimes of benign containment in which the significant questions that concerned consumers about the value and direction of their lives were left unaddressed or obscured. For example, the terms of life offered by psychiatric day services were often judged a dead-end, just one day following the next, without sense or purpose. All the same, going it alone was recognised to be a high-risk enterprise. Above all, subjects wanted access to opportunities that promised to lead somewhere and enable them to establish a direction to their lives. They were persistently haunted by doubts about their worth and much of the time they were engaged in what may be termed a struggle for value. As one subject put it, 'you never actually conquer this problem' and regardless of what is achieved the struggle always has to be renewed. Medical considerations were important but mostly as facets of a broader perspective on their well-being. Considered as patients, people with mental illness may receive exemplary treatment, but such treatment is hardly likely of itself to remedy the complex questions of valuation that trouble them. Subjects often felt that an important dimension of their lives was ignored by the psychiatric officials with whom they came into contact. For example, Ian, a young man in his early thirties, recognises that he is probably not capable of managing a conventional job, yet he feels nonetheless that there must be some socially valued project to which he could contribute usefully. He tried to raise the subject with his psychiatrist who simply told him that he must 'be content to be on the sick and cope and manage as best he could'.

Naturally enough, the stances which people with a history of mental illness adopt within life are as varied as those of any other population group and the people illustrated here are by no means alike: there are wide variations in perception and belief, just as there are marked differences in condition and need. All the same, we can identify a number of common themes and concerns, notably: the pauperisation of lives; the cruel effects of stigma and the 'taint' of mental illness; the barriers to equality with other people, the experience of being made to feel less of a person or even an inferior person; experiences of powerlessness in their efforts to exert some control over their lives, not least in their dealings with the medical profession; and the demoralisation produced by a health and welfare system that treats them as secondary sorts of people or as children.

Mental Hospital Reforms of the 1950s and 1960s

These, then, typify some of the perspectives and circumstances of the 'new' mental patients of the late 1980s and early 90s. Contrast this with the following account by David Clark, reforming medical superintendent of a large mental hospital – Fulbourn, near Cambridge – in the 1950s and 60s, and one of the pioneers of the 'open-door' policy and of what Clark later came to style 'social therapy'.[5] These ideas about how to treat mentally disturbed people derive, broadly, from the tradition of moral treatment, and some of them had been 'reinvented' before the 1950s. Already in the 1920s at Colney Hatch, one of London's largest asylums, there was talk of open-door wards, and of unblocking ground-floor windows. In March 1922 the Medical Superintendent reported that the 'experiment of serving tea in a household manner' had been tried on one female ward and one male, and was 'entirely successful and much appreciated by the patients'.[6] Considering a proposal in the following year that patients be given lockers to store their private belongings, it was reckoned that about one in three of the inmates would be fit to have one, and would appreciate its possession.[7] Still, it was really only in the 1950s that the humanisation of the mental hospital environment really got under way. As David Clark recounts:

> 'In the first 90 years of its existence the Fulbourn Asylum was a social institution devoted to containing madness, to quietening furore, to maintaining the fabric of society and to discouraging change. Patients were sent there to be quietened down...'[8]

Clark describes his own awakening. To start with, he had shown a lamentable tendency to accept:

> the prevailing medical view of patients as pathetic beings, only kept from recovery by the failure of their illnesses to respond to medical treatment, or their wilful inability to do what doctors prescribed for them. It was several years before I even began to consider the possibility that patients could actually help each other – and that there might be patients who could help each other better than the doctors did.[9]

But eventually the message got through and he was brought to realise that:

> when people were held for years in an institution, the forces that changed them, for better or for worse, were social rather than medical. It was the environment, its messages of fear , or hope, or recovery, rather than the pills they were given which determined how they recovered.[10]

He came to recognise that:

> the vitality of a therapeutic culture derived from the people in it ... It was their attitudes that determined whether a person's stay in hospital was a time of change, growth and progress – or whether it was a time of defeat, shame, misery, degradation and brutality, as was common in the old custodial hospitals...[11]

At the end of the 1960s, Clark adopted the term 'social therapy' to denote:

> all that we were doing to help patients progress. This term included activities such as carpentry workshops, play and pantomimes, halfway houses, therapeutic communities, rehabilitation clinics and so on, – everything that used social structures to help patients. It also included the ideas emerging from our therapeutic communities: these were that everyone in the hospital, but especially the patients, had valuable contributions to make, and that while communications, authority and power patterns were an essential part of the treatment process, they must be constantly reviewed, surveyed and changed...[12]

According to Clark, the basic premise of social therapy was that of 'the Moral Treatment pioneers – the belief that the way patients lived in a mental hospital was a potent factor in deciding whether they progressed, became better and took their discharge or whether they sank into stultified, resentful chronicity'.[13] In the 1950s, the quality of life of the long-stay patients in Fulbourn Mental Hospital was immensely improved, 'from being locked up in squalid congestion, they were allowed a life-style providing more freedom and dignity'; and in the 1960s patients began to move out of the hospital and many of them were successfully established in group homes and other forms of sheltered accommodation.[14] As Clark reveals, the hopeful and encouraging message was not simply from the mental hospital to the patient, but also from the wider society to the mental hospital. As he says about his own reforms, 'all this happened at a time when mental hospitals were on the brink of change because English society as a whole wanted authoritarian institutions to become more liberal'.[15]

The Patient's 'Illness' and the Doctor's 'Disease'

Now, it is evident that in certain respects the experiences of contemporary mental patients mark a reversal from the hopeful trends which Clark delineates, for the messages from the contemporary environment are not altogether encouraging and hopeful. I shall return to this aspect later, but it is also important to mark the continuities in the current scene in the orientation towards mental suffering that David Clark and his team rediscovered in their social therapy experiments. So, for example, the tradition of resettling long-stay patients has been maintained relatively successfully over three decades and more, most recently in a number of mental hospital closure programmes.[16]

More especially, patients' ideas about, and perspectives on, their illness have reassumed a prominence and topicality that over a long period had been foreclosed. In the idiom of the American anthropologist and psychiatrist Arthur Kleinman, there is begrudging recognition that the patient's 'experience of illness' does not necessarily coincide with the doctor's attention to 'disease'. Illness, in Kleinman's account, 'refers to how the sick person and the members of the family or wider social network perceive, live with and respond to symptoms and disability'. Disease, by contrast, is the problem from the doctor's perspective.[17] This distinction is enormously important. Some years ago, in a remarkable study of a British mental hospital, another anthropologist, Elizabeth Bott, described how 'admission to hospital, especially for the first time, is a catastrophe. It alters one's sense of oneself irrevocably, a fact that people who work constantly in hospitals tend to become almost unaware of'.[18] In a similar vein, David Clark describes how for many people:

> admission to Fulbourn Hospital in the early 1950s was a terrifying and degrading experience. After weeks of mounting tension, mental disorder and distress, things came to a crisis. There were secret conclaves of relatives and doctors; doctors whom they did not know came to talk to the patient. Finally, policemen, ambulances, motor cars and a Magistrate all arrived at the house, to the fascination and horror of the neighbours. The patient was dragged into the ambulance and whisked off to Fulbourn, there to be stripped, bathed, roughly examined and drugged. Little wonder that many of them were confused, angry, paranoid and resentful by the time I saw them'.[19]

It can plausibly be claimed that one of the aims of mental health policy in Britain over the past three decades or so has been to try to moderate the catastrophe of a life shattered by a mental breakdown by taking more serious account – notionally, at least, if not always in actuality – of what it means for the person to go through the ordeal of becoming a mental patient. Though modern medicine tends to look upon illness as a random event striking from outside, and to disparage concerns with meaning, in their narratives patients may legitimately want to make sense of an episode of illness within a wider meaning of life.[20] Peter Campbell, who describes himself as a 'recipient' of psychiatric services, talks about the damage he has sustained across twenty-five years of psychiatric treatment: 'a great part has been a result of psychiatry's failure to give value to my

personal perceptions and experience. Psychiatry has always chosen
to consider some aspects of my person and rebuff or ignore others.'
As he continues, people in his situation 'spend much time searching
for meaning and grappling with the consequences of experiencing
the types of distress that the majority classify as signs of "mental
illness" or "madness". It is no joke to find yourself perpetually
trapped within such negative frameworks'.[21]

Here is a brief example from a follow-up interview with Ben,
one of my research subjects, in which he describes how he has
struggled to reclaim the moral meaning of his experience of mental
illness, without at the same time denying the validity of medical
interventions and perspectives. According to Ben, by dint of
repeated hospitalizations over a period of fifteen years or so, he has
been brought to accept that vulnerability to mental illness is an
integral part of him, rather than something that happens from time
to time, and that he can put behind him when he leaves hospital:

> I realise that some of my fantasies and ideas were as a result of my
> illness really: you see, my illness questions things about truth and
> knowledge and existence, because its such a shattering experience,
> and I find it a bit religious ... it questions what I can think of as
> being truth, in social terms ... I have come a lot more, perhaps,
> towards accepting what the doctors have said ... in terms of it being
> some kind of chemical reaction in the brain ... I have come to
> accept that I need an injection, I have reluctantly come to accept that.

For Ben, at this point in his life, there appears to be a kind of
reassurance and stability in accepting a 'material' in preference to an
'existential' explanation, at least in part. The 'existential' in its
plenitude is, perhaps, too much to handle: too many questions, no
planks to stand upon. As Ben puts it, 'if you just take the various
choices you have in, say, religion – there are a whole host of
dilemmas there, and if you're a thinking kind of person those
dilemmas can create terrible tensions in your head in trying to cope'.
But then having having offered the material account, he distances
himself from it and returns with his own explanation:

> I found 'schizophrenic', which I was diagnosed as, a difficult word
> to understand. My own personal view of schizophrenia, what
> happened to me, I call it a psyche-social [*sic*] religious experience,
> which may not mean much to you but it means a lot more to me:
> and what happened, which includes something to do with my head,
> something in society and religion, but also an experience that has

happened to me, and I find that happens to other people, there are a lot of religious problems ... . Maybe we are experiencing something about existence.

It would be a mistake, I believe, to view the co-existence of these explanations as contradictory, or as a sign of Ben's confusion. Ben evidently wants to maintain intact the integrity of his spiritual outlook on life, but it is also apparent to him that his experience of mental breakdown has not been a very reliable instrument in his spiritual development. He is now willing to permit himself more acknowledgement of illness, yet he is determined at the same time to maintain the integrity of his life project. By comparison with five or so years ago he is 'much calmer' about his illness, and prepared to talk about it with people:

> I like to show that even though I have the illness, I can function as a person. Whereas, before, I would like to think that I havent really got the illness, "Look I'm alright!" It's a slightly different emphasis.

He is anxious to ensure that by acknowledging an "I have" illness, he does not find himself surreptitiously transformed into an "I am" condition. He puts it very plainly:

> In a joking way, I say, well, if I had a broken leg, I wouldn't say "I am a broken leg". In the same way, we shouldn't say "I am a schizophrenic" ... . We should say something like, "I have a schizophrenic illness". Because it's defining. You don't say "I am a broken leg"... I might limp or something ... but it shouldn't define your life.

'If we are to become part of the community', he continues, 'we need to be there as people in our own right with skills and failings, not as the local schizophrenic. I don't want to be a schizophrenic "doing well": "Isn't he good even though he's had a mental illness?" I just want my illness to be forgotten about. I'm not proud of it, its a bloody nuisance. I hate being called a schizophrenic.'[22]

The Challenge to Welfare Paternalism

Arguably, the egalitarian ideals of the social therapy movement have resurfaced, and been refashioned, in contemporary challenges to the tradition of welfare paternalism in which the beneficiaries were the passive recipients of care and the voice of the mentally ill was all but silenced. From what contemporary users of mental health services say, it is apparent that the reproduction of client docility under new professional auspices, no matter how well resourced, is not what is sought after. This is the voice of a young woman called Sarah:

> I think the hospital encourages you to take on the tag, to go to groups and to live the life according to schizophrenia ... its a way of controlling you, where you are. I suppose its a way of helping you in a way but it doesnt really help you and I have been institutionalized in that way and I want to break out of that mould now.... It creates half the schizophrenic's problems by doing that, by forcing them into a certain role or a certain mould or a certain way of life... They hate you doing something stressful in your life, ... And they just expect you to be a dummy and sit in groups and drink coffee all day...

And this is how Vaughan describes his experiences with psychiatrists in attempting to negotiate his concerns after recovering from a relapse:

> That's the big battle, the battle with the doctors, when you're feeling better and you feel its time to cut down your tablets... The doctor I saw said: "You're going to need injections for the rest of your life". I said I was going to look for a job and he said: "I wouldn't bother looking for a job, just get an hour or two's rest every day". I said: "That's no good I want to get out and get a job". He said: "Oh no, I should take it easy"...

Writing in 1989, Michael Ignatieff described the welfare mould from which many users want to break and nicely castigated those who tried to defend the welfare state by contrasting the 'uncaring' policies of the conservative government with their own 'caring' attitudes. The 'citizenship ideal of post-war liberals and social democrats', Ignatieff argued:

> stressed the passive quality of entitlements at the expense of the active equality of participation. The entitled were never empowered, because empowerment would have infringed the prerogatives of the managers of the welfare state.

As a political question, Ignatieff went on to say, welfare is about rights not caring. To 'describe the welfare state in the language of caring is to misdescribe it, and to misdescribe is to deceive'. To do so is to reinstate Poor Law principles and to understand the welfare state as a civic pact between haves and have-nots, care-givers and care-receivers, in which entitlements are a matter of moral generosity rather than of right. As Ignatieff aptly remarks, 'only someone who has not actually been on the receiving end of the welfare state would dare call it an instance of civic altruism at work'. Notions of the 'caring society' evoke for Ignatieff 'the image of a nanny state in which the care we get depends on what the "caring professions" think it fit for us to receive'. He would, he goes on, much 'prefer to live in a society which struggles to be just, which respects and enhances people's rights and entitlements'. Simon spoke for a number of my research subjects when he described how demoralising it felt to be part of the community mental patient system, 'you're sort of tied to the strings of the hospital, the apron strings of the hospital, you're being treated like a child...'. The critical issue, Ignatieff suggests, is not to 'tie us all in the leading strings of therapeutic good intentions' but 'the struggle to make freedom real' through the shared foundation of a 'citizenship of entitlement'.[23]

Strictures like these throw a critical spotlight on some of the liberal psychiatric traditions of the 1960's and 1970's. Consider, for example, the writings of Douglas Bennett, for many years one of the leading figures in the British tradition of social psychiatry. Rehabilitation for psychiatric patients, Bennett tells us, is 'principally directed to the recovery or initiation of appropriate social roles'.[24] Bennett provides a benign and dedicated approach to individualised failings in socialisation for role performance but the problem with it resides in just this – that the failings of mental patients are entirely individualised. Cursory reference is made to secondary handicaps and the impact of stigma but missing is an understanding of the constraints and perplexities of the field of social and cultural forces in which people with a history of mental illness have to try and make something of their lives. Here, for example, is what Sidney, a young man with a history of several hospitalizations for schizophrenia, has to say about his difficulties in striking up relationships with women. In an encounter with a woman in a pub, for example:

> I might have got talking to her but I would have had to cut off at a certain point because I knew that once she found out about the background she'd lose interest ... It would have been more difficult to carry on with the relationship ... I have actually avoided getting into relationships because of the difficulty I would have in explaining what I'd been through, and what it all means, to someone.... . If I met someone in a pub or a club or whatever, and I liked her, if I felt that she'd never known anything about mental illness, never experienced anything to do with it, I'd avoid talking to

her ... because it would seem pointless to me. I'd just stop it dead.

Within Bennett's normative scheme of things, the ability to form relationships with members of the opposite sex is surely to be reckoned an important accomplishment but we entirely misapprehend what Sidney is telling us if we cast his difficulty in this sphere as an individualised failing or weakness. If we want to understand what it is like to be in Sidney's position in his encounter with a woman in a pub, we can only do so on the basis of a reading of the history through which people like Sidney have been brought to see themselves, and have come to be seen by others, in a singularly dismal light. For want of a moral critique of the norms by which people with mental illness have been judged, and the barriers on their participation in social life justified, we are inevitably trapped in a view of the mental patient as a failed, if not broken, individual. Bennett, for example, clearly does not consider it a legitimate part of his business to assist his patients to confront their debased status as second-class citizens.[25]

The Mental Patient and Public Opinion

Writing about the history of a mental hospital, the attitudes of the staff who had worked there, and the sensibilities that had animated it, Diana Gittins explains that 'many staff seemed to genuinely love the patients, though certainly never as equals. They were very much regarded as "other"...'. Many of the staff modelled their conception of the hospital on the analogy of the family in which the patients were invariably the children. The mental hospital regime did not necessarily lack for compassion, but it was certainly an exclusionary universe in which mental patients were 'not like us'. As Diana Gittins explains further, the hospital she studied apparently stopped feeling like a family when the railings came down and the message of reform was received that 'patients were not, in fact, like children at all, but like everyone else'.[26] This, in essence, is the message that, for good and ill, perhaps, has fuelled the enthusiasm for the closure of asylums, and energised the inclusionary counter-visions of contemporary mental health policies which are intent upon affirming 'the humanity and worth of people with severe mental illness, and their rights as citizens'.[27]

But just how committed is public opinion in Britain to an inclusive vision of mental health policy? Public feeling has certainly been stirred in the past by revelation of abuses in mental hospitals, and the principle of a community rather than hospital-based existence for people with mental illness appears to have attracted widespread support. Yet there are reasons to be sceptical about the depth and extent of public commitment to reform, and in recent years it is far from obvious that public thinking about people with mental illness has kept pace with the shifts that have taken place among enlightened sections of the professional community, and among former mental patients themselves. A commitment to equality in principle, perhaps, but with some measure of reserve: in certain respects, former mental patients are still under suspicion; they cannot always be trusted with the children; they are unreliable employees, and so forth. Journalists continue to speak of 'the mentally ill' as of another caste, and whilst policy makers may have decided that mental patients and former mental patients are not like children and are like everyone else, there is a lurking sense that that is still what they are: difficult and 'impossible' children.

The moral imagination of early twentieth century social reformers in Britain evinced a tension between a spirit of compassion and vision of a social order founded on scientific advancement from which 'failures' would be eliminated. Gertrude Himmelfarb has drawn attention to the Fabian distrust of the 'average sensual man', a synonym, as she describes, for the 'ordinary man who was incapable of exercising control not only over political and administrative affairs, but even over his own "sensual nature"'.[28] Supposedly, the Welfare State, with its commitment to a citizenship of universalism, transcended the tensions and discriminations redolent of the late Victorian and Edwardian eras, but as historians such as Mathew Thomson have shown mental health services occupied a very lowly position in the new National Health Service system, and behind the patina of egalitarian rhetoric long-standing divisions and patterns of inequality were waiting to be rediscovered.[29] Concerns about the ability of the discharged mental patient to exercise control over his own nature have not been eroded by the promotion of ideals of common citizenship, and the pronouncement made by Beatrice Webb in 1911 that it was 'no use letting the poor come and go, as they think fit, be helped or not ...'[30] is echoed in contemporary sentiments about the mentally ill as untrustworthy individuals in need of steadfast control by experts, and in influential traditions of psychiatric writing in which the schizophrenic, for example, is represented as a reluctant, incapacitated and largely inarticulate actor who only by the most patient ministrations of psychiatric expertise can be encouraged to do anything at all.

English society as a whole may have wanted authoritarian

institutions like mental hospitals to become more liberal, but if the public is resigned to the closure of mental hospitals, and the exodus of the vast majority of patients into the community, there are plentiful indications that it possesses only limited patience for talk about giving a better deal to mental patients, attending to their rights, transforming their social relationships, and so forth. Yet in this respect public opinion may simply be echoing a long-standing ambiguity within the idea of community care, evident as early as the interwar period as Mathew Thomson has shown, between a critical approach which addressed the conditions of the community, and a simple transfer of the locus of care.[31]

The Psychiatrist as Long Stay Patient

The volatile temper of current opinion towards the mentally ill in the community is illustrated in a recent article by a psychiatrist, writing in the *British Medical Journal*. According to Simon Wessely, over the past few years government policy and influential sections of the psychiatric profession have 'united to promote the concentration of resources on what has become known as "severe mental illness"'. Wessely goes on to attack 'the obsession with severe mental illness' and the 'increasing emphasis on the care of the long-term psychotic patient' at the expense of other areas of potential psychiatric concern. Not only are the psychotics eating all the cake, but psychiatrists are suffering the 'taint' of their association with these mad people. According to Wessely, psychiatry is perceived by the general public to be authoritarian and stigmatizing, and the 'source of that stigma is not hard to find – it is the stigma of "insanity" since psychiatrists are concerned with the care of psychotic patients'. The consequence of such concentration on the psychotic patient, Wessely goes on to say, 'will be an inevitable reduction of the scope of psychiatry, the skills necessary to practise psychiatry and ... the attraction of a psychiatric career'. All of this, Wessely claims, 'marks a return to the world of Victorian psychiatry. The great asylums may have been abolished but psychiatry is reverting to 'the days of alienism: in Victorian terms, the care of "the mad"'.[32]

In this scenario, then, the psychiatrist has become the long-stay patient shackled in the asylum, and the mad have become the jailers. The mad are a hindrance whom the doctors in their professional advancement are all too eager to break free from. Wessely forcibly contrasts his own lot with that of counsellors who appear able to sell their services to increasing numbers of clients precisely by distancing themselves from psychiatry. The pitiful Wessely gazes over the asylum walls into the community to discover that, among other interlopers, his seat in the consulting room has been usurped by priests.

This is certainly a rather disturbing account but it should be stressed that the sentiments underlying it are scarcely new. Since the nineteenth century psychiatry has been anxious to align itself with the curative model of general medicine, and has accordingly demonstrated a highly ambivalent relation to chronic and long-term cases. The irony is, of course, that psychiatrists find themselves isolated with their chronic patients once again just at the moment when the majority of asylums are in process of disappearing. Wessely's lament is, perhaps, the nemesis of the enthusiasm for community care of the 1960s that was most keenly promoted by doctors inspired by the promise of the new drug treatments.

Conclusions: Looking Beyond Psychiatry

Overall, the outcome is certainly a complex one. With the expansion of diagnostic categories in the late nineteenth century, the options available to mentally distressed individuals for making sense of their experience were drastically reduced. Once diagnosed as a sufferer from schizophrenia, an 'individual became, in part, that diagnosis'.[33] Yet in recent years people with a history of mental illness have learned to challenge these designations and to put a distance between themselves and the categories of psychiatry. The permanence and division of 'mental patienthood' has to a considerable extent yielded to identities that are altogether more provisional and negotiable. And quite a few of those who once took tea in a household manner on mental hospital wards have become householders in their own right, either singly or in shared homes with others. Formally, the term 'lunatic' was abolished in 1930, when the stigma of pauperism was at least moderated, and the pauper lunatic became a 'rate-aided person'; and 'madness' disappeared with the Mental Health Act of 1959 in which the 'person of unsound mind' was replaced by the softer attribute of 'mental disorder'. As a sociologist explains, 'these changes were justified on the basis that the old terms of madness, insanity and lunacy did not correspond to the changed perception of the mentally ill in a more tolerant society'.[34] In the contemporary idiom, the former mental patient or sufferer from mental illness, may be reconstructed as a 'person with mental health problems'. It would be premature to claim that these developments presage a new chapter in the troubled history of doctor-patient relations in psychiatry, but it is certainly true to say that the authoritarianism of traditional psychiatry has ceded to styles of relations in which there is increased scope for negotiation and some element of client control.

Still, despite this progressive distancing from their origins, contemporary mental patients in the community for the most part display a recognisable kinship with the poor lunatics of the last century and beyond: they have not succeeded in breaking the ancient association between poverty and lunacy. A report by the Rowntree Foundation published in 1995 showed that since 1977 the very poor in Britain have in fact become poorer, both relatively and absolutely.[35] Inclusionary visions of mental health policy are bent upon redressing the inequalities which restrict the entitlements of citizenship, but it is apparent that in the case of this (and of course other) disadvantaged groups the hour of the citizen has once again been postponed.[36] Release from the stigmatizing discourse of psychiatry may not entail much more than the freedom to be picked up in the stigmatizing discourse of poverty. The options for identity formation and negotiation may have expanded, but the identities of former mental patients in the community are insecurely grounded, and so is the whole idea of the person with a history of mental illness as a trustworthy human being, capable of controlling his own nature. According to a recent estimate, there are about 300,000 people with severe mental illness in England and Wales, but despite the best efforts of self-help groups and associations it would be disingenuous to claim that the benefits of collective solidarity are entirely salutary.

Even in late twentieth century Britain, cultural constructions of madness are enormously protean, and resistant to being packaged and confined within the categories and institutions of modern medicine. As Ruth Padel has remarked in her richly evocative study of the mutation of ideas about madness in Western culture from Greek tragedy through the Renaissance with its notions of 'mad true seeing', such as melancholic divination, and the allied Erasmian conception of Christian folly, down to our own period, there are 'seams of thought, deeply embedded layers in the quarry of ideas that underlie our attitude to madness'.[37] We can thus think of anti-psychiatry as having refurbished for a contemporary audience resources from an extensive cultural repertoire that had been obscured or annulled in the modern psychiatric imagination, but the stress is on the word audience, for the anti-psychiatric moment, as it has been termed, was doubtless far more significant within a cultural history than a distinctly psychiatric one, and in this respect perhaps it recapitulated the use of madness in classical tragedy as Ruth Padel describes it, in which other people rather than the 'maddened person' gets any 'goods' that may arise out of the experience, and ultimately it is the audience who gains.[38]

In addressing the 'maddened person' in contemporary Britain one is likely to discover at the very least an intriguing ambivalence, rather than wholehearted approval, over the 'goods' that are to be found in madness. Sarah is able to say that she is 'guilty of enjoying her schizophrenic experience... You're poor in lot of ways – OK, you haven't got a car and you haven't got a house – but you're a damn sight better off in a lot of other ways ... you are reasonably content most of the time in your illness'; yet she believes at the same time that she would rather have been without the experience. As the example of Sarah suggests, the contemporary psychiatric patient is rather unlikely to conform either to the image of the Laingian rebel or to that of the docile recipient of psychiatric treatment.

But it was not only the division of the 'goods' in mental distress that anti-psychiatry glossed over, but the perpetuation and staying-power of the condition itself. Ironically, for what purported to be an iconoclastic movement, anti-psychiatry was still bound by some very conventional assumptions, not least those of the curative model of medicine in which intensive short-term intervention (drug treatments in the case of conventional psychiatry, therapeutic communities for anti-psychiatry) could bring about or re-activate the individual's capacity for self-determination and independent living. Apposite though the enthusiasm for rescuing wronged individuals from oppressive institutions may have been, we are now perhaps in a position to appreciate that it also carried forward in a new guise long-standing misgivings and uncertainties, in the wider society as much as in the psychiatric establishment, over how to provide for people with chronic conditions.

Stanley Hauerwas has forcibly argued that a medicine led by an ethos of freedom is incapable of giving any reason why as a society we should be willing to care for vulnerable groups such as the long-term mentally ill.[39] Mental health reformers such as David Clark have discerned that medical concepts of cure and discharge are not readily applicable to clients with psychiatric disabilities, even though they may be leading relatively independent lives in the community. Clark and his team accepted a commitment to help their clients for the rest of their lives, yet it is far from clear how such commitments are to be sustained in Britain in the future, and answers are unlikely to be forthcoming from within the narrow confines of psychiatry. It has now become obvious that the idea of a linear passage from charity to state welfare is false, and in the contemporary scene models and perspectives that had seemingly been marginalized or surpassed in the forward march of scientific psychiatry are becoming more salient.[40] For example, there are signs of a belated recognition that the spiritual dimension of patients lives, particularly the use of spiritual resources in the recovery from mental illness, count for rather more than has generally been maintained.[41] Under the influence of positivist models of medicine, the pastoral role in mental health care has typically been trivialised or obscured. Giving evidence to a committee of inquiry in the 1920s, the Revd. Ridler said that the asylum chaplain was considered 'a very subordinate officer ... he is very much at the mercy of his medical superintendent'.[42] The medical superintendent in Ridler's asylum evidently went out of his way to humiliate the chaplain, even to the extent of questioning whether Ridler was in possession of a 'point of view' to represent to the committee. British historians have too readily taken at its face value the pastoral minimalism favoured by many alienists, and in this as in other areas comparison with other parts of Europe such as the Netherlands may prove invigorating. Psychiatry's relationship to the chronic patient seems to me as much unresolved as ever it was in the nineteenth century. And it is here, perhaps, that traditions, such as the pastoral presence in the care of the insane, that have either been overlooked or treated only in their repressive aspects, not only in the major canons of psychiatry, but also in the writings of some of the leading critics of psychiatry, may continue to possess some contemporary relevance. As far as people with long term mental illness are concerned, the future of psychiatry must surely be to look beyond psychiatry itself.

Notes

1. Part of this discussion is based on material discussed at greater length in: P. Barham, *Closing the Asylum: The Mental Patient in Modern Society*, 2nd edn (Harmondsworth: Penguin Books, 1997); P. Barham & R. Hayward, *Relocating Madness: From the Mental Patient to the Person*, 2nd edn (London: Free Association Books, 1995); and P. Barham and R. Hayward, 'In Sickness & in Health: Dilemmas of the Person with Severe Mental Illness', *Psychiatry*, in press.

2. E. Goffman, *Asylums* (Harmondsworth: Penguin Books, 1963).

3. On the idea of the 'part-time psychotic' see especially S. Estroff, *Making it Crazy*, revised paperback edn (Berkeley, California: University of California Press, 1985).

4. See P. Barham & R. Hayward, *Relocating Madness: From the Mental Patient to the Person*, 2nd edn (London: Free Association Books, 1995).

5. See D.H. Clark, *The Story of a Mental Hospital: Fulbourn 1858–1983* (London: Process Press, 1996).

6. Greater London Record Office (GLRO), H12/ CH/ A/ 8/ 1

7. GLRO, H12/ CH/ A/ 8/ 3.

8. D.H.Clark, *op. cit.*, 160

9. *Ibid.*, 161.

10. *Ibid.*, 194.

11. *Ibid.*, 236.

12. *Ibid.*, 193.

13. *Ibid.*, 237.

14. *Ibid.*, 238.

15. *Ibid.*, 239.

16. Some of these are summarised in P. Barham (1997) *op. cit.*, but for a detailed account see J. Leff, ed., *Care in the Community: Illusion or Reality?* (Chichester: Wiley, 1997)

17. A. Kleinman, *The Illness Narratives: Suffering, Healing & the Human Condition* (New York: Basic Books, 1988), 3–5.

18. E. Bott, 'Hospital & Society', *British Journal of Medical Psychology*, 49 (1976), 97–140, p. 119.

19. D. H. Clark, *op. cit.*, 65.

20. On the meaning of illness see R. Porter, 'The Patient in England, c.1660–c. 1800', in Wear, A. (ed.), *Medicine in Society* (Cambridge: Cambridge University Press, 1992); on meaning and medicine see A. Kleinman, 'What is Specific to Western Medicine?' in: W.F. Bynum & R. Porter (eds), *Companion Encyclopedia of the History of Medicine*, Vol. I (London: Routledge, 1993); and A. Kleinman & J. Kleinman, 'Suffering and its Professional Transformation: Towards an Ethnography of Interpersonal Experience', *Culture, Medicine & Psychiatry*, 15 (1991), 275–302.

21. P. Campbell, 'A Survivor's View of Community Psychiatry', *Journal of Mental Health*, 1 (1992), 117–122, p. 120.

22. For further discussion of Ben's revaluation of his experience, see P. Barham & R. Hayward, 'In Sickness & in Health: Dilemmas of the Person with Severe Mental Illness', *Psychiatry*, in press.

23. M. Ignatieff, 'Citizenship & Moral Narcissism', *Political Quarterly*, 60 (1989), 63–74.

24. D. Bennett, 'Some Forms of Psychiatric Treatment', in: J. Wing (ed.), *Schizophrenia: Towards a New Sytnthesis* (London: Academic Press, 1978).

25. For an example of such confrontation, see R. Warner, *Recovery from Schizophrenia* (London: Routledge, 1985).

26. D. Gittins, 'Keep it in the Family', *Health Service Journal*, 25 July

1996, 24–7.

27. Mental Health Foundation, *Creating Community Care: Report of the Mental Health Foundation Inquiry into Community Care for People with Severe Mental Illness* (London: Mental Health Foundation, 1994).

28. G. Himmelfarb, *Poverty and Compassion: The Moral Imagination of the Late Victorians* (New York: Vintage Books, 1992), p. 374.

29. M. Thomson, *The Problem of Mental Deficiency: Eugencs & Social Policy in Britain, c.1870–1959* (Oxford: Oxford University Press, 1998). On the Welfare State, inequality, and patterns of exclusion see especially Ralf Dahrendorf, *The Modern Social Conflict* (London: Weidenfeld & Nicolson, 1988).

30. Quoted in G. Himmelfarb, *op. cit.*, p. 377.

31. See M. Thomson, 'Sterilization, Segregation and Community Care: Ideology and Solutions to the Problem of Mental Deficiency in Inter-War Britain', *History of Psychiatry*, 3 (1992), 473–98.

32. S. Wessely, 'The Rise of Counselling and the Return of Alienism', *British Medical Journal*, 313 (1996), 158–60.

33. C. Rosenberg, 'Framing Disease: Illness, Society and History' in: C.E. Rosenberg & J. Golden, (eds), *Framing Disease: Studies In Cultural History* (New Brunswick: Rutgers University Press, 1992), p. xix.

34. D. Armstrong, "Madness and Coping', *Sociology of Health & Illness* 2 (1980), 293–316.

35. Rowntree Foundation, *The Inquiry Into Income And Wealth*, chaired by Sir Peter Barclay (York: Joseph Rowntree Foundation, 1995).

36. On the struggle for citizenship, and the entitlements of citizenship, see R. Dahrendorf, *op. cit.*

37. R. Padel, *Whom Gods Destroy: Elements of Greek & Tragic Madness* (Princeton, New Jersey: Princeton University Press), p. 94.

38. *Ibid.*, p. 96. The idea of the cultural salience of the anti-psychiatric moment I owe to Colin Jones.

39. S. Hauerwas, *Suffering Presence: Theological Reflections on Medicine, the Mentally Handicapped and the Church* (Notre Dame, Indiana: University of Notre Dame Press, 1986).

40. On charity and state welfare, see C. Jones, 'Charity before *c.*1850' in: W. J. Bynum & R. Porter (eds), *Companion Encyclopedia of the History of Medicine*, Vol. II (London: Routledge, 1993).

41. See for example A. Sims, '"Psyche" – Spirit as Well as Mind?', *British Journal of Psychiatry*, 165 (1994), 441–6.

42. Public Record Office, Kew: MH 59/ 220, Cobb Committee on the Administration of Public Mental Hospitals, 1922: Evidence & Questions.

13

The Battle against Peace-Keeping Frustrations: Psychiatrists and Psychologists in the Dutch Army

Hans Binneveld

Introduction

In the summer of 1995 the Muslim enclave of Srebrenica was captured by the Bosnian Serbs. Since then about five thousand Muslims have been missing. The Dutch battalion of blue helmets, that had been charged, by order of the United Nations, with the security of the area, could only stand by and do nothing. After the embarrassing retreat the soldiers were taken care of by specialized assistance workers, such as psychologists, chaplains and social workers. Some of these were already in the area of the operations, others were hastily flown in from the Netherlands.

This incident demonstrates that the prevalent conviction within the Dutch military that soldiers who are, one way or another, involved in a war may sustain mental injury. This view is not new. The mentally injured soldier is a phenomenon of all time. The first large-scale experiments in setting up a system of care were carried out during World War I. This is how military psychiatry began. Since then psychiatrists and psychologists became a part of military organization. They were present at all the great twentieth-century battles, from the Somme offensive in 1916 to the Kuwait war in 1991.

For various reasons military psychiatry has never really developed in the Netherlands. The big conflicts with Germany and the Republic of Indonesia were fought without psychological assistance. In a recent survey on the history of military psychiatry no attention was given to its development in the Netherlands. However, during the last ten years our forces have started to catch up. Soldiers who are now employed in UN peace-keeping operations are supported by an elaborate system of psychological assistance. In this chapter the main characteristics of this system will be discussed. Because some knowledge of military psychiatry in general is necessary to have a understand this system, a short explanation is given about the history of this field.

Military Psychiatry

Military psychiatry grew up during World War I and has been developing ever since.[1] In this process prevention has received attention as well. Within this field of study contributions from psychologists and sociologists became more and more important. The behavioural disorders that psychiatrists had to face were diverse and they varied for every war and every combat situation. Comparatively minor injuries were observed, such as headaches, loss of memory and gastro-enteritis. In addition, there were severe injuries that could involve complete loss of body functions.

When labeling these syndromes, military psychiatrists were not only led by what civilian psychiatry had to offer, but they were also inspired by the characteristic picture of the war in question. Thus, apart from using terms like *war neuroses* and *Nervenkrankheiten*, they also spoke about *shell shock, combat exhaustion* and *combat stress*.

For the treatment of collapsed soldiers one often fell back to what civilian psychiatry had to offer. Contrary to what is generally assumed, military psychiatry has hardly been innovative. Wars have not led to great therapeutical discoveries. You could say, however, that military psychiatrists made particular selections from the instruments at hand and fitted this into their own work situation. This situation, an army at war, led to a preference for simple, labour-saving therapies. When these therapies were employed normal ethical rules were temporarily brushed aside. Thus military psychiatry took on a specific individual character: simple and harsh. This harshness was not only the result of military necessity. It is obvious that the psychiatrists were eager to make as many soldiers as possible re-deployable. But they also kept a watchful eye on the financial interests of the state. Dr Fritz Kaufmann who became known during World War I for his harsh and merciless treatment methods, was in fact primarily led by these interests. His main goal was the realization of a cut in disability benefits. Even soldiers who were no longer considered re-deployable could expect a harsh regime from Kaufmann.

As has been said before, military psychiatrists did not employ an innovative approach. However this statement requires some qualification, because the care system was set up in quite a creative way. Already during World War I psychiatrists found that their therapies were most successful when certain key practices were employed. Collapsed soldiers were not to be transported to psychiatric institutions, but they had to be treated near the front lines. Their treatment had to be started as soon as possible and it had to be pointed out to the soldier that the whole therapy was above all aimed at his return to the battle. The treatment was to take place within a military setting, with therapists presenting themselves as officers and not as doctors.

These key points, proximity, immediacy and expectancy, form the gospel of combat psychiatry, or *forward psychiatry*. They also form the basis for a specific care system. Within this system the existing treatment facilities are divided into different levels. Although there are some variations in actual practice, in theory three different levels of medical assistance can be distinguished. The first level is situated near the fighting units. Usually these are the divisions, but sometimes also the brigades. Here the ambulant and semi-institutionalized facilities are situated. Only short-term treatments are given here, usually no more than one week. Soldiers who cannot be cured within this period of time will go to the second level. These facilities are preferably still in the close to the front line. This level may involved a longer stay, perhaps weeks rather than days. The base hospitals and specialized clinics situated far from the battlefields form the final level of military psychiatry. Viewed as places of last resort, patients are only sent there when everything else had failed. With their severe doubts about asylum treatment and their rejection of the medical model, military psychiatrists became anti-psychiatrists *avant la lettre*, except that their main concern was not the patient but the army.

Anyone expecting that military authorities have welcomed these new medical specialists with open arms will be disappointed. Psychiatrists and psychologists had to fight for their position and prove their efficacy in military matters over and over again. Traditional military morals were an important barrier. Mentally injured soldiers were traditionally viewed as 'cowards' or 'weaklings'. This aversion concepts of mental injury explains why military psychiatry only developed in fits and starts. This was particularly the case in Anglo-Saxon countries. In these countries psychiatric services had to be set up at the outset of each war. Peacetime would see them shut down or partially dismantled again. This was the case after World War II and also after the Korean conflict.

For the Americans the Vietnam war was the turning point. During the initial stage of the war the military authorities were optimistic. Expectations were that the mental burden for the soldiers would not be that bad. After all, they only had to serve one year and the recreational facilities were excellent. Therefore, no more than a handful of psychiatrists were actually posted in Vietnam.

For a while it seemed as if the mentally injured soldier had become a thing of the past, that it had been a historical phenomenon. But disillusionment followed during the 'seventies. More and more was doubt cast on the information about military psychiatric cases. The conclusions were said to have been too optimistic. For instance, the fact that many psychiatric casualties might have been registered under other labels, such as drug dependence and insubordination, might not have been taken into account. The big surprise, however, was that tens of thousands of soldiers did not show behavioural disorders until after the war. They were suffering from nightmares and experienced substantial social adjustment problems. Since 1980 this has usually been diagnosed as Post Traumatic Stress Disorder (PTSD).

It must be said that after a period of denial and hesitation the US military has been prepared to learn the lessons of the Vietnam war. Since the 'eighties they have begun to take combat psychiatry seriously again. Some allied forces have followed the example of their most important NATO-partner, and the Dutch army is one of these.

The Dutch Frame of Reference

Though there was initially little interest in the mentally injured soldier within the Dutch military, the behavioural scientists of the *Dutch Royal Army* started the process.

These scientists had been brought in since the 'sixties in large numbers and their duties had expanded more and more.[2] In addition to the introduction of selection procedures management training, organizational changes and socio-scientific research were added. In 1973 the Dutch Military Psychological and Sociological Service (*MPSD*) gained independent status. This service employed officers with university qualifications in psychological or sociological sciences in addition to their military education. In addition, a limited number of civilian behavioural scientists were, and still are, employed. By studying specialist literature, attending scientific meetings and participating in NATO working groups, the experts within the *MPSD* had become informed of the developments outside the Netherlands.

In this context it must be noted that there was no Dutch tradition to fall back on. The Netherlands had not taken an active part in World War I. During the May-days of 1940 forward psychiatry was non-existent and the actual fighting was too short to correct this mistake. During the police actions in Indonesia mental care was also insignificant. Only serious casualties could expect treatment. These were sent back to the Netherlands to be admitted into the military neurosis sanitarium at Austerlitz. Popularly speaking these soldiers suffered from 'tropical frenzy'.

Therefore Dutch behavioural scientists had to broaden their horizons beyond their own borders, and the United States and Israel were their main examples. After the disastrous Vietnam war the US military could no longer deny the existence of the mentally injured soldier. Moreover, realistic US army training manoeuvres at Fort Irwin, California in 1980 aroused the suspicion that combat losses might be much heavier in future conflicts and that psychological factors would be one of the reasons.

The Israeli army had not needed such manoeuvres to reach the same conclusion. The Yom Kippur war in 1973 had proved that psychological factors could lead to an enormous drain on forces. In the next big conflict, the invasion of Lebanon in 1982, therefore, combat psychiatry was prepared.[3]

The Dutch military behavioural scientists could use the American theory and the Israeli practice (which, by the way, was also very American-oriented), as their models. In both countries the behavioural disorders that the soldiers showed or might show were diagnosed as stress reactions. The corresponding therapeutical frame was therefore dominated by stress management.

Stress signifies the biochemical reactions occurring in the human body when someone is confronted with a situation that is felt to be threatening. If such a situation occurs certain chemical compounds will be excreted within the various endocrinological systems. Adrenaline is the most familiar of these compounds. As a result of the boom in biochemistry since the 'sixties research into physiological reactions have yielded more and more results. Not only were new chemical compounds discovered, but also more refined measuring techniques were developed, providing more accurate quantification of these compounds.

By then it had become clear that there were substantial individual differences with regard to the reactions to threatening situations. Social and cultural factors, for instance, proved to play an important role in individual perception processes. These variables were incorporated into stress research. The frame of this investigation is therefore more than a specific physiological variant of the medico-biological model. One could actually say that this point of view is rather an invitation to combine various approaches.

Within the stress paradigm it is common practice to make a distinction between minor, serious and severe stress reactions. In fact, we deal with the same cognitive, emotional and functional organic disorders in combination with manifestations of hysteria that have been seen during two world wars. Nevertheless, the interpretation of these symptoms within the modern stress reference frame is different from the past. The important thing is that these disorders are no longer seen as aberrant behaviour, on the contrary, every essay about combat stress reactions indicates actually that these are normal reactions. Only the situation in which the soldiers in question find themselves is abnormal. Everyone, even the highly trained and highly educated soldier will have to deal with it. It does not just happen to those who are mentally or physically predisposed. At the time of shell shock and combat exhaustion most psychiatrists used to have different views about this matter.

Naturally, these more positive views do not alter the fact that certain stress reactions may negatively influence the combat behaviour of the individual soldier and the unit in which he belongs. A therapeutical strategy will therefore remain necessary.

In view of this the American army started a program in 1985 to create an integrated approach to combat stress.[4] In the following year this programme was implemented in the US Army Field Manual by including the training package "Management of Stress in Army Operations". The American approach is integral, because every individual and all units are involved in the stress problems. Furthermore, it is assumed on the basis of historical findings that stress management must be applied not only during combat, but also before and afterwards. Soldiers learn to recognize and control the signs of stress in themselves and in others, under all circumstances. In this context simple self-control techniques are learned that can be used for emergencies. These techniques include relaxation techniques, auto-suggestion and meditation. During stress counselling the soldiers learn to help their buddies in controlling their stress reactions. This system of stress management has been a source of inspiration for the forces in other NATO-countries, including the Netherlands.

Psychologists in the Israeli army had shown that the classic basic principles had not yet lost all value; they had served as a starting point in setting up a care system that had just been finished when the Lebanon war broke out. The successes that the Israelis achieved in limiting combat stress were extensively described in scientific literature. Israeli psychologists became welcome speakers at scientific meetings and symposia about stress management.

With the US Army Field Manual in the one hand and the impressive Israeli therapeutical achievements in the other, Dutch military behavioural scientists started working. At the end of the 'eighties the army command became convinced. The department of behavioural sciences was allowed to make a proposal for setting up a system of psychological care for the army. The department got this order because they had convinced the army command that a large conflict to be fought out at the West German Lowlands would cause an enormous number of mentally injured soldiers. Moreover, they had impressed on the generals that these losses needed only be temporary, if only they would choose the right approach. The army command was also pleased to learn that such a system did not require recruiting new personnel, but that it could be manned by soldiers who did not have war duties, for instance, MPSD behavioural scientists and sports instructors. Until then these categories of personnel had only had a peace-time role. This could now be changed. This devised plan provided among other things a system of levels in which the central point lay with the Recovery Units for Combat Stress Reactions that would be assigned to the stand-by troops (± 4,000 men). For these units the following structure was devised:

- an MPSD officer (head) (lieutenant colonel/major)
- a reserve officer-doctor (captain/lieutenant)
- two (reserve officer) psychotherapists (captain/lieutenant)
- four NCOs (sergeant-majors).[5]

With this structure the American-Israeli line was followed. Other NATO-countries, such as Canada and the United Kingdom who were also in the process of giving shape to forward psychiatry preferred a different approach. In these countries the mentally injured soldier was kept within the medical field. There the recovery units were manned by psychiatrists and psychiatric nurses. There was no significant role whatsoever for psychologists and other behavioural scientists.

In 1989 the Dutch plans were finished, at least on paper. One year later the Berlin wall fell and with it the idea of a large-scale conflict with the Soviet Union diminished. The reports of the department of behavioural sciences could temporarily be put away. The army had to face an uncertain and surprising future.

New Tasks, New Stress Symptoms

The fall of the Berlin wall caused a debate in the Netherlands about the future of defence. Politicians agreed that the time was ready 'to draw some peace dividends'. In addition, the new safety situation seemed to suggest that ground troops in particular would pay this dividend. This part of the army had to deal with drastic reorganization between 1993 and 1997. The following matters in particular are important for this lecture. The army was reduced and in this process the operational part was divided into halves. In the new structure only three of the former six brigades were maintained. In addition, politicians used this opportunity to abolish unpopular conscription. As a result of this decision from 1997 the army would only consist of professional soldiers. Until then there was an interim stage, that pleased hardly anyone.

A final change concerned the role the armed forces were to play. The classic assignment, defending the fatherland and the allied territories, remained. But a second official role was added: military intervention in the wider world. This included carrying out peace-keeping operations and giving assistance at humanitarian actions. This extension of duties resulted primarily from the government's wish that the Netherlands as a small country could play a important role on the world stage, an aspiration supported by all sides in parliament. There were hardly any protests from the military authorities, because they feared that the military machinery would by no means survive the cuts in expenditure, without this new legitimizing of their existence.

So officially, the armed forces now had two main roles. In practice the stress was on the second, new one, especially in the minds of the people concerned. As Russia descended deeper and deeper into morass it hardly represented any threat, whereas peace-keeping operations increased in number and significance during the 'nineties. During the 'eighties about 12,000 soldiers were involved in peace-keeping operations every year. During the next 10 years this number was over 80,000. In the middle of 1995 there were 18 UN missions involving soldiers from almost 50 countries, the Dutch army taking an active part in these actions. Ground troops were present in Iraq, Cambodia, Haiti, Angola and former Yugoslavia, for instance. A total of about 12,000 soldiers, both conscripts and professional soldiers, were involved in these missions.[6]

Soldiers participating in peace-keeping operations are faced with war in a specific way. Their involvement in violent actions is quite different from the parties participating in the war. Take former Yugoslavia, for instance. Every UN soldier had learned even before he was posted abroad that he would risk hitting a mine when leaving the road. Furthermore, observation posts are opened-fire on, purposely or non-purposely. But the risks for these UN soldiers were limited compared to risks of a "real" war. Consequently, the rate of losses remained low, at least until now. Deprivations too can be said to have usually been at an acceptable level. Food and drink have always been available, although one had often fallen back on emergency supplies. In short, risks and deprivations are not the main elements of the observer's life. But more characteristic is the fact that these soldiers have witnessed large-scale havoc and cruelty. Officially these were exactly the situations they were supposed to prevent, but they had neither the means nor the power to do so. This was, of course, not only the case in the Balkans. An investigation among Norwegian UN-soldiers who had served in Lebanon (1978-1991), proved that thirty per cent of the blue helmets there had been forced one time or another to cede the protected territory to one of the fighting parties. Nine per cent had even experienced this regularly. Besides, in Lebanon UN-soldiers were taken hostage.[7]

Consequently, many blue helmets became enormously frustrated. They felt powerless and sometimes even guilt. The pointlessness of the situation is compounded by the powerlessness. Soldiers who are frequently under fire from either of the warring parties, and who are abused by the same civilian population that they are supposed to be protecting will doubt the value of their presence. In Sisal (Croatia) the blue helmets were greeted with the Hitler salute by the youngsters in the streets. In Zagreb the same soldiers were treated to texts such as "UN go home". According to a Dutch blue helmet, powerlessness and senselessness are the overwhelming feelings that soldiers take away from a UN-mission.

In addition to these external factors there is also an internal factor that may put soldiers under stress during peace-keeping operations. During their training the soldiers learn to use violence. They must be able to eliminate their opponent and preferably in the quickest possible way, so that the other will not be able to use his weapon. But in peace-keeping one has to wait for others to take action. Soldiers have to take safety risks, many of which they would normally consider unacceptable. These peace-keeping frustrations may become a serious threat to operational actions. Soldiers may give vent to their feelings individually, or collectively, and the civilian population may become the victim of this. In Canada and Belgium investigations are being carried out on the misbehaviour of soldiers during UN-missions. Television showed pictures of assaults committed by UN-soldiers. Such lapses are not only unpleasant for the victims, but they can also discredit a country. It is also quite possible that such behaviour will ask for acts of revenge, as a result of which the safety of all those involved in the mission will be compromised.

Obviously such direct consequences for operational success will be of primary interest to military authorities. Since the Vietnam war, however, it has become impossible to avoid asking questions about the long-term effects of the frustrations sustained. The investigation into long-term effects of participation in peace-keeping operations has only really started in the last few years. The preliminary results suggest that a significant percentage of UN-solders showed late stress reactions after the end of a mission.

In the Netherlands this has been witnessed in the case of Lebanon veterans, a group of about 8,000 soldiers. Sent to Lebanon between 1979 and 1985 in the scope of the UNIFIL operations, they formed a buffer between the Israeli army and the various Arabic and Palestinian military groups. During their time in Lebanon no major psychological problems were observed within this group. Nobody broke down and nobody had to be repatriated. But after their return to the Netherlands the situation became much less promising. From an investigation carried out in 1987 by the department of behavioural sciences it was found that about 10 per cent of the UNIFIL-veterans suffered from PTSD symptoms.[8] In 1996 340 soldiers had come to seek treatment. To begin with Lebanon veterans found the door closed. Not one of the treatment institutions serving the ground troops was suited to give this kind of assistance. The wife of one of the soldiers involved has written a book about her fruitless efforts with the medical and social institutions involved.[9] This publication shows that personnel care and the medical sector in particular had a chaotic structure. In addition, most experts appeared to be unaware of the fact that stress reactions may show only at a late stage. Not until 1993, after the publication of an article in the *Militaire Spectator*, did Mrs Mentink, the author, discover that her husband was probably suffering from PTSD-symptoms and that he was by far from alone in this.

The article in the *Militaire Spectator* was written by Col. R.W. Jacobs, a military psychologist, who was employed by the *Land Forces Individual Assistance* department. In this department the existence of PTSD was known, but the department lacked the personnel and finances necessary to set up an assistance programme. Finally this small group of clinical psychologists, in collaboration with the department of behavioural sciences, succeeded in convincing the heads of land forces that psychological assistance is also necessary for peace-keeping operations.

In 1991 they started the first experiments and four years later the land forces could proudly show a system of psychological and psychiatric assistance that was strongly manned both quantitatively and qualitatively.[10] During its development they initially focused on the provision of assistance during missions. Then they dealt with prevention. This included psychological preparation to the mission and the selection of personnel. Finally, aftercare was tackled. In the next section the main elements will be discussed.

Stress and Management in the Dutch Army

In 1917 the US army was the first in history to use the services of psychologists.[11] They did this after Gen. John Pershing, commander of the American Expeditionary Force, had insisted on a better selection of the soldiers to be sent to the front lines in France. To meet this wish auxiliary groups of psychologists devised the Army Alpha and the Army Beta tests. With the help of these tests the intelligence level of the recruits could be determined.

There is no doubt that psychologists today would be pleased to have a reliable test to measure stress predisposition, but we are a long way from this and it is questionable whether we will ever reach this point. Nevertheless, psychologists try, as far as possible, to screen soldiers and to test them for their suitability to participate in peace-keeping operations. For this a personality test and a psychiatric interview are conducted. Experiences with UNIFIL soldiers in Lebanon have led to the conclusion that two categories in particular are unsuitable for this kind of action. The first group consists of 'escapists'. These are soldiers who primarily want to join the army to escape their home situation. The second category comprises soldiers with a personal history characterized by a succession of traumatic experiences. This screening was aimed at filtering out these types of personnel and keep them in the Netherlands.

This screening is logically followed by the preparation for the mission. The starting point for this is the fact that every soldier on the ground must be familiar with the following relevant aspects of stress:
1. Lessons about traumatic experiences and stress
2. Training of stress control techniques
3. Training of preventive debriefing techniques

These three subjects are taught to groups during their officer or NCO training. During their basic training the men are mainly instructed in stress control techniques. Before they are sent abroad they get a so-called refresher course. Then they will all receive an instruction card which everyone is obliged to carry with him. This card not only describes the stress symptoms but gives also instructions how to control these. The officers also get another card to help them with the debriefing process.

It is evident that the care given during the missions occupies an important place within the total practice of psychological assistance. For it is at this stage that the soldier will have his traumatic experiences and the connecting frustrations. Assistance must be applied quickly if matters are not to get out of hand. The system devised by the land forces is founded on the basic principles. This means that it has been developed in such a way that it is possible to give immediate therapeutical treatment on the spot. The size and the nature of the peace-keeping operations involved meant that it was impossible to simply fall back on the blue-print of the 'eighties without adjustment. The organizational unit that is now used is no longer the brigade (about 4,000 men) but the battalion (about 600 to 800 men). In the Dutch army every battalion already had a social coordination committee available. This committee was composed of the unit medical doctor, the chaplain, the welfare officer and the personnel officer. But now when the battalion in question was sent out the committee was extended to contain a field psychologist, a clinical psychologist in the rank of major or lieutenant colonel. In 1991, in North Iraq, a psychologist joined the soldiers in the field of battle for the first time. It was just an experiment at the time, but by the time of the Bosnia mission (1994) this had become a standard procedure. When smaller units were sent out, such as platoons (40 men), or companies (about 150 men), there was no support from a field psychologist. But back-up support from a rapid reaction team (RRT) in the Netherlands itself is available, if necessary, providing psychologists and social workers. They can be deployed quickly because they have had all the innoculations necessary. In crisis situations they can be flown in without delay.

The field psychologist can give therapeutical assistance, when necessary. Besides he advises the commander, about matters concerning morale in particular, and gives assistance in debriefing. The latter activity is the core of psychological support in the area of operations. The idea is that the commander takes care after any incident whether it be an accident, a shooting or witnessing a massacre, the soldiers will be provided the opportunity to talk about it. In addition, an end debriefing is held after the mission has been finished. Ideally this is done when they are still in the area of operations. In smaller units that have to operate without a psychologist, end debriefing takes place as soon as possible after return to the Netherlands. The function of this debriefing is twofold. For the soldiers this is the beginning of the adjustment process. At the same time they give the psychologist, and thus the commanders, an insight into any staff problems that may arise in the future. For these end debriefings the psychologist gets assistance on the spot from colleagues who have been flown in especially for this purpose. After the fall of Srebrenica, for instance, four additional psychologists were deployed for the Dutchbat-3 soldiers.

The final step in the psychological assistance process is the so-called reintegration interview. This interview must take place two weeks after return to the Netherlands. The intention is to let the soldiers talk about the mission and about their first experiences after their return. Soldiers with psychological problems can then be referred to the appropriate military or civilian assistance service. The original principle of this assistance was to help the soldiers who were on active service. Veterans who by definition no longer belong to the active forces were not allowed to seek help from the Defence assistance institutions.

For military psychologists this was hard to swallow, because they knew that late stress reactions often do not manifest themselves until 6 months later. They also knew that the victims themselves would not always refer themselves to the assistance service. The same psychologists therefore advocated a more proactive policy, which implied that the soldiers would be approached at the initiative of the Defence department. This attitude was supported from outside. In the middle of 1994 military unions insisted on a similar approach to all conscripts who had participated in crisis control operations. At the same time critical questions were asked in Parliament about the aftercare for UN soldiers.[12]

Both the internal and external pressures were successful. At the end of the same year the Defence staff agreed to a more active and more comprehensive system of aftercare. To get some insight into the likely future demands on aftercare a pilot survey was carried out involving 236 soldiers. These persons were approached either by mail or by telephone about 9 months after their mission had been finished. 24 per cent of the soldiers contacted showed some kind of mental and/or psycho-social problems. Eventually 7 soldiers (4%) were placed under treatment by the department for individual assistance. Four soldiers were diagnosed with PTSD. The history of the current, new style of aftercare is rather limited and it is therefore impossible to give a proper judgement on its functioning. In the following and last section we will give a short enumerative description of the main points of the Dutch stress management system.

Final Remarks

The toll of modern industrial war is substantial. Among the physical casualties there are also soldiers who are mentally injured. Military psychiatry was developed to help this group and to re-deploy them, if possible.

During World War I the stress was on curative treatment. This took the shape of forward psychiatry. The emphasis on prevention became particularly manifest during World War II.

The Netherlands was largely oblivious of these developments. Not until the 'eighties did the army and the land forces in particular begin to worry about the lack of a system of psychiatric or psychological care, prompted by the discussions within the US military after the Vietnam dèbacle. The experiments of the Israeli forces during the Lebanon war also came to the notice of our country.

The American-Israeli views were introduced to the army by behavioural scientists who were members of the Military Psychological and Sociological Service. The absence of a psychiatric tradition enabled them to set up a system that was not included in the medical circuit. In this system the behavioural scientists and the clinical psychologists in particular took a central role.

Central to the theoretical framework is the stress paradigm. This means that the mentally injured soldier is not considered to be aberrant. Rather, the symptoms (stress reactions) are seen as normal reactions to an abnormal situation. Thus the mentally injured soldier is standardized. It is recognised that even the healthiest, strongest personalities can suffer from stress reactions on certain occasions.

The setting up of a concrete system of care happened in two phases. During the first phase the concept of a large-scale conflict with the Soviet Union still dominated. However, the fall of the Berlin wall led to a substantial reorganization of land forces, during which process the aspirations of military psychologists were pushed to one side. By the 'nineties the army was involved in several extensive and less extensive peace-keeping operations. Soon it became obvious that soldiers also on these kind of missions could be mentally damaged. An adapted system of forward psychiatry was developed to cope with this problem. Within this system attention was not only focused on preventive and curative treatments, but also on aftercare.

Currently there is no other NATO country where such a system exists just for peace-keeping operations. Only the Dutch army sends psychologists as stress managers with its UN detachments. Nowhere has psychological assistance service as many personnel as in the Dutch army. Indeed, the department for individual assistance employs no fewer than thirty clinical psychologists, whereas the land forces consist of only three brigades of four thousand men each.

Acknowledgements

I would like to thank the following people for providing useful information: Maj.drs. G. Cloïn, Col.drs. A. Lobbezoo, Dr. R. Moelker and Col.drs. H.W. de Swart.

Notes

1. The following is based on Hans Binneveld, *From Shell Shock to Combat Stress. A Comparative History of Military Psychiatry* (Amsterdam: Amsterdam University Press, 1997).
2. Maj.drs. ing. H.F.M. Vullinghs, *De Militaire Gedragswetenschapper in de Koninklijke Landmacht* (Den Haag: Militair Psychologische en Sociologische Dienst, 1995).
3. Haim Dasberg, 'Trauma in Israel', in: H. Dasberg (ed.), *Society and Trauma of War* (Assen/Maastricht: Van Gorcum, 1987) 1–13, p. 3-7.
4. Binneveld, *ibid.*, p. 174.
5. Lt.col H.W. de Swart, *Human Implications of Modern Warfare. Recovery Units for Combat Stress Victims* (The Hague: Directorate of Personnel (RNLA), 1989) 7.
6. J.M.P. Weerts en L. Weisaeth, 'Epiloog. Stress-factoren, vredeslegers en toekomst-scenario's' in: H.M. van der Ploeg and J.M.P. Weerts eds., *Veteranen in Nederland. Onderzoek naar de Gevolgen van Oorlogservaringen, Tweede Wereldoorlog, Politionele Acties, Korea* (Lisse: Swets & Zeitlinger B.V., 1995), 197–213, p. 205.
7. Weerts en Weisaeth, *ibid.*, 204.
8. Herman W. de Swart, Tessa G.E. Willigenburg, Natasja D. Alkemade, *Contributions of (Military) Psychology to UN/NATO Peacekeeping Operations*. Paper First European Conference on Traumatic Stress in Emergency Services, Peacekeeping and Humanitarian Aid Operations, Sheffield, 18-20 March, 1996, p. 2.
9. Mimi Mentink-Heshusius, *De plicht tot hulp. De Post-traumatische stress-stoornis bij een Nederlandse VN-militair* (Amsterdam, Heuff/Thesis, 1993).
10. B. Peijzel & R.W. Jacobs, 'Stress, trauma en zorg' in: Ted van Baarda and Jan Schoeman (eds), *Werelden apart? Militairen en burgers:*

vredeshandhavers en hulpverleners (Den Haag, SDU, 1997), 161–85, p. 173 ff.

11. The following is based on De Swart, Willigenburg, Alkemade, *ibid.*

12. T. Willigenburg en N.D. Alkemade, *Pilot nazorg Koninklijke Landmacht* ('s-Gravenhage, DPKL/GW en DPKL/AIH, 1995), 10.

Nicely done

14

Moral insanity was used not only to force conformity upon women but to free some from responsibility for committing murder

Anti-Psychiatry and the Family:
Taking the Long View*

Roy Porter

Anti-psychiatry was a revolt against psychiatry but it was not less psychiatry in revolt. But against what? To understand the movement, it is important to establish what it was fighting. This essay examines one aspect of anti-psychiatry's struggle, by setting it within a longer time-frame.

As other papers in this volume show very clearly, debates about the pathogenic role of the family were central to much of 1960s and 1970s European anti-psychiatry – not surprisingly because those were times of the youth revolt, of dropping-out and the 'pill generation', all of which subjected the authority of parental figures to decisive challenge. The mood of the times was summed up with bitter irony by the poet Philip Larkin:

> They fuck you up
> Your mum and dad.[1]

The Billy Graham of that gospel of how families drive you crazy was Ronald Laing, whose views, expressed in best-sellers like _The Divided Self_ (1960) and _The Politics of the Family_ (1971) blamed families, mothers – in particular, for the double binds that trapped the rising generation in what orthodox psychiatry had standardly called schizophrenia.[2] The film that brought such thinking to mass audiences in the UK was inevitably called 'Family Life' (1971).

Though Laing was later to be demonized as antichrist in the British moral panic of the 1990s over the supposed break-up of the traditional nuclear family, received social-psychiatric wisdom in the

---

* A briefer and somewhat different version of this paper is being published in the _Journal of Family History_. I am most grateful to all my colleagues at the Anglo-Dutch conference, and to others, for their incisive comments.

257

post-1950s 'me' society continues to support the individual over and against the fatal attractions of the family; the smothering mother and the absent or incestuous father remain prominent and powerful negative images. Indeed on both sides of the Atlantic we now have an epidemic of clients convinced, arguably by consequence of the suggestions of their therapists, that all their troubles stem from abusive parents, especially fathers. A False Memory Society now exists to help accused parents to fight back against accusing children.[3]

All such developments are, however obliquely, the legacy of Freud – though his is a ferociously contested inheritance, especially amongst feminists, some of whom hail him, while others denounce him as, in Kate Millett's resounding denunciation, 'beyond question the strongest individual counter-revolutionary force in the ideology of sexual politics'.[4] Freud's disclosure of Oedipal wishes – kill your father, sleep with your mother – turned the Holy, Happy Family into a minefield, as may be inferred from the classic case-histories of Dora, Little Hans, the Wolf Man and the Rat Man, where neuroses are revealed to be the scars of spoilt parent-child relations – though Freud's own allegiances in these 'family romances' are controversial.

Family romance was, of course, central to Freud's personal odyssey, his father's death perhaps triggering the world's first self-analysis. During the early 1890s he was elaborating his theory that neurosis stemmed from early sexual traumas. His hysterical female patients, he initially maintained, had been subjected to pre-pubescent 'seduction' – that is, paternal sexual abuse; repressed memories of such assaults were the precipitants of their troubles. He spelt out this 'seduction theory' to Wilhelm Fliess in May 1893, and over the next three years further letters mark mounting enthusiasm for his shocking hypothesis, until on April 21, 1896, he went public in a talk in Vienna on 'The Aetiology of Hysteria'.[5]

The next year, however, on September 21, 1897, he confessed to Fliess: 'I no longer believe in my *neurotica*', that is, the seduction theory. By then Freud had convinced himself that his patients' seduction stories were fantasies, originating not in the perverse deeds of adults but in the erotic wishes of infants.[6] The burying of the seduction theory brought the birth of the idea of infantile sexuality and the Oedipus complex – first disclosed to Fliess a month later:

> I have found love of the mother and jealousy of the father in my own case too, and now believe it to be a general phenomenon of

258

early childhood ... if that is the case, the gripping power of *Oedipus Rex*, in spite of all the rational objections to the inexorable fate that the story presupposes, becomes intelligible ... Every member of the audience was once a budding Oedipus in phantasy ...[7]

Up to his death Freud held fast to its importance: 'if psycho-analysis could boast of no other achievement than the discovery of the repressed Oedipus complex', he wrote in the last year of his life, 'that alone would give it a claim to be included among the precious new acquisitions of mankind'.[8] The twin pillars of orthodox psychoanalytic theory – the unconscious, and infantile sexuality – thus emerged from Freud's *volte face*: had the seduction theory not been abandoned, psychoanalysis could not exist.

The renegade Freudian, Jeffrey Masson, has stood the conventional interpretation on its head, however. His *The Assault on Truth* (1983) argued that Freud got it right first time; it was the *abandonment* of the seduction theory that was the error, a betrayal of the truth and of his patients' trust. This change of mind was in part due to the death of his own father in October 1896: thenceforth Papa Sigmund stood in the father's shoes. Psychoanalysis was a cover-up.[9]

It is not necessary for the argument of this paper to decide whether Masson, or Freud, or neither of them, was right. Either way, the birth of psychoanalysis was bad news for the old-style moral model of the family; from then on, there were not just problem families: the family was itself was the problem. Nor did this creed remain restricted to the magic circle of Freudian shrinks; such convictions were to permeate modern consciousness, becoming canonical to the theory and practices of the social and psychological sciences, in child welfare and family guidance schemes and so forth.[10]

Freud of course was a far cry from the irate, mother-hating Laing. The monogamous Viennese patriarch with his one wife and six children did not come out in favour of alternatives to the bourgeois family – Oedipal struggles, he believed, provided the arduous initiation into the realities of gendered heterosexuality; the family might have its problems but what other solution was there?[11] Some rebel Freudians, admittedly, went further and anathematized the patriarchal family. Blaming it for the mass psychology of fascism, Wilhelm Reich believed it shored up domination by institutionalizing sexual repression. And, like his mentor, Reich too could commandeer anthropological fantasy. Bachofen, Engels, and others had established it as 'a historically proven fact' that

259

matriarchy had been the family system of 'natural society'. To Reich, it was history's tragedy that this idyllic maternal order had yielded to the dictatorship of the father.[12]

Reich notwithstanding, mainstream Freudianism has not, in practice, been about wrecking the family but rescuing it; our therapeutic society has made it its business to buttress the family or, where necessary, to stand in for it, through agencies like juvenile courts and family counselling. In Britain the milestone was the founding in 1920 of the Tavistock Clinic. Extending psychiatry beyond the asylum to the couple in the street, the 'Tavvy' heightened awareness of childhood problems and family psychodynamics. Its Children's Department led to the Child Guidance Council (1927), subjecting family trauma, that Victorian secret garden, to professional inquiry and expert direction. The spread of psychoanalysis sanctioned the view that 'normal' people might have 'complexes', and popularized ideas like juvenile delinquency – the 'crazy mixed-up kid'. Parallel developments occurred in marriage-guidance.[13]

Thus, quite independently of Laing, modern thinking came to identify the family as the prime site, and perhaps the prime source, of personal disorder. In the 'victim' society of the 1990s,[14] the institution that takes the rap is the family, the baddies are the daddies (and even the mammies). But where did psychiatric opinion stand two, three or four hundred years ago? Was the family indicted as pathogenic then? And if not, when did that begin?

The sermons, homilies, plays and proverbs of early modern times, it has been stresed by social historians, undeniably harped on about the fates that might befall families – think of *Hamlet* or *King Lear*,[15] so it will come as no surprise that those we may somewhat anachronistically call psychiatric writers warned that bad families bred troubled minds. Robert Burton's *Anatomy of Melancholy* (1621) for example explained how disordered spirits could arise from faulty upbringing: 'bad parents, step-mothers, Tutors, Masters, Teachers, too rigorous and too severe, or too remisse or indulgent on the other side, are often fountaines and furtherers of this disease'.[16] The perils of sibling rivalry were likewise no secret. 'Even at the tenderest age, in the very cradle', explained George III's physician, Sir George Baker, 'unmistakeable signs of jealousy may be seen…. The child is not to be freed from this grave illness by any art or physician's help unless the rival infant is taken from his sight'.[17] The idea that mental disorder ran in families was also a commonplace of early modern times and its medical mouthpieces. Burton devoted attention to it, and in due course it became restated in the idioms of degenerationist psychiatry and eugenics – biogenetic questions too vast to be further addressed here.[18]

Those seeking help from mental healers, or in a later age from specialist mad-doctors, commonly related how their afflictions sprang from family troubles, as Michael MacDonald's brilliant study of Richard Napier has made clear. An Anglican clergyman-physician active in early Stuart times, Napier left case-notes detailing a couple of thousand consultations with mental patients. These confirm that early modern patriarchal families could be every bit as forbidding as Lawrence Stone has maintained. But rather than the consequence being Reichian psychological armour-plating, the outcome was often despair and breakdown, dread of damnation and suicidal fits. Of the 134 cases of deep depression Napier handled, 58 were attributed to children's deaths. 'Much grief for the death of two children', related one parent. Of Agnys Morton, who had murdered her illegitimate child, it was said: 'This woman is distracted of her wits ... went to make herself away, being tempted as she sayeth thereunto by the Tempter. Will not in any case say her prayers ... Very ravenous and greedy, and will say the foul Fiend lyeth at her heart, that she cannot feed him fast enough'.[19]

Almost forty percent of those who described their anxieties to Napier complained about the frustrations of courtship or of married life. Many wives reported their husbands were brutal, abusive and adulterous. For instance, Mistress Podder told him she had been 'Mightily wronged and beaten by her husband that cannot brook her and calleth her a whore'. But Napier's attitude toward wives who wanted to separate from their husbands was strict. The urge to escape was a sign of a troubled mind. Alice Harvey, then living with her parents, was diagnosed 'mopish' because she could not 'abide to be at home with her husband'.[20]

If we leap forward in time we can hear the plea of the distressed more audibly. Take John Perceval, fifth son of Prime Minister, Spencer Perceval, assassinated in 1812. The father's extreme Evangelical convictions were imbibed by his children, notably by John and the eldest son, Spencer. After abortive military and university careers, John became involved with the Glasgow 'Row' pentecostal sect, and started hearing voices and speaking in tongues; he began evangelizing in Dublin, contracted syphilis from a prostitute he was rescuing, grew delirious, and was dispatched by his family to Brislington Asylum in Bristol, later being transferred to Ticehurst in Sussex. He spent nearly two years in confinement.

Perceval [margin annotation]

Perceval's background seems tailor-made for Freudian analysis: a noble father murdered, a mother who quickly remarried a Lieutenant-Colonel yet who remained the object of her unmarried son's love, even when in his thirties. The Oedipal, indeed Hamletian, echoes hit you in the face. Perceval admitted to a delusion that he was not the son of his 'reputed' parents, but that his father had adopted him from a Bristol woman called Robinson, believing that 'I was ordained to be a herald of the second coming of the Lord, from my conception'.[21]

How far, if at all, did Perceval himself trace his psychic crisis to his family problems? As related in his autobiographical *A Narrative of the Treatment Received by a Gentleman, During a State of Mental Derangement*, the first volume of which appeared in 1838, he found the faith of certain members of his family – in particular, his eldest brother, another Spencer – humbug, professing a love to him that was a mere 'mask of Christianity'. His family made unctuous professions of affection, but only so as to provoke in him insupportable emotional tensions and conflicts of loyalty. In letters he received while in the asylum, he was always being told how much his family loved him and how grateful he should be. Yet he was never grateful enough, and so he was constantly snubbed and slighted. Moreover, the family's role as supplier of love automatically gave it the right of control over him. At thirty, his mother was still addressing him as 'my dear child', and reproving him for the pain his anguished letters were inflicting upon her, while his elder brother would address him 'as if speaking to a child'.[22]

Perceval grew convinced that one of the main reasons his insanity worsened was his abandonment by his family. He loved them 'almost with a romantic attachment', but their neglect convinced him he was the victim of hypocrisy: 'to have been so loved, or so duped by the appearance of my family's love, and to be so abandoned'. Sometimes he explicitly conjoined family, faith and asylum. At Brislington he superimposed the identities of family members upon staff and patients, identifying a particularly pretty maid, called Louise, with one of his own sisters; seeing the hated son of Dr Fox as his eldest brother; while, as for Dr Fox himself, occasionally 'I called him my father'.[23]

The Holy Family, Perceval's natural family and the surrogate asylum family superimposed themselves in a single configuration, one unstable and baffling in Perceval's imagination. He called them all 'manifestations of the Trinity'. By contrast there is no evidence that his doctors – the one-time Quaker Edward Fox in Brislington, or Charles Newington at Ticehurst – embraced aetiological models that read his madness as caused by family strains: the patient approaches closer than his doctors to the kind of psychodynamic reading standard after Freud.[24]

In short, sufferers quite frequently attributed their mental distress to family tensions. Commentators agreed. Novelists from Tobias Smollett in *Sir Launcelot Greaves* (1762) to Charles Reade in *Hard Cash* a century later dramatized the family feuds or machinations that drove some to madness or victimized the sane and led to their sequestration.[25] Doctors, we might say, had family pathology staring them in the face. In this respect I wish to examine the case of Richard Dadd.

Dadd was born on 1 August 1817 in the Medway town of Chatham. He began to draw seriously when he was about thirteen. In 1834 his family moved to London, settling off Pall Mall, then the fashionable art quarter. His father was involved in carving and gilding, and this introduced the young Dadd into artistic circles. One of the most talented young students, Dadd won three silver medals at the Royal Academy. He developed a clear preference for scenes from Shakespeare, and discovered his true *métier* in *A Midsummer Night's Dream*. In 1841 he showed 'Titania Sleeping' at the Academy. He had obviously found the outlet for a most powerful poetic imagination.

He travelled abroad. With his patron, Sir Thomas Phillips, he crossed to Ostend in, to begin a fateful journey. The first month carried them to Venice; then they moved to Ancona, to Greece, then to Smyrna, Constantinople, Rhodes, Cyprus, Beirut, and then on to Damascus. In less than two weeks they toured Mount Hermon, TIberias, Cana, Nazareth, finishing up at Jerusalem. At Jericho they were surrounded by armed arab tribesmen who galloped up with wild gesticulations and brandishing spears, led by a sheik who bargained with their escort for a ransom. Next came Egypt. It was during this whole Egyptian period that Dadd experienced the first symptoms of the illness which was to destroy his reason. Later, he was said to have suffered sunstroke one intensely hot day but to have recovered.

On the way home he developed a terrible feeling of unease: during the passage from Alexandria to Malta, 'I never passed six more miserable days. I scarcely know – perhaps I should say that I am perfectly ignorant of – the cause of the nervous depression that I experienced'.

Throughout the return journey Dadd suffered increasingly from delusions that he was being pursued by spirits, which appeared to him in different disguises; as an old lady in the Vatican galleries, as a priest pretending that he could not understand English, as Sir Thomas Phillips himself on board the steamer from Alexandria, playing at cards for the captain's soul. Towards the end of May 1843, his self-control failed completely, and he showed 'symptoms of aberration of mind' which made Sir Thomas seek medical advice. Dadd fled precipitately home to London.

It was soon obvious to his family and friends that Dadd was insane. He was watchful and suspicious, reserved and gloomy. His actions became unpredictable and occasionally violent, and he believed that he was being watched: he shut himself in his room and waved a knife at visitors; he is said to have cut a birthmark from his forehead, saying it was planted there by the devil. He let slip to a close friend that he was haunted by evil spirits, and was himself searching for the devil.

Dadd felt increasingly under the domination of external powers, whose authority he could not resist, even while still recognising that other people would take them for symptoms of insanity. He felt persecuted by the devil's minions but began to believe in his own mission to rid the whole world of the devil: and intertwined amongst his ideas was a strong element of Egyptian mythology.

He continued working, however, throughout this critical period, and his father resolutely maintained that nothing was wrong except the after-effects of sunstroke, which would pass with rest and quiet. Finally he was prevailed on to consult Dr Alexander Sutherland of St Luke's Hospital, one of the leading mad-doctors of the day. Sutherland advised that Richard was no longer responsible for his actions and should be put under restraint; but Robert Dadd determined to care for him himself.

On Monday 28 August, Dadd called on his father asking him to go down into the country, to his old haunt of Cobham, and promised to 'unburden his mind' when they got there. The two went out together for a walk in Cobham Park, where Richard slew his father with a spring knife. It was premeditated, as Dadd himself explained: 'the idea of a descent from the Egyptian god Osiris, induced me to put a period to the existence of him whom I had always regarded as a parent, but whom the secret admonishing I had, counselled me was the author of the ruin of my race'.

He fled to France and was arrested on the night of 30 August. Under French law he was committed to an asylum without trial on being certified insane. In 1844 he was brought to England. Arriving on 28 July he appeared before the magistrates at Rochester and was remanded to Maidstone gaol. He remained there for another fortnight, alternating between fits of frenzied violence and intervals when he was mild and amenable. At length, on 22 August 1844, he was removed and admitted to the criminal lunatic department of Bethlem Hospital, under an Act of 1840 which enabled the Home Secretary to transfer any prisoner to an asylum on receiving proper certification of his insanity.

The Bethlem of 1844 had come some way since the 'Bedlam' of the era of William Hogarth. From 1815 it had been housed at St George's Fields, Southwark. The use of iron manacles had practically ceased by the 1830s. Dadd was admitted from prison in a strait-waistcoat, but was never again subjected to physical restraint. Dadd began to produce again works of incredible delicacy and beauty, and absorption in art was to sustain him for the next forty years. His first work in Bethlem was in watercolour and consisted chiefly of landscapes and eastern scenes, remembered or worked up from the sketchbook which contained drawings from his Middle Eastern trip – works like 'View in the Island of Rhodes' and 'Bethlehem'. A small oil on panel also dates from the first year, the 'Caravanserai at Mylasa', and he probably went on working over his Middle Eastern material for several years, with paintings such as his 'The Flight out of Egypt' and the 'Caravanserai'.

Bethlem was long presided over by Sir Alexander Morrison, whose portrait Dadd painted. But from around 1850 Dadd was in the hands of a man outstanding in Bethlem's history, Dr William Charles Hood. Appointed at the age of twenty-eight, he was a man of vision and industry, of compassion, culture and commonsense.

Hood was not alone, sharing both work and outlook with the new steward George Henry Haydon, who was little older than himself. In writing up Dadd's casenotes in 1854 Hood spoke of him as being, despite his still deluded state and often unpleasant behaviour, able to be 'a very sensible and agreeable companion, and shew in conversation, a mind once well educated and thoroughly informed in all the particulars of his profession in which he still shines ...'. Hood's admiration for his work is borne out by the fact that he acquired thirty-three of his works of art.

In 1853 Dadd began the series 'Sketch to Illustrate the Passions', of which nearly thirty survive. There is considerable violence and tension in some of these and in other watercolour sketches of the same period, and they seem almost to be used as a vehicle to channel his aggression, which is far less evident in the oil paintings. Of the oils, 'Oberon and Titania' and 'The Fairy Feller's Master-stroke', the two masterpieces of his maturity, are dedicated to Hood and Haydon respectively. They appear to represent his only return to fairy painting after his confinement; the former occupied him for four years and the latter for up to nine.

For many years there had been plans to build a new and much larger state criminal asylum in Berkshire, and when Broadmoor Hospital was finally completed all the Bethlem criminal patients were transferred there. Broadmoor had been designed to allow as much freedom of movement as possible within the outer perimeter. These changed conditions do not seem to have produced much outward change, however, in Dadd's work, which by now was almost entirely the product of imagination; he went on with the fragile and mystical little watercolours of his late period. These were interspersed with a few oils. His major work at Broadmoor is now largely destroyed, the decoration of the theatre in 1874 with murals, an elaborate drop-curtain and other scenery; only a few remnants survive.

Dadd never recovered his sanity, though his intellectual powers were left practically untouched. At Bethlem he was always liable to sudden, if infrequent, outbursts of violence; he would make unprovoked attacks on his neighbours, and apologise afterwards; and his behaviour and conversation were often uncontrolled and disagreeable. His apparently irrational 'impulses' all stemmed from the same source, the feeling of being controlled by Osiris and other Egyptian spirits and this belief remained until he died, on 8 January 1886.

What did the Victorian public make of this mad artist? Few of Dadd's pictures produced after his insanity were publicly exhibited during his lifetime, but there was no attempt to conceal his name or fate. At the Manchester *Art Treasures* exhibition of 1857, three of his oil paintings and three watercolours were exhibited, and the *Manchester Guardian*'s reviewer considered them in relation to the painter's insanity, suggesting that Dadd and Blake might be classed together as 'examples of painters in whom a disordered brain rather aided than impeded the workings of a fertile and original fancy'. But though he was handled sympathetically, there is no sign that Dr Alexander Morison and others who dealt with him entertained models of family pathology when they tried to explain his deed or subsequently to treat him.[26]

I am not, be it noted, suggesting that doctors did not perceive family stresses at all, or that they did not seek to address them. Far from it. In 1753, for instance, Dr George Young recounted a case in which a woman went out of her mind as a result, Young said, of cruel treatment by her husband. He was proud of then successfully dosing her up with opium.[27] At roughly the same time another doctor, Patrick Blair, reported a case in which he had treated a married woman who had gone peculiar and ceased to oblige her husband. Blair tried on her 'frequent bleedings, violent Emeticks, strong purgatives and potent Sudoricks and Narcoticks', and gradually she regained 'the use of her Reason', and showed 'all signs of recovery except that of the dislike to her husband'. Dr Blair knew what to do next:

> I ordered her to be blindfolded. Her nurse and other women stript her. She was lifted up by force, plac'd in and fixt to the Chair in the bathing Tub. All this put her in an unexpressable terrour especially when the water was let down. I kept her under the fall 30 minutes, stopping the pipe now and then and enquiring whether she would take to her husband but she still obstinately deny'd till at last being much fatigu'd with the pressure of the water she promised she would do what I desired on which I desisted, let her go to bed, gave her a Sudorifick as usual. She slept well that night but was still obstinate. I repeated the bleeding and other preparatory doses. A week after I gave her another Tryal by adding a smaller pipe so that when the one let the water fall on top of her head the other squirted it in her face or any other part of her head neck or breast I thought proper. Being still very strong I gave her 60 minutes at this time when she still kept so obstinate that she would not promise to take to her husband till her spirits being allmost dissipated she promised to Love him as before. Upon this she was laid a bed as formerly but the next day she was still obstinate. Evacuations being endeavoured for 2 or 3 dayes more I gave her the 3d Tryal of the fall and continued her 90 minutes under it, promised obedience as before but she was as sullen and obstinate as ever the next day. Being upon resentment why I should treat her so, after 2 or 3 dayes I threatened her with the fourth Tryal, took her out of bed, had her stipt, blindfolded and ready to be put in the Chair, when being terrify'd with what she was to undergo she kneeld submissively that I would spare her and she would become a Loving obedient and dutifull Wife for ever thereafter. I granted her request provided she would go to bed with her husband that night, which she did with great chearfullness ... About 1 month afterwards I went to pay her a visit, saw every thing in good order.[28]

Such success stories reveal a situation in which the mad-doctor seems quite indifferent to delving into what might seem to us the roots of the problem, but undertakes what to his mind is the solution – the restoration by all means possible of the family *status quo*, a strategy earlier evident in Napier's spiritual healing.

Psychiatric practice was thus geared to upholding the family: that is hardly surprising in a social order whose dominant ideologies still thought in terms of nests of family units rather than atomized individuals – take for example the categories in Gregory King's political arithmetic – and which viewed the household as a miniature monarchy.[29] In any case, at least amongst the better-off, eighteenth- and nineteenth-century psychiatric transactions were largely private and initiated through the family hiring practitioners or asylum-keepers.[30] The sick son, wayward wife or delinquent daughter was thus typically a pawn in a transaction between the family and the mad-doctors.

In extreme circumstances, this could involve perfectly lucid if vexatious family members being shut away, through the connivance of corrupt madhouse-keepers, in fulfilment of family strategies: removing embarrassments, seizing fortunes or protecting property. Early in the eighteenth century Daniel Defoe alleged there was

> a vile Practice … in vogue among the better Sort … namely, the sending their Wives to Mad-Houses at every Whim or Dislike, that they may be more secure and undisturb'd in their Debaucheries: Which wicked Custom is got to such a Head, that the number of private Mad-Houses in and about London, are considerably increased within these few Years.[31]

Defoe's allegations were not the lone cry of a scandal-mongering journalist. 'The Case of a Woman perfectly in her Senses brought as a Lunatic by her husband to a House under the Doctor's Direction', was related by the leading mid-eighteenth century mad-doctor, William Battie; the husband 'justified himself by frankly saying, he understood the House to be a Sort of Bridewell, or Place of Correction'.[32] Indeed when Margaret Hunt examined separation suits at the London Consistory Court in the years 1711 to 1713, she found that in half the cases, husbands had threatened to commit their wives to a house of correction or the madhouse.[33]

From 1774 a series of Madhouse Acts aimed to put an end to such iniquities through mandatory certification procedures, but scandals which continued throughout the nineteenth century leave no doubt that family-instigated confinement of those protesting sanity or false imprisonment remained common.[34] Married to the Rev. George Lowe, in 1870 Louisa Lowe had moved out of her matrimonial home. He demanded she return; she refused; he had her kidnapped and taken to Brislington House, Bristol – Perceval's one-time asylum. Though the certificates authorising her committal were found to be invalid, Dr Fox detained her for a further two months. She brought an action against him for false imprisonment, but the Lord Chief Justice ruled it was not a criminal offence to incarcerate a sane individual, provided the intent were not malicious.

There she remained until February 1871, when she was moved to Lawn House, Hanwell, the private asylum of the distinquished Dr Henry Maudsley, who diagnosed her as 'suffering from delusions'. During a visit by the Commissioners in Lunacy in March she demanded to be set free, but on her request that a jury be convened to decide her fate, the Commissioner, Dr Lutwidge, retorted, 'it is very possible but very undesirable'.

In October the Commissioners again visited The Lawn. Mrs Lowe again begged to be released, but they replied that it would be 'contrary to all etiquette', as a suit had been brought by her husband to gain control of her property, then yielding £500 p.a. Overall she was detained for eighteen months. She alleged that the Commissioners had known all along that she was in her right mind, and had failed to do their duty by not supervising her release, warning 'that many sane, and still more merely eccentric and quite harmless persons, are languishing in the mad houses', and going on to found the Lunacy Law Reform Association to protect future family victims.[35]

Doubtless, in suchlike proceedings, some madhouse keepers knowingly behaved in corrupt and mercenary ways. But in handling patients presented by their families, most, like Maudsley, were surely acting in line with their convictions. Orthodox medical beliefs maintained that the root of the problem lay in the disturbed, obstreperous individual, and remedy would come from their restoration to proper conduct.[36]

With such ends in mind madhouse keepers claimed from the eighteenth century that recovery could best be achieved by the temporary detachment of the sick person from family surroundings and removal to an institution – a newish development, since from Greek times lunatics had largely been looked after at home. The madhouse's advantages were obvious – the family got the problem off its hands, and the doctor gained an often lucrative charge. And theoretical rationales were to hand. The best hopes of cure, William Battie and others declared, lay in prompt institutionalization which would grant the doctor total control. Confinement was thus a matter not of punishment or custody but of therapy.[37] Early Victorian experts like Robert Gardiner Hill testified to

> the improbability (I had almost said moral impossibility) of an insane person's regaining the use of his reason, except by removing him early to some institution for that purpose.[38]

'Calmness will come', promised Dr John Conolly in his panegyric on the model asylum of the future, 'hope will revive; satisfaction will prevail... [The asylum is the place] where humanity if anywhere on earth, shall reign supreme'.[39]

The selling of the asylum was facilitated by the claim that madhouses truly were *houses*. David Irish, a madhouse keeper in early eighteenth-century Guildford, stressed that his was indeed a genuinely domestic establishment ('good Fires, Meat and Drink', he promised).[40] At the York Retreat the presiding Tuke family portrayed their institution as domestic, and the superintendent was called 'the master of the family'. Its atmosphere of domestic intimacy was easy to maintain so long as the number of patients remained small. In 1796, the Retreat had just fifteen, but by 1841 that had climbed to eighty-seven, by which time one patient was rueing that 'to one that has always been used to a small family, this is just like being in a show'.[41]

Foucault of course was to mount a critique of the familial tenor of the Retreat, complaining that madness was there reduced to 'childhood' and that 'everything at the Retreat is organized so that the insane are transformed into minors'.[42] The Tukes could have had no quarrel with that. 'There is much analogy between the judicious treatment of children, and that of insane persons', Samuel Tuke happily observed, citing Locke: evidence of how radically the standing of the family was to change between the Georgian Quaker and the modern structuralist.[43]

The upshot of such mythologies of the madhouse as a happy home was that, as Andrew Scull has shown, confinement was made to seem normal.[44] And in turn the availability of the institution reduced tolerance for the disturbed. 'I ... think there is a disposition among all classes not to bear with the troubles that may arise in their own houses', opined Joseph John Henley, General Inspector of the Local Government Board in the late Victorian era:

If a person is troublesome from senile dementia, dirty in his habits, they will not bear with it now. Persons are more easily removed to an asylum than they were a few years ago.[45]

From the eighteenth century, certain precepts and practices thus became authorized. Those deviating from their ascribed family role might be diagnosed as mentally ill; they required treatment from a mad-doctor; and this was best done in an institution. Psychiatric theory and practice thus tended to problematize the family member not the family, often in terms of the diagnosis of 'moral insanity' – roughly speaking, delinquent behaviour – which was developed by James Cowles Prichard. In his *A Treatise on Insanity* (1835), the ex-Quaker Bristol doctor stated that:

> When it happens that the head of a family labours under this ambiguous modification of insanity, it is sometimes thought necessary, from prudential motives, and to prevent absolute ruin from thoughtless and absurd extravagance ... to make some attempt with a view to take the management of his affairs out of his hands.[46]

Examples were presented by Prichard of circumstances in which aberrant family members might be adjudged morally insane (and in some cases better off inside):

> Miss Bagster was a young lady of fortune, and perpetrated a runaway match with Mr. Newton. An application was made by her family to dissolve the marriage, on the ground that she was of unsound mind. The facts urged against her before the commissioners were, that she had been a violent, self-willed, and passionate child; that this continued till she grew up; that she was totally ignorant of arithmetic, and therefore incapable of taking care of her property: that she had evinced a great fondness for matrimony, having engaged herself to several persons; and that, in many respects, she evinced little of the delicacy becoming her sex. Dr. Sutherland had visited her four times, and came to the conclusion that she was incapable of taking care of herself, or her property. She had memory, but neither judgement or reasoning power. Dr. Gordon did not consider her capacity to exceed that of a child of seven years of age. Several non-medical witnesses, who had known her from her infancy, spoke of her extremely passionate, and occasionally indelicate conduct. On her examination, however, before the commissioners, her answers were pertinent and in a proper manner. No indelicate remark escaped from her. Drs.

271

Morrison and Haslam had both visited her, and were disposed to consider her imbecilic or idiotic. She confessed, and lamented her ignorance of arithmetic, but said that her grandfather sent excuses when she was at school, and begged that she might not be pressed. Her conversation generally impressed these gentlemen in a favourable manner as to her sanity. The jury brought in a verdict, that Miss Bagster had been of unsound mind since Nov. 1 1830, and the marriage was consequently dissolved.[47]

Prichard seems to have approved of such family proceedings against a wife adjudged morally insane.

Another classic diagnosis for the disease of disordering the family was hysteria.[48] That is a complex topic, and one instance must serve of the social functions which that diagnosis could serve. Robert Carter was a young general practitioner in the leafy London suburb of Leytonstone. Rejecting somatic theories as 'utterly untenable', his *On the Pathology and Treatment of Hysteria* (1853) argued hysteria was psychological, its aetiology lying in the 'sexual feelings'.

Fear, joy and other strong emotions should find healthy physical release, for example in tears or laughter, he maintained, and sexual passions find discharge in orgasm. Though this rarely posed problems for males, in modern civilization the double standard denied women such relief. Frustrated of such a 'safety valve' by high moral expectations and the 'habitual restraint' imposed by respectability, ladies were forced to bottle up their longings and suffer what Carter called 'repression'. Crises like a broken engagement could easily cause that dam to burst, however, whereupon tension-release might be gained indirectly through hysteria. Sobbing, swooning and the like achieved salutary discharge and calm was restored. This – Carter called it primary hysteria – did not require a physician's services.

The matter did not stop there, however. Unfortunately, 'the suggested or spontaneous remembrance of the emotions' attending the primary fit could easily provoke further attacks, which Carter dubbed 'secondary hysteria'. Women quickly grew habituated themselves to this, finding it provided compensatory pleasures – not least, welcome attention. Worse, such gratifications readily deteriorated into 'tertiary hysteria', an ego-trip that tyrannized others. The tertiary hysteric had descended into moral depravity, manipulating all around her to gratify her domineering spirit and enable her to bask in the 'fuss and parade of illness'. Because this exercise of will assumed somatic expression, it naturally commanded family sympathy – the patient, after all, appeared seriously sick. The greater the sympathy, the more tyrannical she became. Hysterics grew expert in this perverse performance art.

Such a monster of 'selfishness and deceptivity', manipulating a 'self-produced disease', could be overcome only by psychological warfare. The hysteric had to be separated from her family and transferred to the physician's home. There, the doctor must not 'minister to the hysterical desire'. Every bid to use hysterical tantrums to command attention had to be resisted: no notice was to be taken of convulsions, self-starving or self-mutilation; above all, the hysteric's cravings for surrogate sexual gratification, especially through demands for vaginal examinations, had to be resisted. Proper behaviour was, by contrast, to be encouraged.

The physician's most taxing task was to find tactful ways of communicating to the hysteric that the game was up. Diplomatically done, this would afford the shrew the opportunity to surrender with honour, putting herself 'completely in the power of her interlocutor', whereupon she might be reincorporated into normal, bourgeois life – that life whose constraints and double standards, Carter himself had acknowledged, were seedbeds of hysteria in the first place.

Carter was not alone in such views. His contemporary Henry Maudsley agreed that the real bugbear was the over-indulgent family that gave in to an attention-seeking woman. The optimum treatment for a young lady in such an 'extremely perverted moral state' required that 'the patient be removed in time from the anxious but hurtful sympathies and attentions of her family, and placed under good moral control'.[49]

The hysteric's anti-social sibling who also loomed large in nineteenth century family psychiatry was the so-called chronic masturbator, typically male and often said by 1900 to be suffering from dementia praecox. In that diagnostic category championed by Kraepelin, later mutating into what Bleuler called schizophrenia, all the emphasis lay upon the wilful perversity of the sociopathic youngster.[50]

Long afterwards, Laing notably critiqued these early schizophrenia case-histories, questioning and reversing their traditional meanings, and contending that what the diagnosis truly revealed were the pathological abnormalities of families, society and psychiatry. His *The Politics of the Family* (1971) re-examined an account by the French psychiatrist, Benedict Augustin Morel, set forth in his 1860 textbook of psychiatry.[51] To Morel, dementia praecox was an insidious disorder that came over some youngsters. 'I recall with sorrow a disorder of heredity of a progressive form which appeared in a family with whose members I grew up in my youth', he recorded:

> An unhappy father consulted me one day on the mental state of his son, aged 13 or 14, in whom a violent hatred for the author of his being had suddenly replaced the most tender sentiments. When I first saw the child, whose head was well formed and whose intellectual faculties surpassed those of many of his school-fellows, I was struck by the fact that his growth had been arrested in some way. His chief miseries were related to this apparently futile source, which had nothing to do with peculiar anomalies of his feelings. He was in despair because he was the smallest of his class ... Gradually he lost his gaiety, became sombre, taciturn, and showed a tendency to solitariness. One would have thought that he had onanistic tendencies, but it was not so. The child's statement of melancholy depression and his hatred of his father, which was carried to the length of thinking of killing him, had a different cause. His mother was deranged, alienated, and his grandmother eccentric in the extreme.

Morel had the youth put into what was euphemistically called a 'hydrotherapeutic institution' and treated. 'A kind of torpor akin to stupefaction replaced his former activity, and when I saw him again I judged that the fatal transition to that state of dementia praecox was in course of operation'. There was no cure.[52]

This elegant description, comments Laing with icy derision, had been the prototype for millions of comparable diagnoses. The presenting complaint was by an 'unhappy father', reporting that his teenage son had 'suddenly' evidenced 'a violent hatred' of him. Clearly, as Morel and the father could agree, there was nothing the matter with dad. If the boy felt hatred, there *must* be something wrong with the boy. He needed treatment. He must be taken from school and put in an 'institution'. Surely this would stop him hating his father.

The tale, Laing maintained, was still all too common, though nowadays for dementia praecox, read schizophrenia; instead of 'hydrotherapeutic institution', read a good hospital; instead of 'gymnastic exercises, etc'., read group therapy. Add a pinch of psychotherapy, a sprinkling of electroshocks for the depression, and a dab of hormones for his arrested development. Why did he hate his father and why had he even thought of killing him? We would never know, Laing concluded. The direct effect – aim even – of psychiatric intervention was to turn him into a 'young invalid:' to *invalidate* his hatred of his father, in the name of treatment.[53]

•

In this paper I have been tracing a shift in culpabilization. This century has brought powerful currents, within psychiatry and public culture, disposed to see mental illness as generated by dysfunctional families. The solution may differ: it may be deemed to lie in the emancipation of the individual from the family – breaking away; or it may be sought in family therapy, often within wider structures provided by social services. Such views square with the vocational strategies of the psy-professions within therapeutic or welfare states.[54]

Earlier (that is, by way of short-hand: pre-Freudian) psychiatry presents quite a different face. In the world we have lost, the family was hegemonic, the paramount economic, moralizing and normalizing agency. The Filmerian father was the first therapist, and emergent psychiatry was designed and expected to buttress the family unit. Private-sector psychiatry was there to stabilize the family, bringing errant members into line or at least stopping them from being insufferable. In the public sector, as John Walton has shown, there might be considerable give-and-take between families, Poor Law authorities and county asylum doctors respecting the casting out and taking back of mad relatives.[55] In such circumstances psychiatrists were hardly likely to develop theories or practices holding the family itself to be pathogenic. What was problematic, rather, was the family member who did not fit.

As prime minister in the 1980s, Mrs Thatcher applauded – even made a fetish of – Victorian values, and the 'defence of the family' assumed something of the nature of a political crusade in the UK. This marks a further late twentieth-century about-turn in convictions and policy. The tide seemingly turned, and once more, as part of the right-wing 'rolling back of the state' and the backlash against sixties 'permissiveness', the family unit, *pace* Laing, was endowed afresh with sanctity. If, as Mrs Thatcher pronounced, there is no such thing as society, only individuals and families, who other than families can look after individuals?

Notes

1. Philip Larkin, 'This Be The Verse', in *High Windows* (London: Faber and Faber, 1974), 30, reproduced with permission. Larkin, it should be stressed, was no great admirer of Freud. See this extract from a

letter written on 23 July 1941 to his friend Norman Iles:

I am reading Lawrence daily (like the Bible) with great devotion. Guess what Dick Dommett said in Bagley Wood: Griffiths said (talking about an anthology of animal poetry) 'Lawrence's 'Snake' is easily the best poem in the book. Dick Prick said (obviously never having read Lawrence or the poem) 'Oh, he *would* write about a snake, wouldn't he? Freud says the snake is a symbol of debased sexuality'. I was so angry I could hardly hold my axe: I said Freud talked a lot of superficial balls & embarked upon a declamation couched in pseudo-Layardian terms, which bored & puzzled them mightily, I'm afraid'.

Selected Letters of Philip Larkin 1940-1985, ed. Anthony Thwaite (London and Boston: Faber 1992), 19.

2. For excellent biographies see Adrian Charles Laing, *R. D. Laing: A Biography* (London; Chester Springs, PA.: Peter Owen, 1994); Daniel Burston, *The Wing of Madness. The Life and Work of R. D. Laing* (Cambridge, MA: Harvard University Press, 1996); John Clay, *R. D. Laing: A Divided Self* (London: Hodder and Stoughton, 1996); the main relevant works of Laing are: *The Self and Others* (London: Tavistock, 1961); *The Divided Self: An Existential Study in Sanity and Madness* (London; New York: Tavistock, 1969); *The Politics of the Family and Other Essays* (Harmondsworth: Penguin, 1971).

3. For an attempted exposé of 'recovered memory' as a psychiatric fabrication, see Mark Pendergrast, *Victims of Memory: Incest Accusations and Shattered Lives* (London: Harper/Collins, 1997); see also Nicolas Spanos, *Multiple Identities and False Memories* (Washington: American Psychological Association, 1996); Elaine Showalter, *Hysteries: Hysterical Epidemics and Modern Culture* (New York: Columbia University Press, 1997). More broadly on the 'crisis of the family' and its politics, see Michael Neve, 'Nuclear Fallout: Anxiety and the Family', in *The Age of Anxiety*, eds. Sarah Dunant and Roy Porter (London: Virago, 1996), 107-24.

4. Kate Millett, *Sexual Politics* (New York: Doubleday, 1970), 178. For feminist ambiguities about Freud see Juliet Mitchell, *Psychoanalysis and Feminism* (London: Allen Lane, 1974); Jane Gallop, *Feminism and Psychoanalysis. The Daughter's Seduction* (Ithaca: Cornell University Press 1982).

5. This tale has often been told. Full and reliable is Han Israëls and Morton Schatzman, 'The Seduction Theory', *History of Psychiatry*, v (1993), 61-94, which contains a very extensive bibliography. Keith Barrett of the University of London is currently completing a Ph D thesis on Freud's self-analysis.

6. *The Complete Letters of Sigmund Freud to Wilhelm Fliess, 1887-1904,*
    ed. Jeffrey M. Masson (Cambridge, MA: Harvard University Press,
    1986), 264.
7. *Ibid.,* 272.
8. This is quoted and discussed in J. N. Isbister, *Freud. An Introduction
    to his Life and Work* (Cambridge: Polity Press, 1985), 85.
9. Jeffrey M. Masson, *The Assault on Truth: Freud's Suppression of the
    Seduction Theory* (London: Faber, 1984). For the Masson controversy
    see Janet Malcolm, *In the Freud Archives* (New York: Vintage, 1983);
    see also John Forrester, "A Whole Climate of Opinion': Rewriting the
    History of Psychoanalysis', in *Discovering the History of Psychiatry,*
    eds. Mark Micale and Roy Porter (New York and Oxford: Oxford
    University Press, 1994), 174-90; *idem, Lying on the Couch: Truth, Lies
    and Psychoanalysis* (Oxford: Blackwell, 1993); *idem, Dispatches from
    the Freud Wars: Psychoanalysis and its Passions* (Cambridge, MA:
    Harvard University Press, 1997).
10. For some account of how Freudianism penetrated into the psy- and
    social sciences in England, see Sandra Ellesley, 'Psychoanalysis in
    Early Twentieth-Century England: A Study in the Popularization of
    Ideas' (D. Phil. thesis, University of Essex, 1995).
11. Peter Gay's *Freud, A Life for Our Time* (London: Dent, 1988) offers
    an enjoyable cameo of Freud as patriarch.
12. For the radical Freudians see Paul Roazen, *Freud and His Followers*
    (New York: Knopf, 1975); Paul Robinson, *The Freudian Left.
    Wilhelm Reich, Geza Roheim, Herbert Marcuse* (New York and
    London: Harper and Row, 1969); *idem, Freud and his Critics*
    (Berkeley and Los Angeles: University of California Press, 1993).
13. For details and discussion see Nikolas Rose and Peter Miller (eds),
    The Power of Psychiatry (Cambridge: Polity Press, 1986); Nikolas
    Rose, *The Psychological Complex. Psychology, Politics and Society in
    England, 1869-1939* (London: Routledge, 1985); *idem, Governing the
    Soul: The Shaping of the Private Self* (London & New York:
    Routlegde, 1990); *idem, Inventing Our Selves. Psychology, Power and
    Parenthood* (Cambridge and New York: Cambridge University Press,
    1997). For parallel developments elsewhere see Gerald N. Grob,
    Mental Illness and American Society, 1875-1940 (Princeton: Princeton
    University Press, 1983); Françoise and Robert Castel and Anne
    Lovell, *The Psychiatric Society* (New York: Columbia University Press,
    1981).
14. For a piercing analysis see Elaine Showalter, *The Female Malady:
    Women, Madness, and English Culture, 1830-1980* (New York:
    Pantheon Press, 1986).

15. For discussion of family troubles in the drama from a feminist angle, see Lisa Jardine, *Still Harping on Daughters* (Brighton: Harvester Press, 1983).

16. Robert Burton, *The Anatomy of Melancholy* (Oxford: printed by John Lichfield and James Short, for Henry Cripps, 1621), 68; for discussion see L. Babb, *Sanity in Bedlam: A Study of Robert Burton's Anatomy of Melancholy* (East Lansing: Michigan State University Press, 1959).

17. Sir George Baker, *De affectibus animi et morbis inde oriundis* (Cantabrigiae: J. Bentham, 1755), translated in Richard Hunter and Ida Macalpine, *Three Hundred Years of Psychiatry: 1535-1860* (London: Oxford University Press, 1963), 401.

18. See for the development of a biologically-based degenerationist psychiatry Ian Dowbiggin, *Inheriting Madness: Professionalization and Psychiatric Knowledge in Nineteenth-Century France* (Berkeley and Los Angeles: University of California Press, 1991); Daniel Pick, *Faces Of Degeneration: A European Disorder, c.1848-1918* (Cambridge: Cambridge University Press, 1989).

19. Michael MacDonald, *Mystical Bedlam: Madness, Anxiety and Healing in Seventeenth Century England* (Cambridge: Cambridge University Press, 1981), 83. For Stone's views, see Lawrence Stone, *The Family, Sex and Marriage in England, 1500-1800* (London: Weidenfeld and Nicolson, 1977).

20. MacDonald, *Mystical Bedlam*, 101.

21. J. T. Perceval, *A Narrative of the Treatment Received by a Gentleman, During a State of Mental Derangement*, 2 vols (London: Effingham Wilson, 1838-40), i, 126; this work is discussed at greater length in Roy Porter, *A Social History of Madness* (London: Weidenfeld and Nicolson, 1987), 178-80. See also Nicholas Hervey, 'Advocacy or Folly: The Alleged Lunatics' Friend Society, 1845-63', *Medical History*, 30 (1986), 245-75.

22. Perceval, *A Narrative*, ii, 185.

23. *Ibid.*, ii, 157; i, 134.

24. *Ibid.*, i, 121; i, 101.

25. For the dramatization of madness and the family in the novel, see Helen Small, *Love's Madness: Medicine, the Novel, and Female Insanity, 1800-1965* (Oxford: Oxford University Press, 1996).

26. For the source of most of the preceding information on Dadd see, Patricia H. Allderidge's excellent *The Late Richard Dadd, 1817-1886* (London: Tate Gallery, 1974).

27. George Young, *A Treatise on Opium, Founded upon Practical Observations* (London: Millar, 1753), 106.

28. Patrick Blair, 'Some Observations on the Cure of Mad Persons by the Fall of Water', printed in Hunter and Macalpine, *Three Hundred Years of Psychiatry*, 325-9. For similar 'cures' see W. L. Jones, *Ministering to Minds Diseased: A History of Psychiatric Treatment* (London: Heinemann, 1983).

29. G. J. Schochet, *Patriarchalism in Political Thought: The Authoritarian Family and Political Speculation and Attitudes Especially in Seventeenth-Century England* (Oxford: Oxford University Press, 1975).

30. William Llewellyn Parry-Jones, *The Trade in Lunacy: A Study of Private Madhouses in England in the Eighteenth and Nineteenth Centuries* (London: Routledge and Kegan Paul, 1971).

31. Daniel Defoe, *Augusta Triumphans; Or, the Way to Make London the most Flourishing City in the Universe* (London: printed for J. Roberts and sold by E. Nutt 1728), 30.

32. William Battie, quoted in Roy Porter, *Mind Forg'd Manacles: Madness and Psychiatry in England from Restoration to Regency* (London, 1987: Athlone Press, 1990), 151.

33. Margaret Hunt, *The Middling Sort: Commerce, Gender and the Family in England 1680-1780* (Berkeley and Los Angeles: University of California Press, 1997), 161. On houses of correction see Pieter Spierenburg, *The Prison Experience: Disciplinary Institutions and Their Inmates in Early Modern Europe* (New Brunswick and London: Rutgers University Press, 1991).

34. On scandals and the law see N. Walker, *Crime and Insanity in England. Vol 1. The Historical Perspective* (Edinburgh: Edinburgh University Press, 1968); Kathleen Jones, *Lunacy, Law and Conscience, 1744-1845* (London: Routledge & Kegan Paul, 1955).

35. See Louisa Lowe, *Quis Custodiet Ipsos Custodes?* (London: for the author, 1872), 12 and Preface. See also her *The Bastilles of England; or, The Lunacy Laws at Work* (London: Crookenden, 1883), and Michèle Stokes, 'Incarceration of the 'Sane' in Victorian England' (MA thesis, University College, London, 1994).

36. For moral judgmentalism masquerading as psychiatry, see V. Skultans, *Madness and Morals: Ideas on Insanity in the Nineteenth Century* (London & Boston: Routledge & Kegan Paul, 1975).

37. For an illuminating discussion of psychiatric medicalization, see Andrew Scull, *The Most Solitary of Afflictions: Madness and Society in Britain, 1700-1900* (New Haven, CT. and London: Yale University Press, 1993).

38. Robert Gardiner Hill, *Lecture on the Management of Lunatic Asylums* (London: Simkin, Marshall and Highley, 1839), 4.

39. John Conolly, *The Construction and Government of Lunatic Asylums*

and Hospitals for the Insane (London: Churchill, 1847; facsimile edn, Richard A. Hunter and Ida Macalpine eds, London: Dawson, 1968), 143. Conolly is discussed by Scull in Andrew Scull, Charlotte MacKenzie and Nicholas Hervey, *Masters of Bedlam. The Transformation of the Mad-Doctoring Trade* (Princeton, NJ.: Princeton University Press, 1996), especially pp. 69-70.

40. David Irish, *Levamen Infirmi; or, Cordial Counsel to the Sick and Diseased* (London: for the author, 1700), 53.

41. Anne Digby, *Madness, Morality and Medicine. A Study of the York Retreat, 1796-1914* (Cambridge: Cambridge University Press, 1985), 53.

42. Michel Foucault, *La Folie et la Déraison: Histoire de la Folie à l'Age Classique* (Paris: Librairie Plon, 1961); trans. and abridged by Richard Howard as *Madness and Civilization: A History of Insanity in the Age of Reason*, (London: Tavistock, 1967), 252.

43. Samuel Tuke, *Description of the Retreat, an Institution near York for Insane Persons of the Society of Friends Containing an Account of its Origin and Progress, the Modes of Treatment, and a Statement of Cases* (York: W. Alexander, 1813), 160.

44. This is one of the chief arguments of Scull's *The Most Solitary of Afflictions.*

45. Quoted in Scull, *The Most Solitary of Afflictions*, 355.

46. James Cowles Prichard, *A Treatise on Insanity and Other Disorders Affecting the Mind* (London: Sherwood, Gilbert and Piper, 1835), 13; for discussion see Hannah F. Augstein, 'J. C. Prichard's Concept of Moral Insanity – A Medical Theory of the Corruption of Human Nature', *Medical History*, vol. 40, no. 3 (1996), 311-43.

47. James Cowles Prichard, *On the Different Forms of Insanity in Relation to Jurisprudence* (London: Baillière, 1842), 226.

48. For an introduction see Ilza Veith, *Hysteria: The History of a Disease* (Chicago and London: Chicago University Press, 1965); Mark Micale, *Approaching Hysteria. Disease and its Interpretations* (Princeton: Princeton University Press, 1995).

49. Robert Brudenell Carter, *On the Pathology and Treatment of Hysteria* (London: John Churchill, 1853). See discussion in Roy Porter, 'The Body and the Mind: The Doctor and the Patient: Negotiating Hysteria', in Sander Gilman, Helen King, Roy Porter, George Rousseau and Elaine Showalter, *Hysteria Beyond Freud* (Berkeley and Los Angeles: University of California Press, 1993), 262f., and the different reading offered by Elaine Showalter, 'Hysteria, Feminism, and Gender', in the same volume, 301f.

50. For the psychiatrization of adolescent youths, see Kelly Elisabeth Loughlin, 'Framing Schizophrenia: Gender and Professional Identity in

British Psychiatry, c. 1890-c.1930' (University of Essex Ph. D., 1996).

51. For Morel see Jan Goldstein, *Console and Classify: The French Psychiatric Profession in the Nineteenth Century* (Cambridge: Cambridge University Press, 1987), 189f.

52. Quoted in R. D. Laing, *The Politics of the Family and Other Essays* (Harmondsworth: Penguin, 1971), 63.

53. *Ibid.*, 66.

54. See the works of Nikolas Rose cited above in reference 13.

55. John K. Walton, 'The Treatment of Pauper Lunatics in Victorian England: The Case of Lancaster Asylum, 1816-1870', in *Madhouses, Mad-Doctors and Madmen*, ed. Andrew Scull (London and Philadelphia: University of Pennsylvania Press, 1981), 166-200; *idem*, 'Casting Out and Bringing Back in Victorian England: Pauper Lunatics, 1840-1870', in *The Anatomy of Madness*, vol. 2, eds, W. F. Bynum, Roy Porter and Michael Shepherd (London: Tavistock, 1985), 132-46. See also Peter Bartlett, 'The Poor Law of Lunacy: The Administration of Pauper Lunatics in Mid-Nineteenth Century England with Special Emphasis on Leicestershire and Rutland' (Ph.D. dissertation, University of London, 1993). Research on the role of the family in Victorian lunacy policy and practice is currently being undertaken by Dr David Wright and Dr Akihito Suzuki.

15

Raising the Anti:
Jan Foudraine, Ronald Laing and
Anti-Psychiatry

Colin Jones

Ronald Laing is narrating:

The following is an example of the type of examination conducted
at the turn of the century. The account is given by the German
psychiatrist Emil Kraepelin in his own words.

'Gentlemen, the cases that I have to place before you today
are peculiar. First of all, you see a servant-girl, aged twenty-
four, upon whose features and frame traces of great
emaciation can be plainly seen. In spite of this the patient
is in continual movement, going a few steps forward, then
back again; she plaits her hair, only to unloose it the next
minute. *On attempting to stop her movement,* we meet with
unexpectedly strong resistance; *if I place myself in front of
her with my arms spread out,* in order to stop her, if she
cannot push me on one side, she suddenly turns and slips
through under my arms, so as to continue her way. *If one
takes firm hold* of her, she distorts her usually rigid,
expressionless features with deplorable weeping, that only
ceases so soon as one lets her have her own way. We notice
besides that she holds a crushed piece of bread
spasmodically clasped in the fingers of the left hand, which
she absolutely *will not allow to be forced from her.* The
patient does not trouble in the least about her
surroundings so long as you leave her alone. *If you prick her
in the forehead with a needle,* she scarcely winces or turns
away, and leaves the needle quietly sticking there without
letting it disturb her restless, bird-of-prey-like wandering

283

> backwards and forwards. *To questions* she answers almost
> nothing, at the most shaking her head. But from time to
> time she wails, 'Oh dear God! O dear God! O dear
> mother! O dear mother!', always repeating uniformly the
> same phrases.

Here are a man and a young girl. If we see the situation purely in terms of Kraepelin's point of view, it all immediately falls into place. He is sane, she is insane; he is rational, she is irrational. This entails looking at the patient's actions out of context of the situation as she experienced it. But if we take Kraepelin's actions (in italics) – he tries to stop her movements, stands in front of her with arms outspread, tries to force a piece of bread out of her hand, sticks a needle in her forehead, and so on – out of the context of the situation as experienced and defined by him, how extraordinary *they* are![1]

And now Jan Foudraine:

> Imagine a lecture room where a professor clad in a white coat is
> 'demonstrating' a patient. The professor talks over the patient's head
> to the students and explains to them what 'syndrome' the patient is
> exhibiting. He gives a circumstantial account of the patient's
> behaviour and world of experience. Then the patient suddenly
> shouts out, 'I'm made out of wood! I'm made out of wood!' The
> professor, kindling with enthusiasm, can now explain to the students
> that this expression is likewise typical of the syndrome (for instance.
> 'schizophrenia'). In a situation of this sort, one may indeed ask (with
> Laing): 'Who is really wooden here, the professor or the patient?'[2]

These two anecdotes had a leading place in the mythology of anti-psychiatry as exemplified in the persons of R. D. Laing and Jan Foudraine, the British and the Dutch high priests of the movement. Laing's anecdote, recounted in *The Politics of Experience,* became a commonplace of the alternative and underground cultures of the late 1960s and early 1970s in which anti-psychiatry flourished – its influence on the poignant final scenes of Ken Loach's Laing-influenced feature film, *Family Life* (1971), for example, is patent.[3] The patient's response in the anecdote provided Foudraine with the suitably quizzical title for his best-selling volume.

The two anecdotes have something of the force of an anti-psychiatric parable. Scales fall from the reader/observer's eyes, as though in sweeping gesture of unmasking, a Damascan experience, a Situationist *détournement*[4], or else in a drug-induced trance, the fundamental meaning of the encounter is reversed. The power and authority of a founding father of modern psychiatry (Kraepelin) are placed on a kind of semantic turntable: the patient becomes a truth-telling victim; the scientist, either (for Laing) a crazed pin-wielding sadist or (for Foudraine) an unlistening and uncaring denier of human misery. Through a kind of fictive delegitimation, psychiatry becomes not a putative set of solutions to the problems of mental illness, but rather part of the problem – indeed, to a considerable extent, the problem itself.

In this paper, drawing on the contents of the volume and focussing on the careers of the two figures most centrally connected to the phenomenon of anti-psychiatry in Britain and the Netherlands, I wish to examine the act of negation and inversion at the heart of the movement – to explore, so to say, in a volume which has focused on the *psychiatric* context of the movement in the two countries, the *'anti'* element in anti-psychiatry. The 1960s, after all, were a decade in which searching, questioning and motivated rejection of standard models of authority were the norm in a wide range of social and cultural domains. The youth movement in particular repudiated established family norms, social and educational conventions and political orthodoxies and utilised strategies of symbolic inversion in the delegitimation of established authority: Parisian *soixante-huitards* turned the Gaullist jibe against student leader Daniel Cohn-Bendit into the political chant, 'we are all German Jews'; American student hippies and British campus militants represented US involvement in Vietnam not as a defence of the free world but as a horrible techno-fascist assult on a peasant nation by imperialist forces; and in the Netherlands, the Provos proved past-masters in carnivalesque mockery of established authority.

Anti-psychiatry proudly took a place within these wider struggles in the name of 'anti-ness'. As is widely known, the term 'anti-psychiatry' was coined by Laing's collaborator, David Cooper, at the issue of the 'Dialectics of Liberation' conference held in 1967 at the Roundhouse in London which grouped together an astonishing galaxy of 'nay-sayers' – including marxists Lucien Goldman (the literary theorist), Ernest Mandel and Paul Sweezy, both economists, Herbert Marcuse, the veritable guru of American campus radicalism, the veteran anarchist Paul Goodman, the gay anti-poet, Allen Ginsberg and Black Panther organiser and ideologist Stokely Carmichael. What these individuals had in common was not psychiatry – indeed, of the speakers, besides Laing himself, only American sociologists Erving Goffman, originator of the concept of 'total institutions', and widely perceived as a critic of mental hospitals, and Gregory Bateson, anthropologist and populariser of the concept of the 'double-bind', had a connection to the discipline. Rather, all shared a pronounced tendency to negate and to refute political, racial, sexual and gender norms. Laing's biographers have tended to use the episode to show his uncomfortableness with some of the other celebrities involved – notably Stokely Carmichael, to whom he proffered racial insults – but have perhaps lost sight of what an astonishing and avant-garde phenomenon Laing had orchestrated.[5] Even though the event had little direct impact within anti-psychiatry, it illustrated the broader social, political and cultural worlds to which the movement seemed to belong.

That the context in which anti-psychiatry evolved is crucial to an understanding of the movement is demonstrated by the lack of novelty about much of what the movement's proponents had to say. One of the striking features of the essays in the present collection is to highlight how many of central features of anti-psychiatry were found in the period pre-dating it and gestating under the aegis of what the anti-psychiatrists were to attack. The biomedical model of mental illness and the centrality of the asylum may have been hegemonic features of the profession of psychiatry as a whole. The history of as prominent an institution as Bethlem in this period, as Keir Waddington shows, can be written with only a scintilla of reference to the anti-psychiatric movement as a whole: bus-stops, dairy-herds and pre-prandial sherry figure more frequently in the minute-books of the hospital board than the ideas of psychiatry's critics.[6] Yet the values and assumption on which conventional psychiatry rested could still be assailed from within. As Joan Busfield shows, in the late nineteenth and early twentieth centuries, 'custodialism' rather than institutionalisation was the target for reformers' ire; and she also highlights the degree to which as early as the early 1950s community mental health services were offering new models for psychiatric care, thereby putting the traditional mental hospital on the defensive.[7] For Mathew Thomson and Leonie de Goei, the late 1940s were something of a turning-point in both Britain and the Netherlands, as the impact of Hitlerism deterred psychiatrists from locating mental health problems solely within the individual, and pushed them towards more societal explanations, thus providing a heritage which anti-psychiatrists could utilise (if not acknowledge).[8] Group work in mental hospitals dating from the fifties of which both Laing and Foudraine were aware and indeed in which they participated – as Jonathan Andrews and Gemma Blok show[9] – as well as work in

286

community care demonstrate that the claim that 'pre-anti-psychiatry' psychiatry was unreconstructedly wedded to the biomedical model are far off the mark. The impact which Foudraine's writings elicited from nurses also underline the extent to which that model was already being undermined from within the psychiatric community even before the late 1960s.[10]

None of these earlier movements and tendencies within psychiatry had labelled themselves 'anti-psychiatry'. Nor had they penetrated much beyond the professional and institutional carapace under which the individuals in question worked. Yet their existence shows the extent to which anti-psychiatry was surfing a wave of pre-existent discontent with existing paradigms and models, and utilising arguments which had a history before the proclaimedly revolutionary caesura proclaimed by Laing, Cooper, Foudraine and their ilk. Like any movement seeking to establish its novelty, anti-psychiatry had a tendency to construct a heavily contrastive version of its opponent: like other would-be revolutions before it, it built up a model of an 'ancien régime' which was a simplified, flattened-out and rather distorted representation of the state of affairs before its appearance on the scene.[11]

The language of radical opposition utilised by anti-psychiatry, its *en bloc* rejection of the past, have also perhaps obscured the extent to which both Laing and Foudraine still tried to maintain their links to the profession in whose practices they found so much to condemn. Foudraine, as Gemma Blok shows, maintained a perennial love-hate relationship with professional psychiatry, while Laing's career was replete with efforts to maintain the esteem of those very peers whose precepts he assailed. He found it more congenial to be a plenary speaker at an international psychiatry conference than to storm all but the most cerebral of barricades.[12]

In many ways it was less what antipsychiatrists were saying which was new than the ways in which they were saying them and the nature of the audience they were addressing. Crave acceptance by their professional peers as they occasionally might, both Laing and Foudraine differed strongly from their predecessors within the world of psychiatry on whose ideas they were elaborating by the context in which they were operating. The influence of anti-psychiatry in the culture of the 1960s and early 1970s owed less to proceedings of psychiatric conferences or to articles in medical and scientific journals or to intra-professional struggles than to general-market publications. The paperback world (notably, in the English-speaking world, Penguin Books), the underground press, posters and popular visual imagery and an 'event'-seeking popular press all found grist for their mills in anti-psychiatry. Just as one would not seek to write the history of alternative medicine in these years through the pages of the *British Medical Journal* or the *New England Journal of Medicine,* so an over-concentration on the archives of mainstream psychiatry will produce a highly selective and minimalist reading of the significance of anti-psychiatry. Formerly local and intra-professional debates had gone public – and global.

The very term, 'anti-psychiatry', though coined by David Cooper, was essentially a media term, at first vehemently rejected by Laing as a misunderstanding of his ideas.[13] It served as a flag of convenience for the media – and one moreover which often carried pejorative, reprobatory and even abusive connotations. It might signal, for example, a variety of ideas and practitioners – covering for example Thomas Szasz in the United States, and Michel Foucault in France – who were far from all accepting the term: Laing's existentialist approach conflicted with Foucault's well-known distaste for Sartrean phenomenology.[14] Labelled the guru of anti-psychiatrists whether he liked it or not, Laing joined that secondary pantheon of newsworthy 'anti' personae (way behind Mao or Che of course) like Herbert Marcuse or Timothy Leary, whose faces adorned a thousand student walls. They thus joined a cohort of figures known less for the formal content of their ideas than for their faces and the general fact of their existence. To a degree, then, with anti-psychiatry – to adopt another of the clichés of the 1960s generation, popularised by the work of Canadian media-guru Marshall McLuhan – 'the medium was the message'.[15]

The mediatisation of its arch-proponents signalled both the *splendeurs* and the *misères* of anti-psychiatry as a cultural movement (rather than as just a movement within psychiatry itself). The very newsworthiness and chic-ness of the 'anti' in the late 1960s and early 1970s offered a window of opportunity for change which the predecessors of Laing, Cooper and Foudraine who had criticised mainstream psychiatry had never enjoyed. Laing noted – as Stephen Snelders records above – that society was living through an age 'in which the ground is shifting and the foundations are shaking' – and that what he and others were searching for was 'a sure foundation on which we can live'.[16] Yet the accompanying risk was that once anti-ness was no longer current and newsworthy, then the views of the anti-psychiatrists would no longer carry cultural and political clout. Only time and effort could secure this 'sure foundation' – yet time was short, and the moment was now. In this context, one can better understand the tendency of anti-psychiatry movement to oscillate perennially between a serious content-based critique of conventional psychiatry and a gestural politics of carnivalesque inversion and symbolic performance aimed at both highlighting its 'now-ness' and its place within the contestatory counter-culture, and exploring new paradigms of knowledge about human subjectivity. The anti-ness of anti-psychiatry thus chimed with a whole string of other antis, equally under media glare and equally committed to the exploration of new ways of thinking and knowing. The movement came to owe something of its success to its leaders' sense that they were not merely – like their predecessors within psychiatry – attacking psychiatric power *per se,* but also assailing it as an outpost of a more general complex of power – the kind of complex of power whose contours the 1967 'Dialectics of Liberation' conference had sought to delineate. It took seriously the task of unmasking psychiatry in its existing form as a weapon of social control and human domination, and helping people to live differently, and better. Though propounded by trained psychiatrists, anti-psychiatry aimed – in the fashionably Young-Marx language of the day – less to interpret the world of psychiatry than to abolish it.

This oscillation between ideological content and context, plus the very grandiosity of its over-arching project, helps explain many of the apparent contradictions and paradoxes at the heart of the anti-psychiatry movement. It highlights both the futility of the historian seeking to 'essentialise' anti-psychiatry around a set of ideological positions (a task made difficult anyway by the endless spats and fallings-out between the movement's leaders) and the need to attach any analysis of the movement to an exploration of a whole range of issues, sites, procedures, protocols, languages, publications, reverberations, resonances and diffusions in mainstream culture as well as in the counter-culture of the 1960s where it had enriched itself.

The problem of language was never far away in a movement which stressed both the controlling functions of professional psychiatric discourse and the primacy of an experience aimed at transcending the limits of the quotidian. Finding a language to express the aims of the movement was always a conundrum for Laing in particular: his *The Divided Self* renovated psychiatric language by heavy borrowings from Sartrean existentialism; parts of *The Politics of Experience and the Bird of Paradise* read like a drug trip; while much of his later writing (as, most pertinently, in *Knots*) took language tricks and games as its subject and the gnomic as its mode of expression. Though the latter showed an awareness of the power of language in shaping perceptions, more classically anti-psychiatrists appeared to privilege experience over language and to view insanity as a narrative rather than an illness in ways whose links to Romanticism were sometimes openly acknowledged. The quest for the new and the cult of experience put a strain not only on denotative but also on metaphorical language. Given their rejection of the family as a pathogenic institution, anti-psychiatrists found it problematic using the language of family to evoke the new sense of affective community which they stressed. This was all the more so given the largely unproblematised versions of gender roles to which Laing and others adhered: anti-psychiatry – like much of the 1960s counter-culture – was very largely boy's stuff, a guy thing. The feminist movement which grew out of the counter-culture would, significantly, look to Lacan rather than Laing and Cooper as its theoretical guides.[17] The language of the body was also something of a problem for thinkers like Foudraine and Laing who were soon stressing out-of-body experience, and making a headlong rush into eastern mysticism, aided by a convenient guru.

Anti-psychiatry presented a picture of the self ravaged by the technological fixations of late capitalism and the juggernaut of modernisation. The generously humanistic and individualistic critique it developed of psychiatric power as an instance of these broader structures failed to effect durable links to the other critiques of capitalism emerging in the 1960s. Although the very act of naming the beast – along the lines of the passages at the start of this chapter – marked the beginnings of political wisdom, there was often a tendency within anti-psychiatry to assume that it was also its end. For individuals as avowedly committed to politics – a politics 'of experience' – both Foudraine and Laing showed a quite astonishing political naiveté when it came to going further than rhetorical acts of 'unmasking'. Other radical strands within the counter-culture and the *soi-disant* revolutionary Left were impatient with anti-psychiatry's Romanticism and its lack of connection to other struggles: Trotskyist free spirit Peter Sedgwick's corruscating opposition to Laingian ideas was well known in the counter-culture before the publication of his swingeing assault, *Psycho-Politics*.[18] To a degree one can see in Laing's swift passage into eastern mysticism and Foudraine's surrender into the arms of the Baghwan Shree Rajneesh telling signs of anti-psychiatry hitting the political buffers, so to speak, and definitively foreclosing on contact with related movements for change in either the public sphere or the underground world of the counter culture.[19]

The contradictions in and the structural limitations of anti-psychiatry became increasingly – and painfully – glaring. The anti-technological, anti-consumerist, anti-capitalist and anti-modernising impulses within the movement sat uneasily alongside the jet travel, the book profits, the Sunday newspaper profiles, the showbiz and TV appearances, and the joining of the hippy trail to an India, home of 'timeless' wisdom allegedly beyond the embrace of world capitalism. The attacks on drugs as a means of psychiatric and social control within the mental hospital was juxtaposed against a hedonistic indulgence out of which the new entrepreneurs of drug culture were making fat profits: sedating was repressive and bad, seemingly, but tripping on LSD was life-enhancing, good and society-challenging. London and Amsterdam owed their international reputation in the counter culture less to anti-psychiatry than to their role in the trafficking of soft recreational drugs. A movement so thoroughly confused and which progressively cut its moorings from other radical movements could scarcely have survived without the oxygen of publicity offered by the media of mass society.

The crystallisation of the movement onto its leaders which was achieved – with help from the individuals themselves – through the media set a savage agenda for both Laing and Foudraine personally when the movement went into decline. The power of the media to turn public opinion against anti-psychiatry was instanced in the Dennendals experiment highlighted in these pages by Ido Weijers.[20] The glare of media demonisation was all the more severe in that establishment psychiatry – though itself undergoing some degree of turmoil[21] – offered no place for the profession's black sheep to hide. The movement's crystals were soon transformed into cultural fossils, sad vestiges of an earlier, near-forgotten age. The psychological damage this wreaked on both men was patent: Foudraine with his Baghwan proselytising and homophobic rantings, Laing with his showbiz flirtations, drunken posturing and intermittent *folie de grandeur*. Individuals whose identity had become set by the media became the victims of those identities, even as they rejected them out of a spirit of sincerity and authenticity.

The poignant, even tragic parallel personal fate of anti-pychiatry's leading exponents highlights many of the ironies attaching to the movement viewed with historical distance. A movement which had sought to unmake the old and to fashion the new was hijacked by a new it would almost certainly have rejected. The anti-psychiatric quest for personal authenticity has been domesticated by the forces of consumer capitalism to which the movement had, as I have suggested, been profoundly ambivalent. As the 'now' generation was subverted and replaced by 'me' and 'wannabe' impulses, the radical and liberatory hedonism of the 1960s turned into the altogether more passive consumerism of a 'society of the spectacle'[22] which leaves no place for the creative and liberatory moves which had been at the heart of anti-psychiatry. Drugs and sex transmuted from innovatory channels of self-discovery into big pharmaceutical and pornographic business.

One of my main aims in this article has been to emphasise that, in order to understand the anti-psychiatry movement, we must not take at face value anti-psychiatry's story about the past. The agenda of the movement had been fashioned long before the 1960s by a variety of developments within mainstream psychiatry. By the same token, it would be just as misleading to judge the movement simply by what has happened since its demise to the messages it proclaimed so fervently. In retrospect, the movement seems to have been far less an active agent of change, than a symptom of transformations in society and culture taking place from the 1960s onwards which largely transcended it. The movement's claims have been largely recuperated, distorted or made to look anodyne (or just plain silly) by later developments. Yet sometimes it is important not to let hindsight cloud our view. To do so in the case of anti-psychiatry is to miss one of the reasons for its cultural resonance in the late 1960s and early 1970s, namely its sense of belonging to and in some senses emblematising a more profound call for change. The historian of anti-psychiatry will always need to remember the almost electric charge of that 'anti-psychiatric moment' across the world at which the very name of R.D. Laing was 'a byword for a whole system of ideas the central theme of which was a challenge to the recognised order'.[23] To reduce anti-psychiatry to a set of largely *dépassé* ideas and concepts misses the dimension of the movement which was a carnivalesque celebration of the symbolic inversion of medical authority and established legitimacy, and to underestimate the force and the freshness of the 'anti-psychiatric moment' in western culture.

Notes

1. R. D. Laing, *The Politics of Experience and the Bird of Paradise* (Harmondsworth: Penguin, 1977 edn), pp. 88-9.
2. Jan Foudraine, *Not Made of Wood: A Psychiatrist Discovers His Own Profession,* Eng. trans. (London: Quartet Books, 1974), p. 87.
   Foudraine is drawing attention to the Laing passage here cited. The passage continues: 'The professor's attitude is aloof and objectivising

(reducing the person to a thing). In his investigatory and descriptive approach, therefore, and in the dehumanising setting of the lecture room, it does not occur to the psychiatrist that the person sitting there, being gazed at by the students, is saying something perfectly sensible, namely, 'I feel I'm being treated like a piece of wood.'

3. The scene at the end of *Family Life* representing the 'heroine' schizophrenic as subject of a clinical lecture could have been scripted on the basis of the Laing passage cited. And it possibly was.

4. For the Situationist movement, see now S. Plant, *The Most Radical Gesture: The Situationist International in a Post-Modern Age* (London, 1992).

5. See esp. D. Burston, *The Wing of Madness. The Life and Work of R.D. Laing* (Cambridge, Mass.: Harvard University Press, 1996), p. 106ff.; A. C. Laing, *R.D. Laing: A Biography* (London: Peter Owen, 1994), 106-7.

6. See above, chapter 10; and Tilly Tansey's remarks on drug-use: chapter 5.

7. See above, chapter 1.

8. See above, chapters 3 and 4.

9. See above, chapter 7 and 8.

10. See above, esp. Chapters 9 and 12.

11. For a discussion of this tendency in the progenitors of the term 'Ancien Régime', the Revolutionaries of 1789, see the intelligent discussion in R. Chartier, *The Cultural Origins of the French Revolution* (Durham NC: Duke University Press, 1991).

12. For Foudraine, see above, p. 000. The biographies of Laing highlight his partiality for international conferences and keynote speakerships.

13. Burston, *Wing of Madness,* pp. 62, 107, 232; Laing, *R. D. Laing,* p. 138. See too B. Mullan, *Mad to be Normal: Conversations with R. D. Laing* (London: Free Association Books, 1994), esp. p. 356.

14. On Szasz, see Laing, *R. D. Laing,* p. 184; on Foucault, see accounts of his relations with Laing, Cooper and anti-psychiatry in D. Eribon, *Michel Foucault,* Eng. trans. (London: Faber & Faber, 1994), pp. 47, 122-3, 312.

15. M. McLuhan & Q. Fiore, *The Medium is the Message* (Harmondsworth: Penguin 1967).

16. See above, chapter 6, p. 111 (citing Laing's *The Politics of Experience*).

17. This owed something no doubt to Laing's predatory sexuality. For feminism, see esp. J. Mitchell, *Women's Estate* (Harmondsworth: Penguin, 1971); and idem, *Psychoanalysis and Feminism* (London: Allen Lane, 1974).

18. Peter Sedgwick, *Psycho-Politics: Laing, Foucault, Goffman, Szasz and*

the Future of Mass Psychiatry (New York: Harper & Row, 1982).

19. For Foudraine, see above, p. 163.

20 . See above, chapter 9.

21. See esp. above, the chapter by Ooosterhuis and Walters, pp. 203 ff.

22. See, classically, G. Debord, *La Société du Spectacle* (Paris: Gallimard, 1971).

23. Laing, *R. D. Laing*, p. 134.

16

The View from the North Sea

David Ingleby

This book represents a unique attempt to piece together the jigsaw-puzzle of developments in the field of mental health since World War II and to match up the pieces on the Dutch side with those on the British. Having tinkered with this puzzle for fifteen years in Britain and then for another fifteen in Holland, the book has a special fascination for me. In it, we view developments in both countries as it were from somewhere high above the North Sea, and from this vantage-point both histories appear in a new perspective.

By the end of the book, however, it has become clear that any attempt to restrict one's focus to these two countries is doomed to failure. Large gaps in the puzzle will remain unfilled if we do not take into account developments elsewhere. Apart from the obvious influence of the Frenchman Michel Foucault, many of the contributors to this book have referred to crucial American influences in this period on both the mental health services and their critics. Because of their common language, British and American workers in the field of mental health have always enjoyed a 'special relationship'. Anti-psychiatry in particular was just as much an American invention as a British one (think of Szasz, Scheff, the Palo Alto group and Timothy Leary). The relationship between post-war Holland and the U.S.A. was also a special one, but for a different reason: alongside the substantial injection of American financial capital which helped the Dutch to reconstruct their war-torn economy, large quantities of cultural and professional 'capital' were imported to further the modernisation of Dutch society. Nowhere is this process more visible than in the field of mental health. Whereas pre-war Dutch psychiatrists and psychologists had borrowed heavily from their German neighbours, 'continental' approaches steadily lost ground during the 1950s to Anglo-American models of mental health. In psychology, empiricism ousted phenomenology[1]; in psychoanalysis, the work of Anna Freud and her followers came to the fore.

Anti-psychiatry Reassessed

A major theme running through the foregoing chapters is the significance of the anti-psychiatry movement. At first sight this preoccupation may seem to flatter anti-psychiatry: after all, in some respected current textbooks of psychiatry, the movement and its star, R.D. Laing, do not even earn a footnote. However, the contributors to this volume show that reassessing anti-psychiatry is a complex business, full of pitfalls for the unwary. Regarded as an attempt to reform psychiatric care in Britain, anti-psychiatry achieved if anything the opposite of what it set out to do. But what did it really set out to do? As Colin Jones argues in Chapter 15, from about the mid-sixties Laing and his allies were mainly engaged in promoting the new 'counter-culture'. Jonathan Andrews convincingly shows us in Chapter 7 that instead of seeking to forge an alliance with his progressive colleagues, Laing hijacked their findings and denied their progressiveness – thus bolstering his image as a media messiah, but putting paid to his career as a reforming psychiatrist. Other authors in this book have shown that anti-psychiatry was deeply rooted in the profession itself: Mathew Thomson (Chapter 3) relates it to the new thinking on mental hygiene brought about by World War II and Roy Porter (Chapter 14) shows that Laing was far from being the first to posit that families drive people mad.

So it is not the clashes between Laing and the Kraepelinian old-timers within the psychiatric establishment which turn out to be historically significant: viewed at a distance of nearly three decades, these contests have a predictable, exaggerated, almost slapstick character which calls to mind the ding-dong battles in a Laurel and Hardy movie[2]. No: how Laing treated the 'baddies' within psychiatry was of far less consequence than the way he dealt with the 'goodies'. In fact, he did a splendid job of isolating himself from his potential sympathisers within the profession. This was not simply a question of his personality, though Laing's talent for stealing the limelight seems to have been with him practically from birth. It also reflects, as Colin Jones puts it, the need of a movement seeking to establish its novelty "to construct a heavily contrastive version of its opponent" (p. 287). The image which Laing tried to purvey of a lonely, heroic struggle to liberate the schizophrenic from psychiatry would have been far less convincing if he had admitted that others within the profession were trying to do the same. Because he denied this, a split developed rapidly between anti-psychiatry and the 'liberals' within both psychiatry and psychotherapy. The therapeutic community movement, for example, was seen by Laing's followers not as an attempt to 'empower' mental patients, but as a grotesque reincarnation of early nineteenth-century 'moral treatment'.[3] (Foucault's earlier debunking of Tuke in *Madness and Civilisation* played an obvious role in this evaluation.)

It is instructive to compare Laing's approach with that of his Italian contemporary, Franco Basaglia. Whereas Basaglia managed to forge a broadly-based alliance of progressive psychiatrists, nursing staff, trade unionists, artists, journalists and politicians, Laing succeeded only in arousing the suspicion of most of these groups. Of course, the comparison is an unfair one: Basaglia's 'democratic psychiatry' *could* only flourish in the cultural and political soil of Northern Italy.[4] But most of the alliances Laing formed ended in tears. Already as a psychiatrist in Glasgow, he had begun his career as a professional outsider: in London, not even the élite culture of London psycho-analysis could contain him.[5] His preferred companions were other outsiders – philosophers, writers, and above all Americans who, often to escape the Vietnam war, had exiled themselves to London. As a participant in the meetings at Kingsley Hall which led up to the 'Dialectics of Liberation' conference in 1967, it was made clear to me that psychiatry was unequivocally the enemy, too rotten to be worth saving, and politics was not much better. What had to be changed was society as a whole. The view of left wing politicos.

Laing may have started out with serious ambitions of changing psychiatry, but these ambitions soon came to stand in the way of the larger goal of changing the world. Despite his protestations to the contrary, 'anti-psychiatry' was, after the mid-sixties, the right name for this movement. And a canny instinct seems to have told Laing that in Britain and the U.S.A. at least, a charismatic, visionary leader standing out on his own could influence people more effectively than a straggling band of brothers and sisters – the 'sibling solidarity' model which the Left had traditionally relied on, and which in Northern Italy proved itself to be still capable of delivering the goods. In this sense, Laing anticipated the style of contemporary politicians: he was much more of a Berlusconi or a Blair than a Basaglia. Perhaps this makes him sound a calculating con-man, but I do not think either his goal or his strategy for reaching it were consciously chosen. His own grasp of politics was muddled and at times disastrously naïve: it was more a case of allowing himself to be thrust into the role of charismatic leader by a movement which, by the time he allied himself with it, already had the force of a tidal wave. Once in this role, his enthusiasm and talent for it proved formidable.

Psychiatry and the Schizophrenic as Icons

As anti-psychiatry ceased to be a reform movement and became a vehicle of the counter-culture, its images of psychiatry and the mental patient became steadily less literal and more figurative. These images became, in fact, a pair of *icons* – a sort of diptych symbolising the relationship between a sick, corrupt society and the individual caught in its thrall. Psychiatrists were not only the maintenance-men of this society, patching up its victims and silencing its enemies: their reifying and dehumanising mentality epitomised everything that was wrong with it. As the authors in this book show, this image of psychiatry, while it might not have been completely far-fetched, was over-simplified and incomplete. However, it is also worth examining the other icon of the pair: the image of the mental patient.

This representation turns out to be no less stylised and selective. Laing set out to show that where the mental patient was 'at', in human terms, was completely understandable. For rhetorical reasons, he chose not to dwell on less understandable aspects of the patient's behaviour and experience: after all, he was out to change our perceptions and not to reach an 'objective' conclusion. The point I wish to dwell on, however, is not whether Laing exaggerated the extent to which the experience and behaviour of the schizophrenic 'makes sense'. It is the fact that he chose the schizophrenic, in the first place, as the paradigmatic mental patient. In practice, as I argued in *Critical Psychiatry*[6], the 'normalising' approach which Laing stood for can be much more convincingly demonstrated by reference to the other conditions which make up the bulk of the psychiatrist's case-load: the housewife's depression, the schoolchild's behaviour disorders, the elderly person's disorientation, and so on. Why, then, did Laing chose to focus on the very condition – schizophrenia – in which his thesis was most difficult to demonstrate?

I believe this has to do with the central role which the concept of 'reality' plays in the definition of schizophrenia. It is his (or her) 'loss of contact with reality' which sets the schizophrenic apart from the rest of society. And it is precisely because 'reality' was the target of the counter-culture that the schizophrenic became adopted as its hero. 'Reality', for this movement, was the name for a collective illusion *(maya)* which had sanctioned 100 million murders in this century alone: it was not something anyone in their right mind would take seriously. What we had to liberate ourselves from was not simply the power of parents, teachers and politicians, but the 'reality' which held both them and us in its grip.

Thus it is the schizophrenic – not the depressive, the phobic or any other group of sufferers in the sad litany of psychiatric diagnosis – with whom we are invited to identify, because the schizophrenic has made the break with 'reality'[7]. However, Laing's choice of the schizophrenic as icon is replete with ironies. *Families of Schizophrenics*[8] was one of his best-selling studies, and one which it was impossible to read without seething with indignation at what the parents in the study were doing to their children. The central issue was the schizophrenic's rejection of the 'reality' which their parents, backed up by psychiatrists, were blackmailing them into accepting. The fact that all the patients were female and that many of their conflicts had to do with the pressures put on them *as girls and women,* was not even commented on by Laing and Esterson: only the struggle between the individual and the authorities was salient, not the power-relations between men and women.

Another intriguing facet of this study is the story of the 'control group' which Laing and Esterson investigated, without ever publishing their findings. Their problem with this data was that what went on in 'normal' families turned out to be every bit as alarming, if not more so, than the families of schizophrenics. In 1966 Laing told me that he and Esterson sometimes ended their recording sessions in such despair and indignation that they had an irresistible urge to throw the tape-recorder into the Thames! Of course, publishing the data on the control group would have been a formidable indictment of 'normal' family life, but it would have undermined the proposed account of schizophrenia. However, a more important consideration, in my view, was that a tragedy with schizophrenics as the protagonists is a much more powerful drama than an everyday story of family life. In the book as it was published, we saw parents doing the things parents always do – *and driving their children mad.* Seeing the children *not* being driven mad would have watered down the critique drastically. Paradoxically, 'normal' readers could discover their own victimisation more easily in a schizophrenic protagonist than in a 'normal' one. Thus, even if

Laing and Esterson starting out intending the book to be a story about schizophrenics, it was *read,* by the tens of thousands of 'normal' people who bought it, as a story about themselves.

My contention, in short, is that the images of the mental patient and of psychiatry which Laing propagates in his work are, from the mid-sixties onwards, increasingly subordinated to the *symbolic* function of representing the relationship between individual and society. It did not matter that, as Siegler *et al.*[8] pointed out, Laing's three models of schizophrenia were hopelessly incompatible with each other: all the models were equally serviceable in what Colin Jones calls "the carnivalesque celebration of the symbolic inversion of medical authority and established legitimacy" (p. 292).

The Impact of Anti-psychiatry on British Psychiatry

My argument so far has been that Laing's role as evangelist for the new counter-culture undermined whatever ability he might have had to stimulate reform in the mental health system. His presentation of himself as the one good apple in a barrel full of rotten ones alienated not only the Kraepelinian diehards, but – more crucially – those who were attempting from within the profession to further more humane approaches and to understand mental suffering in its social context. The point is, as many contributors to this book have stressed, that psychiatry in Britain in the 1950s was a broad church. A purely organic, reductionist approach never dominated British psychiatry, however much its supporters (egged on from the wings by the pharmaceutical industry) may have wanted it to. Nick Isbister[9] has argued that the strength of the profession lay precisely in its ability to tolerate differences and contain factionalism. This eclecticism enabled it, for example, to boost its status by forming a Royal College in 1970. Even at the present time, when brain technology has reached a level of sophistication undreamt of in the 1950s, the temptation to restrict psychiatry to an organic approach is resisted.

This eclecticism is not based on intellectual liberalism but on shrewd common sense. Firstly, the demand for non-organic forms of treatment such as psychotherapy or social psychiatry is well established and is unlikely to go away. That being so, it would be unwise for psychiatry to leave this sector of the market to rival professions such as psychology. (In Holland, we even see today a tendency for psychiatry to take over ambulant care provisions which it lost control of more than twenty years ago.)

Secondly, psychotherapy – the 'talking cure' – and the

hermeneutic approach have an image in the eyes of the public which
is far too attractive for psychiatry to discard. As with psychology[10],
the 'hard' and the 'soft' wings of the profession have a symbiotic
need for each other: even though the majority of psychiatrists may
practice a brand of treatment entirely different from Sigmund
Freud's, they are not so stupid as to disown his legacy. It says a great
deal for the PR skills of the American psychiatric profession that the
public still sees psychiatry as a repository of interpersonal skills and
compassion, while psychotherapy is in fact a fairly marginal activity.
The psychiatrists Taylor Hayes and James Warwick in the
enormously popular TV soap *The Bold and the Beautiful* are the
moral heroes of the series, and what they peddle are not pills but
that good old Freudian product, self-knowledge.

The most effective counter to anti-psychiatry was not the
outraged reaction of positivists such as Sir Martin Roth[11], who saw it
as merely irrational and inhumane, but the soft-spoken approach of
Anthony Clare[12], who teasingly ridiculed its exaggerations: Irish
charm as a foil to Laing's Scottish rancour. However, if the analysis
offered in this book is correct, Laing was not really interested in a
showdown with the psychiatric profession. His message was aimed
over their heads at the people who bought his books – the bearers of
the new counter-culture.

By the mid-seventies Laing's message for psychiatry, far from
having inspired a wave of reforms, seemed in Britain to have been lost
without trace. The therapeutic community movement had ceased to
be a critical force and psychotherapy remained a very limited option
except for those who could pay for it. About the only development
anti-psychiatrists could take comfort from was the closing down of
many mental hospitals – but as in the U.S.A.[13], the logic of this was
primarily economic and the 'community care' provisions which were
supposed to replace the hospitals were ill thought-out and
understaffed. It was a very different story in Holland, as I shall argue
below: there, a sympathetic social climate and generous funding of
mental health services made it possible to put many, though certainly
not all, of anti-psychiatry's ideals into practice.

Thus, in Britain at least, Laing lost the battle with psychiatry.
However, he won the war with 'reality' – or at any rate, he
positioned himself on the winning side: for the counter-culture
which he contributed to ushered in the post-industrial, post-modern
era. The 'legitimation crisis' of Western capitalism, the increasing
powerlessness of its *grands récits* to convince and inspire, deprived
'normality 'and 'rationality' of their self-evident character. Gone was

the belief in objective truths, the faith in scientists as impartial guardians of those truths and the belief in progress through increasing material prosperity. In their place came relativism, the pursuit of the personal ('inner space') and anti-materialism. Hierarchical and authoritarian social relations, even in the medical encounter, were replaced by *negotiation,* with the patient in the role of finicky customer. It may not have been the utopia which Laing had dreamt of, but it certainly spelt the end of 'reality' as the 1950s had known it.

The Reception of Anti-psychiatry in Holland

In Holland, anti-psychiatric ideas fell on more fertile soil. The accounts presented in this book suggest this was because anti-psychiatry's two agendas – the reform of psychiatry and the promotion of a counter-culture – were less in conflict with each other. In Holland, more mental health workers were in search of an 'emancipatory' approach which would seek to understand patients in their social context. The notion that psychiatry had a social, perhaps even a political dimension seemed less far-fetched than it did in England. This has to do with the fact that the social transformations which fostered anti-psychiatry and the counter-culture were occurring much more rapidly and dramatically than in England. As several contributors have pointed out, the debate about anti-psychiatry took place in Holland against the background of unprecedented social and cultural upheavals. In 1945 Dutch society could be characterised as traditional and confessional: in the subsequent decades, this society was modernised with all the energy and determination which former generations had put into changing the coastline. By the end of the seventies, Holland had become a byword for liberalism and progressive social policies.

The sympathetic reception accorded to anti-psychiatry by the prominent psychiatrist Trimbos was in stark contrast to the reaction of Laing's colleagues in Britain. The front cover of Trimbos' book[14] depicted the execution by drowning of medieval witches, thereby linking anti-psychiatry with the struggle against social exclusion and discrimination which stood high on the political agenda at the time. The blurb warned the reader not to imagine that the popularity of anti-psychiatry was just a fad: "after all, anti-psychiatry is also psychiatry!" Laing was presented not as a prophet or a mystic, but as a champion of human rights with challenging theories about the social roots of mental illness. Intra-mural psychiatry, however, was not the setting in which these ideas would take root, although many nurses and auxiliary workers in the institutions were sympathetic to anti-psychiatry. In Holland, no dramatic emptying-out of the mental hospitals took place and there were few drastic reforms of these institutions. 'Dennendal' (see Chapter 9) was newsworthy precisely because it was atypical. It was mainly in the burgeoning sector of *ambulant* mental health care that ideas opposed to traditional psychiatry took root.

There were, then, two main reasons for the greater success enjoyed by anti-psychiatry in Holland. Firstly, the size and influence of the ambulant sector was growing much more rapidly than in Britain.[15] As Paul Schnabel points out in Chapter 2, a major factor here is money. Humanising mental health care requires not only ideas but the cash to implement them, and compared with the meagre resources available in England, provisions in Holland in the seventies end 'eighties were positively luxurious. In these halcyon days, before the system became overburdened by its own success, one could receive full-time psychoanalysis for as long as ten years at the expense of the State! The setting up of a nation-wide system of American-style Community Mental Health Care centres (RIAGG's) was accompanied by a rapid growth in the professions flanking psychiatry – psychotherapy, clinical psychology, social work and many others, some of which (such as 'andragogy') are now defunct. For these professionals, Laing's hostile portrait of psychiatry was not at all uncongenial. Far from antagonising them, it provided extra legitimation for their goal of expanding their own influence in the mental health services. Moreover, as Harry Oosterhuis and Saskia Wolters point out in Chapter 11, psychiatry in Holland was much more narrowly identified with a neurological approach than in Britain or the U.S.A.

The second factor is the cultural climate of Holland in the seventies. Liberal, democratic and 'emancipatory' values were promoted with a fervour unknown in Britain (ironically regarded by some Dutch progressives as the source of these values). This concern for individual and group rights was not simply a by-product of modernisation: it was rooted in the tradition of tolerance which has been a feature of Dutch society since even before the Golden Age[16]. From the the end of the nineteenth century the policy of 'pillarisation' (*verzuiling*) ensured harmony in a pluralistic society and prevented the type of conflicts which have plagued Northern Ireland. Concern for human rights was intensified by the ordeal of occupation by the Nazis, which gave the Dutch first-hand experience of a racist, authoritarian régime[17].

The social transformations which accompanied post-war economic modernisation presented a challenge to traditional authorities and institutions, in particular church and family. This, in combination with the tradition of tolerance, provided an ideal setting for anti-authoritarian ideas to flourish in the seventies. Far more than their counterparts in France, Britain and the United States, Dutch authorities preferred consensus to conflict and were cautious in their handling of social protest. The challenge to traditional authorities was not confined to a small group: in society at large, hierarchical social relationships were increasingly replaced by relationships based on negotiation. (It can hardly be a coincidence that the 'Amsterdam School' of sociology became the experts on this process.) Even something as seemingly incontrovertible as a traffic-light became, in this climate, an invitation to negotiate. Hofstede's characterisation of Dutch culture as 'feminine'[18] refers among other things to this conviction that rules are not made to be rigidly applied, but to be sensibly interpreted.

Of course, these transformations did not occur uniformly: especially in rural areas, many traditional habits and values remained intact, resulting in a degree of cultural heterogeneity that made tolerance more necessary than ever. Even without the presence of a sizeable immigrant community, generalisations about *the* Dutch culture would be doomed to failure. However, the fact that this diversity has not led to endemic inter-group violence points, paradoxically, to the strength of the underlying consensus about the need for tolerance.

We can thus be more precise about the aspects of anti-psychiatry which appealed to the culture of the seventies in Holland. Firstly, for a generation committed to the freedom of the individual, accusations that psychiatry was a mechanism of social exclusion or an apparatus for suppressing deviance had to be taken very seriously. Secondly, the authoritarian, even dictatorial image of psychiatry presented by Laing and his supporters made the profession seem totally out of place in a sophisticated modern society. In the emerging ideology of the health services, doctors would become *partners* and patients would become clients or consumers. Any form of violence, whether using physical or chemical means, would be inadmissible. (One unintended side-effect of this ideology has been that the violence which does take place in caring for the mentally disturbed or handicapped is often simply covered up.) The new forms of mental health care developed in Holland were more closely modelled on the non-directive, client-centred approach of Carl

Rogers than on traditional psychiatry. And, as a logical consequence of the reduced distance between professionals and their clients, ordinary people came to identify themselves with the professionals, even to the point of reading their books (a process labelled 'proto-professionalisation' by Brinkgreve et al.[19]).

Thus, the rise of a new mental health ideology was stimulated by cultural developments, and in turn this ideology came to shape the culture itself. Whereas anti-psychiatry saw the mental health system as bolstering up the *status quo*, in this situation it was often the 'psy-professionals' who were at the forefront of liberalisation – for example in relation to sexuality, male and female roles, child-rearing, drug use and crime. Psychological notions offered a new normative framework for a land which had only just left the moral certainties of organised religion behind. (According to Castel, Castel and Lovell[20], psychoanalysis had fulfilled a similar function for New England ex-puritans in the first decades of the century.)

Nevertheless, as Ingrid van Lieshout has pointed out[21], the influence runs in both directions: professionals were also keen to respond to the changing priorities of their clientèle. Whatever its true dynamics may be, the process of 'psychologisation' is perhaps more advanced in Holland than in any other society[22]. This clearly reflects an American model – indeed, programmes such as the Oprah Winfrey Show enjoy high viewing figures. Yet the accessibility of therapy and psychological ideas is probably even higher in Holland than in the US: Kittrie's[23] 'therapeutic state' has become a *fait accompli*.

To What Extent Did Dutch Mental Health Care Adopt the Ideas of Anti-psychiatry?

As Gemma Blok describes in Chapter 8, the huge and unexpected popularity of Foudraine's work in 1971 revealed that many people in Holland were receptive to the ideas of anti-psychiatry. Moreover, many of the subsequent changes in mental health care were in directions favoured by anti-psychiatry. This does not, of course, entitle us to conclude that anti-psychiatry was *responsible* for these changes. And although anti-psychiatry certainly helped to persuade the public that things could not go on as they were, it had less influence over the precise agenda for change than other movements and ideologies, in particular mental hygiene. In two important respects, however, the changes accorded well with the views of anti-psychiatrists.

The Relationship Between Client and Professional

As we argued above, the authoritarian role of the traditional psychiatrist was bound to come under fire in a culture increasingly based on negotiation, and in the whole field of health care there have been marked changes in the norms governing the interaction between professionals and clients[24]. In line with Rogerian precepts, the mental health professional today is more likely to adopt the stance of a sympathetic friend and good listener than that of an omniscient expert. Moreover, numerous organisations exist to protect the rights of patients and deal with their complaints.

These changes have important consequences for understanding the power of the (mental) health care system. In the 'eighties, anti-psychiatry came under strong attack from a new generation of critical thinkers inspired by the later Foucault and post-structuralism: elsewhere,[25] I have analysed these disagreements. The most important objection concerned the nature of psychiatric power. Whereas anti-psychiatry had conceptualised this power in terms of *repression,* the new generation of critics argued that Foucault's notion of *productive* power was much more relevant to modern mental health systems: after all, most treatment is anxiously sought and gratefully accepted, and lay people respect and avidly consume the views of the 'psy-professionals'. To some extent, anti-psychiatry has been in this respect a victim of its own success, because the adoption of its views has lessened the relevance of its critique.

'Social' versus 'Medical' Models of Illness

Models of mental illness were identified by Trimbos as the main issue dividing supporters and opponents of change in the seventies. At the time, social approaches were widely favoured over medical or organic views: the criminologist Buikhuisen, who dared to suggest that crime had a genetic basis, was literally hounded out of the universities because of the supposedly racist nature of his views. (For a movement supposedly dedicated to individual freedom this was, of course, an ironic achievement.) Today, the pendulum has swung again in the opposite direction – but more importantly, the whole 'either/or' approach to physical or social explanations has been superseded by interactional (or even 'transactional') models. The new discipline of 'health psychology', for example, has been keen to demonstrate that psychological factors can still be important in illnesses with a known physical cause. Conversely, the *absence* of such a cause is for psychiatrists no reason to withhold physical treatments: nowadays, drugs are frequently prescribed even for symptoms regarded as an understandable reaction to a social event.

However, the shifts that have taken place concern not only the supposed *causes* of psychic problems, but also their *conceptualisation*. At the time when Laing was writing, only a person whose behaviour and experience were not *intelligible* in common-sense terms was considered a 'suitable case for treatment'[26]. Today, however, the definition of illness is much broader: the view has gained ground that 'normal reactions to abnormal situations' can also be regarded as illnesses. (An example of this is the psychological approach to war traumas described by Hans Binneveld in Chapter 13.) Castel, Castel and Lovell describe such an approach as 'therapy for the normal' (see note 20, page 313).

Since anti-psychiatrists aimed to 'normalise' the behaviour of patients by showing how it made sense in its social context, one might conclude that their work had contributed to the rise of this approach. However, in one very important sense the reverse is true. Whereas anti-psychiatrists attempted to show that behaviour was understandable in order to *remove* it from the sphere of illness, the new approach seeks to extend the concept of illness to include even that which is understandable. Not unintelligible behaviour, but behaviour which threatens 'quality of life', has become the target of treatment: your 'symptoms' may simply reflect frustrations at home or work – but if they prevent you, your family or your colleagues from functioning effectively, then they must be treated. Thus, mental health has come to be defined in terms of *adaptiveness* rather than intelligibility. Such a broad definition leads, of course, to a potentially unlimited demand for treatment, and in response to the enormous overloading of ambulant care services in Holland there have been calls recently for a return to the traditional psychiatric criterion of mental *disorder*.

Even in the seventies, the models of mental illness proposed by anti-psychiatrists were accepted only up to a point. As Leonie de Goei points out in Chapter 4, complete social determinism was rejected by Trimbos in favour of a 'dual' view, in which individual factors also played an important role. This shows again that it was mental hygiene, rather than anti-psychiatry, which called the tune in Holland. From its inception at the start of the century, the Mental Hygiene Movement had limited its agenda to the removal of specific social problems: few of its supporters harboured the notion that there was anything *inherently* pathogenic about basic social structures. Particular stresses and strains in society had to be relieved, but this was not a programme for radical political change. Thus, mental health workers were not simply adapting people to society, but neither were they political activists. They might have been more interested in becoming so if Laing's critique of modern Western society had been a little less nebulous: but anti-psychiatry never bothered to develop theories as explicit as those of, say, Reich or Fromm. It was not so much Laing's radical social critique which attracted interest in Holland as his innovations in psychiatric theory and practice.

In particular, Dutch mental health workers saw little in the notion of re-opening the 'dialogue with unreason' which, according to Foucault, had been suppressed since the Age of Reason. Laing's notions about such a dialogue were regarded as interesting, but no more than that. As we have noted above, tolerance in the sense of 'reluctance to repress' does not necessary imply respect or acceptance. Thus, schizophrenics – like junkies, foreigners, prostitutes and radical students – are treated with full respect for their human rights: this does not mean, however, that anyone has to enter into a dialogue with them or take seriously what they have to say. The limitations of this notion of tolerance – which, to a large extent, is the legacy of *verzuiling* – are today becoming painfully visible through the failure of the policy of 'integration' of ethnic minorities. Simply allowing cultural differences to exist has done nothing to prevent the marginalisation and social exclusion of migrant groups.

Developments Since the 1970s

There is no space here to analyse in detail what has happened in Dutch mental health care during the 'eighties and 'nineties, but certain developments are worth noting. One is the decline of interest in the social context of 'mental illness'. Although nobody seems to have realised this at the time, the wholesale importation of psychological theories and methods of therapy from the USA actually *presupposed* that the social, cultural, political and historical dimensions of mental problems could be ignored. Once the textbooks were in use, these dimensions continued to be ignored, because they were virtually invisible in the American approach to mental health. American textbooks and diagnostic manuals talk confidently about *'the* family', *'the* child', *'the* mother-infant relationship' – as if mental health care, like Coca-Cola or Big Macs, can be exported according to a standard formula. Mrs. Thatcher's remark that "there is no such thing as society, only individuals and families" is precisely the conclusion one would draw from a reading of this literature.

Whereas in the seventies, psychologists seemed to offer a socially critical alternative to psychiatry, it may even be that the tables are now turned. The debate about mental health care for ethnic minorities is a case in point. It is (social) psychiatry which has been at the forefront of the campaign for adequate and 'culturally sensitive' provisions for immigrants[27]: clinical psychology has dragged its feet on this issue and remains extremely reluctant to acknowledge that its approach is mainly relevant to the white middle class. Like the counter-culture which helped it to expand, clinical psychology has mainly dedicated itself to liberating its own social group. Now that homosexuals enjoy full rights and feminism has obtained a niche in the universities, it would seem that for most psychologists, the limits of social progress have been reached. And in recent years the dominant position of psychology as a partner to psychiatry has been strengthened, while the involvement of other social sciences such as sociology and anthropology has declined. This has been accompanied by a noticeable shift among academics away from socially critical perspectives, which are increasingly regarded as an embarrassing hangover from the seventies[28]. Critical reflection on the history of psychology, its place in society and its normative content has been elbowed out of the curriculum to make way for more training in statistics and computer use.

The conclusion which all this leads to is a sobering one. In the 1970s, encouraged by the writings of anti-psychiatrists, Dutch mental health services contributed to fundamental social changes. This ushered in a society in which the chief interest of these 'psy-professionals' became precisely the *maintenance* of the status quo and their own powerful position within it. The highly bureaucratised and rationalised character of the mental health professions today contrasts strongly with the heady atmosphere of 25 years ago. What began as part of the counter-culture has become a technology of adaptation: debates about moral and political issues are today replaced by discussions about the regression coefficients which best predict mental health scores. It can hardly be a coincidence that 'health' is consistently rated by the Dutch as their highest priority in life.

What of developments in Britain? My reasons for concentrating on recent developments in Holland are largely autobiographical – but judging from the chapters by Joan Busfield and Peter Barham, the development of mental health services in Britain has been nothing like as vigorous as in Holland. I suspect, too, that British culture in general has been less thoroughly 'psychologised' (that is, Americanised) than Dutch.

However, there are signs that Britain may be catching up. Judging by the political rhetoric which accompanied the funeral of the Princess of Wales in 1997, and the extraordinary scenes accompanying the funeral itself, the rise to power of Tony Blair has been accompanied by a spasm of frustration with traditional British cultural values. Lady Di, of course, had started the rot by talking on television about her therapy, and by portraying the Royal Family as an emblem of everything British we wanted to be rid of: callous, unfeeling, uptight, uncommunicative and rule-bound. Blair seized the moment of her death (or should we say martyrdom) to announce the dawn of a new era in Britain of caring and feeling. Foreigners could not help thinking that the British were simply waking up to the fact that they had missed out on cultural changes which had long been under way in other parts of the Western world. Far. from showing the rest of the world the way forward, as Blair described it, Britain was belatedly trying to catch up.

Perhaps, however, this very 'backwardness' – if that is how we should view it – could be an asset in the future development of mental health care services in Britain. Examining the developments in Holland over the past thirty years shows that many innovations have had unintended consequences and few have been as radical as they were claimed to be. If, as George Santayana remarked, those who do not remember history are condemned to repeat it, then policy makers in Britain today would do well to examine what has been happening on the other side of the North Sea.

Notes

1. Something resembling a phenomenological approach did, however, manage to re-enter Dutch psychology through the back door in the guise of the 'third force' psychology of Rogers and Maslow. The emphasis on the autonomous individual in this approach was not only congenial to the emerging Dutch consumer society; it was also more acceptable to the churches, which had always preferred phenomenology to the 'dehumanising' approaches of behaviourism or psychoanalysis. It was hardly a coincidence that Carl Rogers had initially set out to train as a priest. For explorations of the interface between religion, psychology and psychiatry see Ruud Abma, 'De katholieken en het psy-complex', *Grafiet*, 1 (1983), 156-97;

Dymphie van Berkel, *Moeders tussen zielzorg en psychohygiëne. Katholieke deskundigen over voortplanting en opvoeding 1945-1970* (Assen: Van Gorcum, 1990).

2. M. Siegler, H. Osmond and H. Mann, 'Laing's Models of Madness', *British Journal of Psychiatry,* 115 (1969), 947-58, commented thus on the tendency of bright young schizophrenics to read Laing's *The Politics of Experience*: 'The authors, like other members of the 'square', older generation, are of the opinion that they know what is best, and that this book is not good for these patients.'

3. The therapeutic community I worked in during 1964 (Phoenix Unit at Littlemore Hospital, Oxford) received regular visits from an inhabitant of David Cooper's 'Villa 21'. At Littlemore we regarded ourselves as mightily progressive: had not two of our patients committed the ultimate act of desecration by copulating one day on the cricket pitch? Our guest, however, was not impressed. Only if a patient had done 'it' with a member of staff would it count, for a true anti-psychiatrist, as a revolutionary deed.

4. See S. Ramon, 'The Italian Psychiatric Reform', in S. Mangen (ed.), *Mental Health Care in the European Community* (London: Croom Helm, 1985), 170-203.

5. The advice of his analyst Charles Rycroft, that Laing was in effect too clever to be subordinated to the rules and regulations of the psychoanalytic training body, shows how adept Laing was at seducing others into colluding with his definition of himself.

6. D. Ingleby, 'Understanding "Mental Illness"', in *Critical Psychiatry: The Politics of Mental Health* (New York: Pantheon, 1980; Harmondsworth: Penguin, 1981), 23-71.

7. The first person to write a critique of reason through an analysis of unreason was – once again – Michel Foucault. Because Foucault wanted to understand the history of Western rationality, he decided to write its antithesis: a history of madness. The ideals of a society can be read off from what it rejects as being foreign to its nature. In the Age of Reason, this turns out to be laziness or uselessness, disobedience and subversiveness.

8. R.D. Laing and A. Esterson, *Sanity, Madness and the Family: Families of Schizophrenics* (London: Tavistock, 1964; Harmondsworth: Penguin, 1970).

9. N. Isbister, *Contemporary psychiatry and its conception of science.* Unpublished Ph.D. thesis, University of Cambridge, 1982.

0. See Ruud Abma, 'Meer dan de som der delen. Over het nut van een integratieve benadering', in Louk Hagendoorn, Aafke Komter and Robert Maier (eds.), *Samenhang der sociale wetenschappen: beloften en*

problemen van een interdisciplinaire werkwijze (Houten: Bohn Stafleu van Loghum, 1994), pp. 166-81.

11. M. Roth, 'Psychiatry and its Critics', *British Journal of Psychiatry*, 122 (1973), 373-8.

12. A. Clare, *Psychiatry in Dissent: Controversial Issues in Thought and Practice* (London: Tavistock, 1976).

13. See A. Scull, *Decarceration: Community Treatment, A Radical View* (second edition) (Oxford: Polity Press, 1984).

14. K. Trimbos, *Antipsychiatrie: een overzicht* (Deventer: Van Loghum Slaterus, 1975).

15. Two tables illustrate this expansion dramatically. Firstly, concerning the Instituut voor Medische Psychotherapie in Amsterdam:

	1960	1977
Clients dealt with	133	2,430
Therapists	47	262

The expansion of psychotherapy continued in the 1980s but reached a ceiling in the 1990s. The same figures for all ambulant health care services:

	1982	1989	1993
Clients dealt with	88,000	217,000	240,000
Therapists	3,100	4,500	5,100

Sources: Denise de Ridder, *De klinische rationaliteit: Diagnostische redeneringen en therapiekeuzes in het Amsterdamse Instituut voor Medische Psychotherapie, 1968-1977* (Utrecht: Nederlands Centrum Geestelijke volksgezondheid, 1991); C. Jacobs & R. Bijl, *GGZ in getallen 1991* (Utrecht: Nederlands Centrum Geestelijke volksgezondheid, 1991); C. Jacobs, R. Bijl & M. ten Have, *GGZ in getallen 1995* (Utrecht: Nederlands Centrum Geestelijke volksgezondheid, 1995).

16. See Kees Schuyt, 'Continuïteit en verandering in de idee van tolerantie', in N. Wilterdink, J. Heilbron & A. de Swaan (eds.), *Alles verandert. Opstellen voor en over J. Goudsblom* (Amsterdam: Meulenhoff, 1997), 167-78. Schuyt emphasises that the continuity of the tradition of tolerance masks important shifts in the way the concept has been interpreted. The concept of tolerance developed by religious humanists and enlightenment philosophers made freedom of thought a *right*, implying a certain respect for one's opponent. The segmented structure of *verzuiling*, however, was based on more pragmatic considerations, as is the contemporary reluctance of authorities to enforce the law strictly on matters such as possession of

drugs, prostitution, abortion and euthanasia *(gedogen)*. Under *verzuiling*, different social groups had their own schools, churches, entertainment and leisure facilities, employers' and employees' organisations, and even old people's homes: people did not so much tolerate as ignore each other. Looked at in this way, *verzuiling* reminds one inevitably of another policy known to the world mainly through a Dutch word: *apartheid*.

17. The true impact of Nazi occupation did not emerge, however, until long after the war was ended. In the 1950s and 1960s an increasing number of books documented the extent of Dutch complicity with Nazi policy, in particular with the deportation and extermination of the Jews. (A very high proportion of the Jewish population in Holland was deported during the war, of whom most died in the concentration camps.) Against this incriminating background, the need to show oneself to be on the right side was even greater than it had been in the war. In a sense, the fervent defence of minorities and human rights during the seventies helped to purify the national conscience. It also helped the younger generation to define their own identity in opposition to that of their parents: the revelations of war historians proved the rottenness of the establishment and the moral bankruptcy of the older generation. Perhaps this explains some of the Dutch authorities' reluctance to clamp down on demonstrations and 'alternative' activities. You could shout 'fascist' at a policeman in the USA, but this was unlikely to impress him: in Holland, however, you would be delivering a mortal insult.

18. G. Hofstede, *Cultures and organizations, software of the mind: intercultural cooperation and its importance for survival* (New York: McGraw Hill, 1991).

19. Ch. Brinkgreve, J. Onland and A. de Swaan, *De opkomst van het therapeutisch bedrijf (Sociologie van de psychotherapie, deel 1)* (Utrecht/Antwerpen, Aula/Het Spectrum, 1979).

20. F. Castel, R. Castel and A. Lovell, *The Psychiatric Society* (New York: Columbia University Press, 1979).

21. Ingrid van Lieshout, *Deskundigen en ouders van nu. Binding in een probleemcultuur* (Utrecht: De Tijdstroom, 1979).

22. See Ruud Abma, 'Back to normal: opkomst en ondergang van de psy-kritiek', in K. Schaafsma (ed.), *Het verlangen naar openheid. Over de psychologisering van het alledaagse* (Amsterdam: De Balie, 1995), 68-78.

23. N. Kittrie, *The Right to be Different* (Baltimore: Johns Hopkins University Press, 1971).

24. See René Stüssgen, *De nieuwe patiënt op weg naar autonomie* (Amsterdam: Thesis Publishers, 1997).

25. D. Ingleby, 'Professionals as Socialisers: The "Psy Complex"', in A. Scull and S. Spitzer (eds.), *Research in Law, Deviance and Social Control 7* (New York: Jai Press, 1985), 79-109.

26. See D. Ingleby, 'Understanding "Mental Illness"' (cf. note 6); 'The Social Construction of Mental Illness', in A. Treacher and P. Wright (eds), *The Problem of Medical Knowledge: Examining the Social Construction of Medicine* (Edinburgh: Edinburgh University Press, 1983), 123-43.

27. R. Littlewood and M. Lipsedge, *Aliens and Alienists. Ethnic Minorities and Psychiatry* (London: Unwin Hyman, 1989).

28. Whereas Dutch mental health services and universities in the seventies were hotbeds of political debate, this is much less the case today. One of the most concrete legacies of the seventies was the law governing university management, which accorded far-reaching powers (at least in theory) to students and junior staff. This 'democratisation' recently became the scapegoat for the manifold ills of Dutch universities, and in 1997 new legislation came into force effectively restoring 'top-down' control. Government-appointed 'supervisory councils', composed for example of captains of industry and retired politicians, took the place of elected University Councils.

    Utrecht University received (literally) a taste of things to come when a director of the local coffee factory, newly appointed to oversee the running of the university, objected to the environment-and-third-world-friendly brand of coffee then in use on the grounds that universities 'should not dabble in politics'. Of course, he was quickly ruled out of order: nevertheless, it was announced shortly afterwards that for 'technical' reasons, new coffee dispensers would serve only the local brand. Nothing could provide a more piquant illustration of how much has changed since the seventies.

Index

317

318